THE FRENCH ECONOMY AND THE STATE

THE FRENCH ECONOMY AND THE STATE

BY WARREN C. BAUM

A *RAND* CORPORATION RESEARCH STUDY

PRINCETON, NEW JERSEY
PRINCETON UNIVERSITY PRESS
1958

L.C. Card 58-7120

Printed in the United States of America
By Princeton University Press, Princeton, N.J.

PREFACE

This study is part of a program of research in the natural and social sciences sponsored by The RAND Corporation. Companion studies on France, dealing with political behavior and foreign policy, are in preparation. The present volume is focused primarily on economic issues. In view of the widespread interest in French affairs and in the general question of the economic role of the state, an attempt has been made to make the discussion understandable to both economists and non-economists. It is hoped that the latter will be able to make their way through the simplified treatment of those theoretical problems germane to the inquiry.

It is a pleasure to acknowledge the help received from RAND colleagues. My greatest obligation is to Roland McKean, who labored patiently through several drafts of the manuscript and offered countless valuable suggestions for improving it both in form and content. My thanks also go to Sam Schurr, now with Resources for the Future, and to Malcolm Hoag for reading the manuscript and providing many helpful criticisms. Oleg Hoeffding, Nathan Leites, William Capron, and Harold Barnett gave me the benefit of their comments at numerous places.

Officials of several agencies of the French government, notably the Ministry of Finance and Economic Affairs and the General Planning Commission, gave generously of their time and provided me with insights and information which would not otherwise have been available. It is with regret that I do not make specific acknowledgments, respecting their desire for anonymity. B. E. Lane Timmons kindly gave me access to unclassified material in the U.S. Foreign Operations Mission to France; I am indebted to Deane Hinton and other members of the economic staff, including Carter Ide, Harold Lubell, Donald McGrew, and Leon Goldenberg, for many criticisms and suggestions. Val Lorwin, of the University of Chicago, Henry Ehrmann, of the University of Colorado, and James Houghteling, Jr., of Carnegie Institute of Technology, commented on all or parts of the manuscript in some one of its stages.

Last in this order but perhaps first in importance is the acknowledgment due to two French economists who assisted me on several parts of this study during my eighteen months' stay in France. Raoul Gross, now with the Organization for European Economic Cooperation, did research and analysis and drafted preliminary materials on Parts I and IV. Similarly, much of the material contained in Part V is based on research and initial drafts prepared by Denis Bergmann of the Institut National Agronomique. It is no detraction from their valuable contributions to indicate that I must remain responsible for the final version, with whatever errors of omission or commission it may contain.

Washington, D.C.
December 1957

W. C. BAUM

CONTENTS

PART II

THE STATE AS PUBLIC FINANCIER

TABLES

CHAPTER 1

INTRODUCTION

I PURPOSE

SOME observers of French behavior in national and international affairs have characterized the country as "the sick man of Europe." In diagnosing the malady, they have suspected that the malfunctioning of the economy was an important element. These suspicions have received some confirmation from French leaders. Former Premier Mendès-France has observed:

> If we must sometimes deplore that our voice is not heeded sufficiently in international discussions, it is in large measure because we appear to be weak, if not backward, because our economic power is declining relative to that of other countries, because our social, political, financial instability, our difficulties in the French Union, are so many handicaps which paralyze our action and make foreigners doubt our chances, our strength, and our resolution.*[1]

That the French economy should not be performing well is paradoxical when considered in the light of the country's basic resources. France enjoys a climate, terrain, and geographical location which, on the whole, are quite favorable; its soil is suited to the growing of a large volume and variety of crops; industrial resources include abundant iron ore deposits and a large quantity of low-grade coals, as well as bauxite and phosphate. Water power resources are ample. While the economy is deficient in coke, petroleum, non-ferrous metals, and textile raw materials, some of these deficiencies have been remedied, at least partially, by imports regularly available from French overseas territories or foreign countries. When an industrious and inventive population is added to these favorable natural conditions, it appears that France ought to enjoy a relatively high level of economic prosperity. Yet most evidence indicates that such prosperity has been only a rare occurrence in modern times.

Despite official and popular interest in the question that has sometimes been put, "What's wrong with the French economy?", there have been few comprehensive studies of how the economy works. This book undertakes to fill part of the gap in our under-

* Bibliographical notes, arranged by chapter, appear at the end of the book.

standing of modern France. However, an attempt to analyze the many interrelated problems of the French economy can easily become unmanageable. The present volume therefore focuses attention on a single unifying theme, the role of the state in the French economy. The intervention of the state is so pervasive that there is virtually no important economic problem that does not bear its strong imprint. State intervention should therefore provide a good vantage point from which to observe the economy in action. At the same time, concentration on the role of the state permits some selectivity in the problems to be considered, and some uniformity in the way these problems are treated.

A study of state intervention may also shed some light on a question that has provoked one of the livelier controversies of modern times—what the economic role of the state should be. John Maynard Keynes observed in 1926 that "perhaps the chief task of Economists at this hour is to distinguish afresh the *Agenda* of Government from the *Non-Agenda*."[2] The substantial increase in the items on the "agenda" of most governments since that date has led some groups in the United States to apply the political epithet of "creeping socialism" to encroachments of the government upon the private economic sphere. Other groups, if not open advocates of the principle of increased state intervention, have not been reluctant to call upon or demand the services of the state as new occasions have arisen. In scholarly circles, the controversy has been touched off anew by Professor Hayek's book, *The Road to Serfdom.*[3] Hayek's central thesis is that the trend toward economic planning by the state inevitably leads democratic nations down the primrose path to totalitarianism. Some of the subsequent titles—*Freedom Under Planning*, *Road to Reaction*, *Ordeal by Planning*, and *Alternative to Serfdom*[4]—reflect in capsule form the divergent views of the authors who have taken part in this debate.

It is not intended to discuss here in any detail the various doctrines which underlie the debate on the proper role of the state. By inquiring into the objectives, methods, and results of state intervention in the particular case of the French economy, however, this book may provide some assistance in the task of determining the appropriate "agenda."

II METHOD

The general approach of this book is to examine some of the principal economic activities in which the state engages, and to ask three questions about these activities. The three questions, briefly stated, are: (1) Why did the government act? (2) How did the government act? (3) What were some of the significant results of government action? These questions are applied to the government's activities in dealing with major postwar problems such as economic reconstruction and the fight against inflation, and in performing certain long-standing roles such as the regulation of business and agriculture.

The first two questions, concerned with objectives and methods, are indispensable steps in arriving at any appraisal of the results of state action. They are also of considerable interest in their own right to anyone attempting to understand the complicated process of state intervention as it has evolved in France. In many instances, moreover, comparatively little about the results of the state's activities can be concluded from an economic analysis, and the bulk of the discussion will necessarily be devoted to answering the first two questions. In other instances, more attention will be given to results and conclusions. Thus, the relative emphasis to be placed on each of the three questions varies for different activities or roles of the state.

A. WHY DID THE GOVERNMENT ACT?

Why intervention took place will be explored by considering the particular problems confronting the government and the aims or objectives fixed by the government in connection with them. The most general problem facing the government is that of choosing among alternative and at least partially conflicting objectives. It has been observed that "to govern is to choose," for if more of one objective can be obtained without sacrificing other objectives there is no "problem." For example, one of the hard choices of early postwar years was between more rapid economic growth and more effective control of inflation. Why particular decisions were taken can only be understood in the light of the main objectives that the government appeared to hold.

Naturally, the reasons for state action cannot be described in their full complexity. It is necessary to rely heavily on the aims that public officials professed or appeared to have. Some unavowed but important aims of government action may thus be underemphasized or neglected entirely. Also, we can only examine the most important objectives and not the whole panoply of considerations entering into each decision. Despite these limitations, it will be useful to explore briefly, with respect to each set of government activities, the nature of the problems and objectives that brought about the intervention of the state. Why the government intervened seems to call for less background explanation in connection with some activities (e.g., measures taken to curb inflation) than in connection with others (e.g., the postwar nationalizations).

B. HOW DID THE GOVERNMENT ACT?

The second question—how did the government act?—involves a description of the methods (or policies) adopted by the government. This description is central to the whole inquiry, both for understanding and for evaluating state intervention, and a large part of the book is devoted to it. The presentation of materials is necessarily selective; to describe French policies in photographic detail would tend to overwhelm rather than enlighten, and is in any case precluded, even for any one policy, by limitations of space. The materials to be included were chosen, in large part, because they had a bearing on the extent to which certain objectives, identified below, were achieved.

C. RESULTS OF STATE INTERVENTION

The third question examines the results of government action. We cannot hope to provide a definitive evaluation of the role of the state in the aggregate or even in particular activities. There is no satisfactory criterion of "correct" state action that would make such an appraisal possible. We can, however, see to what extent certain of the main objectives have been realized in practice. The objectives which will be used for this purpose are four in number and are concerned primarily with economic performance. They relate to the rate of economic growth, the stability of economic activity, the equity of income distribution, and the efficiency of resource use. In addition, some effects of the state's performance of its economic missions upon political behavior will be observed, though in a less systematic fashion.

We shall thus attempt to identify some of the gains that have been realized—that is, progress toward the achievement of particular objectives—and some of the costs that have been entailed—that is, sacrifices of other objectives. But, as has been noted, the objectives of state action may be contradictory, and there is no acceptable method of weighing the gains, in terms of some objectives, against the costs in terms of others. While the observed results of state intervention are important ingredients in the process of evaluating the state's role, they do not by themselves add up to a definitive conclusion.

The four objectives of economic performance used to examine the results of state action all figure prominently in statements of French policy. They are also considered by most outside observers to be important objectives from the standpoint of appraising French policies, although the weight that outsiders attach to individual ones might be greater or less than that given to them by Frenchmen. In most cases it is necessary to define the objectives with somewhat more precision than occurs in official French pronouncements before results can be considered in terms of them. It might be stressed that the extent to which other (and important) objectives of state intervention, such as the advancement of personal security, are achieved will not be taken into account.

1. *Rate of Economic Growth.* A high rate of economic growth has become an important goal of most societies. France is no exception to this general rule. A rapid expansion of resources and incomes helps to ease some of the social tensions and to reduce the pressures of various groups for larger shares of the national income, both by enlarging the size of the income to be distributed and by providing expectations of higher incomes in the future. Also, differences in the rate of economic growth in France and elsewhere play an important part in Franco-German relations, always a key problem, and in France's role generally in the international scene.

A number of policies of the French government have implications for economic growth. Government efforts to influence the size of the investment program and the allocation of investment resources among alternative uses are perhaps the most outstanding. The rate of growth is also influenced, if less directly, by policies that affect incentives to innovate and invest or that bear on the mobility of resources.

In most cases, the direction in which a policy works is all that can be identified. What the "correct" level of investment may be cannot be determined. It is not possible to measure the loss of competitive pressures or the impairment of incentives, nor can one quantify the resultant effect on the growth process. However, it is possible at least to indicate whether certain policies operate in the direction of promoting investment and growth or of discouraging growth by protecting and preserving the status quo. And such conclusions are in themselves of considerable significance.

2. *Stability of the Economy.* What is meant by "stability" is not

always clear. How "full" employment should be, and whether the price level should be constant or slowly rising or falling, are still matters of debate. But it is generally agreed that "wide" fluctuations in the levels of prices, output, and employment are highly undesirable and should be prevented by government action. Without defining the optimal conditions of stability, therefore, it should be possible to indicate whether particular government policies help to alleviate or to intensify the instability of the economy.

The problem of equilibrating the foreign exchange position may be considered as a special or external aspect of the general question of stability. The foreign exchange goal has generally been conceived of as "viability"; that is, the ability of a country to pay its own way while maintaining a "high" volume of trade. Again, some evaluations can be made of the net direction of the impact of French policies affecting the "dollar gap," even though a more precise formulation of the goal of balance-of-payments equilibrium is eschewed.

3. Equity of Income Distribution. A major preoccupation of modern governments has been to remedy some of the alleged inequities in the distribution of income. In France, the tax and social security systems have been constructed in part with this goal in mind; subsidies and various other government actions may also affect the distribution of income, intentionally or otherwise.

We will not presume to tackle the formidable task of defining what an "equitable" distribution of income might be. Most French policies contain few tangible clues as to the particular conceptions of equity on which they may rest. Two widely accepted objectives can be used, however, to make partial evaluations. One objective is to move in the direction of a more nearly equal distribution of income through a "progressive" system of taxes and expenditures which redistributes income from the richer to the poorer. This objective might be called the "unequal treatment of unequals"—that is, differential taxes and benefits for persons who are in dissimilar circumstances. Without any attempt to devise a measure of progressiveness or to define how progressive a tax-expenditure system ought to be, it is sometimes possible to indicate whether or not policies operate in this direction.

The second objective is "equal treatment of equals." It is generally considered inequitable to impose markedly different tax burdens or to bestow markedly different benefits on persons who are in similar circumstances. How "similar" the circumstances are is not always beyond dispute, but extreme cases can usually be identified.

4. Efficiency of Resource Use. "Economic efficiency" is the allocation of existing resources among different uses in the way which will maximize the real national product for a given distribution of income. Economic efficiency in this sense is not an end in itself, but, by getting the most out of the resources which are available, it is a means towards the achievement of many objectives (e.g., the desire for food and shelter). Thus, while efficiency of resource use is not of value for its own sake, it is of value because it represents the maximum achievement of certain things that *are* desired for their own sakes.

This is not to say that economic efficiency is all-important. There are other considerations that are closely related to material well-being, such as the development of new resources that did not previously exist; the control of fluctuations in the level of resources that are employed; and the creation of a more equitable income distribution. In addition, there are "non-economic" considerations, such as spiritual aspirations, personal security, freedom of the individual, and the preservation of tradition.

Equal significance is not attached to economic efficiency by different societies. Some countries, such as India, apparently are prepared to sacrifice a good deal of economic efficiency for the sake of holding onto traditional modes of life. France too is sometimes considered to value efficiency less highly than does, say, the United States. But at least some French officials do place a high premium on economic efficiency. Moreover, the attainment of various goals of French policy is in fact dependent on the efficiency with which resources are used. French foreign policies are oriented towards maintaining France's position as a world power. It is often urged—in national debates over policies in Indo-China and Africa—that France is "over-extended" in terms of its resource base. This view is reflected in the statement of Finance Minister Pflimlin that "our current difficulties have as their essential cause the disequilibrium between the obligations and responsibilities of France, on the one hand, and its resources and possibilities on the other."[5] Increasing the level of the real national product, not only by creating new resources through economic growth but also by using existing resources more efficiently, is therefore important for the realization of many French objectives.

5. Implications for Political Behavior. Aims with respect to political behavior are certainly no less elusive than those bearing on economic performance. Needless to say, we cannot offer unimpeachable definitions of the most desirable political system or of the ideal relationship between citizen and state. Nevertheless some significant political consequences of the state's role in economic affairs can be pointed out. For example, the interventions of the state may prove to have significant implications for the extent of the pressures to which the government is subjected, for the stability of individual governments in the face of such pressures, and for the attitude of voters and taxpayers toward the state.

III SCOPE

The substantive portions of the study are divided into five parts. Attention is directed first towards the actions of the state in connection with several broad and interrelated problems confronting the nation in the postwar period. These problems were the need for reconstruction and development of the war-devastated economy, the need to control sharp fluctuations in the level of economic activity, and the need to close the large balance-of-payments gap.

In the subsequent parts, several specific roles of the state are examined. The first is the state's traditional role of public financier in determining the size and structure of the budget with respect to both expenditures and taxes. Part III is concerned with the less orthodox role of the state as entrepreneur in the large sector of the economy which is now under public ownership. The next two parts deal with the role of the state as regulator of private enterprise, in industry and agriculture respectively. Some concluding remarks are made in the final chapter.

In view of the wide range of topics to be covered, many points are sketched in with broad brush strokes. Moreover, a number of interesting and relevant subjects are deliberately ignored or treated only incidentally. Thus, the focus being on the postwar period, the prewar history of state intervention is examined only to the extent necessary to clarify the origins of postwar problems or government actions with respect to them. The time span is essentially the first decade of the postwar period, which encompasses some twenty individual governments. The statistical "books" have been closed as of the end of 1954, while the record of government policies ends with the downfall of the Mendès-France government, early in 1955.[a] The analysis is confined primarily to Metropolitan

[a] A partial exception has been made for agricultural policies, the discussion of which extends through the crop year 1954-1955.

France. The rather specialized subject of the economic relationships between Metropolitan France and the rest of the French Union is not discussed except insofar as these relationships are reflected in the budgetary situation or foreign trade accounts.

The reader may often wonder to what extent the state's intervention and the consequences thereof are peculiar to France. This is a highly interesting question, but our purpose is not to show to what extent the role of the state is different in France from what it is in other countries. Comparisons among countries are often either impossible to make or misleading because of inherently disparate situations. Inter-country comparisons are therefore confined for the most part to cases where the data are readily available and where special effort has been made to render them comparable (as by the Organization for European Economic Cooperation).

The term "state" is used, somewhat loosely, to refer to any one or all of the various organs of government which comprise the national state. Unless particularly relevant, the separate roles performed by the legislative, executive, or judicial branches of government are not identified. The problems thus excluded are, again, interesting but outside the central purpose. Local governmental bodies and their relationships to the national or central government are excluded for similar reasons. Also, the "state" is treated as an entity separate from the French people. Public policies grow out of a complex process of interaction between the state and various groups or forces in society. We do not go behind particular state actions to identify all of the forces operating upon the government or the extent to which these forces find expression in the actions of the state. Where the "responsibility" for the state's performance may lie, in some ultimate sense, is not explored.

The book is concerned solely with the economic missions in which the state engages. The conduct of foreign affairs, the performance of cultural services, and other non-economic activities of the state are not considered as such.

A general warning is in order on the use of statistics. A government report has observed that: ". . . of all the developed nations, France is no doubt the one which is least informed on its economy. Most of the analytical instruments which modern nations have developed are still lacking in our country."[6] This situation is being steadily improved through the efforts of the *Institut National de la Statistique et des Etudes Economiques* (INSEE), but data on some important problems are still almost entirely lacking, while on others those available are incomplete or of doubtful value. For example, there has been no industrial census since 1931, and there was no agricultural census between 1929 and 1954.[b] Some of the problems involved in the use of particular statistical materials are identified where they occur, but these general cautions should also be borne in mind.

[b] One reason for the infrequency of such censuses may be the strong popular suspicions and resentments which they arouse. In order to effectuate the general population census of 1954, it was necessary to publish explicit guarantees that the forms would be destroyed after the population data had been complied, and under no circumstances would be made available to the tax authorities.

PART I

THE STATE AND SOME GENERAL PROBLEMS OF THE POSTWAR ECONOMY

CHAPTER 2

RECONSTRUCTION AND MODERNIZATION

I INTRODUCTION

EVENTS during the thirties and the war years left France with relatively bare cupboards and a heightened demand for goods. Tasks such as reconstruction and economic growth were urgent and called for a considerable share of available resources. An upward surge of private bids for goods and services was to be expected, chiefly on account of the pent-up desires of consumers and the large stock of money in their hands. The excess of these demands over available supplies, at the prices which existed immediately after the war, gave rise to several broad and inter-related problems.

First, there was the problem of ensuring that available resources would go to their most valuable uses. Some demands would have to be curtailed, since the available resources were not adequate to meet all of them. And, unless the state exercised its choices carefully, the least important demands might be satisfied at the expense of more essential ones.

Second, there was the problem of controlling price inflation. Allowing prices to rise was one method of restricting demand; purchasing power would not go as far as otherwise and eventually the quantities that people (or the government) wished to buy at the higher price level would be reduced. Unfortunately, however, inflation would curtail demand in a manner which was disruptive and generally regarded as undesirable.

Third, there was the problem of settling the balances due each year to foreign countries. The heightened demand and depleted resources in France tended to increase imports and decrease exports. This resulted in a reduction of internal inflationary pressures, but at the same time led to an increased demand for foreign currencies to pay for French imports, and a decreased supply of foreign currencies earned by French exports. The result was another imbalance, this time with respect to foreign exchanges.

These problems were closely inter-related. Decisions about which demands were to be met might either ease or aggravate the other difficulties. If certain demands for resources (e.g., for reconstruction) were regarded as vitally important and were stimulated, the difficulties of curtailing other demands, of controlling inflation, and also of settling balances due to other countries would be worsened. Similarly, decisions about the control of inflation would affect the severity of other problems. Inflation, if permitted, would curtail all demands in an inequitable fashion; it might prevent high-priority demands from being satisfied and would aggravate the difficulty of settling balances owed abroad. Finally, decisions that affected directly the amount of foreign exchange supplied and demanded had repercussions on the problems of getting resources to their most valuable uses and of controlling inflation.

The French government had to choose its post-war policies in the light of these difficulties. What might the government have done? Broadly speaking, three courses of action, or some combination thereof, were possible: to restrict purchasing power at the source (by monetary reform, higher taxes, or lower government spending) and then allow freely-moving prices and exchange rates to decide which demands were to be met; to suppress inflationary pressures and satisfy high-priority demands through a pervasive network of direct controls, such as price ceilings, rationing of consumer goods, allocation of materials, and rationing of foreign exchange; and to allow the inflation to take its course, and let the higher price level eventually restrict demands in real (rather than in money) terms.

Part I describes what the French government actually did about these problems. Chapter 3 deals with the efforts of the state to cope with the post-war inflation, and with subsequent fluctuations of prices and employment. Chapter 4 describes the post-war foreign exchange situation and the actions intended to influence it. The present chapter examines one of the most significant of the heightened post-war demands on French resources—the need for reconstruction and modernization. This was a major facet of the problem of determining which post-war demands were the most valuable uses for French resources. In the war-devastated and stagnant French economy, it was not unnatural that the government attached a high premium to growth. Reconstruction and modernization were not the only measures that had a bearing on economic growth, but they had a major impact on the growth process during the post-war period.

II THE PROBLEM: THE ECONOMY AT LIBERATION

A. PREWAR STAGNATION OF THE ECONOMY

Over most of the 19th century, and of the 20th century prior to the second World War, the French economy grew at a slower pace than that of other major western European countries. In part this was due to the relative decline in the French population compared with that of the rest of Europe, and in part to the slower increase of productivity in industry and agriculture. At the time of Colbert, France held the lead in industrial development. A century before the outbreak of World War II it was probably still the most highly industrialized country on the continent.[1] Industrial development was rather sluggish, however, and it has been said that France lived through most of the 19th century without experiencing a genuine industrial revolution.[2] The French birth rate fell significantly below that of other European countries during the first half of the century; in the second half, the rate of natural increase in the population was close to zero in France, while remaining around one per cent a year in the rest of Europe.[3]

Industrialization began to assume a swifter pace towards the close of the century. The period 1905-1913 witnessed a "revolution" in French industry, which expanded more rapidly than that of other western countries.[4] At the eve of the first World War, the transformation that was taking place gave some promise that the gap in industrial development separating France from Germany and Great Britain might eventually be bridged. On the other hand, the relative stagnation of the French population continued, and French agriculture, which had been developing only slowly, was further retarded by a prolonged series of crises dating from the 1870's.

France suffered a major loss of population, especially of able-bodied males, during the first World War. The recovery of industry was nevertheless fairly rapid, and by 1929-1930 industrial production was about 40 per cent above the prewar (1913) level.[5] Unlike most other countries, however, France had failed to recover from the depression of the 1930's by the eve of the second World War. Industrial production in 1938 was 20-25 per cent below the peak of 1929-1930. Domestic capital formation, which in the past had suffered from what has been described as "the disinclination to undertake productive investment," declined to the point where there was probably no net investment during the 1930's.[6] The agricultural situation was more favorable, but the stagnation of the economy during the interwar period is indicated by the fact that the gross national product increased by only 6 per cent during the 25 year span 1913-1938.[7]

The relatively slow growth of the French economy before the second World War is highlighted by the comparative studies of Colin Clark. While the following data on the movement of real national income in France, Germany, and Great Britain are subject to many reservations, the orders of magnitude are presumably correct. The period between 1911-1913 and 1929 is the only one

REAL NATIONAL INCOME IN BILLIONS OF "INTERNATIONAL UNITS"[a] [8]

	France	*Germany*	*Great Britain*
1870-1876	7.66[a]	7.69[c]	8.14
1911-1913	10.91[b]	19.72	18.26
1929	14.35	20.84	23.22
1938	12.38	35.7	27.55

[a] For the period 1870-1879.
[b] For the year 1911.
[c] For the year 1876.

in which the movement of real national income in France compares favorably with the other two countries. Over the 60-odd year period as a whole, real national income rose more than four fold in Germany and more than three fold in Great Britain; in France, it less than doubled.

This situation presented the post-war French governments with a serious problem. As the Organization for European Economic Cooperation (OEEC) observed, "it was imperative to restore, renew and expand the nation's capital."[9] The dimensions and urgency of the problem were sharply altered, however, as a result of the economic damage suffered during the war and occupation.

B. EFFECTS OF WAR AND OCCUPATION

France incurred a heavy loss of resources during the years 1940-1944. 1,400,000 persons were killed, and the supply of manpower further reduced by mass labor deportations to Germany. The loss of capital equipment as a result of war damage, sabotage, and looting was severe (crudely estimated by one source at about twice the gross national product of 1938). Major damage was inflicted on the transportation network: 21 per cent of the steam locomotives and 65 per cent of the freight cars had been destroyed, and large numbers of locomotives and cars damaged or removed. Much of the capital equipment left standing had been inadequately maintained throughout the war.

The damage to French agriculture, while less spectacular, was also serious. Substantial areas were withdrawn from farm use as a result of mining, fortifications, military requisitioning, and flood-

[a] An international unit is defined as the average value of the U. S. dollar over the period 1925-1934. Real national income includes farm consumption imputed at retail prices. Data for Great Britain exclude Ireland.

ing. The number of horses over three years of age (the main source of draught power on most French farms) had been reduced by half. Perhaps more unfortunate was the drop in productivity caused by the lack of fertilizers and the wearing out of machinery which had not been replaced during the war.[10]

As a result of the wartime damage and dislocation, the French economy was almost prostrate at the time of liberation. Available resources were unbalanced; shortages of raw materials, especially coal, were acute, and those materials which had to be imported from abroad were virtually unobtainable. The labor supply had suffered from a quantitative and qualitative deterioration. Inventories at all stages of production and distribution were depleted. Owing chiefly to Allied bombardments, the rail transportation system was almost completely disrupted; only 17 per cent of the rail network was immediately utilizable. Industrial production, which had been systematically reduced by the Germans during the occupation, had fallen to 20 per cent of 1938. Agricultural production was at less than 70 per cent of the prewar level, and many farm products were no longer passing through official channels.

C. OBJECTIVES OF GOVERNMENT ACTION

Reconstruction of the damaged economy and the undertaking of a long-range program of modernization became major objectives of public policy after the war. During the first years these objectives appeared to enjoy an overriding priority. As conflicts with other objectives became evident, difficult problems of choice were presented. All of the objectives were at least partially compromised, as will be seen in this and the following two chapters. Indeed, reconstruction and modernization themselves competed for resources. In practice, the reconstruction and modernization programs were pursued more or less independently of each other—although the modernization and equipment plan did attempt to embrace the reconstruction program in a rather loose fashion—and they will be discussed more or less separately here.

III RECONSTRUCTION ACTIVITIES

A formal "reconstruction" program, providing public financial assistance for the replacement of damaged facilities, was voted in 1946. Perhaps more important was the variety of emergency measures (which do not fall under any program label) adopted by the government to rehabilitate the productive sector of the economy.

A. EMERGENCY MEASURES

Public efforts were first devoted towards the removal of land mines and the clearance of debris and rubble. In plants that had been closed down as a result of the hostilities, the Ministry of Industrial Production (later the Ministry of Industry and Commerce) assumed considerable responsibilities for the resumption of production, including the direction of emergency reconstruction.

A comprehensive set of direct controls, carried over from the Vichy period and supplemented by new legislation, was applied to the production process. Allocations and priorities were used, rather than the "free" price mechanism, in an effort to direct critical materials to the tasks deemed most urgent. Most raw materials were subject to this rationing system, which was gradually abandoned as supplies became more plentiful after 1947. The use of building materials was controlled through a system of permits; in addition, a special government authorization was required for business construction beyond a certain size. A series of short run production plans were drawn up to serve as guides in the establishment of priorities.

Stringent controls were applied to foreign trade; imports became a virtual monopoly of a variety of government organizations, while the exportation of a long list of "essential" commodities was prohibited. During the winter of 1944, the flow of imports had dwindled almost to the vanishing point. By the spring of 1946, the volume was back to the prewar level, financed in large part by Lend Lease and a number of emergency loan arrangements.

As production began to recover, the first "bottleneck" to be encountered was transportation. During the winter of 1944, economic activity in many sectors was at a standstill because of the dislocation of rail transportation. Energetic steps were taken by the National Railway Company (*Société Nationale des Chemins de Fer Français* or SNCF)—in which the state has owned a majority share since 1937—to repair damaged facilities and bring the rail system back into emergency operation. By the spring of 1945, the immediate transportation crisis had been relieved.

The next production problems to which the government addressed itself were the shortages of coal and of manpower.[b] In the

[b] Since the terms "bottleneck" and "shortage" are sometimes used rather loosely, it may be helpful to attempt a more precise definition. A "bottleneck" or "shortage" is assumed to exist for a product or service when the supply is less than the

coal industry, the urgency of the task of reconstruction was advanced as a reason for nationalization, and the new public enterprises concentrated their first efforts on achieving a rapid increase in output. In the spring of 1945, coal production was 60 per cent of prewar (1938); by the beginning of 1946, the prewar level had been attained.

Several measures were adopted in order to ease the manpower shortage. The work week was extended;[c] large numbers of German prisoners of war were introduced into the coal mines and agriculture or used for the clearance of war damage; and emergency programs to encourage the immigration of free German and Italian workers were implemented.

A rapid recovery of production took place, presumably in considerable part as a result of these measures, during the first years after the war. When the war in Europe ended, industrial production in France was at about 40 per cent of the 1938 level.[11] Less than two years later, by the spring of 1947, the 1938 level had been regained (see Table 1). Agricultural production recovered more slowly, in part because of unfavorable weather conditions as in the poor harvest of 1947. The prewar levels, both of 1929-1930 and of 1934-1938, were about reached by the harvest of 1948.

B. THE "RECONSTRUCTION" PROGRAM

Of the major European countries, France is the only one that has accorded to its war-damage victims the right to complete reparation.[12] Moreover, the generous terms of the law of October 28, 1946 provide that indemnities should be in the form of grants rather than loans and should be based on cost of replacement, with a maximum allowance of 20 per cent for depreciation and obsolescence. Inasmuch as the average age of French housing was about 60 years, and of French industrial equipment 25 years, at the time of Liberation,[13] these provisions have enabled the beneficiaries of reconstruction payments to acquire new facilities of considerably greater value than those that were destroyed.

The total cost of this reconstruction program has been officially estimated at some 5,000 billion francs (in 1950 prices).[14] By the

---

quantity demanded either at the prevailing price or for uses which are regarded as essential.

[c] The legislation of February 25, 1946 restored the 40-hour week and made overtime pay (at a higher rate) compulsory for work beyond 40 hours. However, the government emphasized that the legislation was designed to increase effective wage rates and that a 48-hour week should be considered as "normal" during the emergency period.

TABLE 1

INDEX OF INDUSTRIAL PRODUCTION, 1946-1954
(Base: 1938 = 100)

	1946	*1947*	*1948*	*1949*	*1950*	*1951*	*1952*	*1953*	*19*
				General Index (Including Building)					
January	66	91	107	119	125	135	148	139	14
February	75	96	111	125	125	138	149	142	14
March	78	99	114	127	112	136	151	144	1[illegible]
April	85	106	115	128	122	140	150	145	1[illegible]
May	90	106	118	131	128	144	148	147	1[illegible]
June	90	101	116	129	125	142	147	147	1[illegible]
July	85	98	109	117	117	133	138	132	14
August	73	87	95	102	101	113	116	105	1[illegible]
September	88	101	110	122	125	137	142	139	1[illegible]
October	95	105	103	123	132	143	149	143	1[illegible]
November	94	99	113	124	136	147	147	147	1[illegible]
December	92	93	117	126	131	144	143	150	1[illegible]

Sources: 1946-1948: INSEE, *Bulletin de la statistique générale de la France*, August-Septem
issues of 1947, 1948 and 1949.
1949-1954: INSEE, *Bulletin mensuel de statistique*, various issues.

Note: The major components of this index comprise capital goods (including building), consu
goods, and fuel and power.

end of 1954, expenditures had amounted to about 3,000 billion francs, or 60 per cent of the total. Originally the funds were used mostly for de-mining, clearance of rubble, and provisional construction; almost all of the funds are now being devoted to the permanent reconstruction of damaged property.

With the underlying principle of the reconstruction program being the compensation of damage victims, not much attention has been given by the government to the part which its expenditures do or might play in the development of the economy. Some increase in industrial capacity has undoubtedly resulted from the replacement of old by new facilities. But it has been pointed out that the program has tended to solidify the economic structure along previously existing lines, regardless of the obsoleteness of the industry in question or of the disadvantages of its geographical location.[15] A part of the reconstruction program, covering rehabilitation of the national railways and the merchant marine, has been under the general aegis of the modernization and equipment plan described below. Also, plan officials were able to have the reconstruction of private housing postponed, in large part, until the reconstruction of industrial facilities was well advanced. For the rest, however, there does not appear to have been much coordination in the direction of the reconstruction program and of the modernization and equipment plan.

These are important considerations, since the reconstruction program is a major component of the total investments financed with public funds. Thus, in the 1953 budget, appropriations for reconstruction were scheduled at 335 billion francs, plus an undisclosed amount included in the equipment budget of the civil services. Appropriations for projects financed through the modernization and equipment fund were 300 billion, to which might perhaps be added the 120 billion of equipment loans by public enterprises which bear the guarantee of the state.[d] Each of these forms of investment thus took a significant volume of resources from the other one, as well as from other possible uses.

IV MODERNIZATION AND EQUIPMENT PLANS

A. THE PLANNING FRAMEWORK

At the time of liberation, there appeared to be a strong popular sentiment in favor of centralized planning of the development of the economy. The National Resistance Council, meeting in Algiers during the war, had developed a program of "indispensable reforms," calling for "a rational organization of the economy assuring the subordination of special interests to the general interest" and a state plan for "the intensification of national production."[16] A Ministry of National Economy (later merged with the Ministry of Finance) was established shortly after the liberation in 1944, with the responsibility, *inter alia*, of preparing a national plan and controlling its execution. The large-scale nationalization of industry between 1944 and 1946 was rationalized in part by the need for centralized planning, and a number of advisory and planning bodies were established as adjuncts of the nationalized enterprises.

The framework for centralized planning of production and investment emerged only gradually, however, through a process of trial and error. During the first year after the liberation, a number of piecemeal and uncoordinated programs were developed by individual agencies concerned with specific, shortrun "bottleneck" problems. Dissatisfaction with these programs gave impetus to the drive for a national economic plan extending over several years. Also, United States loan negotiators were pressing the French

[d] It might be noted that in particular cases the line between a "reconstruction" expenditure and one for new investment or modernization may be difficult to draw. These data were taken from the discussion of the 1953 budget in Chapter 5.

representatives for a more systematic presentation of the economic objectives towards which the aid funds would be utilized.[17]

The planning movement culminated, in January 1946, in the creation of a General Planning Commission (*Commissariat Général du Plan de Modernisation et d'Equipement*)[e] originally headed by Jean Monnet. The *Commissariat Général* was instructed to prepare a multi-purpose plan which would "increase production; increase foreign trade, especially in those industries in which France holds a favorable advantage; increase the rate of production to the level of the highest competing countries; provide full employment; raise the standard of living; and provide for reconstruction of public and private equipment damaged or destroyed by the war."[18] By the end of the year a four-year modernization and equipment plan (covering the period 1947-1950) had been drafted. The first plan, popularly referred to as the "Monnet Plan," was later extended to 1952. After some delay, euphemistically called a period of "transition," a second or "Hirsch Plan" (named after the incumbent "commissioner general") was launched to cover the period 1954 through 1957.

B. THE "MONNET PLAN" (1947-1952)

1. Elaboration of the targets. The fundamental concept of the plan was that investment resources should be concentrated on an expansion of the "basic sectors" or "means of production" that were essential to industrial and agricultural development as a whole. In 1946 these were identified as the chief "bottlenecks" that were impeding the recovery of activity throughout the economy. Initially six sectors were selected as basic: coal, electricity, steel, cement, farm machinery, and transportation. In these sectors, to which fuel and fertilizers were added shortly, the production–investment objectives were "imperative"; in others, they were only "indicative." The fact that coal, electricity, and rail transportation had been nationalized and that some investment plans in these sectors were already in existence undoubtedly also figured in their selection.[19]

The production–investment objectives were fixed initially by large, unwieldy planning commissions, one of which was established for each of the sectors of the plan. Each commission was largely independent of the others in the determination of the original objectives. Essentially, the procedure adopted by the commissions was to estimate in physical terms the maximum production possible over the four-year span of the plan, taking into account

[e] After several years, the name of the organization was changed, presumably for some esthetic reason, to Commissariat Général *au* Plan.

estimated availabilities of labor and raw materials and with some assumptions on the evolution of market demand. The amount of new productive capacity necessary to realize the production target was then calculated and translated into a financial estimate of the amount of investment required.[20]

The integration of the individual production–investment targets was the weakest link in the planning process. Some cross-checking did inevitably take place, in view of the obviously competing claims for scarce physical resources such as coal. To a considerable extent, however, the over-all plan was arrived at simply by the addition of its separate component parts. Although the primary interest of the planners was in the "basic sectors," the reconstruction program and other public and private investments were loosely folded into the "plan" and taken into account in arriving at its aggregate investment and production targets.

No systematic studies were attempted of the comparative costs and benefits of alternative investment projects. Some rough pragmatic judgments along these lines must have been made, but the over-all criteria were never made explicit. Little attention was given to the implications of the investment program as a whole for the foreign exchange position of France; direct import requirements were estimated, but it was generally assumed that the increased production would be consumed internally, and that there would not be an induced demand for imports. Similarly, no comprehensive study was made of how the use of resources by the investment program would affect consumption standards, or how the necessary resources could be diverted to the program without adding to inflationary pressures.[21]

It should be pointed out that the planning officials were seriously handicapped by the lack of precise knowledge of the extent of war damage to industrial plants, the size of existing inventories, and the quantitative and qualitative deficiencies of the manpower supply. No official set of national accounts data existed into which the aggregate investment effort could be fitted, nor were there even rudimentary statistics on interindustry production relationships.

The 1946 version of the plan called for an increase in production by 1950 to a level 25 per cent above 1929.[22] This was, of course, only a very approximate target, and it is not even clear from the language of the report whether it applied to industrial production or to the gross national product (including agriculture and services). The total of new investment (net of current maintenance and renewals) was projected at 2,250 billion francs or 23-25 per cent of estimated national income over the four-year period. This projection applied to all new investment, whether made under the aegis of the plan or by individuals and public authorities independently of the plan.

With a highly pragmatic philosophy of trial and error adopted, by choice or by force, frequent revision of the plan was envisaged and in fact quickly proved necessary. The goals for cement, coal, and rail transportation proved to have been based on over-optimistic forecasts of the evolution of demand. Technical difficulties of launching investment projects appear to have been underestimated. The advent of the Marshall Plan in 1948 provided an opportunity for a general downward revision of the goals of the program. The more modest goals were a 10 per cent increase in industrial production over 1929, a 25 per cent increase in agricultural production over the 1934-1938 average, and an increase in gross national product (GNP) to 14 per cent above 1929.[23]

At the same time, the period for the realization of the plan was extended two years to match the terminal date of the European Recovery Program (1952-1953). In the new context of European economic cooperation, greater emphasis was placed on the achievement of dollar viability by the end of the program. New basic sectors (agriculture, tourism) were added for this purpose. In terms of constant prices, the total investment effort contemplated over the revised life of the plan (1947-1952) appears to be roughly equal to that originally fixed for the four-year period 1947-1950.[f] The production targets of the original and revised plans in some of the basic sectors are given in Table 2.

2. *Methods of execution.* The original plan was particularly vague on the sources of financing to be used, and on the control techniques necessary to assure an adequate flow of investment resources to the priority sectors. When the plan was established, the *Commissariat Général* was assigned a coordinating function with respect to the various measures that might be required for its implementation. Partly because of the resistance of other agencies, however, this function could not be exercised effectively.

During the time that direct controls over productive resources were in effect, the priorities assigned by the modernization and equipment plan were used in allocating scarce materials and in

[f] In average 1949 prices, calculated by the use of the index of equipment goods, the investment total was 6,220 billion francs under the original plan and 4,260 billion for the period 1949-1952 under the revised plan. Actual investments in 1947 and 1948 (in 1949 prices) were 1,830 billion francs.

TABLE 2. OBJECTIVES AND RESULTS IN "BASIC SECTORS" OF FIRST MODERNIZATION AND EQUIPMENT PLAN, 1947-1952

Sector	*Unit*	*Actual 1929*	*Actual 1938*	*Objective 1950*	*Actual 1950*	*Objective 1952-1953*	*Actual 1952*
Energy							
Coal[1]	mill. tons	55	47.6	65	52.5	60	57.4
Electricity	bill. k.w.h.	15.6	20.8	37	33.1	43	40.8
Petroleum Products	mill. tons refined	0	7	8.1	14.5	18.7	21.5
Industrial Means of Production							
Steel[2]	mill. tons	9.7	6.2	11	8.7	12.5	10.9
Cement	mill. tons	6.2	3.6	13.5	7.2	8.5	8.6
Agricultural Means of Production							
Tractors	thousands	1	1.7	50	14.2	40	25.3
Nitrogenous fertilizer	thous. tons	73	177	320	236	300	285

Source: Commissariat Général au Plan, *Rapport sur la réalisation du plan de modernisation et d'équipement de l'Union française, année 1952* (Paris, 1953), p. 13, and *General Report of the First Plan of Modernization and Equipment, November 1946-January 1947* (Paris, 1947), pp. 37-39. Figure for 1950 objective in tractor production from *Journal officiel, Avis et rapports du Conseil Economique*, January 27, 1951, report by J. Ménard on "Investissements pour l'exercice 1951."

[1] Excludes Saar; includes lignite.

[2] Excludes Saar.

authorizing building construction. As these controls were abandoned, the principal methods of directing and implementing the plan were threefold: limiting the use of private funds for unauthorized investment purposes; encouraging the use of private funds for authorized investment purposes; and providing public funds, under favorable conditions, for authorized projects. Of these methods, the third proved by far to be the most important.

The flotation of private stock or bond issues in amounts exceeding a specified minimum required prior authorization of the government. A detailed statement of the purpose of the investment had to be submitted, on the basis of which the government attempted to ascertain the usefulness of the project. Little activity took place on the capital market during the years immediately after the war, however. A system of qualitative, and later quantitative, controls on the extension of bank credit was instituted. As will be indicated in the next chapter, the controls had only a limited effect in enabling the banking authorities to prohibit private investments that they considered to be unsound. Moreover, none of these measures designed to restrict the amount of low-priority investments could affect investments financed from internal business funds.

The government encouraged private investments in "approved" sectors by guaranteeing the bond issues of certain firms. These guarantees were extended to some private firms whose projects came under the modernization and equipment plan, but most of them applied to the bond issues of nationalized enterprises. More important, the government sometimes used its influence to obtain medium-term bank credit for private or nationalized firms, and the extension of medium-term credit by the banking system involved such elaborate rediscount and guarantee arrangements by the government as to make these credits quasi-governmental in character.

In quantitative terms, the principal method for implementing the investment plan in the early years was the provision of public funds under favorable conditions from a number of budgetary or parabudgetary accounts. It was envisaged at the outset that some public funds (in unspecified amounts) would be required for financing the investment program. In practice, the combination of a variety of factors resulted in large-scale recourse to budgetary funds. The capital market, anemic before the war, had practically vanished. The frugal savings habits of the "average" Frenchman had been discouraged by the almost continuous depreciation of the value of the franc since the first World War. With long-term credit virtually unattainable, medium-term bank credit was resorted to on a large scale in 1946 and 1947, but this type of borrowing was unsatisfactory for the major investment projects. The early price policies of the nationalized enterprises[g] precluded any extensive recourse to self-financing of their modernization programs.

The difficulties of obtaining private funds were intensified by the inflation which got under way shortly after liberation. Individual and business savings were wiped out; this was particularly damaging since the family enterprise (typical of large parts of French industry and trade) traditionally resorted to internal financing of its investments. Early government efforts at price control, described in the next chapter, reduced profit margins and possibilities of self-financing in the larger industries. The inflation did, of course, lead to large profits, but they did not flow to productive investments in substantial volume. A large share of the funds was devoted, instead, to inventory speculation, gold hoarding, luxury consumption, and capital flight, or, if invested, was placed in enterprises offering quick turnover. Continued lack of faith in the currency impeded the recovery of the capital market, where fixed-interest obligations were traditionally the principal form of investment. Once large-scale public financing had been established, the flow of private funds (particularly from the banking system) was diverted, directly or indirectly, to finance the massive Treasury deficits to which the investment program was contributing.

All of these factors played a part in the scarcity of loanable funds which persisted throughout most of the period of the first plan. With private funds for investment projects generally obtainable only at high market rates of interest, the provision by the government of public funds at lower rates or on more favorable terms constituted an important "subsidy" to approved projects. This was particularly the case for long-term investments (such as hydroelectric dams) in the "basic" sectors, most of which were under public ownership. As will be seen later, investments financed by "public" funds (variously defined) represented a high proportion of total investments during the years 1947-1952.

Within the "basic" sectors of the modernization and equipment plan, most of the public funds were disbursed through a modernization and equipment fund (MEF) established in 1948, as a special treasury account, to make long-term loans for productive purposes. For direct recipients, such as the nationalized industries, the terms were customarily 4½ per cent interest for 30 years. Some of the money allotted to the fund, earmarked for approved projects in

[g] See Chapter 8.

private industry and agriculture, was administered through specialized public and semi-public credit institutions controlled by government agencies. These institutions also made loans from their own resources; in both cases, the rates were generally the same in order to avoid "discrimination" among recipients. The interest rates charged by these institutions varied widely with the purpose of the loan, but in many cases might be considered to be below the "market" rate.

Not all of the public funds used for investment purposes were, of course, devoted to projects financed by the modernization and equipment fund or directed by the *Commissariat Général au Plan.* The spending of all of the investment funds voted by Parliament was under the general supervision of an interministerial Investment Committee (*Commission des Investissements*) in which the Ministry of Finance and the *Commissariat Général* were the main participants. As has been noted, a substantial part of public investment funds went to reconstruction, which enjoyed a somewhat ambiguous status with respect to the "plan" as a whole. Most of the appropriations for this purpose were disbursed by a separate reconstruction fund or through budgetary accounts. Expenditures for public works and for the equipment of the civil services were handled through regular budgetary accounts. A low cost housing program, which also led a somewhat independent life with respect to the "plan," was financed in part by public funds administered by a specialized agency.

C. THE "HIRSCH PLAN" (1954-1957)

1. Elaboration of the targets. Prior to the official termination of the first plan, preparations had begun for a second one to cover the period 1952 through 1956. The plan had not emerged from the committee stage by the end of 1953, which was consequently labelled a year of "transition." Cabinet endorsement of the Hirsch Plan, now scheduled for the period 1954-1957, was obtained in April 1954. Unlike its predecessor, the second plan was submitted to the Parliament for approval in principle. After a year of examination in committee, followed by a desultory debate, the National Assembly authorized the plan in May 1955.[h] This act in itself does not have much significance apart from facilitating the planning of long-range projects. Parliament decides each year, as under the first plan, what the volume of appropriations should be;

[h] Between 20 and 50 of the 627 members of the National Assembly attended the debate on the plan. (*Le Monde*, May 12, 1955, p. 6.)

this procedure was also followed in 1953 and 1954 when the plan still lacked official "approval."

The second plan, like the first, was described as both "an instrument for orienting the economy and the framework of the investment programs" for the period 1954-1957.[24] The principal difference was a shift in emphasis away from the basic sectors of the first plan (notably power and transportation) toward a more general diffusion of investment activity throughout the economy. Main attention was focused on four sectors: "secondary" industries (manufacturing); housing; the development of the overseas territories; and agriculture (which acquired the status of a "basic" sector under the first plan in 1948).

A 25 per cent increase in the gross national product over the 1952 level was projected. This was to come about through a 20 per cent increase in agricultural production, a 25-30 per cent increase in industrial production, and a 60 per cent rise in construction. These increases were expected to provide for the full employment of labor. The foreign trade accounts were to be balanced by a 40 per cent rise in exports, primarily of raw materials and selected agricultural products, with imports remaining constant in the aggregate. The projected levels of investment necessary to reach these goals are listed, by sector, in Table 3.

In elaborating the second plan, more attention was devoted to the implications of the level of investment for the over-all pattern of resource allocation and for the financial stability of the economy. The so-called "vertical" committees, organized by individual sectors, were supplemented by "horizontal" committees, which examined and attempted to reconcile the projects with respect to their manpower or financial requirements. "For the first time," points out the bill requesting authorization of the Hirsch Plan, and "thanks to the progress of national accounting, it has been possible . . . to evaluate the volume and the rhythm of investments compatible with the general equilibrium, both internal and external, of the French economy."[25]

A number of questions have nevertheless been raised, and doubts expressed, concerning the methods followed by the planning authorities and the consistency of some of their assumptions. In preparing the individual production and investment targets, inadequate attention was apparently paid to prospective market demand and to levels of existing capacity. The export goals were not based on detailed market studies of the commodities for which enlarged outlets were assumed. The possibility of an induced demand for

TABLE 3

INVESTMENT FORECASTS BY SECTOR UNDER THE SECOND MODERNIZATION AND EQUIPMENT PLAN (1954-1957)
(billions of 1953 francs)

Sectors	Actual 1953	FORECAST 1954	1955	1956	1957	Forecas total 1954-19.
I. *Investments covered by projects of the Planning Commission*	1892	2057	2195	2350	2510	9112
A. *New Investment*	1365	1501	1600	1740	1881	6722
Agriculture and fisheries	220	232	270	300	333	1135
Housing and related activities[1]	375	417	455	490	534	1896
Manufacturing industries	115	140	175	210	250	775
Energy and mining	271	302	310	325	325	1262
Iron and steel	99	91	65	60	51	267
Chemical industries	39	42	40	40	43	165
Transportation, communications and tourism	186	195	200	225	250	870
Education and health	60	82	85	90	95	352
B. *Replacement and maintenance*	527	556	595	610	629	2390
II. *Investments not covered by projects of Planning Commission*	768	753	755	790	820	3118
A. *Government*	430	453	755 (A and B)	790 (A and B)	820 (A and B)	3118 (A and B)
B. *Miscellaneous*	278	300				
TOTAL INVESTMENT	2660	2810	2950	3140	3330	12230

Source: Journal Officiel, Documents Parlementaires, Assemblée Nationale, Deuxième Législatu 1954, Annexe No. 8555, *Projet de loi portant approbation du deuxième plan de modernisation d'équipement*, p. 932.

[1] Excluding housing construction undertaken by agriculture, the iron and steel industry, c mining and the SNCF.

[2] Covering activities not included elsewhere, as well as investments in the Saar.

imports as national income rose appears to to have been discarded too lightly. Also, the expected rise in industrial production as a whole (25-30 per cent) was greater than that of most of its components (manufacturing—24 per cent, chemicals—25 per cent, energy—20 per cent). The rise in energy production was particularly out of line with that of industry as a whole.[26]

The planning authorities stated that more attention was given in the second plan to the "profitability" of particular investment projects. In some cases, such as the choice between hydro and thermal sources of power, detailed studies were undertaken of expected costs and returns of alternative investments. How systematically such criteria were applied in reaching decisions on the size of the various investment projects has not been indicated.

A striking feature of the second plan is the modest character of its goals. A 25 per cent increase in gross national product during four years is appreciable, but the base year for the calculation (1952) was marked by stable industrial production and a poor agricultural harvest. No increase in the share of the GNP devoted to investment over the comparatively low levels of 1952-1953 (see below) was projected. Some observers have suggested that unemployment might actually rise during the course of the plan.[27] The watchword of the plan was "expansion with stability." Its modest goals no doubt reflect concern over the frequent allegations that the first plan "failed" to reach its goals and was "responsible" for the postwar inflation and financial instability.

2. *Methods of execution.* The plan is being realized in an increasingly "unplanned" economy. The principal method of controlling or directing investments under the first plan—the provision of public funds—was expected to play a less important part. Except in the nationalized industries, which account for a smaller share of total investments than under the first plan, the majority of the projects were to be financed by private funds. In view of the uncertainty attached to an estimate of the probable volume of private investment, the global target of 6,700 billion francs of investments in projects supervised by the plan was described as "indicative." Various parts of the legislation authorizing the second plan extoll the virtues of "flexibility."

The planning documents outline a number of measures to encourage private investment. Several steps have subsequently been taken by the government along these lines, among them: a reduction in the excise tax rates, which had previously discriminated against purchases of equipment goods; tax advantages to personal savings invested in certain kinds of activities; a general lowering of bank rates; and a raising of the ceiling above which private capital stock flotations require prior government approval. Measures to encourage self-financing by changes in depreciation and price-control regulations have also been undertaken.

The plan also stressed a number of "basic actions," which it compared in importance to the emphasis on "basic sectors" under the Monnet Plan. These were considered necessary to reform the structure of the economy and to make possible a more rapid economic expansion. Five basic actions were identified:

(1) Development of scientific and technical research, and the diffusion of modern production methods;

(2) Specialization and regrouping of industrial firms;

(3) Lowering of production and investment costs through normalization, standardization, and long-range programming;

(4) "Organizing" (i.e., sheltering) of markets for agricultural products and modernizing distribution circuits; and

(5) Reconversion of obsolete firms and the retraining of displaced manpower.[28]

Nothing more than policy "guidance" along these lines was provided by the plan. The government has initiated (or continued) some action on all of the basic points, however, as will be indicated in chapters 9 and 11 dealing with private industry and agriculture.

Procedurally, the most significant change relative to the first plan is that the *Commissariat Général* was placed under the administrative jurisdiction of the Minister of Finance (now officially the Minister of Finance, Economic Affairs, and Planning). The modernization and equipment fund was abolished in 1954, but in its stead was created a similar fund for "construction, rural equipment, and economic expansion."

V ACTUAL INVESTMENT AND PRODUCTION UNDER THE PLANS

It is perhaps inevitable that the results of the modernization and equipment plans are customarily measured relative to their targets. This is a useful comparison, but its significance is limited because the targets themselves may not have been appropriate. For, as the investment plan proceeded, the hard choices which the government faced became more apparent. In order to have more investment, something else—such as personal consumption or defense—

had to be reduced. As will be seen in the next chapter, the government's failure to decide just what should be cut permitted inflation to inflict cuts in real terms on all spending, including that under the plan. Moreover, almost all components of the plan were deliberately cut back, either voluntarily by the planners or (more frequently) by Parliament in the annual struggle for appropriations, in order to obtain a more rational choice than that provided by the inflationary process. Important reasons for the discrepancies between "targets" and "results" may thus have been that the former were chosen too uncritically or that various anti-inflationary policies were ineffective, although delays in implementation and estimating errors were also involved. Nonetheless, we shall examine results in relation to targets, at least in part of the discussion.

A. INVESTMENT EXPENDITURES AND TARGETS

Unfortunately, there are serious discrepancies in the various official statistics on French investments, especially for years prior to 1952, with different statistics published by the *Commissariat Général au Plan*, INSEE, the *Commission des Investissements*, and the statistical services of the Ministry of Finance.[1] According to data of the *Commission des Investissements*, actual investments over the period of the revised Monnet Plan (1947-1952) were below the original targets but about equal to the revised targets. Thus the total volume of funds invested over the period 1947-1952 (about 6,500 billion 1949 francs) corresponds roughly to the objective fixed originally by the planning commission for the shorter time period 1947-1950. On the other hand, the revised financial targets for the period 1949-1952 were slightly exceeded by the actual results.

The movements of new investment funds, together with a breakdown between public and private sources of financing, are given in Table 4. Two alternative definitions of "public" funds are necessitated by the fact that the dividing line between public and private

[1] In part the disparity is due to varying degrees of completeness, to different concepts of "gross" or "new" investment or capital formation, or to different estimating methods. For example, statistics on capital formation may include or exclude: investment inventories; repairs and maintenance; capital formation in the Saar; and direct investments by government agencies, such as the building of schools. In addition, the concepts themselves undergo frequent revision, but revised data for earlier years are not always published. In 1954, for example, the *Commission des Investissements* published a new series of investment data differing, for 1952 and 1953, by 25 per cent from those published previously. The revisions were not carried back to any earlier years, nor was the basis of the revisions made clear except that the data were reconciled with those published in the national accounts series by the addition of a column of "all others."

TABLE 4. NEW INVESTMENT IN METROPOLITAN FRANCE BY SOURCE OF FUNDS, 1947-1953
(billions of francs)

	1947	*1948*	*1949*	*1950*	*1951*	*1952*	*1953*	*Total 1947-1953*
I. Funds invested at current prices								
Public funds:[1]								
A.	236.1	498.9	704.5	720.5	675.1	708.7	734.2	4,278.0
B.	80.8	67.5	95.0	90.6	142.0	238.3	307.0	1,021.2
Private funds	119.7	274.5	296.0	405.7	816.1	842.7	758.8	3,513.5
Miscellaneous	–	–	7.9	–16.6	16.8	22.1	–	30.2
Total	436.6	840.9	1,103.4	1,200.2	1,650.0	1,811.8	1,800.0	8,842.9
Index of equipment good prices, 1949=100	50	88	100	107	138	157	155.4	
II. Funds invested at 1949 prices								
Public funds:[1]								
A.	472.2	566.9	704.5	673.4	489.2	451.4	472.5	3,830.1
B.	161.6	76.7	95.0	84.7	102.9	151.8	197.6	870.3
Private funds	239.4	311.9	296.0	379.2	591.4	536.8	488.3	2,843.0
Miscellaneous	–	–	7.9	–15.5	12.1	14.1	–	18.6
Total	873.2	955.5	1,103.4	1,121.8	1,195.6	1,154.1	1,158.4	7,562.0
III. Public funds as per cent of total (in constant prices):								
A.	54.1	59.3	63.8	60.0	40.9	39.1	40.8	50.6
B.	18.5	8.0	8.6	7.6	8.6	13.2	17.1	11.5
Total	72.6	67.3	72.4	67.6	49.5	52.3	57.9	62.1

Source: Ministère des Finances, *Sixième rapport de la Commission des Investissements* (Paris, 1953), p. 88-1.

[1] Public funds are sometimes narrowly defined as "A" alone, and sometimes broadly defined as "A plus B." "A" includes modernization and equipment loans, housing loans, reconstruction grants made by government agencies, and the public works and equipment budget of the administrative services. "B" comprises loans made by specialized public and semi-public institutions from their own funds and medium-term bank credit.

financing is difficult to draw in practice. The narrower concept generally followed includes modernization and equipment loans, housing loans, reconstruction grants made by government agencies, and the public works and equipment budget of the administrative services. Under the broader definition, two items are added: loans made by specialized public and semi-public institutions from their own funds; and medium-term bank credit.[j]

Total expenditures on new investments increased continuously (in constant prices) between 1947 and 1951. In 1952 and 1953 they were slightly below the 1951 peak; the estimate for 1954 shows about a 10 per cent rise over 1952 and 1953.[k] The proportion of public funds (narrowly defined) was particularly high in the early years, representing some 60 per cent of total investments; in 1951-1953 this proportion was reduced to 40 per cent, concomitant with a shift of public funds from investment in industry to the rearmament program.

Two developments not evident from Table 4 may be worth noting. During the period 1949-1954 investment in housing increased, while the volume of investment in industry was constant or declining. (It may be noted that while the volume of investment in housing increased, the rate of housing investment as of the end of 1954 was low relative to the needs of France and low relative to housing construction in other countries, such as Great Britain and Germany.) Investments in inventories (not shown in Table 4) comprised a substantial share of total capital investment in the earlier years; such investments totalled 300 billion francs in 1949 (in current prices) but only 150 billion francs in 1954 (in current and much higher prices).[29]

As a proportion of the gross national product, the trend of investment expenditures is slightly different. Gross domestic capital formation (which includes inventory as well as fixed capital formation) reached its peak in 1949;[l] according to the OEEC, it declined

[j] The case for including the former item is that these institutions are so closely directed by the state that they may be considered, for practical purposes, as "public" in character. The Ministry of Finance has included loans from these institutions among those "decided by public authority" in its own studies (cf. *Economic Report for 1951 and 1952*, p. 87). With respect to bank credit, the argument for its inclusion is twofold: (a) some of the leading institutions are nationalized; and (b) the government is intimately involved in the provision of these credits, and has established a complex system of guarantees, endorsements, and rediscounting arrangements without which the banking system has been reluctant to invest.

[k] Data are not available for 1954 on a basis comparable to those given in Table 4. The OEEC shows gross domestic fixed capital formation in constant prices as 10 per cent higher in 1954 than in 1952-1953. (*General Statistics*, April 1956, p. 107.)

[l] Data from INSEE show the following proportions: 1947—15.0%; 1948—17.9%

from 18 per cent in 1949 to 16 per cent in 1952 and 15 per cent in 1954.[30]

The 1948 level of investment in France, measured as a percentage of the GNP, may have been higher than the average of the OEEC countries as a whole. In 1954 it appears to have been appreciably lower: capital formation was only 15 per cent of GNP in France, as against 18 per cent for the OEEC countries combined.[30] [m] Over the period 1947-1954 as a whole, it seems probable that the French investment effort was lower than the average for European countries. Yet, as the OEEC points out, France "is one of the countries where the need to modernize equipment is most urgent, and the housing situation is also extremely serious."[31]

These comparisons are not intended to suggest that the French government's efforts have had a negative effect on investment levels; it is possible that these levels might have been lower in the absence of state action. The comparisons do suggest, however, that the objective of a high rate of investment was realized only in small part. They highlight the fact that in the overall context of the postwar situation and government policy, reconstruction and modernization proceeded within definite constraints in the form of important and competing objectives.

B. COMPOSITION OF INVESTMENTS

In the absence of comprehensive controls over the implementation of the investment plan, the actual composition of investments differed somewhat from that originally envisaged. As can be seen from the following figures, the portion of funds going to industry and commerce (mostly private) was larger than that contemplated in either version of the plan, primarily at the expense of agriculture and housing.

PERCENTAGE BREAKDOWN OF INVESTMENT EXPENDITURES BY SECTOR[32]

	1946 Plan	*1948 Revision*	*Actual 1947-1952*
Energy	13.1	22.2	18.2
Transportation	10.2	15.6	15.2
Agriculture	15.8	15.2	11.6
Industry and Commerce	15.5	13.6	23.8
Housing	29.3	33.4 (Housing and Others)	24.4
Others	16.1		6.8
	100.0	100.0	100.0

1949—19.1%; 1950—17.7%; 1951—18.3%; 1952—15.2%. INSEE, *Annuaire statistique de la France*, 1952 (Paris, 1953), pp. 332-335.

[m] Comparisons such as the above are particularly hazardous.

The basic sectors did nevertheless receive a large share of total investments, and the government did influence the allocation of investment resources in their favor. Depending on the definition of "public" funds, between 60 and 70 per cent of the investments in the energy sector, and between 85 and 90 per cent of those in the transportation sector, were provided by the government.[83] The Economic Commission for Europe has described France as "the [non-socialist] country where the influence of the State in the development of basic industries was the most systematic and the most pervasive."[84]

Whether this emphasis on the basic sectors was correctly placed has been the subject of controversy. The French government has sometimes been criticized for "overdeveloping" the basic sectors of the economy, while neglecting transformation industries, housing, and (to a lesser extent) agriculture. The early emphasis on the basic sectors is easy to understand in view of the "bottlenecks" in these sectors that were impeding recovery throughout the economy. Some investments, perhaps on a large scale, appeared to be necessary to achieve substantial increases in the output of goods and services by these sectors. On the other hand, some of the investments (such as electrification of railroad lines and construction of hydroelectric dams) had only delayed effects on production, and were presumably based on longer range judgments with respect to cost and prospective demand. In either case, the most "efficient" allocation of the investment resources available during any planning period would require an analysis of the expected costs and returns of increments of investment funds placed in alternative uses. Perhaps all that can be said by way of generalization is that the procedures that were adopted, and the available data, were not such as to provide, at best, more than a rough approximation to an "efficient" composition of investments.[n]

C. PRODUCTION TRENDS AND TARGETS

The actual increase in industrial production fell substantially short of the original target and slightly short of the revised one. The original plan called for an increase in industrial production to 125 (based on 1929) by 1950; the actual index was 93. The more modest target of the revised plan (110 by 1952) was not quite reached. The production index was 108 in 1952 and 105 in 1953.

[n] Some comments on allocative decisions within the various sectors of the investment program are given in the chapters dealing with the nationalized industries, private business, and agriculture.

Similarly, virtually all of the particular targets of the original plan were missed, and most of those of the revised plan. The production results in some of the basic sectors of the plan are given in Table 5. Petroleum refining was the only sector in which the 1950 plans were realized on schedule. The 1952-1953 objectives were reached in cement and exceeded in petroleum refining, but were not attained in coal, electricity, steel, tractors, or fertilizers. Among the sectors of the plan for which "imperative" targets were not fixed, the rate of housing construction was particularly disappointing in relation both to the urgent needs of the nation and to the expectations of planning officials.

The same situation prevailed with respect to agricultural production. In its 1948 version, the first plan called for an increase in agricultural output to 16 per cent above the 1934-1938 average by 1952. The overall index in 1952 was appreciably below the target, and none of the particular targets for individual commodities was reached, as can be seen from Table 6. Weather conditions were unfavorable in 1952, however, and agricultural production in the following year was close to the 1952 target.[o]

Again, these shortfalls are not necessarily evidence of failures in implementing the plan, since part of the explanation lies in the deliberate sacrifice of a high rate of investment. Also, the growth of production is dependent on other factors than the level of investment, although this level is a major element.

If industrial and agricultural production continue to expand at the rates achieved in 1954 and 1955, the second plan may prove to be outstandingly successful in hitting its targets in most sectors. But some of this "success" will have to be attributed to the selection of targets that were within easier range.

Over the postwar period as a whole, the rise of industrial and agricultural production, while appreciable, has not been impressive in comparison with the record of other European countries. Such comparisons are subject to many qualifications, and the results depend in part on the years which are selected. Thus each of the comparisons shown in Table 7 presents a somewhat different picture. Data on a per capita basis would make the French performance appear in a considerably better light, but such an adjustment does not seem appropriate since the slower rise in population is an im-

[o] The index of agricultural production has been unsatisfactory and is being revised by INSEE. The index for 1952, originally shown as 109 (on the prewar base) has since been changed to 112. The index for 1953 is 115. The OEEC Statistical Bulletin *General Statistics* (April 1956), gives indices of 110 and 120 for 1952-1953 and 1953-1954 respectively.

TABLE 5. OBJECTIVES AND RESULTS IN "BASIC SECTORS" OF FIRST MODERNIZATION AND EQUIPMENT PLAN, 1947-1952

Sector	*Unit*	*Actual 1929*	*Actual 1938*	*Objective 1950*	*Actual 1950*	*Objective 1952-1953*	*Actual 1952*
Energy							
Coal	mill. tons	55	47.6	65	52.5	60	57.4
Electricity	bill. k.w.h.	15.6	20.8	37	33.1	43	40.8
Petroleum Products	mill. tons refined	0	7	8.1	14.5	18.7	21.5
Industrial Means of Production							
Steel	mill. tons	9.7	6.2	11	8.7	12.5	10.9
Cement	mill. tons	6.2	3.6	13.5	7.2	8.5	8.6
Agricultural Means of Production							
Tractors	thous.	1	1.7	50	14.2	40	25.3
Nitrogenous fertilizer	thous. tons	73	177	320	236	300	285

Source: Commissariat Général au Plan, *Rapport sur la réalisation du plan de modernisation et d'équipement de l'Union française, année 1952*, (Paris, 1953) p. 13; and *General Report of the First Plan of Modernization and Equipment, November 1946-January 1947*, (Paris, 1947) pp. 37-39. Figure for 1950 objective in tractor production from *Journal Officiel, Avis et rapports du Conseil Economique*, January 27, 1951, p. 10, report by J. Bénard on "Investissements pour l'exercice 1951."

TABLE 6

PRODUCTION OBJECTIVES AND RESULTS OF THE FIRST MODERNIZATION AND EQUIPMENT PLAN (1948 VERSION) FOR AGRICULTURE

Commodity	*Unit*	*1934-1938 average*	*1952 objective*	*1952 results*	*195 resul*
Wheat	million quintals	81	95	84	90
Barley	" "	11	23	17	22
Oil seeds	" "	0.2	3.5	2.5	1.
Potatoes	" "	159	179	111	136
Sugar beets	" "	88	124	95	125
Sugar	thousand tons	769	1,300	910	1,500
Meat (beef, lamb, pork)	" "	1,700	2,200	2,065	2,270
Milk	million hectoliters	146	170	150	170

Source: Commissariat Général au Plan, *Rapport sur la réalisation du plan de modernisation d'équipement de l'Union française, année 1952* (Paris, 1953), p. 29; and INSEE, *Etudes conjoncture* January-February *1955*, pp. *50-56*.

portant factor to consider in studying the slower rate of economic growth of the country.

The comparison between 1946 and 1953 may be misleading since the level of industrial production was particularly low in France in 1946 as a result of heavier wartime damage and dislocation. Relative to 1938, France shows up rather poorly when it is recalled that industrial production was lower in France in that year than it was in most other countries, as a result of the continued recession. (On the other hand, the problem of recovery from the effects of the war and occupation was more severe in France.) Perhaps most significant for the long-run welfare of France is the comparison with 1929, which was a year of high production in most countries. During the 25-year span, 1929-1954, industrial production increased in France only by 24 per cent, hardly an impressive rate of growth. Only Belgium has failed to grow more rapidly than France in the intervening period, and the increase in industrial production in most countries has far outstripped that of France.

Relative to prewar, the growth of agricultural production is essentially similar to that of other European countries. According to the OEEC, which computes indices of agricultural production for each of its member countries on the basis of statistical information submitted by the country, using uniform weights, the preliminary results for the crop year 1954-1955 show French total agricultural

TABLE 7

INDEX OF INDUSTRIAL PRODUCTION[1] IN FRANCE AND OTHER COUNTRIES IN 1954

	INDEXES		
Country	*1946=100*	*1938=100*	*1929=100*
France	195	154	124
West Germany (excluding West Berlin)	[2]	178[3]	[2]
Belgium	169	150	117[7]
Denmark	141[5]	[2]	[2]
Italy	[2]	176	173
Norway	196	186	[2]
Netherlands	239	177	200
United Kingdom[4]	149	151	[2]
Sweden[6]	127	170	260
Europe[6, 7]	214	151	191
Canada	142	239	265
United States[6]	139	258	211

Source: United Nations *1955 Statistical Yearbook*, pp. 115, 117, 118, 123-126, 128-131.
1 Without building.
2 Not calculated.
3 Relative to 1936.
4 Including building.
5 Relative to 1947.
6 Excluding electricity and industrial gas.
7 Excludes USSR, Bulgaria, Czechoslovakia, Hungary, Poland, Romania, and Eastern Germany.

output as 125 per cent of prewar, and total agricultural output for the member countries combined as 126 per cent of prewar.[35]

VI SUMMARY

Faced with a war-devastated and stagnant economy, the government assumed responsibility for major programs to bring about its reconstruction and modernization. The programs at first had an overriding priority, but reconciliation of the need for investments and growth with other urgent needs soon became a continuing preoccupation, and some sacrifices were imposed on these as well as other objectives.

It appeared initially that reconstruction and modernization would be implemented by a tight system of direct controls over the allocation of productive resources, adopted within the framework of a national economic plan. Such a plan was eventually developed and later revised, but direct controls over resources were quickly abandoned. The principal method of achieving the plan became the provision of public funds for approved investments at preferential interest rates (or the provision of grants for reconstruction projects). With some revival of personal and business savings, and with growing pressures for other uses of public funds, this method declined in importance. The second modernization and equipment plan, apart from projects in the nationalized industries, was largely "indicative" and relied in the main on indirect incentives to stimulate private investments.

The emergency efforts of the government to reconstruct the economy contributed to the rapid recovery of production in the years immediately after the war. Over the life of the modernization and equipment plan, actual investments have been lower than the targets of the original or revised plans. The production realizations have also, in almost all cases, been below the original or revised goals. Some of the shortfalls were due to technical defects of the plan, or to its methods of implementation, but many were due to the failure to recognize, in setting targets, the conflicts among growth, stability, defense, and other objectives. The composition of investments, including those for "reconstruction" projects, was influenced by the government, but without very clear or precise notions of what the most efficient pattern of investments might be.

By European standards, the actual level of investments during the postwar period as a whole has not been high, and the growth of production has not been rapid. The economy has not grown at a pace that has permitted France to maintain its relative standing among European countries, let alone to make up for the interwar stagnation.

CHAPTER 3

CONTROL OF ECONOMIC FLUCTUATIONS

THIS chapter is concerned with efforts of the French government to control fluctuations in the levels of prices, output, and employment during the postwar period. It was during the years 1944 to 1948 that institutions were established, and policies adopted, that have carried over into subsequent years. Hence a more rounded description will be given of governmental policies during this period.

Although the government's efforts to achieve stabilization were not always closely correlated with the general economic situation, it is convenient to discuss the policies with reference to the economic background. The postwar evolution of the economy has not always been sharp or clear-cut, but for purposes of analysis the first decade of the postwar era can be divided into four periods: 1944 to 1948—inflation; 1949 to mid-1950—stabilization; mid-1950 to Spring 1952—the "Korean" inflation; and, since the Spring of 1952—stabilization, recession, and recovery.

I INFLATION (1944-1948)

A. THE PROBLEM

The years 1944-1948 were characterized by a large excess of money income and demand over available supplies, with acute shortages of consumer and equipment goods and rapidly rising prices.

Important elements of the inflationary situation confronting the government during this period were inherited, not only from the war and occupation but, in some instances, from the economic crises of the 1930's or earlier periods. On the demand side, the legacies were a swollen volume of liquid purchasing power, pumped into the monetary system by the occupation authorities,[a] the government's resolve to promote reconstruction and modernization, and the pent-up demand of a population anxious to enjoy the material fruits of victory. Consumer behavior was also influenced

[a] The money supply had increased about four-fold during the occupation, while the "official" price level (wholesale) rose about two and one-half times, and production levels dropped sharply. (R. Delouvrier and R. Nathan, *Politique économique de la France*, Cours à l'Institut d'Études Politiques de l'Université de Paris, 1953-1954, Vol. IV, pp. 114-117, Delbert A. Snider, "French Monetary and Fiscal Policies Since the Liberation," *American Economic Review*, Vol. XXVIII, No. 3, June 1948, p. 310.)

by an inflationary psychosis acquired in the prolonged periods of monetary instability between the two wars.[b] Moreover, the civilian population had developed considerable skill in circumventing direct economic controls, which had become highly unpopular during the Vichy period when evasion was exalted to a patriotic duty.

On the supply side, the legacy was an economy that was near prostration. The heavy loss of capital resources, the imbalance of remaining resources, and the low levels of current production have already been described. With the war still being fought on French soil in 1944 and early 1945, a substantial proportion of the slim margin of available resources was being devoted to the feeding and equipping of military forces.

Various factors continued to stimulate demands relative to supplies for several years after the war. Despite the steady rise of industrial production, availabilities of consumer goods remained well below the prewar level in 1945, 1946, and 1947. War-depleted inventories had to be built up at all stages of production and distribution. There was also some expansion of business inventories for speculative purposes or as a hedge against a further depreciation of the currency. Agricultural production recovered more slowly, in part as a result of the poor weather conditions in 1946 and 1947. The availability of foodstuffs to urban consumers was further reduced by the need to reconstitute livestock herds and by an increase in on-the-farm consumption. In view of the predominant part of food in the budget of the French workingman (generally about 60 per cent), the low food supplies prior to the second half of 1948 were a major element in the prolongation of the inflationary process.

Among the few factors acting to curb inflation might be mentioned the foreign trade deficits of early postwar years, which tended to offset domestic inflationary pressures by absorbing disposable incomes. The deficit that is relevant in this regard is that of Metropolitan France with the rest of the world (including the French overseas possessions). Even this factor was significant only immediately after the war, for in subsequent years the deficit in trade of Metropolitan France with foreign countries was largely offset by the surplus in Metropolitan France's trade with its overseas possessions.[c]

[b] Thus, wholesale prices by the end of 1938 had risen to 6.7 times the 1914 level. (INSEE, *Annuaire statistique* 1951, p. 227.)

[c] Data from INSEE (*Annuaire statistique* 1952, pp. 332-335) show ratios of the deficit to gross national availabilities of 5 per cent in 1946, 2.5 per cent in 1947, and 1.5 per cent in 1948. These figures are only very rough orders of mag-

The inflationary "gap" between money demands and available resources at *ex ante* prices was not measured statistically by the government before 1948, when the inflation was almost at an end. For 1948, a Commission on National Accounts made a very crude estimate. The gap, measured in terms of the price level at the beginning of the period (i.e., in November 1947) was estimated at 8.7 per cent of total available resources during the first half of the year and 5.5 per cent during the second half. It had to be filled by an increase in voluntary savings, by higher taxes, or by a rise in the price level. While the accuracy of the projections is open to question, it is interesting that when the gap had disappeared (*ex post*) the price level had risen by 35 per cent. The key figures in the estimate were as follows:[1]

	1948 (billions of francs)	
	Projected (Nov. 1947 Prices)	*Actual (Current Prices)*
A. *Resources*		
Agricultural products	1,762	
Industrial products	2,212	
Government services	387	
Other services	271	
Gross domestic production	4,635	6,253
Imports[a]	437	844
Exports[a]	178	566
Net imports	259	278
Total Resources	4,894	6,531
B. *Demands*		
Current government expenditures	552	725
Public and private investment	968	1,322
Private consumption	3,739	4,484
Total Demands	5,259	6,531
C. *Inflationary "Gap"*	365	—

[a] The large differences between estimated and actual import and export values are presumably due in part to the devaluations of the franc during 1948.

Thus, aggregate demand exceeded aggregate supplies of goods and services at the going level of prices, both as of the end of the war and as of various subsequent dates. Something had to give.

nitude. The data from the Commission on National Accounts, referred to below, show a ratio of 4 per cent for 1948. "Gross national availabilities" are defined as gross national product plus imports.

Unless purchasing power could be siphoned off at the source or the rise of prices suppressed by direct controls, inflation was bound to occur. Open inflation was known to have serious disadvantages. It would divert the effort of individuals to the protection of their positions against price increases, and in the end would curtail the demands of those persons or agencies who left themselves relatively unprotected. In other words, inflation would bring aggregate demand and aggregate supply into balance by inflicting cuts in demand (in real terms) inequitably, almost haphazardly. Also, inflation would raise the price of French goods, tending to reduce sales to, and to increase purchases from, other countries. This would aggravate the foreign exchange deficit, which, while offsetting some of the internal inflationary pressure, was difficult to finance. On both internal and external accounts, therefore, vigorous action to curb the inflation seemed imperative.

Of course, policies to control inflation were by no means easy to apply. Simple suppression of price increases, if effective at all, could also inflict haphazard cuts in demand—by allocating materials on the basis of vague and erroneous criteria, by allocating nothing to purchasers who got in line last or were least vociferous. And to shrink purchasing power at the source would mean facing head-on the painful (and politically difficult) problem of deciding which demands should be cut.

The postwar governments in France tried to use the techniques both of mopping up excess purchasing power and of forcibly suppressing price increases. But, as will be seen, they had great difficulty in facing and resolving the hard choices that were required to implement an effective anti-inflationary policy. The dimensions of their problem, and their success in attacking it, may be gauged by the fact that wholesale prices increased more than sevenfold between mid-1944 and the end of 1948 (Table 8).[d]

B. THE POLICIES—DIRECT CONTROLS

A comprehensive system of direct controls over income and spending was carried over from wartime and, in some cases, enlarged. Ceilings on prices and wage rates, rationing of consumer goods, compulsory collection of some foodstuffs, and subsidies constituted the full range of controls. In view of the government's

[d] The sharp increases in the indexes in 1947 and 1948 shown in Table 8 are in large part deceptive, and reflect primarily the relaxation of legal controls; the official indexes during the earlier years are under-estimated by virtue of the ubiquitous black market in which many transactions took place at prices up to two or three times the legal ones.

TABLE 8. INDEX OF WHOLESALE PRICES, 1944-1954

Year	*Jan.*	*Feb.*	*Mar.*	*April*	*May*	*June*	*July*	*Aug.*	*Sept.*	*Oct.*	*Nov.*	*Dec.*
					A. 1944-1950 (Base 1938 =100)							
1944	253	254	254	255	267	268	271	271	267	265	272	276
1945	277	286	290	327	366	375	377	393	429	447	462	469
1946	479	488	548	559	624	604	571	699	727	824	810	846
1947	874	889	860	847	946	904	888	1,004	1,096	1,129	1,211	1,217
1948	1,463	1,537	1,536	1,555	1,653	1,691	1,698	1,784	1,791	1,887	1,977	1,974
1949	1,946	1,898	1,872	1,846	1,890	1,812	1,854	1,918	1,958	2,002	2,005	2,002
1950	2,063	2,057	2,102	2,098	2,082	2,035	2,123	2,207	2,237	2,270	2,204	2,409
					B. 1949-1954 (Base 1949 = 100)							
1949	102.9	100.3	99.5	98.1	98.8	96.3	96.9	98.5	100.6	102.8	102.5	102.6
1950	103.9	103.1	104.6	104.6	104.3	103.4	106.1	107.3	111.6	113.2	116.6	120.5
1951	123.0	130.0	134.0	140.2	140.7	137.6	134.7	133.9	137.5	145.5	150.7	151.5
1952	152.5	152.0	149.3	146.8	144.6	142.6	143.5	143.7	142.6	140.6	140.1	140.5
1953	140.8	139.2	139.7	139.0	139.3	138.6	137.3	137.3	136.9	136.3	137.4	138.0
1954	137.9	137.8	136.3	136.8	138.9	134.8	134.4	135.9	134.6	133.9	134.7	135.2

Sources: 1944-1945: INSEE, *Bulletin de la statistique générale de la France*, 1945-1946.
1946-1951: Ministère des Finances, *Inventaire de la situation financière*, 1951, p. 144.
1949 (new base): INSEE, *Annuaire statistique de la France*, 1952, p. 269.
1952-1954: INSEE, *Bulletin mensuel de statistique*, February 1953, p. 19; February 1954, p. 25; February 1955, p. 28.

monetary and fiscal policies and the extent of the inflationary pressures, whether or not these direct controls could have worked if applied vigorously and consistently is questionable. But there can be little question that the government did not so apply them.

Several early decisions played an important part in setting the pattern that was to be followed throughout most of the period. One of these was the granting of massive wage increases, which immediately strained the control mechanism. Prior to the Allied landings, the resistance leaders in Algiers had decided upon a general wage increase, as a liberation "gift" to workers, whose controlled wages had lagged behind prices during the occupation. In August and September of 1944, upon the liberation of Paris, wage increases of about 40 per cent were granted, together with a 50 to 80 per cent increase in the system of family allowances. Prices were blocked at a level that did not incorporate the effects of the wage increases; the government hoped that the increase in costs would be taken out of profit margins, but was prepared to grant subsidies if necessary to hold down the price level. A further round of substantial wage increases was granted in the spring of 1945. This time it proved necessary to raise industrial prices as well, and when agricultural crops began to be marketed in the summer large increases were in turn provided (50 per cent for beef, 65 per cent for wheat, 60 per cent for wine).

Another key factor was the inability or unwillingness to control meat supplies and prices at the farm level, and therefore at wholesale and retail levels. As in the case of other farm products, the large number of meat producers and their geographical dispersion made it difficult, at best, to enforce a program of compulsory meat collection. The farmers strongly opposed the program, and they exercised an important voice in postwar political affairs; their widespread evasion of the controls contributed to the rapid breakdown of the program. As Lorwin has observed, "Farmers who during the occupation had found it patriotic to sell on the black market, now simply found it natural."[2] Compulsory collection of meat at the farm level was abandoned in August 1945, thereby inserting a major loophole into the control system. An interminable series of "meat plans" was subsequently attempted, none of which was able to bring adequate supplies to the large urban centers except at highly inflated prices. Since meat occupies a large place in the budget of the French workingman, the continual rise in its price became a significant element in the mounting cost of living. The meat price also tended to act as the bellwether for other agricultural prices.[3]

The system of consumer rationing, which had been both unpopular and largely ineffective, was progressively dismantled in 1945 and 1946. A flourishing black market thus continued to be an accompaniment of attempts to fix consumer prices at wholesale and retail. Because of the inadequate controls over the distribution of consumer goods, and particularly of food products, the action of the price control authorities consisted in part of the *de jure* ratification of increases which had already taken place. Where prices could be effectively controlled, as in the case of basic industrial products or agricultural products at the farm level, the rapid increase in other prices made adjustments necessary. Nevertheless, since most prices and all wages were under its authority, the government's decisions influenced the magnitude of the inflationary process and imparted a distinctive pattern to it.

The government proved unable to arbitrate the conflict among the different economic groups for a larger share of the national income except by capitulating to each in turn (or in some cases to several simultaneously). The result of this process of "log-rolling inflation"[4] was a wage-cost-price spiral proceeding at a cadence strongly influenced by the government's decisions. At periodic intervals, the government would adjust whichever element was lagging most, thereby giving a new impulse to the spiralling process. Thus an increase in farm prices following a bad harvest would raise urban living costs; workers would successfully press their claims for higher money wages; because of rising wage costs, an increase in industrial prices would be granted; the higher industrial prices would raise the cost of living of workers and farmers, who would demand further increases in wages and farm prices, and so forth. Once the pattern had become established, expectations that further price and wage increases would be authorized by the government acted to intensify the inflationary movement.

A celebrated instance of early government wage-price policies was the conference at the Palais Royal, convoked by the Bidault government in July 1946 to resolve simultaneously the problems of adjusting prices, costs, and wages. The conference was made up of national representatives of trade unions, farm organizations, and businessmen's trade associations. The government adopted a strategy of aloofness, in the hopes that the conflicting claims of the groups would cancel out. Instead, the interested groups succeeded in cumulating their claims. A program for a 25 per cent increase in wages and a 50 to 60 per cent increase in agricultural prices was agreed upon. With respect to industrial prices, it was piously hoped that an increase could be avoided by reduced margins and increased subsidies, but the possibility that further increases in industrial prices might be necessary was recognized. The government having accepted the results of the conference, an average increase in industrial prices of 20 per cent took place in September.[5]

It is not necessary to trace the subsequent steps in detail. Authorized price increases took place too frequently and unsystematically for easy enumeration. With respect to wage rates, the government undertook six major readjustments from the liberation to the end of 1947. Meanwhile, the general level of wages tended to move upwards as some employers provided "black market" wage increases or reclassified workers to achieve the same result.[6]

Subsidies of industrial and food products were resorted to on a large scale in 1945, 1946, and 1947. They represented 16.4 per cent of budgetary expenses in 1946 and 12.4 per cent in 1947.[7] Since subsidies, while holding down particular prices, inject additional purchasing power, they are not likely to be an effective anti-inflationary weapon; in any event, they were not used systematically, because of the resultant increases in the budgetary deficit, which had come to be regarded as the heart of the inflationary problem.

An interesting departure from the standard pattern took place in January 1947, when the Blum government attempted to roll back prices while holding wages constant. An immediate 5 per cent reduction in almost all prices was ordered, with a further 5 per cent reduction announced for no later than March 1. The government was apparently relying primarily on the psychological impact of the well-publicized rollback, particularly on those holding inventories for speculative purposes. Some wage increases were granted in the lowest categories, but the general wage level was frozen. Increased subsidies were provided for industrial products, some of which had benefited from substantial price increases just before the program was announced. The second 5 per cent reduction, on a more selective basis, was ordered late in February by Blum's successor, Ramadier. The Blum experiment succeeded in reversing temporarily the upward spiral of official prices. Whether "unofficial" prices also followed the downward trend is more difficult to ascertain. In any event, the experiment was short lived.

Because of the continued meat shortages, an increase in meat prices at the consumer level was authorized. In April, labor pressure resulted in the granting of further wage increases in the form of a special bonus. Shortly thereafter the upward process resumed.[8]

By the end of 1947, Parliamentary sentiment had shifted away from direct controls and a "managed" economy towards a more "liberal" approach. The shift paralleled a political swing toward the Right; it also reflected both a general recognition of the failure of the control mechanism to curb the inflationary pressures and an impression that the period of most acute postwar shortages was now past. Some relaxation of price controls took place in 1948, in accordance with a new regulatory system described below. Wage controls were not relaxed until early 1950, however.

C. FISCAL POLICY

An effective anti-inflationary policy in the fiscal field would have called for a combination of measures designed to create a cash surplus or at least to reduce the deficit sharply from the prodigious levels carried over from wartime. With its deficits widely regarded as a prime mover of inflation, and the favorite target of critics, the government made numerous gestures in this direction by cutting some expenditures and increasing tax yields. But the deficits persisted, if on a somewhat reduced scale, and were at least 30 per cent of government expenditures in each year. The government's fiscal policy therefore generated additional incomes and an increase in the stock of liquidity throughout the period.

"Economies" in government spending were ordered by a "hatchet" committee (in 1946) and a "guillotine" committee (in 1947). Across-the-board percentage reductions in expenditures of civil ministries were attempted on some occasions, while on others the executive was given special powers to carry out economies by decree. But the ordained cuts in civil expenditures were often swamped by the frequent revisions in personnel and procurement costs prompted by the inflation. Some increases in subsidy payments were also authorized—contrary to the initial budgetary intentions of the government—in an unsuccessful effort to stem the inflationary tide. While the data on budgetary expenditures and receipts of the central government, given in Table 9, show a large increase in the level of civil expenditures between 1945 and 1948, it is likely that in real terms such expenditures decreased.

Important reductions in military spending were possible after 1945, when the major direct costs arising from the war and

TABLE 9. CENTRAL GOVERNMENT BUDGETARY EXPENDITURES AND RECEIPTS, 1945-1954
(billions of current francs)

Expenditures and Receipts	*1945*	*1946*	*1947*	*1948*	*1949*	*1950*	*1951*	*1952*	*1953*	*1954*[1]
Operating expenditures of civil services	296	345	444	681	842	1,114	1,297	1,394	1,559	1,736
Capital expenditures:										
Equipment of civil services	14	43	70	98	150	121	140	145	179	500 (Equipment and Economic and social investments combined)
Economic and social investments[2]	3	39	77	280	432	426	303	332	350	
War damage and construction	35	83	92	200	246	285	312	332	330	312
Total capital expenditures	52	165	239	578	828	832	755	809	859	812
Military expenditures	175	171	231	332	377	463	857	1,269	1,242	1,110[3]
Deficit of special treasury accounts[4]	–	–	–	–	–	–	–	70	62[5]	55
Total expenditures[6]	523	681	914	1,591	2,047	2,409	2,909	3,542	3,722	3,713
Total receipts[7]	238	462	685	1,050	1,487	1,952	2,161	2,698	2,940	2,903
Budget deficit	285	219	229	541	560	457	748	844	782	810

Sources: Data for 1945-1951 inclusive from Ministère des Finances, *Inventaire de la situation financière* (Paris, 1951), pp. 17, 258-259; for 1952 from Assemblée Nationale, *Rapport de la Commission des Finances sur le projet de loi des finances pour l'exercice 1953* (No. 4794), pp. 57, 85; for 1953 from *Revue d'économie politique*, July-October 1954, pp. 579, 589; for 1954 from Ministère des Finances, *Statistiques et études financières*, No. 73, January 1955, p. 16, except for military expenditures which are based on the finance law of December 31, 1953.

1 Provisional results.

2 Does not include loans floated by nationalized enterprises after 1950 and guaranteed by the state. The amount of these loans has ranged between 85 and 120 billion francs during the years 1951-1954 inclusive.

3 Estimated from the Finance Law of December 31, 1953.

4 Not available prior to 1951.

5 Estimated from the Finance Law of July 11, 1953.

6 Data do not include expenditures still in special treasury accounts or annexed budgets in 1951. However, the data do include many important expenditures, such as payments of war damages, that were covered in the special treasury accounts (rather than in the budget proper) prior to 1951. Data for the years 1952-1954 have been adjusted by the writer to make them roughly comparable to the figures for 1945-1951.

7 Includes receipts from ordinary taxes, customs duties, and exceptional taxes (confiscation of illegal profits, National Solidarity tax), and from industrial operations and miscellaneous revenue sources. Does not include the counterpart of American aid.

occupation had been liquidated. The military component of the budget would have declined in relative importance even more rapidly had it not been for the campaign in Indochina, which began in December 1946.

The most distinctive feature of the early pattern of government spending was the sharp increase in capital expenditures. The reasons for the devotion of public funds to reconstruction and investment activities have already been commented upon. Capital expenditures, which were only 10 per cent of the budget in 1945, had risen to more than 35 per cent by 1948.[e] Some reductions were made in the publicly-financed portions of the investment program after 1947 in the interests of budgetary economy and the fight against inflation. In these early years of the program, however, the government was reluctant to cut its financial support more sharply on several grounds. One was that the modernization goals were considered to be sufficiently important that a "mild" inflation was acceptable in order to achieve them. Also, a considerable proportion of the investments was regarded as being particularly valuable because these investments brought about increases in supply in the short run and assisted in the prompt recovery of production throughout the economy. Finally, it was believed, at least in some government circles, that a shift of the resources used in the investment program to the production of consumer goods would only have increased that production slowly.[9]

On the revenue side of the budget, several exceptional measures were taken to increase tax receipts, and later to raise basic tax rates. These measures seem to have had less effect than the increases in yields arising more-or-less automatically from the high proportion of expenditure taxes in the French tax structure.

Immediately after the war, a series of "exceptional" revenue measures was adopted to finance the swollen volume of public expenditures, also considered to be exceptional and therefore temporary. The first of these, decreed in October 1944, was a confiscatory tax on illegal profits, defined as those having arisen from trading with the enemy or from infractions of the price control and rationing systems. The tax was not seriously enforced, and had only a small yield. To this was added, in August 1945, a "national solidarity tax" intended to provide for an equitable sharing of the

[e] The data on capital expenditures in Table 9 are derived from different sources than those used in estimating "public" investment funds in Table 4. The results are not comparable, *inter alia*, because of differences in the definition of public funds, in the concept of investment, in the date on which the figures for a given year are prepared and possibly also in the precise time period to which they apply.

national burden of war damage reconstruction. The tax contained two elements: a tax on capital assets, with broad exemptions and a moderate increase in the tax rate; and a tax on capital gains during the wartime period, with considerably steeper rates. Despite a subsequent increase in the tax on capital assets, the return fell below expectations. Over the period 1946-1949, the total yield from the tax was only 3 per cent of budgetary receipts.[10]

The temporary increase in the level of expenditures proving to be more permanent, the government was shortly obliged to consider ways and means of increasing its revenue from ordinary tax sources. The principal action was directed at increasing the rates of existing taxes rather than at overhauling the tax system as a whole. As a result of increases in rates and of the fact that returns from taxes on production and sales followed the upward movement of economic activity and prices with a shorter time lag than did returns from taxes on income, excise taxes accounted for an increasing proportion of total tax yields. Thus, the yield on all of the excise taxes (including custom duties) rose from 39 per cent of total budgetary receipts in 1945 to 56 per cent in 1948.[11] An advantage stemming from the heavy reliance on excise taxes was that receipts from these sources increased more rapidly than did most items of government spending during the inflation. This was an important factor contributing to the reduction in the size of the deficit in comparison with 1945. Nevertheless, while the relative size of the deficit was reduced, it remained substantial throughout the years 1945 to 1948. It did not fall below 30 per cent of total expenditures in any year, and was 36 per cent in 1948.

The government endeavored to finance its deficits with long and medium-term borrowing, the method of borrowing believed to increase the liquidity of the public to the smallest extent. But the public proved to have little confidence in the longer-term issues while the inflation was proceeding. An exception was the liberation loan of November 1944, which benefited from the particular psychological climate at the time of its issuance. The loan brought in 164 billion francs, of which 127 billion were new receipts of money and 37 conversion of shorter-term treasury certificates.[12] Attempts at medium or long-term borrowing in subsequent years met with less success. In 1948, an "exceptional anti-inflationary levy" was adopted by Parliament, through a procedure which amounted to a forced loan directed towards those groups which were believed to have profited most from the postwar inflation. The loan received subscriptions of 108 billion francs, a smaller sum than had been anticipated.[13]

Short-term borrowing from the public, in the form of treasury certificates, was tried with varying success. Subscriptions were at a very high level in 1945, when economic activity was close to a standstill and alternative methods of investing liquid savings were limited. During the ensuing inflation, however, there was a net liquidation of public short-term holdings.

In addition to its direct borrowing from the public, the government made effective use of a well established technique, still applied, for channeling the savings of individuals and businesses into its exchequer. The postal checking system has been obliged to deposit its holdings with the Treasury, which pays interest of 1 per cent on sums attributable to private depositors. The private savings institutions and the National Savings Fund (*Caisse Nationale d'Epargne*) have been depositing their funds with a semi-public institution (the *Caisse des Dépôts et Consignations*), which may in turn subscribe to government securities or leave funds on deposit with the Treasury. In this way the Treasury has built up what has been described as a "veritable banking department."[14] The movement of these funds was erratic, varying with the economic situation and (in 1945 and 1948) with the techniques used in connection with certain monetary operations described below. Their importance is indicated by the fact that, over the years 1945-1948, net receipts from these sources were equal to those from all long, medium, and short-term public borrowing combined. (The various resources used by the Treasury in covering its deficits are listed in Table 10.)

Despite these various forms of borrowing from the public, the government had to rely heavily on the less attractive alternatives of borrowing from the Bank of France and from other parts of the banking system. The remainder of the banking system provided short-term funds to the Treasury through direct subscriptions to treasury certificates (an operation prohibited the Bank of France) and through the discounting of short-term public expenditures drafts (*traites*) used by the Treasury as a means of deferring cash payments to its creditors. A substantial volume of banking funds was invested in these forms of treasury paper in 1945, but the volume dropped off in 1946 and there was a net liquidation in 1947. Since 1948, the system of quantitative credit controls (see below) has formalized the banks' participation by obliging them to keep a prescribed portion of their assets in the form of treasury paper.

TABLE 10. SUMMARY OF TREASURY OPERATIONS, 1945-1954
(billions of current francs)

Operation	*1945*	*1946*	*1947*	*1948*	*1949*	*1950*	*1951*	*1952*	*1953*	*1954*[1]
Expenditures	532	780	951	1,593	2,081	2,466	2,850	3,609	3,837	3,891
Revenues	224	427	659	1,023	1,470	1,896	2,346	2,737	3,020	3,118
Balance	–308	–353	–292	–570	–611	–570	–504	–872	–817	–773
Treasury resources:										
Counterpart of foreign borrowing and American aid	59	143	156	124	289	185	150	204	159	109
Borrowing from business and individuals:										
Long-term loans	40	34	4	127	123	42	9	228	27	
Medium- and short-term loans	61	–5	2	45	10	57	91	83	94	
Private savings in bank, postal, and treasury accounts	104	42	38	153	130	147	119	145	215	
Total	205	71	44	325	263	246	219	456	336	
Borrowing from banking system:										664
Bank of France advances	–14	73	115	17	7	–12	–2	15	228	
Other banking resources	100	38	–19	89	52	61	86	116	51	
Total	86	111	96	106	59	49	84	131	279	
Deposits of local and other administrative agencies	–37	–2	14	38	28	110	63	69	80	
Miscellaneous	–5	30	–18	–23	–28	–20	–12	12	–37	
Balance of Treasury operations	308	353	292	570	611	570	504	872	817	773

Sources: 1945-1949: Ministère des Finances, *Inventaire de la situation financière* (Paris, 1951), pp. 489, 492.
1950-1953: Ministère des Finances, *Statistiques et études financières*, No. 66 (Paris, June 1954), pp. 543, 545.
1954: Ministère des Finances, *Statistiques et études financières*, No. 78 (Paris, June 1955), p. 577.

[1] Complete data for 1954 have not been published on a basis comparable to the data for earlier years.

The principal form of postwar assistance from the central bank has been the "provisional" advance, the volume of which is limited by a ceiling fixed by the Parliament. Through these advances, the Bank of France has acted as a "lender of last resort" to the Treasury. Heavy recourse to Bank of France advances took place in 1946 and 1947. Advances in these two years totalled 188 billion francs; it was necessary to raise the ceiling on advances from 100 billion francs to 150 billion in June 1947, 175 billion in September and 200 billion in November. This direct recourse to the central bank, which may have the same effects in practice as the printing of currency, became the symbol of inflationary financing and has since been looked upon with increasing disfavor.

The government also resorted to borrowing from the Bank of France through the legerdemain of the "counterpart" accounts, representing the local currency counterpart of the balance of payments deficit. Despite a popular myth to the contrary, the net effect of the complicated transactions involved is tantamount to direct central bank advances to the Treasury.[f] The Treasury has used this operation, in one form or another, almost continuously since 1940. When the European Recovery Program was instituted, the local currency equivalent of American aid was set up in a special "counterpart fund" in accordance with the ECA legislation. In countries with more "austere" financial policies (the United Kingdom, Netherlands, and Norway) these counterpart funds were sterilized or used to retire part of the public debt, on the grounds that their release would be inflationary (or would offset the original deflationary effect of the imports paid for in the local

[f] The use of one deficit to cover another might appear to be one of the seven wonders of modern finance. Briefly stated, the operation runs essentially as follows. The Treasury receives foreign exchange from the reserves of the Bank of France in return for treasury certificates (*bons du trésor*). The foreign exchange is then ceded to the Exchange Stabilization Fund. As the exchange is sold to importers, the francs received by the ESF are deposited in an account in the Treasury, where they are disbursed for current operations. This operation is described in Ministère des Finances, *Inventaire de la situation financière* (Paris, 1951), pp. 79, 82, 479, 483, 486 and *Statistiques et études financières, supplément finances comparées*, No. 10, 1951, p. 392. The Treasury also appropriated the local currency proceeds of loans floated abroad by the government. Each time that the franc was devalued, the bookkeeping profits arising from the re-evaluation of the Bank of France's holdings of foreign exchange were also used by the Treasury, to reduce its indebtedness to the Bank of France.

A favorable shift in the balance of payments situation in 1949 began to have a reverse effect on the Treasury, which found itself obliged to provide francs to the ESF for its acquisitions of foreign exchange. A new agreement was therefore adopted in June 1949, divorcing the ESF from the Treasury and linking it directly with the Bank of France. The Treasury has continued to use the counterpart of American aid, however, and to benefit from the local currency proceeds of foreign loans.

currencies). In France, however, the counterpart funds were released for budgetary expenditures almost as fast as they accumulated.

The counterpart of the foreign deficit was a particularly important source of treasury funds during the years in question. In 1947, for example, more than half of the deficit was covered in this fashion. Over the period 1945-1948 as a whole, close to 60 per cent of the deficit was financed by recourse to the banking system in this and more conventional forms.

On balance, it must be said that the government's fiscal policies, by failing to reduce the deficit to manageable proportions and by financing it primarily through the banking system, served more to aggravate than to alleviate the inflationary problem. One rough indication of the magnitude of the government's contribution to the inflationary situation is that the increase in government borrowing from all sources amounted to about 40 per cent of the increase in the money supply in 1946 and 1947, as can be seen from Table 11.

D. MONETARY AND CREDIT POLICY[g]

Throughout this period the stock of money increased rapidly, by 33 per cent in 1946, 24 per cent in 1947, and 29 per cent in 1948. The monetary policy of the government was dominated by two viewpoints: that the origins of the inflation lay outside of the monetary system; and that an "adequate" supply of money was indispensable to a recovery of production which might eventually bring the inflation to a halt. To the extent that credit controls were attempted by central banking authorities, the measures that were used could not have had more than a minor effect as an anti-inflationary weapon. Also, the selective controls on which the government primarily relied proved to have serious deficiencies. Credit policy therefore did not prevent an increase in the money supply, which was an important element in the inflationary process in that it permitted the financing of economic activity at a continually rising level of prices.

A key decision, which followed the pattern already observed in the case of other controls, was the early rejection of a strong currency reform.[15] During the occupation period, the money supply

[g] The term "fiscal policy" has been used to include the financing of government deficits and their effects on the stock of money. "Monetary and credit policy" is used to refer to other monetary measures such as currency reform and actions directly affecting the volume of bank credit and the conditions under which it is available to private borrowers.

TABLE 11. SOURCE OF MONEY SUPPLY, 1938, 1945-1954
(billions of current francs)

	December 31										
Source	*1938*	*1945*	*1946*	*1947*	*1948*	*1949*	*1950*	*1951*	*1952*	*1953*	*1954*
Gold and foreign exchange holdings[1]	92	144	144	152	152	241	477	289	240	229	398
Loans to Government:											
Bank of France advances[2]	32	441	517	633	676	681	695	732	798	927	943
Government securities in portfolios of the banking system	15	274	304	293	354	420	431	513	626	702	768
Postal checking system deposits	3	43	62	85	143	187	209	262	304	352	437
Deposits of individuals and businesses with treasury agents	–	7	10	15	17	22	28	33	31	35	37
Total loans to Government	50	765	893	1,026	1,190	1,310	1,363	1,540	1,759	2,016	2,185
Loans to individuals and businesses[3]	53	118	308	490	850	1,189	1,355	1,905	2,271	2,518	2,840
Gross total	195	1,027	1,345	1,668	2,192	2,740	3,195	3,734	4,270	4,763	5,423
Adjustment[4]	–3	–14	+4	+8	–27	–36	–75	–56	–111	–133	–168
Total money supply	192	1,013	1,349	1,676	2,165	2,704	3,120	3,678	4,159	4,630	5,255

Sources: 1938-1950: Ministère des Finances, *Inventaire de la situation financière* (Paris, 1951), pp. 524-525.
1951-1954: Ministère des Finances, *Statistiques et études financières*, No. 76, April 1955, p. 397.

[1] Of the Bank of France, including treasury bills representative of gold holdings.

[2] Including Bank of France deposits with postal checking system and discount of tax certificates ("traites fiscales"); including treasury bills representative of gold holdings.

[3] Excluding medium-term loans extended by specialized credit agencies and not rediscounted by the banks.

[4] Balance of non-monetary assets and liabilities in the balance sheet of the banking system.

had increased at a rate almost double that of the general price level. Immediately after the liberation, a dispute arose within the government on the best means of carrying out a currency conversion operation to mop up the excessive holdings of liquid assets which constituted a serious inflationary threat. The group headed by Mendès-France, then Minister of National Economy, favored a drastic operation similar to that of Belgium, where the exchange of bank notes in October 1944 had been combined with partial blockage of the notes in new accounts subject to subsequent taxation and only gradually unfrozen. Opponents of the drastic operation, headed by Minister of Finance Pleven, objected on a variety of grounds: theoretical (that a reduction in the money supply would only increase the velocity of its circulation); technical (that it would be difficult to administer such a reform); psychological (that it would ruin the state's credit); and economic (that it would paralyze business activity). In practice, political considerations, among them the desire not to antagonize the peasants who were believed to be holders of substantial monetary hoards, played an important part in the eventual decision.

It was not possible to carry out a currency conversion before early 1945 owing to the lack of new banknotes. When the liberation loan was launched in the autumn of 1944, it was announced that upon its success would depend the need to carry out a more drastic measure. The dispute was renewed in the beginning of 1945 with the arrival of the new banknotes. After several months' time lost in debate, it was decided to conduct only a simple exchange operation. All old bank notes in denominations above 50 francs (representing 98 per cent of the currency in circulation) were called in, declared valueless, and exchanged almost immediately for new ones. This decision was an important one, since it set the tone for subsequent monetary and financial policies.

Advocates of the simple note conversion expected it to achieve several results. The government would receive a "profit" on the notes which, for various reasons, would not be exchanged; an opportunity would be provided to "photograph" currency holdings, as a basis for a future capital levy; and idle cash holdings would be converted into Treasury bonds, either directly or through the medium of increased bank deposits.

The conversion was carried out in June 1945. The Treasury netted a profit of 35 billion francs on notes which were not exchanged. The note circulation declined from 589 billion francs in May to 444 billion in August. On the other hand, deposit money increased by 110 billion francs, as individuals placed their cash in bank accounts to avoid the need for conversion. Shortly thereafter, the increase of currency in circulation resumed at its old rate. The effect of the operation on the total money supply was therefore very slight. Not unexpectedly, it proved to be a bonanza for the Treasury, which made use of the bank deposits to finance its operations through increased sales of treasury bonds. The exchange was followed by the imposition of the national solidarity tax (capital levy) with the disappointing results already noted.

In its other monetary policies, the government sought ambivalently to facilitate the use of credit for the recovery of business activity while attempting to discourage its use for "inflationary" purposes. Adjustments of the discount rate alone might not have had a decisive effect in curbing the volume of credit, but it is significant that a "cheap" money policy was pursued throughout almost the entire inflationary period. While hostilities were still under way, in January 1945, the Bank of France reduced the discount rate from the occupation level of 1.75 per cent to the unprecedentedly low rate of 1.625 per cent. This step was taken on the grounds that large-scale bank credit was indispensable for financing the recovery of production. At the same time, banks were permitted unlimited rediscounting at the Bank of France and at semi-public credit institutions. The first significant increase in the discount rate was not made until October 1947, with a dual rate established to penalize borrowing for inventory speculation. It was only in September 1948, when the price inflation was virtually over, that the Bank decided to use the discount rate, along with stronger qualitative credit controls and new measures of quantitative control, as "defensive weapons."[16]

The principal device upon which banking officials originally pinned their hopes was the application of qualitative or selective credit controls. By a policy that was "discriminatory, but not systematically restrictive," the National Credit Council[h] and its alter ego, the Bank of France, hoped to facilitate the recovery of production while forestalling the use of bank credit for speculative purposes. The system established progressively over the period 1946 to 1948 had two main elements: instructions to banks to screen all loans above a certain size in accordance with prescribed criteria; and the requirement of prior authorization by the Bank of France

[h] The National Credit Council is a central planning and advisory body set up under the law of December 2, 1945 which nationalized the Bank of France and the four largest deposit banks.

for loans above a certain (larger) amount. Commercial paper was not subject to the regulations, however, and the bankers were not persuaded to follow the vague criteria laid down by the Bank of France.

First in the form of "recommendations" and later as "instructions" couched in stronger language, the lending banks were advised to set up extensive dossiers of information on prospective loans above 2 million francs. These dossiers might be examined *ex post* by the Bank of France to see whether the credits had in fact been adequately justified. In deciding upon the merits of an individual loan, two new criteria were added to the conventional ones of financial security and prospective earnings: the indispensability of the loan (that is, whether it was possible for the borrower to obtain the necessary funds from any other source); and the economic utility of the loan (that is, whether it contributed to the recovery of the productive sectors of the economy). While strongly warning the banks against any curtailment of funds necessary for the economic life of the country, the National Credit Council and the Bank of France issued general or specific injunctions against the use of credit for consumer purchases, for inventory speculation or commodity hoarding, and for purchases of stocks or real estate.[17]

The more important requests for credit (in amounts in excess of 30 million francs, later raised to 50 million) were made subject to advance approval by the Bank of France. The central bank followed the same criteria, but concentrated on the question of economic productivity or utility, leaving the financial aspects of the dossier to the bank which transmitted it. An important exception to the requirements both for review and for advance approval was made for the discounting of commercial paper, on the dubious grounds that this paper represented goods in production or transit and therefore unlimited discounting of such paper was not inflationary.[1]

The experiment with selective controls proved largely unsatisfactory.[18] An increasing proportion of bank credit escaped from the regulations, as borrowers turned from banking overdrafts to the discounting of commercial paper. Even greater difficulties arose from the uncertainties attached to the notion of economic utility. At the local level, banking officials openly professed themselves incapable of determining the importance of an individual enterprise to the national economy. Under pressure from their habitual clients, the temptation was great to resort exclusively to the orthodox con-

[1] This notion is generally referred to as the "real bills fallacy."

siderations of risk and profit. The guidance from public banking authorities was necessarily vague, and became more so as the priority sectors of the original modernization and equipment plan were extended. The experience of the Bank of France did not differ significantly. In the approval or rejection of loan requests, how were bank personnel to interpret the imprecise concept of economic utility? In practice, decisions were made pragmatically on the basis of more conventional financial yardsticks. Less than 10 per cent of the loan requests were rejected by the Bank in 1947 and 1948.[j]

In September 1948, when the inflation was almost over, the qualitative controls were strengthened by the inclusion of commercial bills in the review process of individual banks (but not in the prior authorization procedure of the Bank of France). This action was taken concurrently with the institution of a new system of quantitative controls and the adoption of a "dear" money policy. Specific instructions were also issued in the second half of 1948 against loans for particular inventory purposes.

The banking authorities shied away from quantitative restrictions on the volume of credit during the years 1945-1947. It was believed that such measures would be difficult to administer during a period of rapidly rising prices, and might cause "undue" hardship to businesses because of their inflexibility.[19] By the autumn of 1948, the economic situation appeared to warrant their application; industrial production had passed the 1938 level and an abundant harvest was in prospect. The quantitative measures adopted in September had two main elements. One was the institution of a formal system of reserve requirements, the first in French banking history. Its purpose was to prevent the banking system from expanding credit by selling government securities, directly or indirectly, to the Bank of France. Formalizing a set of "gentlemen's agreements" which had grown up between the Bank of France and the commercial banks, the new provision obliged the banks to maintain in their portfolios at least 95 per cent of the government securities held as of September 30, 1948. In addition, 20 per cent of any increase in deposits had to be invested in government securities.

The 20 per cent figure was a moderate one, somewhat below the actual practice of most banks in times of increasing deposits.

[j] It is possible, of course, that some loans were rejected in advance by the commercial banks or that some prospective borrowers were deterred by the regulations.

Its effectiveness as a means of sterilizing this small proportion of new deposits depended on the source of the government securities and the uses to which the Treasury put its newly acquired funds. Thus there was no provision to prevent the banks from acquiring government securities from non-Treasury sources, thereby returning the funds to circulation. A similar result would occur if the Treasury used the proceeds of its additional sales for any purpose other than retiring the public debt held by the Bank of France. In this connection, the government did assume a "moral" obligation not to increase its borrowing from the Bank of France.

The second element was a more widespread application of the rediscount ceilings which the Bank of France had previously applied to some commercial banks. A global limit for rediscounting was fixed, on the basis of an individual ceiling for each bank. The global limit was 188 billion francs, as against 159 billion in actual rediscounts as of September 30; the margin was smaller than the observed increase of rediscounting during previous quarters of 1948. The commercial bill was therefore no longer to be treated as self-liquidating paper that could be permitted an unlimited expansion. It will be seen later that the system of quantitative controls had some deficiencies as a device for limiting the volume of credit. With respect to the period under review, however, it was applied too late to have had more than a psychological effect upon the inflationary situation.

Another note exchange was undertaken in 1948, but in a halfhearted fashion. Early in the year the Schuman-Mayer government agreed to a second operation in order to obtain socialist support for its anti-inflationary program as a whole. The exchange concerned only 5,000 franc notes, the common medium of exchange on the black market and the largest denomination in circulation, which represented about 36 per cent of the currency in circulation. The exchange was combined with a temporary blocking of the new notes, but Parliamentary pressure compelled the government to agree in advance both not to impose taxes on the blocked notes and to limit the period of blockage to a maximum of five months. The decrease in the amount of currency in circulation resulting from the blocking was offset by an increase in the velocity of circulation and by an increase in deposit money.[k] After the operation was completed,

[k] Between December 31, 1947 and March 31, 1948, currency in circulation declined by 142 billion francs while deposit money rose by 107 billion. (Ministry of Finance data.)

the fiduciary circulation gradually resumed its proportionate place in the total money supply.

The money supply did not increase as rapidly as prices during most of the inflationary period; between December 1945 and December 1948, the increase in wholesale prices was double that of the money supply. But bank credit to businesses and individuals, the principal source of increase in the money supply, expanded more rapidly than prices and production. In December 1948 these loans were at 7.2 times the December 1945 level, while ("official") wholesale prices had increased 4.2 fold and industrial production about 1.8 fold. The government's policies in this field made it possible for economic activity to be financed with rising prices. They must therefore be cited as a decisive factor in permitting the inflation to continue.

E. THE END OF THE INFLATION

The end of the inflation caught government officials somewhat by surprise. An inflationary gap in 1949 of 475 billion francs, or almost 6 per cent of available resources, had been forecast by the Commission on National Accounts. The principal factor in bringing the inflation to a close was a sudden increase in the supplies of foodstuffs and industrial goods at the consumer level. When the very good harvest of 1948 reached the market in the last half of 1948 and the early months of 1949, the availability of food was close to prewar. The influx of consumer durables and non-durables was due both to the results of early investments and to the natural "ripening" of the production process, which had virtually started anew at the end of the war.[20] By the end of 1948, inventories had been reconstituted at all stages of production and distribution. A change in business expectations, stimulated in part by the decline in world prices and the growing fears of a business recession in the United States, resulted in some unloading of these stocks on the market.[21]

France was the last of the major West European countries to bring its postwar inflation under control, and the resultant level of prices was higher than in most other countries.[1] The situation confronting postwar French governments was also more difficult, but

[1] In December 1948, for example, the index of wholesale prices (on a 1937 base) stood at 2,219 in France, in comparison with 221 for Denmark, 269 for the Netherlands, 392 for Belgium, 180 for Norway, 193 for West Germany, and 203 for the United Kingdom (United Nations Statistical Office, *Statistical Yearbook*, 1948, pp. 357-362.)

most of the government's actions in the fiscal and monetary area, as well as in that of direct controls, would seem to have contributed more to prolonging than to curbing the inflation. A qualification should be added: many of the government's investments did contribute to increasing production and supplies in the short run, although the methods chosen to finance them were largely inflationary. Also, while the inflation was prolonged by the unwillingness to cut investments more drastically (or to adopt a more suitable tax policy for financing them), later levels of production and real income may have been higher than would otherwise have obtained.[22]

II STABILIZATION (1949 TO MID-1950)

A. THE PROBLEM

The year 1949 and the first half of 1950 were characterized by an unwonted stability of prices and production. In June 1950 both wholesale and retail prices were only 1 or 2 per cent higher than in January 1949. This stability was in marked contrast to the previous four-year period, when prices were rising at the rate of 50 per cent or more per year. Industrial production in June 1950 was 5 per cent higher than in January 1949, but 3 per cent lower than in June 1949.[23] Again, this stability was in marked contrast to the previous four-year period, when the smallest year-to-year increase of industrial output was 14 per cent. The progress of the economy appeared to be at least temporarily halted, and there were some signs, particularly in the sector of consumer goods, that a recession might be developing.

B. THE POLICIES

For the most part, the government continued to be preoccupied with the possibility that the rapid price rise might resume. General awareness of the danger of recession did not long precede the external events (most notably the Korean war) which brought the period to a close. The gradual and selective relaxation of price controls, begun in 1948, was continued, but wages were not "freed" until in February of 1950 when the principle of wage determination through collective bargaining agreements was reestablished. The government retained the power to fix the minimum wage.

Fiscal policy was still dominated by concern over the size of the budgetary deficit. A "law of maxima" was adopted in 1948, and has since been continued in one form or another, to prevent Parliament from voting increases in expenditures without corresponding reductions in other expenditures or increases in new revenue. Substantial cuts were made in new investment authorizations, although expenditures remained high as a result of earlier program authorizations. The deficits were relatively smaller in both 1949 and 1950 than in 1948. However, the deficits were substantial in both years and (probably unintentionally) exerted an expansionary effect on the economy, especially since they were financed largely through the expenditure of the local currency counterpart of American aid and foreign loans.

The monetary stock continued to increase rapidly during 1949, at a rate of 25 per cent, but during the first half of 1950 the increase fell to an annual rate of 9 per cent. Credit policy was mostly out of phase with the economic situation. The discount rate was not lowered from its "defensive" level until June 1950. Greater emphasis was placed upon quantitative credit controls, although a slight increase in the global ceiling on rediscounts was permitted. However, these controls contained serious loopholes. Thus, the ceilings applied to bank statements as of the end of the month; during the month the ceilings were often exceeded by substantial amounts which were covered by "window-dressing" operations at the month's end. More important, the ceiling contained several exemptions, and a massive increase in the rediscounting of the exempted categories took place.[m] While the continued imposition of qualitative and quantitative restrictions on the supply of credit during a period of recessionary dangers might be regarded as anomalous, the laxity of the controls makes it unlikely that they hampered economic activity to a serious extent.

III THE "KOREAN" INFLATION (MID-1950 TO SPRING 1952)

A. THE PROBLEM

The Korean war transmitted a new impulse to the economy. With the skyrocketing of prices of internationally-traded raw ma-

[m] Originally the three exemptions were medium-term obligations of a specialized credit agency (the *Crédit National*) for equipment purposes, commercial paper used to cover the financing of the wheat harvest, and certificates of tax indebtedness. Later, treasury paper used to supply working capital to exporters was also exempted. In 1948 exempted securities represented only 15 per cent of total bank portfolios; in 1949, only 26 billion francs of ordinary commercial paper was rediscounted, in contrast with 118 billion francs of "safety valve" operations. (The 1948 figure was obtained from private sources; 1949 figure is given in Conseil National du Crédit, *Quatrième rapport annuel, 1950*, p. 57.)

terials following the outbreak of the Korean war, an upward surge of prices was a common phenomenon in Western Europe, but the ensuing inflation in France had a distinctly national character.

A factor in the process was the rapid expansion of private investment. Government orders for military procurement stimulated the demand for equipment goods. In large part, however, the spurt of private investment occurred in anticipation of the large rearmament programs expected to take place in France and elsewhere. These investments were financed in considerable measure by internal business funds.

Part of the rapid increase in the French price level can be attributed to the speculative behavior of consumers, producers, and middlemen, whose recollections of past inflations were still fresh. After a brief flurry, consumer hoarding ceased to be a significant factor as it became apparent that there would not be a pervasive shortage of consumer goods. Producers and middlemen augmented their stocks, even in sectors where consumer demand was slack. Manufacturers of consumer goods increased their output in anticipation of a revival of demand, which did not always take place, and put through price increases that resulted in a reduced volume of sales and a growth of unmarketable stocks in some sectors. Farmers began to withhold their livestock from the market and to delay crop deliveries. As a result of the excellent harvest of 1950 and the very good one of 1951, however, the availability of foodstuffs increased substantially in 1951, and was an important element in preventing a more serious inflation from occurring.[24]

No official measure of the inflationary "gap" was published. The dimensions of the inflationary situation can be suggested by the fact that wholesale prices had climbed by February 1952 to a point almost 50 per cent above the pre-Korean level. Once the renewed dangers of inflation had become apparent, various instruments of public policy were directed towards its control. The objective of controlling inflation was given a high priority, but again it had to be pursued concurrently with several others, among them the defense of France's positions in Western Europe and Indochina. It cannot be said that the government's efforts were crowned with much more success than during the first postwar inflation.

B. THE POLICIES

On a somewhat reduced scale, the government's wage-price decisions fed the inflationary process through the same "log-rolling" procedure observed during the first postwar inflation. Price controls had been relaxed, but key industrial and agricultural prices remained in the "fixed" category. Despite the restoration of collective bargaining, the government continued to exercise a large influence over wage decisions, primarily through its ability to fix the minimum wage on which much of the wage hierarchy depended. Experience has demonstrated that changes in the general wage level have closely followed those in the prescribed minimum wage. The government's continued influence over wage decisions also arose from its key role as the largest employer in France. In addition, social security payments of various kinds, which are a large component of the total remuneration of the wage earner, are a matter of legislative determination.[n]

Faced with a rising price level, the government fixed the minimum wage in August 1950 at a point which brought about a 10 to 12 per cent increase in most wage rates. In October a general price freeze was re-introduced, to limit the impact of rising raw material prices, but the measure was only temporary. A further wage increase of 10 per cent was provided in the spring of 1951 by a revision of the minimum wage. At the same time, the government raised those prices that remained "fixed" (e.g., coal, electricity, steel). In the summer, prices of the main agricultural products were fixed at considerably higher levels (the wheat price was raised 38 per cent); the prices of basic industrial products were again raised by the government; and (in September) another increase in the minimum wage was granted. Some increases in subsidies were voted as a means of holding down prices, although not on the scale of 1945-1947.[25] While the government viewed its wage and price increases as necessary "adjustments" following the price rises which had already taken place elsewhere, some of its increases included a margin against possible further price and cost rises. The resultant increases in costs touched off subsequent rounds of price increases, and the apparent disposition of the government to permit the rapid price spiral to go unchecked added to the speculation in favor of inflation.

The fiscal and monetary policies of the government did not exert an anti-inflationary impact on the economy. The budgetary situation was favored by the time lags between authorizations and expenditures under the intensified military programs for NATO and Indochina; military expenditures rose substantially in 1951, but did not reach their peak until 1952-1953 when the inflation had

[n] These points are discussed more fully in Chapter 10.

come to a halt. As a result of the cuts in the investment program and some selective increases in tax rates, the deficits in 1950 and 1951 were smaller on a cash basis than in 1949. They were nonetheless appreciable, and an expansionary factor. Also, the expectation of larger budgetary deficits in the future when the rearmament program was fully under way may have contributed to the psychological factors underlying consumer and producer behavior. It was widely assumed not only that the rearmament program would stimulate economic activity but that the means used to finance the program would generate strong inflationary pressures.[26]

Covering the deficit obliged the government to resort to a considerable volume of borrowing from the banking system, both directly and through the intermediary mechanism of the counterpart arrangements. Government borrowing accounted for about one-third of the increase in the money supply in 1951, a slightly lower proportion than during the first inflation.[27] A ten-year loan was floated by the Pinay government in the spring of 1952 as part of a program to restore "confidence." The loan contained the exceptional guarantee (against monetary depreciation) that reimbursement would be tied to the free market price of gold. While nominally floated at par, earlier public issues were again accepted in payment at par rather than market value. Of total proceeds of 428 billion francs, net receipts from the public were only 195 billion since 233 billion came from conversion of earlier issues.[28]

Monetary policy was again an important factor in the inflationary process. The supply of money increased at an annual rate of 21 per cent in the last half of 1950 and by 18 per cent during 1951, thus supporting the rising level of costs and prices. Despite the rapid acceleration of bank credit to business, the low rediscount rate adopted on the eve of the Korean war was held until the price rise was almost over (i.e., until October and November of 1951). The adjusted rate of 4 per cent, officially termed one of "monetary defense,"[29] was combined with a "tightening" of credit restrictions. Even then, however, the National Credit Council rejected a "brutally restrictive" policy which would have been counter to the general economic policies of the government.[30]

The "tightening" of credit policy was concerned primarily with the ceiling on rediscount facilities. The global ceiling, which had been raised from 200 to 250 billion francs in September 1950, was raised to 500 billion francs in October 1951. This increase, which would appear to be a "loosening" of controls, was explained on two grounds: (a) the increase in the price level in the interim;

and (b) the fact that "window dressing" operations, which had reached the level of 150 billion francs, were no longer to be permitted.[31] In practice an additional margin of temporary assistance from the Bank of France, in amounts up to 10 per cent of the individual bank's ceiling, was permitted at a penalty rate higher than the standard rediscount rate. More important, none of the exceptions or safety valves was changed; rediscounting of securities exempted from the ceiling, which amounted to 118 billion francs in 1949, had risen to 669 billion by the end of 1952.[32]

The leniency of the government's monetary policy can be inferred from the fact that the growth of bank credit to business, which had been continuous since the last quarter of 1950, was more rapid following the policy changes of October 1951. The relative abundance of bank credit played an important part in the rapid expansion of equipment orders and the rise of inventories during the inflationary period.

How, one may well ask, did the price inflation come to an end? The psychological climate had changed by the spring of 1952 as a result of some relaxation of international tensions and of more evidence on the actual dimensions of the French military effort. Prices of imported raw materials had peaked almost a year earlier and fell appreciably in the third and fourth quarters of 1951; some time lag (although probably not of this duration) was necessary for the impact of these price reductions to be felt on the domestic price level. Producers of consumer goods had miscalculated the extent of the rise in demand, and the administered price increases had brought about a widening slump in the consumer goods industries.

When the inflation ended, it had again lasted longer, and been more intensive, in France than in most European countries. OEEC data show that wholesale prices in the first quarter of 1952 were 40 per cent above the 1950 level in France, as against 20 per cent in Belgium, 22 per cent in Germany, 10 per cent in Italy, 23 per cent in the Netherlands, 27 per cent in the United Kingdom, and 9 per cent in the United States.[33]

IV STABILIZATION, RECESSION, RECOVERY (SPRING 1952 TO 1954)

A. THE PROBLEM

After reaching their peaks in the spring of 1952, domestic wholesale and retail prices began to move downward. The average level of production in 1952 was higher than in 1951, but largely as a result of the higher output of equipment goods; the production of consumer goods was lower than in the preceding year, with distributors and producers drawing down their inventories. As the decline in orders spread from the consumer goods industries to those producing equipment goods, the recession became more generalized. In 1953, the average level of industrial production was 3 per cent below that of 1952; the work week was reduced, and unemployment was on the rise. Farm prices and other prices continued to decline slightly.

This business recession of late 1952 and 1953 may have been in part a "normal" adjustment to the unbalanced expansion which had taken place during the earlier period of inflation. The situation was aggravated by the structural adjustments necessitated by the shift of productive resources to the rearmament program in 1951. Despite the high volume of defense contracts placed by the government, the total level of investment was lower in 1952 and 1953 than in 1951 (in real terms). A further complicating factor was the large harvest of 1953, arising from good weather conditions and increases in farm productivity. Surpluses were accumulating in crops the prices of which were supported by the government.

Some time was again required before government attention shifted from concern with inflation to recognition of the dangers of recession. Beginning in 1953, however, "expansion" became the keynote of government policy. The Mayer government announced its intention to "revive" (*relancer*) the economy; its successor, under Laniel, offered a program of "economic recovery" (*redressement économique*), in which full employment was to be guaranteed by economic expansion. The program was presented in February 1954 by Finance Minister Faure as the "Eighteen Month Plan for Economic Expansion." His plan called for a 10 per cent increase in industrial production (from an index of 150 to 165 based on 1938) and a similar increase in the gross national product. The essentials of the Faure plan were taken over, in a slightly enlarged and better orchestrated version, by Mendès-France, who labelled his abortive program one of "financial equilibrium, economic expansion, and social progress."[o] In agriculture, the emphasis was less on "expansion" than on "market organization" to bolster sagging farm prices.

o The continuity of the essentials of the Faure plan under the Mendès-France government can undoubtedly be attributed in part to the continuation of Edgar Faure as Minister of Finance in the new cabinet.

B. THE POLICIES—DIRECT CONTROLS

The Pinay government, formed in March 1952, was mostly preoccupied with restoring "confidence" and "safeguarding the franc." While the tone of its policies may have contributed to the restoration of "confidence" and a reversal of the inflationary expectations of businessmen, the stabilization of prices was under way considerably in advance of the adoption or implementation of most of the policies.

In July 1952 the Pinay government established an automatic link between movements of the minimum wage and of the price level, notably of prices entering directly into the cost of living. The law provided for a "sliding scale" of adjustments of the minimum wage in accordance with increases in the cost of living index beyond a reference point which had not yet been reached. The sliding scale was intended to give workers a guarantee that wages would not lag behind consumer prices during another inflation, while forestalling demands for wage increases in the absence of a generalized price rise. During a period of intense inflation, the sliding scale might have accelerated the spiralling of costs and prices; in its actual context, it probably added to the stabilization process by easing the pressure for wage and price increases. The Pinay government also attempted to reinforce the downward movement of prices by a series of voluntary price reductions negotiated with representative business organizations. These were coupled with reductions in the prices of the commodities and services provided by the nationalized enterprises. At the end of the voluntary campaign, which had met with little success in the selected areas where it was applied, prices were frozen by executive decree in September 1952.

Under successive governments, the focus of policy shifted in favor of a readjustment of prices and wages as a means of increasing the purchasing power of the working classes, whose money income had lagged behind prices during the inflationary periods. This was to be accomplished by a gradual increase of wages while prices were held constant or forced downwards. The primary objectives of the increase in real wages were twofold: to calm the continued social unrest, which had erupted in the general strike movement of August 1953; and to stimulate consumer demand as a means of promoting economic expansion. Thus, a series of voluntary and selective price reductions at the wholesale and retail level was negotiated by the Laniel government in September 1953, partly by granting special tax benefits. At the same time, the government increased wage rates in the lowest categories of public employees and used its considerable influence to see that the increase was extended to comparable categories in private enterprise.

When the "18-month plan" was launched in February 1954, one of its major components was a wage increase to workers in the lowest categories, in the form of a "bonus" applied to the minimum wage, which nominally remained unchanged in an effort to prevent the wage increase from spreading throughout the entire wage hierarchy. Another key element was a new freeze on prices at the February level. The price freeze was intended to consolidate the general downward movement of prices, which had occurred as a result of the recession, since the similar action taken by Pinay in August 1952. It contained a number of exemptions, the principal one being farm products at the production level. By keeping prices constant while production and wages rose, the Faure plan hoped to achieve at least a 10 per cent increase in real wages over the 18-month span. The Mendès-France government carried over this program, and formalized it through semi-annual consultations between government and labor to provide for increases in wages as production rose.

These wage-price policies were accompanied by, and may have contributed to, an increase in real wages and in consumption. The "voluntary" price reduction campaigns had been unspectacular. But, while virtually all earlier efforts in this direction had failed, the price controls of the years 1952-1954 were "successful" in the sense that price increases did not occur during this period. This was achieved despite the almost complete dismantling in the interim of the administrative mechanism for enforcing the controls. The explanation seems to lie in the fact that the strongest pressures on the price level were deflationary, arising from the declining level of world raw material prices and the abundant supplies of agricultural products. There is not likely to have been pressure against the price ceilings except in isolated cases. Also, some increase in labor productivity undoubtedly took place between 1952 and 1954, making possible higher wage rates without higher prices.

Substantial increases in wage rates did take place, partly under the initiative of the government, in the public sector and in much of private industry. There was a 7.8 per cent increase in hourly wages during 1954; at the same time, employment was up slightly (1.7 per cent) and the work week lengthened (0.4 per cent).[34] Prices remained stable or declined slightly. Between 1952 and 1954, wages rose by 12.5 per cent, with most of the rise taking place in 1954; national income and profits increased more slowly (9 per cent and 5.5 per cent respectively), while consumption increased by 9 per cent.[35]

The government was not completely consistent in its effort to raise money incomes while lowering prices. Thus, in its agricultural policies, the government was more concerned with placing a floor under, than a ceiling above, the movement of prices. To this end, a variety of price support, production control, and surplus disposal programs were developed for individual commodities.

C. FISCAL POLICY

In part by intent and in part by accident, the government's fiscal policies were expansionary. Concern was still voiced frequently over the size of the budgetary "*impasse*" (i.e., deficit) and the inflationary dangers which it entailed. The deficits were nonetheless substantial in both 1953 and 1954. The high level of expenditure was largely due to the military program decided upon earlier.[p] Publicly-financed investment expenditures were kept at their reduced levels; in 1954, the increase in government loans for selective investment purposes (housing, agricultural equipment) was more than offset by the decline in reconstruction and equipment loans. An appreciable rise in civil operating expenses took place, however, primarily on three counts: higher payments on the public debt; higher administrative costs arising from wage increases to civil servants; and increased subsidies for export promotion, farm surpluses, and the deficit of the national railways.

The government's tax policies also helped to preserve a substantial deficit. No general rise in tax rates took place after 1952, when Pinay came into office with a pledge not to increase taxes. In 1953 and 1954, several measures were adopted to lower tax rates as a means of encouraging private investment and certain kinds of economic activity. Tax relief was also afforded in order to improve the income position (and purchasing power) of certain classes. Excise taxes on purchases of investment goods were lowered; tax advantages were given to personal savings invested in stipulated kinds of economic activity; more favorable depreciation allowances

[p] Table 9 gives a somewhat misleading impression of the movement of military expenditures since 1952. Actual military spending may have been higher in 1953 than in 1952, and the drop between 1953 and 1954 is probably not as sharp as that shown in the table. The statistical problems arise partly from questions of what constitutes "military" spending (thus, by NATO definitions French military spending was higher in 1953 than in 1952) and partly from differences in the way in which expenditures financed by American aid are presented.

were permitted; firms engaging in mergers or product-specialization agreements designed to increase business efficiency received special tax benefits; and tax rebates were allowed on farm purchases of fertilizers and agricultural equipment. Wage earners benefited from a reduction in income tax rates. Some tax relief was provided to producers and distributors in connection with the government's price-reduction campaigns.

Covering the deficit posed difficult problems for the Treasury in 1953. A protracted Treasury crisis necessitated heavy recourse to direct borrowing from the Bank of France; the 228 billion francs of advances from the Bank required a further increase in the authorized ceiling. The situation of the Treasury improved with the recovery of 1954, making it possible to repay some of the new advances on the schedule which the Bank of France had insisted upon as a prior condition. Medium-term (i.e., 10 year) "investment loans" floated by the government had a moderate success, but most of the Treasury's resources came from short-term borrowing from the public, the counterpart of American aid, and the siphoning-off of savings deposited with the banking system.

D. MONETARY AND CREDIT POLICY

Throughout this period the monetary stock increased at about the same rate each year: 13 per cent in 1952, 11 per cent in 1953, and 14 per cent in 1954. As in earlier periods, a considerable time interval elapsed before the government's policies were adapted to the changing situation. In September 1953, the discount rate was lowered from its "defensive" level (4 per cent) to 3½ per cent; two subsequent reductions, in February and December of 1954, brought the rate to 3 per cent. This easier credit policy was combined with measures to lower the general structure of interest rates, as a means of stimulating private investment or facilitating the recovery of production. No significant modification of the system of credit controls was undertaken. However, in this situation the controls had the virtue of their defects. There is no evidence that maintenance of the controls hampered the recovery, which in 1954 was accompanied by an expansion of bank lending to business over the 1953 level.

E. THE END OF THE RECESSION

The recovery was first felt in the consumer goods industries towards the latter part of 1953. As the increase in demand was transmitted to the capital goods industries, the recovery became more widespread. By mid-1954 a general recovery of the economy was well under way,[q] with the output of consumer goods at record levels.

How much of the recovery was due to a "normal" cyclical movement of the economy? It is significant that the relative prosperity of 1954 was shared by virtually all European countries. France's recovery up to that time, while appreciable, was described as "modest" by European standards.[36] A meaningful international comparison is difficult to draw, since the post-Korean expansion (and inflation) did not last as long in most other countries, nor did they suffer the same setback of production in 1953. Taking 1950 as the base year, industrial production was at an index of 119 in France in 1954, in comparison with the average index of 126 for the OEEC countries as a whole.[37]

The French recovery was favored by a number of circumstances, among them the downward pressure on prices as a result of the large harvest and the stable or declining level of world prices. The European-wide boom, taking place under conditions of freer trade within the OEEC countries, also assisted by stimulating the foreign demand for French products. Nevertheless, the actions of the French government undoubtedly contributed to the expansion process.

V SUMMARY

Throughout the postwar period, a major goal of government policy has been to promote the expansion of economic activity at a stable level of prices. Pursuit of this objective has been made difficult, however, both by the conflict with other objectives (such as defense) and by the serious and complex problems inherited from the past or introduced from abroad.

In attempting to stabilize economic fluctuations, the government has had recourse to a very broad range of policies, running the gamut from verbal persuasion and indirect incentives to direct control of prices, wages, and the allocation of resources. Some tendency to relinquish direct controls in favor of more "global" fiscal and monetary controls or indirect incentives can be observed, in part because of the difficulties experienced in the enforcement of direct controls and the antagonisms which they aroused. But while some direct controls (subsidies to reduce internal prices, rationing of consumer goods, priorities and allocations of industrial goods) were largely abandoned, the government retained a substantial measure of in-

[q] The expansion continued at an impressive rate throughout 1955 and 1956.

fluence over prices and wages. France is one of the few countries in the Western world to have had comprehensive price ceilings in effect during the years 1952-1954. While the broad outlines of fiscal policy have remained essentially unchanged, the monetary interventions used by the state have become more rather than less extensive with the passage of time, notably in the area of quantitative credit controls.

With respect to the results of state action, both of the postwar inflations lasted longer and were more intensive in France than in most other European countries. Some extenuating circumstances existed, at least during the early postwar inflation, in view of the heavy damage inflicted by the war. Over the first decade of the postwar period as a whole, in only two years (1949 and 1954) was price stability realized under conditions of relative prosperity.[r]

Despite the extensiveness of its controls and the frequency of its efforts, the government, at best, had little success in curbing the postwar inflations. Both the need for domestic stability and the balance of payments situation called for disinflationary action. But the government's policies were not strongly anti-inflationary, and in important instances they assisted or accelerated the inflationary process. The government was unable to arbitrate the conflict among social groups inherent in the application of direct controls. Its weaknesses in this area were conducive to the widespread habit of settling income distribution by group pressures on the government. Its monetary policy characteristically tended towards inflation of the monetary stock, partly on the questionable grounds that ample credit was necessary for rising production. When credit controls were applied, the vagueness of the criteria employed and the extent of the loopholes permitted made them largely ineffective. In its fiscal policies the government recognized more clearly the connection with inflation but had great difficulty in facing or enforcing the hard choices to cut spending on investment, defense, or consumption. It was necessary to finance the large deficits by frequent recourse to the banking system, directly or in various guises, because of the continued lack of public confidence in government securities.

The government's actions appear to have been better conceived and executed in the case of recession, the periods of which have been short-lived. Recovery from the recession of 1952-1953 was favored by external circumstances, but the government's policies in

[r] 1955 and 1956 can be added as years of "expansion with stability," although in the latter year inflation again became a serious danger.

the wage-price and monetary fields contributed to the process. Fiscal policies were also expansionary, although preoccupation with the elimination of the budgetary deficit has largely been independent of the economic cycle. The more favorable results achieved in combatting recession may be due in part to the fact that the French economy, over the past four decades, has become hyper-sensitive to inflation. Also, an expansionary policy has apparently involved less painful decisions and open group conflicts for an unstable government.

CHAPTER 4

BALANCE OF PAYMENTS PROBLEMS

THROUGHOUT the postwar period the French government has had to grapple with a major balance of payments problem. In connection with this problem, it is important to realize that the balance of payments position of Metropolitan France with the rest of the world consists of two quite different elements: relations with the rest of the "franc area"[a] (that is, with the French overseas possessions), in which the Metropole has shown a surplus on current transactions during most of the postwar period, and relations with foreign currency areas, in which there has been a large deficit during most of this period. A surplus in Metropolitan France's position within the franc area does not provide foreign currencies with which to settle the deficit with foreign countries; in fact, trade between the rest of the franc area and foreign countries has also shown a deficit, and this gap has added to the serious foreign currency problems with which the "franc area" as a whole has been faced.

We shall be concerned almost exclusively with the balance of payments relationship between the franc area as a whole and foreign countries, and with the efforts of the French government to reduce the payments "gap." There are several ways of defining the balance of payments "gap," each of which has its significance and uses. The gap under discussion here will be (unless otherwise specified) the net deficit or surplus on current account, plus the net deficit or surplus on private capital transactions. In other words, it is the deficit to be covered by a net increase in the foreign indebtedness of the French government, by the receipt of aid from other countries, or by a drawing down of gold and foreign currency reserves. Most of the gap has had to be filled by settlement in gold or dollars, hence the popular emphasis on the problem of the "dollar gap."

The announced aim of the French government was not only to close the gap, but also to achieve "viability" in its international trading relations. By this it was meant that trade should be balanced

[a] The "franc area" consists of Metropolitan France, the Saar, and all the French overseas possessions (except for French Somaliland, whose currency is pegged to the dollar). Several currencies are in use within the franc area (Metropolitan francs, North African francs, etc.) but these are freely convertible into French francs at fixed exchange rates (except for payments with Indochina, to which certain exchange restrictions apply).

at a high level of imports and exports, a level maintained without extraordinary foreign assistance and without rationing of imports and special stimuli to exports. The mere size of the balance of payments gap or the absence of such a gap is therefore not the only measure of the success of the French government in meeting its international economic problems.

I THE PROBLEM

A. ITS ORIGINS

During the inter-war period, the balance of payments of the franc area was characterized by a chronic deficit on merchandise account. The merchandise deficit was generally small during the 1920's, and was more than covered by the net surplus on invisibles (notably tourism and investment income). In the 1930's, the commercial deficit increased and could no longer be offset by invisible earnings. The deficit on current account, while substantial, had not reached critical proportions. It was covered by a drawing down of foreign exchange reserves and some liquidation of foreign investments.[1]

Virtually all aspects of the French payments position deteriorated under the impact of the war and the early postwar inflation. Reconstruction of the economy required a heavy volume of imports; as a result of the wartime disruption of trade channels, an unusually high proportion of these had to be purchased in the dollar area. (France imported 53 per cent of its merchandise from the Western Hemisphere in 1947, as against 28 per cent in 1938.)[2] Goods were available for export only in limited quantities. The domestic inflation increased the demand for imports, and the rising price level made it difficult for exporters to compete in world markets (in the absence of frequent adjustments of the exchange rate). As the inflation progressed, exporters were diverted from seeking foreign markets by the attractive profits to be earned within France.[b] The movement of the key elements in the postwar balance of payments may be observed in Table 12.[c]

The position with respect to invisibles also deteriorated. One of the principal elements was the loss of investment income as a result

[b] The 1938 volume of imports was regained in March 1946, while the volume of exports did not reach the prewar level until two years later.

[c] While Table 12 is a summary balance of payments of the franc area with foreign countries, most of the entries refer to the balance of payments of Metropolitan France with foreign countries. The Overseas Territories appear as a single line entry, which gives the net position on current and capital account in transactions with foreign countries.

TABLE 12. SUMMARY BALANCE OF PAYMENTS OF THE FRANC AREA WITH FOREIGN COUNTRIES, 1945-1954

(millions of current dollars)

	1945	1946	1947	1948	1949	1950	1951	1952	1953	1954
Payments on current account										
Trade:										
Exports	42.5	452.8	1,040.0	1,082.0	1,567.2	1,880.0	2,496.4	2,024.1	2,155.2	2,544.7
Imports	903.9	1,980.0	2,491.7	2,510.3	2,034.8	1,958.3	3,266.7	2,642.6	2,493.7	2,724.1
Balance of trade	−861.4	−1,527.2	−1,451.7	−1,428.3	−467.6	−78.3	−770.3	−618.5	−338.5	−179.4
Invisibles:										
Receipts	244.9	324.7	713.8	617.0	633.0	620.2	686.8	877.9	1,060.6	1,311.7
Expenditures	499.4	549.6	775.2	718.8	704.6	656.8	886.5	850.3	838.7	870.3
Balance of invisibles	−254.5	−224.9	−61.4	−101.8	−71.6	−36.6	−199.7	+27.6	+221.9	+441.4
Transportation and misc. services[1]	−31.7	−233.3	−257.8	−281.4	−222.4	−131.3	−237.2	−150.3	−122.4	−84.9
Tourism[1]	−20.2	−18.6	+9.3	+70.1	+120.6	+141.2	+77.3	+24.4	−6.2	+61.0
Interest and dividends[1]	−22.1	+71.5	+86.1	+57.0	+23.0	−22.7	−29.8	−19.1	−23.4	−24.7
Receipts and expenditures of foreign governments[1]	+109.6	+11.8	+142.0	+38.9	—	—	+72.3	+257.2	+468.0	+565.7
Wage transfers[1]	−14.7	−35.0	−55.4	−79.8	−55.1	−42.5	−56.1	−69.5	−78.2	−81.0
Other invisibles[1]	−275.4	−21.3	−5.6	+93.4	+62.3	+28.7	−26.2	−15.1	−15.9	+5.3
Net balance of payments of Overseas Territories with foreign countries[2]	−374.6	−296.7	−162.6	−207.5	−167.3	−123.1	−88.0	−61.1	−95.1	−55.0
Balance of payments on current account	−1,490.5	−2,048.8	−1,675.7	−1,737.6	−706.5	−238.0	−1,058.0	−652.0	−211.8	+207.0

(*continued on facing page*)

TABLE 12 (*concluded*)

	1945	1946	1947	1948	1949	1950	1951	1952	1953	1954
Payments on capital account										
Net private investments	−7.1	+186.6	+94.7	+204.7	+55.7	+160.4	+68.3	+106.3	+130.1	+80.3
Net public investments (official loans)[3]	+844.1	+762.6	+1,213.8	+450.8	+126.7	−262.8	+164.7	+230.0	−104.6	−327.8
Foreign aid[4]	–	–	–	+754.0	+855.4	+508.7	+477.5	+343.0	+341.4	+507.2
Movement of gold and foreign exchange holdings[5]	+680.3	+1,104.9	+367.9	+335.2	−330.2	−170.2	+311.6	−20.7	−161.6	−506.3
Errors and omissions[6]	−26.8	−5.3	−0.7	−7.1	−1.1	+1.9	+35.9	−6.6	+6.5	+39.6
Balance of payments on capital account	+1,490.5	+2,048.8	+1,675.7	+1,737.6	+706.5	+238.0	+1,058.0	+652.0	+211.8	−207.0

Source: INSEE, *Bulletin mensuel de statistique*, supplement, January-March 1953, pp. 69-70.
Ministère des Finances, *Statistiques et études financières*, August 1954, No. 68, pp. 722-728; September 1955, No. 81, pp. 917-932.

1 Net balance.

2 Net balance of operations on current and capital accounts with the exception of "Miscellaneous private credits and investments."

3 Net loans received (+) or net amortization paid (—). Including changes in the credit or debit balance with the European Payments Union.

4 Including reimbursement of French military expenditures in Indochina ($321.0 million in 1954).

5 From 1952 onwards, including "current operations" (net balance of foreign exchange in process of collection or disbursement by the Exchange Stabilization Fund).

6 Including "current operations" for 1951.

of the large-scale liquidation of assets held abroad by French nationals, in part through the requisition operations conducted by the French government (see below). The small net surplus of investment income during the period 1946-1949 (less than 5 per cent of the trade deficit) may be contrasted with that during the period 1927-1931 when the surplus covered more than half of the trade deficit.[3] In addition, a large deficit on shipping services emerged, in contrast with the surplus of most prewar years. The reversal of the shipping position was caused by the increase in the volume of imports, the need to import bulk commodities such as wheat and coal from the United States (partly in American vessels, in accordance with ECA legislation), and the damage to the French merchant fleet during the war. Finally, tourist receipts, which were an important source of revenue before the war, fell off in the early postwar period. In addition to the unsettled international conditions, exchange restrictions were imposed by other countries on foreign travel.

B. ITS DIMENSIONS

There is no way of measuring how large the deficit would have been in the absence of government policies which influenced it. Nevertheless, while data on the evolution of the actual deficit reflect the impact not only of exogenous factors but also of government policies, they give some impression of the dimensions of the problem facing successive governments.

The currrent account balance of the franc area with all foreign countries showed a huge deficit in 1945, close to $1.5 billion. In 1946, the current account deficit rose to about $2 billion. Some idea of the significance of these deficits can be gained from the fact that they were larger than the total volume of imports in both years. In 1947 and 1948 the current account deficit dropped somewhat, to about $1.7 billion. Despite the large-scale liquidation of foreign private investments between 1946 and 1948 and the negotiation of various emergency loan and aid arrangements (described below), there was a heavy loss of gold and foreign exchange reserves. During the years 1945-1948 the loss amounted to about $2.5 billion. By the time that the European Recovery Program got under way, French reserves had declined precipitously to a level far below the conventional "danger mark." The gold holdings of the Bank of France had fallen from 4,900 tons in 1932 and 2,160 tons in 1938 to 487 tons in 1948.[4]

The current account deficit fell off sharply in 1949 and 1950, as exports and the tourist trade resumed. The payments situation was further improved by a net inflow of private investments. Some accumulation of reserves took place, but it was almost wiped out with the large deficit of 1951 resulting primarily from the unfavorable impact of the Korean war on the value of imports and on shipping costs. The deficit declined again in 1952 and 1953; in 1954, for the first time since the war, there was a surplus in the franc area's current account. This improvement was due in part to a revival of French exports, but a more important factor was the exceptional (and, in some respects, temporary) earnings of foreign currency arising from United States military expenditures in France (for offshore procurement, NATO infrastructure, and maintenance of United States armed forces). With the continued provision of American dollar aid to support the French military effort in Indochina, there was a small increase in foreign exchange reserves in 1953, and an appreciable one in 1954. The dependence of the payments position on extraordinary sources of foreign currency can be gathered from the fact that receipts from expenditures of foreign governments (primarily the United States) and from foreign aid were over $1 billion in 1954.[d]

The above figures give an imperfect picture of the character of the French postwar payments problems, since they do not distinguish among the different currencies in which, in the absence of general currency convertibility, financial settlements had to be made. The most critical payments problem of the early postwar years was that arising from the widening "gap" in exchanges which had to be settled in gold or dollars. The total deficit on current account with the "dollar area"—about $1.4 billion in 1946 and 1947—was between two-thirds and four-fifths of the entire current account deficit in those years.[5] By 1952, the "dollar gap" on current account had been reduced to $170 million, and in 1953 and 1954 surpluses were registered for the first time in the postwar period.

Another payments problem arose from the large deficits incurred by France in its trade with other European countries and their allied monetary systems, including the sterling area as a whole. Other OEEC countries were obliged to extend heavy credits to France under the two intra-European payments schemes, and, more re-

[d] Derived from Table 12. In addition, there are some French dollar receipts under the United States offshore procurement program which appear in the table as French exports (if the goods are produced by private firms).

cently, under their successor organization, the European Payments Union (EPU).[e] Within the EPU, the French cumulative deficit had reached $0.8 billion in December 1953 (at the end of three years of operation), necessitating gold payments by France of $0.5 billion. The EPU position of France began to be reversed in 1954, and surpluses in its trade and payments with other OEEC countries were earned towards the end of the year.

C. OBJECTIVES OF GOVERNMENT POLICY

In the face of the huge deficits of 1945 and 1946, closing the balance of payments gap quickly became one of the key objectives of public policy. Whatever advantages the deficits may have had as anti-inflationary weapons, they were luxuries which the French economy, in the depleted state of its foreign exchange reserves, could ill afford.

A complete closing of the balance of payments gap was not envisaged during the period of reconstruction and economic recovery. The various members participating in the European Recovery Program adopted "viability" as their common goal, to be achieved by the end of the program in 1952-1953. In the meantime, economic aid from the United States was apportioned on the basis of the "necessary minimum" dollar gap associated with the desirable allocation of national resources to investment, consumption, and exports, and with the level of imports necessary to support this allocation of resources. Following the Korean war, the advent of the Mutual Security Program required a postponement of the date for achieving the viability goal. But the foreign exchange objectives have always been to keep the deficit as narrow as possible and to close it as soon as possible, consistent with other objectives. While the favorable payments positions of 1953 and 1954 have provided a temporary breathing spell, the low level of reserves and the dependence of the present position on a high volume of extraordinary receipts have necessitated continuing preoccupation with the balance of payments situation.

How might the government have gone about tackling the balance of payments problem? The possible courses of action, in very general terms, were as follows: (1) to check the domestic inflation, thus removing one force which stimulated imports and discouraged

[e] The European Payments Union provides a system whereby each member's payments position can be cleared multilaterally with all other member countries (and their associated monetary areas) as well as a system for settling deficits by a combination of gold or dollar payments and credits.

exports; (2) to keep the exchange rate constant, and let the dwindling supply of foreign exchange go to those who were "first in line"; (3) to keep the exchange rate constant, bringing the supply of and demand for foreign exchange into balance by means of direct exchange controls on imports and special stimuli to exports; (4) to let the exchange rate move to the level which would balance the demand for and supply of foreign exchange, with the exchange rate determining to what uses the supply of foreign exchange would be put; (5) to finance a continuing gap, at least for some time and to some extent, by getting further credit from foreign governments. The government's efforts to check the inflation have already been discussed. With respect to the other possible actions (or combinations thereof), what the government did in fact do will be examined under three headings: emergency and special measures to finance the gap; exchange rate adjustments; and exchange controls and commercial policy.

II THE POLICIES

A. EMERGENCY AND SPECIAL MEASURES TO FINANCE THE GAP

At the time of liberation, the French economy was almost completely deprived of imports; in December 1944 the index of the volume of imports of Metropolitan France was less than 2 per cent of the 1938 level (Table 13).[f] With the shortage of imported raw materials and equipment impeding industrial and agricultural recovery, and with a large volume of imported foodstuffs required to supplement the slim margin of resources available for feeding the civilian population, the government undertook emergency action to organize a flow of imports and to arrange for its financing.

"State trading" was heavily relied upon to get the procurement process under way. The French Supply Mission in Washington, which had functioned during the war under the Lend-Lease program, was transformed into a government purchasing mission. Other government purchasing missions were established in Canada and Great Britain in 1945. Because of the dislocation of shipping, port facilities, and payment procedures, a government organization known as IMPEX was set up to handle the receipt, delivery and billing of a large volume of imported products.[6] Government purchasing missions and the IMPEX organization became less important as

[f] Indexes of the volume of imports and exports are not published for the franc area as a whole.

TABLE 13. INDEXES OF THE VOLUME OF FOREIGN TRADE OF METROPOLITAN FRANCE, 1944-1954
(Base: 1938 = 100)

Year	*Jan.*	*Feb.*	*Mar.*	*April*	*May*	*June*	*July*	*Aug.*	*Sept.*	*Oct.*	*Nov.*	*Dec.*	*Annual Average*
						Imports							
1944	11.2	11.0	9.9	9.2	8.3	7.1	5.4	4.1	3.5	2.4	1.8	1.7	6.3
1945	2.1	3.0	4.6	7.0	10.9	15.2	19.9	32.1	44.7	60.2	72.0	84.8	29.7
1946	92.2	99.6	104.7	106.1	123.8	125.3	127.1	125.0	120.1	105.5	99.8	99.1	110.7
1947	105.0	106.1	121.4	126.6	131.3	129.8	127.7	125.6	117.7	107.1	[1]	[1]	119.8
1948	74	74	114	112	101	119	101	101	113	118	97	108	103
1949	104	106	109	116	109	98	97	93	105	98	97	110	104
1950	115	115	112	113	97	110	86	91	89	103	114	113	105
1951	109[2]	115	115[3]	117	115	127	123	115	118	128	134	141	121
1952	141	158	126	133	116	132	114	102	116	114	115	131	125
1953	129	134	132	142	115	140	124	102	121	118	127	129	126
1954	142	133	132	145	142	138	127	120	121	120	131	136	132
						Exports							
1944	48.6	50.7	48.3	44.6	39.2	33.3	26.3	17.9	12.3	8.8	5.8	3.1	28.2
1945	2.0	2.5	3.5	4.4	6.3	8.6	10.7	12.5	14.1	15.7	16.8	18.4	9.6
1946	19.6	23.9	27.9	32.6	36.4	39.2	42.8	44.5	48.8	53.7	57.6	64.6	41.0
1947	69.4	76.0	79.9	82.7	86.4	85.5	85.4	84.9	83.8	81.7	[1]	[1]	81.6
1948	55	55	97	102	102	116	89	89	103	107	99	111	94
1949	114	135	131	145	137	130	126	116	119	146	143	156	133
1950	145	159	147	153	149	179	165	148	162	220	230	225	173
1951	195[2]	236	214[3]	214	183	216	184	170	206	207	203	199	202
1952	175	182	168	175	184	165	152	151	161	180	186	192	173
1953	162	183	186	194	179	194	168	145	159	194	214	202	182
1954	192	212	196	206	203	203	186	195	189	217	231	241	206

Sources: 1944-1947: *Bulletin de la statistique générale de la France*, monthly issues, December 1945-February 1948. 1948: *Bulletin de la statistique générale de la France*, Supplement October-December 1949, p. 376. 1949-1954: INSEE, *Bulletin mensuel de statistique*, monthly issues. [1] Adjusted indexes have not been published. [2] Since 1951, the indexes have been calculated from the base index, 1949 = 100. [3] From March 1951, the indexes have been calculated on the basis of a revised method.

the supply of imported products became more abundant. To a considerable extent, the control over the process of import procurement formerly enjoyed by the purchasing missions and IMPEX is still vested in the state or in semi-public organizations, but for reasons essentially unconnected with the balance of payments situation.[g]

Financing the desired imports required both the establishment of a framework within which payments could be made and the acquisition of foreign exchange resources through the requisitioning of private assets and the negotiation of foreign loans and financial assistance.

Trading relations had been seriously disrupted by the war, and a new network of payments agreements had to be created. In the absence of a general currency convertibility, these payments agreements were originally negotiated between governments on a bilateral basis. The agreements fixed the official rate of exchange between the two currencies, arranged for payments through the central bank of each country, and provided for settlement between the central banks of uncovered balances. They generally included a credit margin in the case of payments disequilibrium; settlement of the balances beyond this margin was made in gold or "hard" currencies.[7] This system of individual agreements has been superseded, insofar as trade with OEEC countries and their monetary zones is concerned, by the two intra-European payments agreements and, more recently, by the European Payments Union, which specifies the conditions under which payments are to be made.

An important contribution towards financing the flow of imports was made by requisitioning and liquidating French private investments abroad. The government resorted both to voluntary repatriation of private holdings of gold, foreign currencies, and securities through various schemes (such as tax amnesties and favorable exchange rates for capital repatriation) and to forced repatriation. According to one estimate, nearly $500 million of private foreign exchange assets were requisitioned by the French government and used in 1946-1948 to cover the foreign exchange deficit.[8] This source of foreign exchange virtually had dried up by 1949.

Several emergency loans were floated between the American and French governments in 1945 and 1946 to make possible the importation of essential materials from the dollar area. Close to $2 billion was provided through the Blum-Byrnes agreement, two Export-Import Bank loans, and a loan from the Maritime Com-

[g] Cf. the discussion in Chapter 10 of the role of semi-public organizations and trade associations in the import field.

mission. Loans were also negotiated with the Swiss and British governments. With the inception of the European Recovery Program, foreign aid grants replaced loans as the principal form of American assistance. An emergency grant of $325 million of "interim aid" was extended in 1947-1948 prior to final congressional approval of the program. At the end of 1953, "economic aid" from the United States (sometimes packaged under different labels) totalled $2.8 billion of grants and $225 million of loans.[9]

By the summer of 1945 the government's efforts to organize and finance the import program began to bear fruit. Imports rose rapidly, and by March 1946 had passed the 1938 volume. The volume of imports rose further in 1947 with the recovery of domestic production and the continuation of a strong demand for foreign goods. The annual average was 20 per cent above 1938, but fell off in 1948 to about the 1938 level. While these imports made a substantial contribution to the prompt recovery of the economy, their immediate effect on the foreign payments position was, of course, to increase the size of the deficit. A heavy financial cost was consequently entailed, through the liquidation of foreign investments, the increase in foreign indebtedness, and (despite these measures) the loss of foreign exchange reserves.

B. EXCHANGE RATE ADJUSTMENTS

Throughout the postwar period, the rate of exchange between the franc and foreign currencies has been under tight government control. It is possible to distinguish two general stages in the development of government policy with respect to the role of the exchange rate in the external payments position: (1) a period of occasional adjustments of the franc, including experiments with discriminatory exchange rates (1944-1949); and (2) a period of stable exchanges (since 1949). During both periods the franc appears generally to have been "overvalued," insofar as can be determined from the relative movements of prices and exchange rates.

1. 1944-1949. An inter-allied agreement of November 1944 fixed the exchange rate at 1 dollar to 49.63 francs (and 1 pound sterling to 200 francs). This represented a devaluation of only 13 per cent since 1940, although French prices had risen much more rapidly than those in the other two countries over this time period. The devaluation was limited in extent as a means of keeping down import prices and of restricting the purchases of Allied troops stationed in France. A second and larger devaluation took place in December 1945, when the rate with the dollar was changed to 119.1. Once again, the devaluation did not take full account of the relative movement of prices within and outside France, although the government hoped that a stabilization of the domestic price level would make further devaluation unnecessary.[10]

No further adjustments of the exchange rate took place in 1946 and 1947, despite the fact that the internal price level continued to rise considerably more rapidly than in the countries which were France's principal trading partners. Why was not the franc devalued further during these years? It was argued that the system of import licensing (described below) reduced imports to the minimum "essential" to the recovery of the economy, so that a devaluation would not reduce the volume of imports while it would exert an upward pressure on the domestic price level. Conversely, exports were generally considered to be limited by the production possibilities at home, so that a reduction in their prices in foreign currencies would not increase sales abroad. The government also wished to restrict the exporting of key industrial materials or of consumer goods which could be used to offset inflationary pressures at home. (As will be seen below, however, some selective inducements to exporting were provided during these years.)

Several exchange rate adjustments were made in 1948 and 1949. The recovery of production and (in 1949) the easing of inflationary tensions made it appear more feasible to restrict the volume of imports and to stimulate exports through devaluation, while the exhaustion of foreign exchange reserves heightened the desirability of taking action. How much closer the new rates were to the "equilibrium" level, and whether the discriminatory rates had their intended effects, cannot be judged; external events (notably the Korean war) disrupted the trade and payments situation before the devaluation could take full effect.

The first of these devaluations occurred in January 1948, when the official rate with the dollar was fixed at 214. In addition, a "free" market in certain "hard" or convertible currencies—the American and Canadian dollars, the Portuguese escudo, and (shortly thereafter) the Swiss franc—was established. The Foreign Exchange Office controlled the demand on the free market via its system of import licensing, and controlled the supply by compelling exporters to give half of their earnings to the Office, which would use them to intervene in the free market as necessary. The free market rate was allowed to climb to about 306-310 francs to the dollar. The purpose of this system was to make discrimination possible according to the currency area and the nature of the transaction. Thus, non-commercial transactions in "free" currencies were permitted at the free rate, as a means of encouraging tourism and capital repatriation. In order to stimulate exports to these areas, exporters received what amounted to a middle rate. French importers could acquire foreign exchange at a variety of rates in accordance with the degree of essentiality of the product. Subsequently, "non-essential" imports from the free currency areas were conducted at the middle rate and essential imports at the lower official rate of 214.

With minor exceptions, the only rate applicable to all transactions in all other currencies was the "cross-rate" calculated on the basis of the official rate of 214 francs to the dollar. This introduced a disorderly system of exchange rates with respect to the quotations of these currencies in other markets and, under pressure from the United Kingdom, brought about the official "non-acceptance" of the French scheme by the International Monetary Fund.

In October 1948, the system was modified by "aligning" (i.e., devaluing) the franc with respect to all foreign currencies not traded on the free market. The October alignment-devaluation eliminated the system of disorderly cross rates on commercial transactions and shipping, although preserving it on non-commercial transactions still taking place at the free market rate in certain currencies.[11]

In April 1949 the exchange control authorities undertook a further devaluation by permitting the free market rate for the dollar to move to 330 francs. Following the devaluation of the pound in September 1949, the exchange system was completely unified. The free market rate for the dollar, fixed at 350 francs, applied to all transactions and was used as the base for the calculation of all cross rates.

2. 1950-1954. During the period 1950-1954 there were no further adjustments of the exchange rate. Widespread speculation concerning an imminent devaluation occurred on several occasions after the end of the Korean inflation. But the government consistently decided against devaluation, and its unwillingness to attempt this approach has been a matter of controversy, both at home and abroad. The attitude of the government towards an exchange readjustment can be reviewed in conjunction with two pertinent questions. Is the franc "over-valued"? And, if so, would a devaluation help to restore balance of payments equilibrium?

With respect to the first question, both the relative level of prices in France and elsewhere and the state of the exchange market suggest that the franc has been overvalued. The OEEC cited evidence of a price disparity in the relative movements of prices in various countries over the past several years and in the persistence of the French balance of payments disequilibrium despite import restrictions and encouragements to exports.[12] The notion of a price disparity has been officially consecrated in France by the establishment, at the beginning of 1954, of a commission "for the study of the disparities between French and foreign prices" (the "Nathan Commission"). In its report, the Commission found "disparities, often appreciable, to the detriment of French prices for most of the products examined. . . ."[13] A more detailed study, conducted by INSEE in 1952, revealed a considerably higher level of prices in France than in Great Britain and the United States under some of the statistical measures used. In view of the great dispersion in results, however, the study concluded that "reasoning on the general levels of prices is subject to caution and that a detailed study for each country and each product is indispensable."[14] The fact that the "black market" rate (i.e., the rate on the genuinely "free" markets) has ranged between 365 and more than 500 francs is also cited occasionally as evidence of overvaluation, although the "thinness" of the market reduces the significance of the quotations.

Unfortunately, a comparison of price levels and price-level movements in various nations is a hazardous test for overvaluation. The price indexes that are generally used for this purpose reflect imperfectly the basic relationships. Differences in the quality of a given commodity, and the considerable dispersion which may exist among prices for the same commodity within one country, also make it difficult to arrive at valid generalizations.[15] Finally, capital equipment, productivity, and cost conditions have changed in different ways in the various countries, putting pressures on the exchange rates other than those caused by changes in price levels. Nonetheless it is significant that most French officials have taken for granted the existence of a considerable disparity between French and foreign prices. Also it is undeniably true that balance of payments difficulties did persist for a long time. Why, then, was there not a devaluation to correct what might appear to be a "fundamental disequilibrium" within the terms of the Bretton Woods Agreement?

Several arguments have customarily been advanced by those who believed that a devaluation would not succeed in appreciably narrowing the foreign exchange deficit.[16]

a) The demand for imports was said to be highly inelastic with respect to price, since most of the imports permitted entry under the licensing system consisted of "essential" raw materials, equipment, and semi-finished goods required in connection with domestic production. Consequently only small savings in foreign exchange were likely to result from devaluation.

b) The foreign demand for French exports was also believed to be price-inelastic. In this case, export volume would not increase rapidly enough to offset the reduction in price (in foreign currencies) and receipts of foreign exchange would go down.

c) The supply of exports was said to be inelastic, so that more could be produced only at rising costs and prices which would tend to offset the decline in export prices afforded by devaluation.

d) With import demand inelastic, an appreciable rise in the domestic prive level was likely to follow from a devaluation. This might trigger another inflationary spiral, particularly in view of the strong inflationary psychosis of the population and (since 1952) the automatic linkage of the minimum wage to price increases through the sliding wage scale. An inflation might counteract any initial advantages of the currency depreciation by increasing the demand for imports and raising the price of exports.

The case for or against devaluation, from the standpoint of France, depends heavily on empirical verification of the assumed elasticities of demand and supply. If there are definitive studies that confirm the assumptions, they have not been made public. As partial evidence, it is frequently argued that past devaluations did not bring about a significant improvement of the foreign exchange position. The "Nathan Report" refers in passing to the disappointing results of the 1949 action.[17] Another official study, covering several prewar and postwar devaluations in a highly cursory fashion, concluded that the analysis "did not permit one to affirm that the expected results of these operations have been obtained as far as foreign trade is concerned."[18] An INSEE study observed that: "All of the French devaluations have been disappointing. . . ."[19]

While it may literally be true that none of the past devaluations was followed by the desired improvement in the balance of payments, this may, of itself, be of little significance in considering the present situation. At least with respect to the postwar period, none of the studies referred to above has been sufficiently thorough to permit even a partial isolation of the effects of the devaluation from the many other factors that were concurrently affecting the movement of imports and exports. Also, because of the complex character of the 1948-1949 devaluations, a separate study by currency areas would have to be undertaken before significant conclusions could be reached.

On grounds of internal consistency, the case based on assumed inelasticities is weakened by the fact that some persons who have argued that devaluation would not work have since argued that a disguised or ersatz devaluation has already taken place—and with beneficial effects on the foreign trade position—as a result of the import taxes and export subsidies described below.[20] The assumptions with respect to inelasticities would presumably apply as well to the import taxes and export subsidies, though the two situations are not entirely comparable since the taxes and subsidies can, in principle, be applied selectively to those commodities for which the demand or supply situation is believed to be most favorable. (Another advantage of the disguised devaluation is that it avoids some of the adverse psychological effects of a more widely publicized action.)

With respect to the inelastic supply of French exports, "structural reforms" aimed at improving this situation by increasing efficiency and lowering production costs have sometimes been proposed as an alternative to devaluation. It might be noted that the success of these reforms, insofar as the balance of payments is concerned, also depends upon the elasticity of foreign demand for French goods.

The possibility of a rise in the domestic price level following a devaluation cannot be discounted. How appreciable the rise would be, however, would depend on expectations, other inflationary and deflationary forces at work in the economy, and the steps which the government might take to counteract an incipient rise. The timing of the devaluation is a crucial factor; if undertaken during a period of recession and falling prices, the inflationary danger would be minimized.

Whether or not a devaluation during the years 1952-1954 would have succeeded in improving the balance of payments position can, in the final analysis, be only a matter of conjecture. It is worth noting that France has rejected both of the orthodox methods for correcting balance of payments disequilibrium: exchange rate adjustments and (as seen in the preceding chapter) an internal deflationary policy. To the French government, the external effects of a devaluation have appeared, at best, to be uncertain and its internal effects potentially dangerous. Devaluation could only be accepted as the lesser of two evils, the greater being a serious and continuing drain on the country's foreign exchange reserves. During the period of large deficits (1951-1952), the availability of foreign aid and foreign loans made it appear that the painful choice could be avoided. The subsequent improvement in the balance of payments has weakened the pressures for a devaluation. But full "viability" has not been achieved, since the improvement in France's ability to pay its own way has been dependent to a considerable extent on exceptional circumstances. Also, the import taxes and export subsidies that have provided a partial devaluation are "temporary" and destined to be abandoned. In the absence of more rapid structural reforms than are now taking place, the question of devaluation may be up for future reexamination. This will particularly be so if France wishes to participate more actively than has yet been possible in the European movement towards greater convertibility of currencies.

C. EXCHANGE CONTROLS AND COMMERCIAL POLICY

Since the price system (that is, adjustments in the exchange rate) was not used to ration the supply of foreign exchange, extensive controls on commercial and capital transactions were necessary in order to allocate scarce foreign exchange resources to their most "essential" uses. Most European countries utilized similar kinds of controls, at least during the widespread payments difficulties of the early postwar period, although the degree was not identical in all cases.

The application of exchange controls actually dates from the emergency legislation preceding and immediately following the outbreak of the second World War. This legislation gave the government general and sweeping powers to control and direct foreign trade, and particularly to regulate the movements of foreign currencies and gold through the newly established Foreign Exchange Office. The legislation was strengthened by a series of decrees in 1944 and 1945. Since then the legislative base has remained extremely strict, although its application has been considerably softened by a number of administrative exceptions. The application of these controls to capital movements and imports will be examined, and then the government's efforts to close the balance of payments gap by promoting a larger flow of exports.

1. Capital Movements. A gradual relaxation of controls on

capital movements began in 1949. The modifications, all of a rather specialized nature, were intended to "liberalize" the system of controls without removing those deemed essential to safeguarding the balance of payments position. Progress in the direction of freer exchange has been slow. But, while the extensive controls on capital transactions which remain in force have probably restricted the flow of capital, they have left considerable scope for movements, both legal and illegal, which have intensified the balance of payments problem.[21]

Within the legal framework of controls, short-term capital movements of appreciable proportions have been made by variations in the rhythm of importing and by modifications in the delays in payment. The rhythm of importing is broadly determined by the delivery of licenses, but the permissible delays in their utilization (up to six months) have been sufficient for a considerable acceleration of imports at certain moments. Thus, a "speculative" increase in imports above the normal rate (i.e., an export of capital) occurred between November 1951 and April 1952 to an amount estimated at $200-$300 million. Although the delays in payment are supervised by the Foreign Exchange Office, it has remained possible to effect short-term capital movements by modifying the interval of delay. The export of capital in this fashion during the second half of 1951 has been estimated at about $150 million. As concerns export receipts, the regulations with respect to EFAC accounts (described below) have, until recently, permitted the holding of foreign exchange abroad without time limits; between 1948 and 1951, $130 million of foreign holdings were built up in this way.[22]

One of the conventional methods of exporting capital through extra-legal channels has been the overvaluation of imports and the undervaluation of exports. For a number of reasons, it has been difficult to employ this method in France.[h] The principal means of exporting capital illegally have therefore been the acquisition of foreign currencies sold by tourists on the black market and the exportation of bank notes. In 1948, with the franc probably still overvalued, about 80-90 per cent of foreign exchange from tourist expenditures (and from private non-commercial remittances)

[h] The correct value of imported raw materials, which bulk large in the commodity pattern of French trade, is generally known to customs authorities. Since manufactured products are subject to high customs duties and production and sales taxes, an over-declaration of their value is unprofitable unless the disparity between the "free" and black market rates of exchange is substantial. Undervaluation of exports is also difficult for raw materials and semi-finished products, and its profitability on manufactured products is reduced by the tax advantages which these products receive when exported.

went into the French black market. Some $150-$200 million was lost to the exchange control authorities through this leakage.[23] The loss of tourist receipts between 1949 and 1951 has been estimated at $385 million.[24] The export of bank notes has been involved in the purchase of foreign currencies on exchange markets abroad in order to import gold for private hoards. The same operation has been conducted by the acquisition of foreign exchange on the black market in Paris or by private compensation arrangements, and consequently it is difficult to regulate. Between 1939 and 1949, while the official gold reserve of France was rapidly being depleted, private gold holdings in France doubled in value (from $1.1 billion to $2.2 billion).[25]

2. *Import Quotas and Licensing.* Import restrictions have been used continuously since the 1930's in an effort to reduce imports to the "essential" minimum and to ensure the use of scarce foreign exchange resources for this minimum. In principle, all imports have been subject to an authorizing license by the Foreign Exchange Office, with the number of licenses issued determined by quotas designed to limit imports to the amount of available foreign exchange. Import programs have been drawn up by monetary area and type of commodity. Typically, a bilateral trade agreement has been negotiated with each foreign country, including other OEEC members; an annex to the trade agreement lists the quantities of specific commodities for which import licenses may be granted. Commodity imports financed by American aid have been organized under annual programs subjected to a special set of authorization and procurement procedures. A modification of the standard pattern of bilateral trade agreements has also existed for products "liberated" under the OEEC program (see below) and for countries with which there are no trade or payments agreements (e.g., Communist China). There has been no general waiver of the requirement of import licensing, although the complicated review-authorizing procedure of the Foreign Exchange Office and the technical ministries has been abbreviated in special cases.[1]

How effective have the quantitative restrictions been as a means of controlling the flow of imports? At the level of exchange rates

[1] Imports of products covered by the European Coal and Steel Treaty receive licenses automatically, as do products which have been "liberated" within intra-European trade, and no quotas apply to these products. Simplified procedures have been used for certain "shock" imports admitted during brief periods as a means of exerting a downward pressure on the price level. Licenses are granted outside the quotas in connection with some of the export promotion schemes or with specific "compensation" (i.e., barter) operations.

fixed during most of the postwar period, there was undoubtedly a potential demand for foreign imports substantially in excess of the amounts permitted by exchange control authorities. This would particularly be the case for consumer goods (clothing, electrical appliances, etc.) which were in short supply at home and/or frequently cheaper in foreign countries. While below the level of imports which would have obtained in the absence of import restrictions (*other things being equal*), the long-run movement of import volumes has closely followed the rise of domestic production. Between 1948 and 1953, the index of industrial production rose 23.5 per cent; the volume of total imports into Metropolitan France rose 22.8 per cent while those from foreign sources (to which the quota system applied) rose 28.3 per cent. Relative to 1929, the index of the volume of imports stood at 102 in 1953, while the index of industrial production was at 105. In the European trade area, the OEEC concluded that "French quantitative restrictions have thus had only a limited effect on the volume and value of total French imports from member countries and from the EPU area as a whole."[26] [j]

Several factors may help to explain why import restrictions have not resulted in greater savings on imports, despite the severity of the balance of payments deficits which inspired them. A high proportion of postwar French imports has consisted of: (a) agricultural products required to meet deficiencies of domestic production; and (b) raw materials (coal, petroleum, textile raw materials and non-ferrous metals) required to maintain the levels of industrial activity in France. In 1952, agricultural products and raw materials accounted for 86 per cent of the value of imports of Metropolitan France.[27] In addition, a large part of the "manufactured" products has consisted of equipment goods required for the realization of the investment program. A substantial cutback of imports in any of these categories would undoubtedly have resulted in a reduction of the levels of production and consumption in France. With respect to the substantial volume of imports payable in gold or dollars (including the gold or dollar component of France's

j Import controls have been used particularly to restrict the volume of imports of manufactured articles which are competitive with goods produced domestically and of foodstuffs which compete with the products of French agriculture. Domestic producers in these categories have traditionally been protected against foreign imports by high tariffs and (since 1931) by quantitative restrictions. These products were imported only in limited quantities, therefore, even before the war; this should be borne in mind in considering the comparative statistics (prewar and postwar) on which judgments concerning the efficacy of the import controls are generally based.

deficit in intra-European trade), a major purpose of the American aid programs was to ensure an adequate supply of the foreign products considered to be indispensable for economic recovery or mutual defense.

It is by no means established, of course, that all of the imports permitted into the country have been "essential" to French needs. The import program from the dollar area has been subject to a review and screening procedure by United States officials under the foreign aid programs, and "luxury" goods (automobiles, refrigerators, etc.) have been rigorously excluded. With respect to other imports, special factors may have modified the rules of thumb in various ways. Thus, during periods of world shortages, the supplying countries have sometimes agreed to provide the desired products only if less "essential" ones were included in the package. Conversely, the need to develop outlets for French export surpluses (of agricultural products, for example) has sometimes necessitated the acceptance of non-essential imports in return. The American government has hardly been reluctant to encourage consumption of the surpluses of American farm production, in France as elsewhere. In the absence of clearly defined criteria of "need" as applied to imported products, traditional patterns have undoubtedly also played an important part in the horse trading involved in the negotiation of bilateral trade agreements.

The quota and licensing system has also been used, along with other measures, in an effort to redirect import trade from "hard" to "soft" currency areas. Detailed information on the government's efforts along these lines is not readily available. As can be seen from Table 14, the proportion of metropolitan imports from the dollar area has declined appreciably since 1949, but is about at the prewar levels. It is not clear how much of the reduction since 1949 can be attributed directly to state action, rather than to the restoration of more normal trading patterns and to the gradual decline of American aid.

3. *Trade Liberalization.* The quantitative restrictions on imports have been destined to be reduced or abolished, insofar as European trade is concerned, under the "trade liberalization" program of the OEEC. The OEEC position has been that quotas are the primary obstacle to a free exchange of goods and services within Europe, and that the maintenance of these quotas was not justified, in the case of most countries, by a "structural" balance of payments problem. The French government, which has claimed the initiative in developing the trade liberalization program,[28] was later obliged

TABLE 14

PERCENTAGE DISTRIBUTION OF FOREIGN TRADE OF METROPOLITAN FRANCE BY MONETARY AREA, 1913, 1929, 1938, 1949-1952

	1913	*1929*	*1938*	*1949*	*1950*	*1951*	*1952*
				Per cent of total imports			
Countries							
)ollar area	12.4	15.4	14.8	21.1	15.2	14.1	13.5
Ion-sterling EPU	30.8	30.5	24.8	22.2	24.5	25.6	24.9
'articipating sterling	13.6	10.9	9.0	7.0	8.3	10.8	11.4
Ion-participating sterling	8.6	11.1	10.8	14.0	14.7	17.0	16.1
Ion-dollar American	9.2	8.9	5.8	3.8	6.0	5.8	5.1
astern Europe	6.6	3.9	4.8	2.9	1.9	2.5	2.8
)ther foreign	9.1	7.0	3.1	3.0	3.2	3.4	3.6
Total foreign countries	90.3	87.7	73.1	74.0	73.8	79.2	77.4
)verseas territories	9.7	12.3	26.9	26.0	26.2	20.8	22.6
Grand total	100.0	100.0	100.0	100.0	100.0	100.0	100.0
				Per cent of total exports			
)ollar area	7.2	8.8	7.3	3.3	5.4	7.4	5.4
Ion-sterling EPU	44.2	41.6	37.2	28.4	32.8	28.6	29.6
'articipating sterling	21.3	15.7	12.5	10.1	10.4	10.7	7.8
Ion-participating sterling	1.3	1.7	1.8	2.0	2.8	3.4	3.0
Ion-dollar American	5.7	4.4	4.2	6.0	5.7	5.7	3.5
astern Europe	1.4	2.9	5.7	3.8	1.9	2.1	3.4
'ther foreign countries	4.7	5.9	4.4	4.7	5.0	5.2	5.1
'otal foreign countries	85.8	81.0	73.1	58.3	64.0	63.1	57.8
verseas territories	14.2	19.0	26.9	41.7	36.0	36.9	42.2
Grand total	100.0	100.0	100.0	100.0	100.0	100.0	100.0

)urce: La Documentation Française, *Notes et études documentaires* No. 1807, "L'Evolution du commerce extérieur de la France métropolitaine de 1950 à 1953" (Paris, 1953), pp. 7-8.

to abandon it completely for a time. The original goal of the OEEC program, launched late in 1949, was the removal of half of the quotas on private imports among the member countries and among those parts of their monetary areas participating in the program. The base year for purposes of calculation was 1948; specifically excluded were "state-traded" imports, which in 1952 amounted to 34 per cent of the total intra-European trade of France, a far higher proportion than the European average (7 per cent).[29] Successive increases in the goals raised them to 75 per cent by February 1951. France reached a level of 55 per cent in March 1950, 66 per cent in December, and attained the 75 per cent goal in April 1951.

The French position in EPU deteriorated continuously after March 1951, and in February 1952 the government suspended the liberalization measures and reimposed quotas on all intra-European imports. The removal of import restrictions was not the only cause of the reversal of the French position; other factors, among them speculation on a devaluation of the franc and a decline in exports, played a major part in the process. Despite the reimposition of quotas, the monthly EPU deficits continued, although on a somewhat reduced scale, throughout most of 1952 and all of 1953.

The use of import quotas has traditionally been justified in France solely on grounds of defending the balance of payments position.[30] But the intensive discussions with business and farm groups which precede decisions on the specific commodities to be liberated indicate that the protection of domestic producers in agriculture and industry against foreign competition has been inextricably mixed with this consideration.[31] Trade liberalization again came to the fore under the economic programs of Faure[k] and Mendès-France, but because of the continued overvaluation of the franc, it had to proceed cautiously. The proportion of private imports freed rose gradually to 65 per cent by the end of 1954, the OEEC "minimum" goal of 75 per cent finally being reached in April 1955. However, a "special provisional compensatory tax" of 10-15 per cent was applied to most of the freed commodities. The tax was officially attributed to the need to protect domestic producers against the "shock" of foreign competition which, be-

[k] Finance Minister Faure graphically described the French position in the trade liberalization program in the following terms: "We have built a house, and then locked ourselves outside. Now it is necessary for France to become a full shareholder in the construction of Europe." (Quoted in *Le Monde*, March 20, 1954, p. 14.)

cause of price disparities, might "flood" the French market and cause widespread unemployment (as well as a drain on foreign exchange reserves).[32] The compensatory tax was specifically labelled "provisional," and the OEEC called for its abolition as soon as possible. In November 1954 the rates of 10 per cent and 15 per cent were lowered to 7 and 11 per cent, but the higher rates were applied to most of the products newly liberated in 1955 as the 75 per cent stage was approached.

4. *Export Promotion.* The expansion of exports has appeared to be a particularly attractive solution, both to the problem of the balance of payments gap and, during periods of recession, to the problem of stimulating economic activity within France. The government has bent its efforts toward this end with a general increase in the number and extensiveness of export promotion schemes with the passage of time. The various export promotion measures can be roughly grouped into three categories: provision of special credit and insurance facilities for exporters; export subsidies in the form of tax benefits and rebates of different kinds; and foreign exchange incentives.[33]

a. Insurance and credit facilities. A price guaranty, provided by the government without charge, insures the exporter against an increase in costs during the period of execution of a contract, either from domestic price inflation or from changes in international monetary parities. Originally intended for capital goods requiring a production period of at least eighteen months, the guaranty has been progressively extended to cover a wide range of products. In addition, a public establishment, the *Compagnie Française d'Assurance pour le Commerce Extérieur* (CFACE) has been functioning since 1946 to provide insurance facilities of various kinds to exporters. A guaranty is given to private banks that finance exports, at a commission of 2.4 per cent. Exporters are insured against political risks (war and foreign revolutions), natural catastrophes, and difficulties of transferring funds, at rates which vary according to the country (0.8 per cent for the United States, 4 per cent for Eastern Europe). Exporters may also be insured against the risks of commercial default, for which the premiums are between 2 per cent and 8 per cent. Because of the reluctance of commercial banks to engage in export operations, still other credit arrangements have had to be provided through the mechanism of another public establishment, the *Banque Française pour le Commerce Extérieur* (BFCE). Short, medium and long-term credit is available, at rates ranging from 6 to 16 per cent, under various guaranty, endorsement and discount arrangements made by the BFCE directly or in conjunction with other public credit establishments.

These extensive insurance and credit facilities have undoubtedly contributed to the postwar expansion of exports, by creating a more favorable climate for export operations. This would apply particularly to long-run investment contracts, for which commercial bank financing has been most difficult to obtain.

b. Export subsidies.[34] The exemption of exports from indirect domestic taxes is a widely practiced custom, which has tended to spread as other countries have found it necessary to retaliate in order to maintain their relative position. It has become of particular importance in France, where the large volume of indirect taxes incorporated into prices is considered to be an important element in the international price disparities which have handicapped French exporters. The exemption (or, in most cases, reimbursement) applies in France both to fiscal charges and to social charges (that is, to the employer's contribution to the social security system for social insurance, family allowances and workmen's compensation). The latter is of special significance since the French social security system is financed, in the first instance, largely by employer contributions.[1]

The details of the export subsidies are highly complicated, and the basic provisions and methods of application have been frequently revised. In broad outline, the procedure in force since 1951 involves the reimbursement of a portion (or in some cases the whole) of the taxes or charges paid by the employer for social security contributions, the 5 per cent payroll tax, and the transaction and services taxes on other than the last transaction. A tax credit or exemption is provided for the tax on value added and the tax on transactions at the last stage. The list of products benefiting from this procedure is frequently changed, as is the list of countries to which it applies. The method used in calculating the exemption or reimbursement has also varied widely, in part because of the multiplicity of basic tax rates and of the difficulty of determining the final burden of the tax on value added. In the case of agricultural products, subsidies have been used as simple "dumping" operations, independent of the volume of indirect taxes imposed on the commodities in question.

The effect of the export subsidies on France's competitive position cannot be ascertained precisely, since to measure that effect

[1] Cf. Chapter 10 below.

would require a comparison of actual events with the (unknown) situation that would have existed in the absence of subsidies. The erratic movement of exports since 1951 (see Table 13) may be *prima facie* evidence that other factors—such as the international economic situation, the level of internal demand, import restrictions imposed or lifted by other countries—have had the dominant effect. The substantial sum of about 80 billion francs was spent by the French government in 1953 on export promotion measures, mostly in the form of export subsidies (on a total export trade of 760 billion francs).[35] Fragmentary studies made in 1953 showed little correlation between these subsidies and the movement of export prices or export volumes. The moderate decline in French export prices between the first half of 1952 and the first half of 1953 was not only lower than the average fall in export prices for OEEC countries as a whole; it was also actually smaller, in the case of raw materials and semi-finished products, than the decline in French internal prices over the same period.[36] French exporters were disposed to look upon the export subsidies as a kind of "windfall" profit, partly because the legislation was revised so frequently and extensively as to raise doubts concerning the continuity of the government's efforts. Better results seem to have been obtained from the export subsidies in 1954. French export prices declined more than internal prices, and the volume of exports to foreign countries rose considerably.[37] The increased subsidy of agricultural products apparently played an important part in this expansion.

A general campaign against export promotion schemes was launched at the January 1955 meeting of the OEEC. France (along with Greece and Turkey) was temporarily exempted from the agreement to remove export aids on an "experimental" basis by the end of 1955. If the campaign is carried out, however, there will be strong pressures on the French government to follow suit.

c. Foreign currency incentives. The government has also attempted to encourage the development of exports by permitting exporting firms to retain a portion of their foreign exchange earnings. In most cases the uses to which the foreign currencies can be put have been prescribed, although sometimes quite loosely.

The principal foreign currency scheme has been the system of "EFAC" (*Exportations-Frais Accessoires*) accounts. Under the EFAC system, the exporter has been permitted to retain 10 per cent of his foreign currency earnings (15 per cent in the case of dollar exports). This currency can be used for "accessory" expenses connected with the export business (commissions, publicity, travel) or for the purchase of raw materials and equipment required by the exporter. The currency may also be transferred, under a blanket or specific authorization by the exchange authorities. For a few years, 3 per cent of the total export proceeds (that is, between 20 per cent and 30 per cent of the EFAC account) could be used for any purpose.

There has been widespread speculation in the EFAC accounts,[38] resulting in the use of the foreign currencies for the import of "luxuries" prohibited under the licensing system. Steps were taken in 1954 to limit the use of the accounts to the "normal" requirements of the exporter, while the building-up of foreign currency holdings abroad was restricted by the regulation that 10 per cent of the outstanding balances (above a prescribed minimum) must be repatriated at quarterly intervals.

Under a separate "10 per cent equipment" program, exporters of a specified list of products have been permitted to repurchase foreign currencies from the Foreign Exchange Office, up to a maximum of 10 per cent of their export earnings and subject to the approval of a trade association and of the competent ministry. The foreign currency could initially be used only for the purchase of equipment, but raw materials have subsequently been authorized for importation under the program. Despite the more stringent conditions governing their use, some of the "10 per cent equipment funds" have been used by trade associations for the importation of "nonessential" products.[39] Another incentive scheme has been the IM-EX procedure. This has made possible the importation of raw materials outside of the official import programs and import quotas, if the materials are to be exported after transformation in France. As a general rule, the importer-exporter has been required to demonstrate that the amount of foreign exchange earnings (in currencies of the same or greater "hardness") is at least as great as the foreign exchange cost of the imports.

While the various foreign currency schemes have presumably encouraged the growth of exports, they have been at least partially self-defeating. A substantial portion of the foreign exchange has been used either to build up foreign holdings abroad (which the exchange control authorities have, thus far, had little success in tapping) or to finance imports of "luxury" products which are not otherwise permitted.

III SUMMARY

Closing the balance of payments "gap," particularly with respect to "hard" currencies, has been a major objective of postwar policy. Because of the conflict with other objectives (reconstruction, recovery, defense), complete elimination of the gap has not been considered a feasible goal during most of the postwar period. The balance of payments difficulty appeared to call, first of all, for curbing the inflation, but, as noted in the preceding chapter, the government had little success in doing this. Nor did the government turn vigorously to the orthodox policy of currency depreciation. Instead, primary reliance has been placed on strict control of capital movements, quantitative control of imports, and special stimuli to exports. Hope has also been pinned on "structural reforms" which might lower the cost-price structure of the economy.

External relations have thus become one of the fields of economic activity where the extent of public regulation has been greatest. The government has created the trade and payments framework within which foreign exchange has taken place. Through its system of exchange controls (and through its regulation of the exchange rate), it has strongly influenced the terms of these exchanges. The state has also directly participated in part of the importing process, and subjected both imports and exports to a wide variety of controls and incentive devices. There has been some tendency for the tightness of controls to be relaxed with the passage of time, but this relaxation has been gradual and carefully selective.

Despite some erratic movements, there has been a substantial narrowing of the balance of payments "gap" since the war, and in 1954 there was a surplus on current account. "Viability" has remained a somewhat distant goal, however, since the improvement has been dependent in considerable part on exceptional sources of foreign exchange. French participation in the trade liberalization program, and in discussions on convertibility, has still been handicapped by balance of payments difficulties.

Some success can be observed in the government's efforts to restrict capital movements, to reduce imports (or to keep them from rising), and to stimulate exports. Each of the policies has had defects or limitations, and external factors have played a major part in the postwar evolution of French trade. Implementation of an effective control system has been made more difficult by the continued overvaluation of the franc, which has encouraged capital flight and evasion of controls. Many French officials have doubted that a devaluation would be successful, because of inelastic demand and supply and the susceptibility of the domestic economy to inflation. A "correct" exchange rate policy is not easy to define, especially in light of the interaction of other objectives. But it is not clear that devaluation need have all of the foreseen consequences, nor that some officials have accepted their objections to devaluation at face value.

PART II

THE STATE AS PUBLIC FINANCIER

CHAPTER 5

BUDGETARY EXPENDITURES

1. THE PROBLEM

IN Part I, the actions of the state with respect to some broad general problems of the postwar period were discussed. An important element of these problems, and indeed of the state's activities in general, were decisions concerning the use of public resources (i.e., the budget) for alternative purposes. In Part II, a closer scrutiny will be given to the state's actions in this field—that is, to how the state has collected and allocated the resources channelled through the public finances. The expenditure of public funds for the performance of certain "indispensable" services relating to the general welfare and safety; the use of the revenues of the public domain; and the levying and collecting of taxes to cover these expenditures have long been essential functions of the state. As the responsibilities assumed by the modern state for the economic and social welfare of its citizens have increased, its public finances have grown concomitantly, reflecting this expanding role.

The next chapter considers the tax system. This chapter, concerning budgetary expenditures, deals essentially with two points: the size of the budget (how large a proportion of the nation's resources have been channelled through the government's budget); and the composition of the budget (how these public outlays have been allocated among alternative activities or broad categories of expenditures, with the 1953 budget as the point of reference).

As an index of the extent and character of state intervention, the pattern of budgetary expenditures has certain limitations. While most of the activities of the state are reflected in its public accounts in some form, these accounts do not necessarily measure accurately the significance of some activities. Thus, the effect upon the allocation of resources of the tariff protection given to industry and agriculture cannot be evaluated satisfactorily in terms of either the budgetary receipts that tariffs provide or the slight administrative expenses that they entail. Similarly, some of the instruments of direct economic intervention, such as price fixing, wage controls, and antitrust enforcement do not have important quantitative counterparts in the finances of the state, although they may indirectly influence the level of receipts or expenditures. Nevertheless, with these limitations in mind, it is possible to obtain valuable insights into the political economy of postwar France through the medium of its budgetary expenditures.

II. SIZE OF THE BUDGET

How has the size of the budget changed over time, in absolute terms and as a proportion of the national income? That the volume of budgetary expenditures has grown steadily and appreciably over the past century or more is as evident to common observation as it is difficult to measure accurately. Treasury officials strive for a high degree of "flexibility" in budgetary operations so as to adapt their procedures to changing circumstances.[a] One of the less favorable byproducts of this flexibility is that, in tracing the development of the budget over a considerable period of time, one finds substantial differences in the number and kind of expenditures covered under the heading of the "general" budget. This has been especially true during the postwar period. The almost continuous depreciation of the internal and external value of the franc during the past 40 years also makes comparisons over any extended period a hazardous undertaking.

Unadjusted figures on the growth of expenditures in the "general" budget of the central government over the past 140 years (since 1815) are given in Table 15.[b] With the exception of a few, isolated years of budgetary deflation, they reveal a steady and rapid increase in the volume of budgetary expenditures; a so-called "law of the continual increase in public expenses" has even been discovered to describe their growth.[1] Between 1815 and 1954 the volume of the budget increased over four thousand fold. Critics of state intervention relish the opportunity to point out that the government now spends more in a day than it did in an entire year before the first World War.

[a] Witness the following statement by a former Director of the Treasury: "Experience shows that in budgetary affairs tactics are often more important than strategy: in other words, the Minister of Finance must often change his method in order to obtain satisfactory results and he would run the risk, by being a prisoner of unchanged principles, of losing all flexibility of action." (François Bloch-Lainé, *Le Trésor public et la politique financière*, Cours à l'Institut d'Etudes Politiques de l'Université de Paris, Paris 1953, p. 53.)

[b] Data in Table 15 refer to the fiscal year (*exercice*), covering the expenditures authorized by a particular budget even if they occur after the end of the fiscal year (which in France is also the calendar year). They cover the "general" budget of ordinary and extraordinary expenditures but do not include certain activities which for various reasons are placed in "annexed budgets" (such as the postal, telephone and telegraph service and family allowances to farmers) or in "special treasury accounts" (on the grounds, not always correct, that they are self-liquidating). The broad system of social security and related benefits is administered by an autonomous fund outside of the budgetary accounts.

TABLE 15

BUDGETARY EXPENDITURES OF THE CENTRAL GOVERNMENT FOR SELECTED YEARS, 1815-1954[1]

(billions of current francs)

1815	0.9	1934	49.9
1825	1.0	1938	82.3
1835	1.0	1939	150.2
1845	1.5	1945	465.4
1855	2.3	1946	521.2
1865	2.1	1947	689.5
1875	2.9	1948	992.2
1885	3.5	1949	1,282.0[3]
1895	3.4	1950	2,422.6[3]
1905	3.7	1951	2,631.4[4]
1914	10.1	1952	3,542.0[5]
1918	41.9	1953	3,722.0[5]
1924	42.5	1954	3,713.0[5]
1929	58.9[2]		

Source: 1815-1951: INSEE, *Annuaire statistique* 58th Volume 1951 (Paris, 1952), pp. 302-304. 1952-1954: Table 9.

[1] Except as noted, data refer to the fiscal year (*exercice*), including both ordinary and extraordinary budgets, but excluding annexed budgets, special treasury accounts and the independent social security system.

[2] Fiscal year of 15 months.

[3] Provisional figures drawn from the accounting report at the close of the fiscal year.

[4] Preliminary.

[5] The net deficit of the special treasury accounts is included. Data are not strictly comparable with data for other years.

It is clear from even a casual observation of the figures in Table 15 that the rate of increase in government expenditures has not been constant over time, but it is undesirable to look solely at unadjusted figures; in fact, in their crude form, data on French budgetary expenditures are highly deceptive and difficult to comprehend. The first adjustments which need to be made to the crude figures concern differences in the way that the same activities have been classified over time (for example, as between the central and local government budgets). The net effect of the many changes that have taken place in the classification of budgetary expenditures is to understate the rate of growth during some periods and to overstate it during others.[c]

[c] Prior to 1882, local government expenditures appear to have been included in the central government budget. They have since been shown separately, so that the increase since that date tends to be somewhat understated; on the other hand, there has been a general tendency to centralize more and more public expenses into the accounts of the national government, with the result that some of the apparent increase is due only to differences in reporting. After the first World War

It is also useful to broaden the concept of public expenditures to include items that do not go through the general budgetary accounts of the central government. Expenditures for social security and related benefits are administered autonomously and do not appear in the public budget. Local government expenditures are also excluded. In 1913 these were one-third the size of the central government budget, but their importance has since been declining as the central government has assumed an increasing proportion of the total public charges.

Finally, an adjustment should be made for changes in the level of prices. Price inflation, which has proceeded with few interruptions over the past 40 years, has had a very uneven incidence on the budgetary figures. The official indexes of wholesale and retail prices that should be used to deflate budgetary expenditures are, for all practical purposes, non-existent for the period before the first World War and quite unsatisfactory for the interwar period and for postwar years prior to 1948.[d]

Unfortunately, data reflecting the three adjustments just described are available from official sources for only a limited number of years. The expenditure data in Table 16[e] cover the years 1913, 1938, 1946, 1949, and 1951. It can be seen that the real size of the budget (i.e., expenditures in constant prices) increased about three-fold between 1913 and 1938. This in itself is an impressive figure, the significance of which tends to be lost in the astronomical (but misleading) results of the unadjusted data. The figure for 1946 should probably be disregarded since it reflects the disorganized conditions of the immediate postwar period. Between 1938

a number of important operations previously carried in the budget were withdrawn and shown either on a net basis or not at all; among them, the public debt financing of the Amortization Fund after 1926, the war damage and reconstruction payments made by the *Crédit National* after 1919, and the activities of the Postal, Telephone and Telegraph services and certain "industrial or commercial" organizations. In the early years after the second World War, many important operations, such as the payment of war damages and the public financing of investments, were covered in special treasury accounts rather than the general budget. It was not until 1950-1951 that the general budget incorporated all of the major capital expenditures of the central government; in 1954, some of them were again returned to the special treasury accounts.

[d] Ideally, different categories of expenditures should be deflated by different price indexes, and some (e.g., interest payments on the public debt) should not be adjusted. However, as is evident from inspection of Table 16, The Ministry of Finance has used the same price deflator for each expenditure category, including interest payments.

[e] The statistics on the general budget of the central government in Table 16 are based on the "cash" budget (*gestion*) of the Treasury, which involves different accounting concepts from those used in the authorization budget (*exercice*) shown in Table 15.

TABLE 16. TOTAL PUBLIC EXPENDITURES, 1913, 1938, 1946, 1949, 1951

	(billions of current francs)					(billions of francs in 1951 prices)				
Category	*1913*	*1938*	*1946*	*1949*	*1951*	*1913*	*1938*	*1946*	*1949*	*1951*
Central Government General Budget[1]	5.1	83	547	1,362	2,100	790	1,930	1,560	1,810	2,100
Local Communities[2]	1.7	25	90	352	515	264	580	257	468	515
Amortization Fund for Public Debt[3]	–	6.6	18	31	52	–	155	52	41	52
Special Treasury Accounts[4]										
1. Investments	–	–	13	107	–	–	–	37	142	–
2. Payments to old workers	–	–	–	20	25	–	–	–	27	25
3. Others	0.2	24.4	123	27	135	31	565	350	36	135
Social Security	–	5	120	674	908	–	120	340	900	908
War Damage Indemnities, National Railways, Merchant Marine	–	–	–	310	300	–	–	–	410	300
Modernization and Equipment Fund[4]	–	–	–	264	267	–	–	–	350	267
Total	7	144	911	3,147	4,302	1,085	3,330	2,581	4,171	4,302

Source: Ministère des Finances, *Rapports sur les comptes provisoires de la nation des années 1951 et 1952 et sur le budget économique de l'année 1953* (Paris, 1953), pp. 132-133. The following footnotes are taken from the source:

[1] Based on Treasury situation reports.

[2] Based on statistics of the *Direction de la Comptabilité Publique*.

[3] Represents expenditures of the *Caisse Autonome d'Amortissement* for the amortization of the public debt and for the debts held by the *Caisse*. Excludes transfer to central budget of surplus of receipts.

[4] Based on Ministère des Finances, *Inventaire de la situation financière* (Paris, 1951).

and 1951, the real level of public expenditures increased by about 30 per cent. Comparable data are not available for subsequent years, although it is known that the real volume of public expenditures increased further as a result of the higher military spending for NATO defense and the war in Indochina. It is clear, however, that the major increase in the size of the budget occurred during the 1913-1938 period, rather than as a postwar phenomenon.

One of the most significant measures of the size of the budget is the proportion of the economy's resources channelled through the public finances of the state. Adjusted budgetary expenditures of the central government were about 32 per cent of the net national income in 1951. If the concept of central government expenditures is broadened to include social security payments outside of the budget proper, total expenditures were over 40 per cent of the net national income in 1951 as against 11 per cent in 1913 and 33 per cent in 1938. Including expenditures of local governments, the total public budget has now reached the imposing level of almost 50 per cent of the net national income (48 per cent in 1951).[2]

The growth of the public budget has, of course, been a general phenomenon, and it would be interesting to know whether the development of public expenditures in other countries has kept pace with that in France. International comparisons in this field are often deceptive because of the many differences in the handling of public expenditures within and outside of the central budget. The following figures, while probably the best available, and adjusted at least in part to take care of conceptual differences, are offered with considerable reservations. They represent central government expenditures during the U.S. fiscal year 1952-1953 as percentages of the gross national product (at market prices)[f].[3]

United Kingdom	32.3%
France	30.0
Belgium-Luxembourg	26.9
Netherlands	26.7
Italy	22.1
United States	21.1
Denmark	14.5

While serving as Finance Minister, Edgar Faure claimed for France the admittedly doubtful distinction of holding the international

[f] The percentage for Germany is not shown since it includes expenditures by the Laender.

record for the highest proportion of government expenditures to national income. Mr. Faure's figures, which do not indicate the year in question, are 36 per cent for France, 35 per cent for the United Kingdom, 24 per cent for the United States, and 22 per cent for Western Germany.[4] Statistical problems aside, both sets of data indicate that the level of French public expenditures is among the highest in the Western world.

The more conservative governments which have been in office during the latter part of the postwar period have often described the level of public expenditures as "excessive." Edgar Faure, while Finance Minister under the Laniel government in 1953, asserted: "The tasks of the State are too heavy, too numerous, too costly. Only a profound reorganization will make it possible to lighten the burden of public expenditures."[5] The proposed Finance Law of 1953 echoes similar sentiments, while revealing some of the reasons that the present levels have been reached:

> . . . the public charges still weigh too heavily on the economy of the country for the development of production and consumption to take place as rapidly as possible. The financial situation would be transformed if the Parliament and the Government could consent to the abandonment of one or several of the missions which the country has entrusted to them: assuring its defense, accomplishing its reconstruction, hastening its economic, social, and cultural development, raising its standard of living, associating the populations overseas with this progress, in a word, making it into a modern nation in a modern world.[6]

Even if future governments succeed in reducing particular missions, the trend of public expenditures over the past 140 years gives some a priori grounds for doubting that the aggregate role of the state, as reflected in its budgetary accounts, is destined to be reduced appreciably.

III COMPOSITION OF THE BUDGET

The difficulties of tracing the size of the budget pale into insignificance when contrasted with those involved in the attempt to discover from a detailed analysis of its contents how the state has allocated among different activities the resources at its disposal. In each of the three fiscal years 1952, 1953, 1954, for instance, a different classification of some of the major categories of expenditure has been adopted. In particular, the handling of investments financed by the general budget and the special treasury accounts has been frequently changed since the war. In order to minimize the likelihood of confusion or error, the following discussion will focus primarily on the budget for a single year, 1953. Some discussion of the trend of major categories of expenditure during the postwar period was given in Chapter 3.

The 1953 documents introduced a new nomenclature for the principal headings of the budget, designed to clarify the functional purposes of the expenditures. The new system of classification, while a marked improvement over earlier presentations, is not yet in a form which provides a complete and satisfactory answer to the popular inquiry, "Where does the money go?" It has therefore been necessary in a number of cases to work from the basic budgetary accounts, a kind of research bordering on detective work. The resulting rough estimates, summarized in Table 17, can only be considered an exploratory attempt at a more rational economic classification of the budget.

The establishment of the definitive 1953 budget was realized in successive stages over a period of 10 months, which spanned the premierships of three men (Pinay, Mayer, and Laniel), two of whom fell from office on issues immediately bearing on it. The original requests drawn up by the various government agencies totalled 4,049 billion francs.[g] These were reduced in the government sponsored bill to 3,804 billion. The expenditures authorized by Parliament, following closely the recommendations of the Finance Committee of the National Assembly, were slightly higher—3,831 billion francs—as a result of a number of "rectifying letters" introduced by the Finance Ministry, largely at the request of Parliament.[h] The basic budgetary documents were placed in the Parliamentary machinery between September and November 1952 and the finance law voted on February 6, 1953. This was a postwar record for prompt legislative action, for in most years it has not been possible to obtain Parliamentary approval until well into the fiscal (and calendar) year to which the budget applies. The record was unfortunately marred by the major revisions subsequently found

[g] We shall respect the French aversion to stating financial figures in "trillions" of francs.

[h] The powers of the Legislature to increase budgetary expenditures have been strictly limited by law, but various Parliamentary maneuvers have enhanced the influence of the Parliament at the expense of the politically unstable Executive. One of these maneuvers is to vote a token reduction in items for which an increase is desired, with the implied threat that the budget as a whole will be delayed or rejected if the increase is not obtained. The Executive frequently responds by a "rectifying letter" in which the expenditures in question are increased.

to be necessary. The budgetary forecasts proved to be unduly optimistic, as regards both the receipts from certain taxes and the possibility of compressing certain expenditures. After subsequent changes, which included increasing other receipts and reducing other expenditures, the budget authorizations in their final version amounted to 3,814 billion francs.[1] From preliminary figures it appears that actual expenditures were in the neighborhood of 3,842 billion, very close to the original estimate.

These figures relate to the general budget incorporating the civil expenditures of the government, investment and reconstruction, and military operations. The net deficit of the special treasury accounts is included, but not the gross figures, which appear separately in the legislation. The annexed budgets enter only indirectly, to the extent that they contribute a net surplus to the Treasury or receive a subsidy to cover a net deficit. The gross expenditures of the annexed budgets and special treasury accounts should be included, however, in any definitive economic analysis of the composition of public expenditures, as must certain operations which for legal or administrative reasons are not part of the budget proper (the Public Debt Amortization Fund and the Social Security Funds).

The following discussion describes in turn each of the principal categories of public expenditure, reorganized along functional or economic lines. Unless otherwise noted, the information applies to the finance law of February 6; the cost of regrouping all of the subsequent adjustments along functional lines is prohibitive. The brief discussion is intended primarily to identify the principal kinds of expenditures and to give some indication of their relative importance, since most of the principal items have been or will be treated at greater length elsewhere in the text.

A. INTEREST AND AMORTIZATION OF THE PUBLIC DEBT

Expenditures connected with the public debt are found in the general budget, the annexed budgets, and the extra-budgetary accounts of the Public Debt Amortization Fund. In total, they amount to 263.3 billion francs, or about 5 per cent of total public expenditures, of which 166.3 billion francs are for current interest payments and 97.0 billion for amortization of the debt.

These charges apply to a public debt which totalled 5,417 billion francs as of December 31, 1953.[7] The public debt of France is only about 40 per cent of the country's gross national product, in

[1] The estimated deficit of the special treasury accounts and the guaranteed loans of the nationalized enterprises (120 billion francs) are included in this figure.

TABLE 17. PUBLIC EXPENDITURES OF THE CENTRAL GOVERNMENT IN 1953[1]

(billions of francs)

Category	*General Budget*[2]	*Annexed Budgets*	*Special Treasury Accounts*[3]	*Amortization Fund*	*Autonomous Social Security Funds*	*Total*
Interest and Amortization of Public Debt	150.3	16.0	–	97.0	–	263.3
Operations of Civil Services:[4]						
Personnel—Salaries	363.6	115.6	n.a.	–	–	n.a.
Personnel—Pensions, Allowances, Social Charges	175.6	17.3	n.a.	–	–	n.a.
Materiel and Maintenance	85.8	39.6	n.a.	–	–	n.a.
Operating Subsidies	43.5	–	n.a.	–	–	n.a.
Miscellaneous	22.9	9.7	n.a.	–	–	n.a.
Total	691.4	182.2	30.1	–	–	903.7
Transfer Payments:[4]						
Social Transfers	275.9	102.7	20.0	–	1,205.9[5]	1,604.5
Economic Subsidies and Public Interventions	205.1	–	96.2	–	–	301.3
Total	481.0	102.7	116.2	–	1,205.9[5]	1,905.8
Capital Expenditures:						
Reconstruction and Equipment of Civil Services	191.8	9.3	–	–	–	201.1
Economic and Social Investments—Loans and Advances	299.8	–	–	–	–	299.8
Economic and Social Investments—Guaranteed Loans	120.0	–	–	–	–	120.0
Economic and Social Investments—Low-cost Housing	52.0	–	–	–	–	52.0
Reconstruction of War Damage	336.7	–	–	–	–	336.7
Total	1,000.3	9.3	–	–	–	1,009.6

(continued on facing page)

Category	General Budget[2]	Annexed Budgets	Special Treasury Accounts[3]	Amortization Fund	Autonomous Social Security Funds	Total
Military Services:[6]						
National Defense and Civil Protection	863.0	–	–	–	–	863.0
Associated States (Indochina)	373.6	–	–	–	–	373.6
Overseas France (North Africa)	42.4	–	–	–	–	42.4
Military Pensions	82.2	–	–	–	–	82.2
Expenditures for NATO Countries[7]	–	–	65.4[7]	–	–	65.4
Total	1,361.2	–	65.4	–	–	1,426.6
Grand Total	3,684.2	310.2	211.7	97.0	1,205.9	5,509.0

Sources: Data for general budget obtained from Finance Law of February 7, 1953 (No. 53-79) and related development laws, printed in the *Journal officiel* of February 4, 7, and 8, 1953, *Lois et décrets*, pp. 1011-1058, 1151-1172, and 1234-1276 and summarized in Ministère des Finances, *Statistiques et études financières* No. 52, April 1953. Breakdown of annexed budgets obtained from *Journal officiel, Lois et décrets* February 4, 1953, pp. 1061-1074 and February 7, 1953, pp. 1205-1207 and from Report No. 4888 of the Finance Committee, National Assembly, November 27, 1952, Vol. II, p. 59. Data on special treasury accounts were obtained from *Journal officiel, Lois et décrets*, February 7, 1953, No. 53-75, pp. 1179-1191. The figure for the Autonomous Amortization Fund was taken from Ministère des Finances, *Rapports sur les comptes provisoires de la nation des années 1951 et 1952 et sur le budget économique de l'année 1953* (Paris, 1953), p. 202. Operations of the social security funds based on data from Finance Committee of National Assembly, reprinted in *Le Monde* January 17, 1954, Financial and Economic Supplement; revised with more recent figures from *Agence économique et financière*, March 19, 1954, p. 4.

1 Excludes expenditures of local communities and central government contributions to these communities.

2 As voted on February 6, 1953. Except as noted below in (4), it does not take account of blocked credits or subsequent reductions in credits. Expenses offsetting receipts, amounting to 64.6 billion francs, are not shown.

3 This is only a partial tabulation of the numerous special treasury accounts. It covers: the economic subsidies included in the commercial accounts; all of the special purpose accounts; none of the foreign government or monetary operations accounts; the principal accounts providing loans and advances.

4 16 billion francs of blocked credits have been deducted from the operations of civil services and transfer payments; the itemized breakdown of these credits is not available.

5 Data based on actual expenditures in 1953 or projected from actual expenditures during first half of 1953. Figure includes general social security system and special funds of public enterprises and farmers not covered elsewhere. Does not include government subsidies to social security funds, social payments made directly by the state, or social payments by local communities.

6 Approximately 55 billion francs of military expenditures are also included in the operations of civil services and in transfer payments.

7 These expenditures are reimbursed by the recipient governments, except for a contribution from the general budget which has been deducted.

contrast with a proportion of 75 per cent in the United States, and payments on the debt account for a smaller proportion of total budgetary expenditures in France. Those who might be inclined to envy this feature of the French budget should bear in mind the process of almost chronic inflation through which the (relatively) low level of public debt payments has been achieved.

B. CURRENT EXPENDITURES FOR CIVIL OPERATIONS

Under this heading are included the current costs for operating the administrative services of the central government. These costs were projected at 903.7 billion francs or 16 per cent of the total in 1953, including the gross expenditures of administrative activities covered in the annexed budgets and the special treasury accounts.

The largest single element in this total (about 215 billion francs) is accounted for by the public education system, which is entirely financed by the central government. It is followed in importance by the costs of operating the state-owned postal, telegraph, and telephone services (about 150 billion). Expenditures of the Ministry of Interior for internal security, police, etc., are about 80 billion.[j]

In view of the nature of the operations covered, personnel salaries naturally play the largest part, although social payments to personnel also figure prominently, as can be seen from the summary data in Table 17.

The cost of operating the civil services has been increasing slightly (in real terms) since the war, following the closely related trends of population and economic activity. There is, of course, no way of determining whether this cost is "high," but it is instructive to observe the trend in the number of civil service personnel. The number engaged in traditional administrative functions was 682,000 in 1936. In the following decade the personnel rolls were increased by 276,000; since then, however, the number has fallen by 113,000. Over a period of about 16 years, therefore, the increase in personnel performing these functions was under 25 per cent.[8] On the other hand, the largest increases in personnel relative to prewar have been in connection with the operation of the nationalized industries and the autonomous system of social security. These personnel do not appear in the above figures, nor are the operating costs of these activities included in the general total.

[j] It is not possible to arrive at precise figures for the operating costs of different ministries, since the sizable payments to government personnel for pensions and allowances are not broken down by ministry.

C. TRANSFER PAYMENTS

Disbursements that are intended, not to pay for purchases of goods or services, but to subsidize or assist someone can be thought of as transfers from the taxpayers to the recipients. These disbursements, which are usually called transfer payments, have become one of the most significant features of a modern budget. The transfer payments contained in the general budget amount to 481.0 billion francs, or 13 per cent of the general budget, of which 275.9 billion are social transfers (that is, transfers intended to assist certain social groups) and 205.1 billion economic subsidies and miscellaneous activities described in the budget as "public interventions." The full volume of transfer payments is considerably larger, but more difficult to measure.

1. Social Transfers. The principal social transfers included in the general budget voted on February 6, 1953, are listed below (in billions of francs).[k]

Veterans and war victims	152.1
Family, maternity, medical, old age assistance	53.2
Fellowships and financial aid to students	16.0
Contribution to railroad retirement fund (SNCF)	13.2
Contribution to miners' retirement fund	10.9
Contribution to merchant marine social insurance	9.4
Increase in state annuities (*rentes viagères*)	8.3
Adult education and training	4.0
Unemployment assistance	3.1
Subsidy to paupers (*économiquement faibles*) to compensate for rent increases	3.0
Miscellaneous social contributions	2.7
Total	275.9

The most important social transfer payments, however, are found in other public funds, some of them outside the budget proper and financed from special receipts. The annexed budgets include an autonomous fund for family allowances to farmers, financed primarily by taxes on agricultural products. In 1953 the fund was expected to make payments of 102.7 billion francs. The special treasury accounts include family allowances administered by the Ministry of National Education amounting to 20.0 billion francs. The complex system of social security, administered by a series of autonomous funds outside of the budget, disbursed the very substantial amount of 1,205.9 billion francs in 1953. This total consists of 677.8 billion francs of payments for social in-

[k] It will be recalled that pensions and social benefits paid by the government to its employees are included in the current operating costs of the civil services.

surance and retirement, 437.8 billion for family allowances, and 90.3 billion for workmen's compensation. Payments were disbursed by "general" funds and special funds for farmers and for miners, railroad employees and other employees of nationalized industries.

The grand total of social transfers from public funds was thus expected to exceed 1,600 billion francs in 1953. These transfers represent almost 30 per cent of total public expenditures, and more than 15 per cent of the 1953 national income. By way of comparison, similar social transfers by the United States government amounted to about 15 per cent of the Federal budget and 4 per cent of the United States national income in 1954.[1] If social payments made by the French government as employer and by local communities are added, the total is raised to almost 2,000 billion francs or close to 20 per cent of the national income.[9] Whether or not these transfers result in a redistribution of income in the direction of greater "equity"—a complicated question which will not be entered into here—they create a situation in which a sizable proportion of personal income is distributed on a "fixed" basis rather than varying in accordance with productivity. In view of the magnitude of these transfers, there is a danger that the Frenchman's search for greater security may have the effect of dulling incentives to greater efficiency. Also, as will be seen in later chapters, the "acquired rights" or fixed claims against the government implicit in this system as well as in the many direct and indirect subsidies provided by the government tend to beget still other claims and privileges.

2. *Economic Subsidies.* The economic subsidies provided by the state are considerably more elusive than the transfer payments, as regards both their definition and their identification in the various parts of the budget. Some of the more important subsidies, such as the reduced rates for rail transportation or electricity charged by the public enterprises to favored industrial or social groups, appear in the public budget indirectly, if at all, through the part they play in any net deficits or reduced profits of these enterprises. Other public expenditures that have important subsidy effects, such as reduced interest charges on housing or equipment loans, do not appear as expenditures, nor do the subsidy benefits pro-

[1] In the derivation of these figures, the social transfers in the *Budget of the United States, 1954* (similar in nature to the items included in the calculation for France) were summed up. The figure for the total Federal budget came from the same source. The estimate of U. S. national income was taken from *Survey of Current Business, 1954*, U.S. Dept. of Commerce.

vided by the system of rent controls. Some important *de facto* subsidies, such as the aid to ship builders, to farm cooperatives, and to civil aviation, appear instead in the investment accounts, while others are classified as operating expenses if they relate to public enterprises administered directly by the state. A number of funds, some of them equivalent to subsidies, financed through "parafiscal" measures escape entirely from the budgetary records.[m] Although fragmentary, the list of economic subsidies appearing as such and financed directly from public funds is nevertheless long and varied.

Within the general budget, economic subsidies and miscellaneous forms of public interventions (the latter amounting to 17.4 billion francs) were 205.1 billion francs. The special treasury accounts are a rich source of public subsidy funds containing some 96.2 billion francs of grants, loans, and advances which would appear to warrant classification under this heading. The total of direct subsidies (identifiable as such) and miscellaneous interventions is therefore 301.3 billion francs, or about 6 per cent of total expenditures of the central government. It will be recalled that subsidies were of considerably greater importance in earlier postwar years, when they were used in substantial amounts in an effort to control the domestic inflation.

The national railways (SNCF) received the lion's share of public subsidy funds in 1953; except in the field of transportation, the need for operating subsidies to the public enterprises has been decreasing. The second largest subsidy went to exporters under the program of export promotion. Both of these expenditures were underestimated in the February law, and had to be increased through subsequent authorizations (the SNCF by about 18 billion francs and export subsidies by 25 billion francs). The costly alcohol program, the special fund for road construction.[n] and the subsidy to producers who use imported coal were next in importance. The following lists the principal economic subsidies in the general budget and the special treasury accounts (in billions of francs).

Subsidies to Public Enterprises and Establishments	
SNCF	106.3[o]
Merchant marine	3.6
Paris transport system (RATP)	2.9

m The parafiscal system is discussed in Chapter 10.

n A portion of highway expenditures, financed by a special gasoline tax, is listed as a subsidy although it could also be shown as a public works expenditure.

o A part of the government's subsidy to the SNCF appears under social transfers. To calculate the net subsidy, it is necessary to deduct the "toll" paid to the state by the SNCF, which is estimated at about 12 billion francs in 1953 (see the discussion in Chapter 8).

Air France	2.4
Press association (*Agence France-Presse*)	1.6
Productivity association	0.5
Autonomous ports	0.3
Total	117.6
Subsidies to Economic Groups	
Aid to exporters	40.0
Alcohol program (loans and advances from treasury accounts)	35.0
Subsidies to road construction	21.9
Compensation on imported coal	18.0
Subsidy to fuel producers	14.2
National forestry fund	8.8
Rebate on agricultural fuels	8.0
Textile compensation fund	5.3
Miscellaneous compensation funds	5.0
Rebates on housing construction	3.5
Agricultural cooperatives	1.8
Miscellaneous agricultural subsidies	1.4
Sugar subsidy	1.2
Advance to movie production industry	1.0
Others	1.2
Total	166.3

D. CAPITAL EXPENDITURES

The massive increase in the expenditures of the government on capital formation is the most striking feature of postwar French budgets. From small sums amounting to less than 5 per cent of the 1938 budget, public capital expenditures have risen to 1,000.3 billion francs in 1953,[10] or 27 per cent of the general budget. The breakdown of this figure into its major components is as follows (in billions of francs):

Reconstruction and equipment expenditures of civil services		191.8
Investments executed by the state	71.1	
Investments executed with state assistance	120.7	
"Economic and social" investments		471.8
Loans and advances of Modernization and Equipment Fund	299.8	
State-guaranteed loans of public enterprises	120.0	
Low-cost housing loans	52.0	
Reconstruction of war damage		336.7
Payments of Autonomous Reconstruction Fund (CAREC)	261.5	
Guarantee of securities	20.0	
Reconstruction and equipment of SNCF and merchant marine	55.2	
Total for general budget		1,000.3

These figures do not take account of military investments, which are presented under the rubric of military expenditures. The annexed budgets contain 9.3 billion francs of civil investments (for the PTT and *Radiodiffusion Française*). Capital expenditures of the central government as a whole represent about 18 per cent of total expenditures. The inclusion of the state-guaranteed loans of the nationalized enterprises (120 billion francs) as public "expenditures" is questionable, however, since only a fraction of these loans are likely to represent an eventual charge against the public budget (unless they are eventually converted into capital grants, as the enterprises have requested).

The emergence of these capital expenditures as a major element of postwar budgets has been described in Chapter 2. At the relative height of these programs, in 1949, capital expenditures represented about 40 per cent of the general budget. The completion of the more urgent reconstruction and modernization projects, together with the shift of public funds to the military effort following the outbreak of the Korean war, resulted in a drop in the proportion to about 30 per cent in the period 1951-1953.[p]

Among the 191.8 billion francs of expenditures for the reconstruction and equipment of the civil services of the government, the largest items are equipment expenditures in the overseas departments and territories (48.7 billion) and expenditures for public educational facilities (43.8 billion). Various public works activities account for 22.0 billion, and investments in civil aviation and the merchant marine for 28.1 billion. The category of "economic and social" investments covers: loans and advances disbursed under the authority of the Modernization and Equipment Fund (which, it will be noted, account for only 30 per cent of capital expenditures in the general budget); 120 billion francs of state-guaranteed loans, representing the maximum amount of bond issues bearing the guarantee of the Treasury that the nationalized industries were authorized to float in 1953; and the low-cost housing program, long the step-child of the French capital budget. The third of the major components of capital expenditure is the program of reconstruction of war damage, the generous provisions of which have already been described.

E. MILITARY EXPENDITURES

The extensive French military commitments in Europe, North Africa, and the Far East are reflected in the level of budgetary

[p] See Table 9.

expenditures for purposes of defense. The initial 1953 finance law authorized expenditures of 1,276 billion francs under the military budget. About two-thirds of these expenditures (860 billion francs) were intended for European defense, and one third (416 billion) for defense overseas (of which the Indochina war accounted for 373.6 billion francs and North Africa the remainder). The total military credits were reduced later in 1953 by 43 billion francs, to 1,233 billion. Certain expenditures recognized to be of a military character, and so defined by the North Atlantic Treaty Organization, are included in civilian expenditures. These amount to about 140 billion francs;[q] when they are added, the defense budget is raised to 1,416 billion francs[r] or 39 per cent of the general budget voted on February 6. In the final version of the 1953 budget, the total defense effort was 1,373 billion francs.

Military expenditures projected in 1953 amount to more than 10 per cent of the gross national product. France and the United Kingdom were, in 1953-1954, the two countries with the largest defense efforts, on a relative basis, of the NATO members other than the United States.[11] France is also providing installations and services on its territory to other NATO countries, on a reimbursable basis, expected to amount to 65.4 billion francs in 1953 and handled as a special treasury account. With these included, defense expenditures amounted to about 25 per cent of the total expenditures of the central government.

Military spending in connection with the war in Indochina, which was in full sway in 1953, was larger than the 373.6 billion francs inscribed under this heading in the defense budget. The costs of air and naval operations in the Associated States are shown under the national (European) defense budget; in 1953 the Indochinese component of these costs was 47 billion francs.[12] Also, an indeterminate amount of the equipment costs of French forces in Indochina is included in the national defense budget.

Past as well as current military activities had an important impact on the direction of government spending in 1953. In order to measure this impact, 152.1 billion francs of social payments to veterans and war victims (shown under transfer payments) and

[q] This total is made up of military pensions (80-85 billion francs), payments to the SNCF for reduced fares for military personnel, costs of civil defense, expenses of national defense included in the budget of the Premier's office, and the military share of public works projects of common use.

[r] This total differs from the one shown in Column 1 of Table 17, since it has not been possible in the table to identify in detail about 55 billion francs of military expenditures still included in the civil budget.

336.7 billion francs of payments for reconstruction of war damage should be added to the 1,416 billion francs of military items identified above. An appreciable (but indeterminate) proportion of the payments on the public debt might also be attributed to the financial deficits incurred as a result of heavy military expenditures in the past. It thus appears that at least half of the expenditures in the general budget may be said to arise, directly or indirectly, from the effects of past military conflicts and current defense. If all expenditures of the central government are taken into account, the proportion is about 35 per cent. What the pattern of public spending might have been in the absence of these military requirements is, of course, unknown, but it is clear that they have in practice had a decisive effect on the current size and structure of the budget.

IV SUMMARY

The government has attempted to control the use of an increasing proportion of the national resources through its public finances. As a result of the growth of the budget over the past century and a half, over 40 per cent of the net national income now passes through the budgetary accounts (broadly defined) of the central government. France has relatively one of the largest budgets of the Western world.

The outstanding features of the contemporary (1953) pattern of public expenditures are: the heavy volume of social transfers (with its implications for incentives and the spread of "acquired rights"); the large capital investment program financed by the government; and, of paramount importance, the cumulative effects of past wars and present-day defense requirements. The operating costs of the civil services are not a relatively high or increasing proportion of the budget, if the public ownership and management of nationalized industry and the administration of social security are excluded. As a result of the almost chronic inflation, payments on the public debt are relatively low.

CHAPTER 6

THE TAX SYSTEM

I THE PROBLEM

An important problem of choice is that of determining the proper combination of taxes by which to finance the activities of the state. No tax system has yet been devised that is immune to criticism, nor is there general agreement on how a tax system might do the least damage or the most good in raising a given amount of revenue. It is possible, however, to identify some of the key variables or considerations involved. Thus, tax policies may support or violate popular conceptions of equity in several ways. It is generally assumed that persons in equal circumstances should be treated equally. If tax policies accord markedly different treatment to persons in essentially similar circumstances, they may have important effects on the development of pressure groups and on popular attitudes toward law and order. Equity considerations are also involved in the extent of progressiveness or regressiveness of the tax structure; that is, in the extent to which persons in unequal circumstances (with respect to income) are treated differentially. The tax system may also affect the efficiency of resource use in various ways, through its impact on incentives and on relative prices.

This chapter orients an examination of the French tax structure around these considerations. It begins with a brief description of key features of the individual parts of the tax system and of one special aspect—evasion and fraud. The implications of the tax system for equity (i.e., the equal treatment of equals and the extent of progressiveness) and efficiency are then discussed. Finally, the agitation for, and the obstacles to, reform of the tax system are described.

II DESCRIPTION OF THE TAX SYSTEM[1]

It is customary for discussions of the French tax system to begin with a statement of what is not to be discussed. We shall not deal with the tax system in all its breathtaking complexity (there are, for example, more than two thousand articles in the *Code Général des Impôts*) nor with tax procedures. Treatment of the historical evolution of the tax system will be omitted, while the use of the tax system as an instrument of fiscal policy has been discussed in Chapter 3. The present chapter focuses on the tax structure as it existed in 1953.[a] The focus on a single year makes it possible to describe some of the complications and special provisions which permeate the tax structure, affecting the equity of the tax system and the efficiency of the economy.

Attention will be devoted mainly to the taxes which account for the bulk of receipts. These are six in number: the personal income tax and the corporate profit tax (which together accounted for 26 per cent of estimated budgetary receipts in 1953[b]); the employer's tax on payrolls (7 per cent); the production tax (30 per cent); the transaction tax (and miscellaneous indirect taxes) (13 per cent); and capital taxes (6 per cent). These and other sources of budgetary income are listed in Table 18.

A striking feature of the French tax structure is the high proportion of excise taxes. When the income tax was introduced, late in the first World War, it was hoped that it would eventually become the principal source of revenue. This has not proven to be the case. The proportion of excise taxes is higher in France than in any Western European country other than Italy. The contrast with Great Britain and the United States, which use income taxes as the primary source of tax revenue, is particularly striking, as indicated by the following data for 1949:[c]

Country	*Excise Taxes as Per Cent of Total Tax Revenue*[2]
Italy	70
France	65[d]
West Germany	56
Belgium	56

[a] The tax system is, of course, continually being revised. The principal changes made in 1954 and 1955 are identified throughout the text by footnotes, and referred to again in the section on tax reform.

[b] In 1951, the personal income tax amounted to about 55 per cent of total income tax collections and the corporate profit tax 45 per cent. Data derived from Ministère des Finances, *Statistiques et études financières, supplément finances françaises* No. 18, 1953, pp. 328-329, 350-353, except for proportional tax on securities which was obtained from *supplément finances comparées* Nos. 19-20, 1953, p. 314.

[c] Data from another source give the following percentages for 1952: France (63.6); West Germany (54.2); Great Britain (45.0); Italy (79.6). (Rapport *général de la commission créée par arrêté du 6 Janvier 1954 pour l'étude des disparités entre les prix français et étrangers* (the *Nathan Report*) Paris, 1954, p. 17.

[d] This result is not necessarily inconsistent with that of Table 18. If the payroll tax be deemed an excise tax (see note [a] to Table 18) the per cent of total budgetary receipts accounted for by excise taxes is raised from 54 to 61. Of the total budgetary receipts shown in Table 18, 92 per cent are due to taxes (categories 1 through 5), and hence excise plus payroll taxes account for 66 per cent of total tax receipts.

Country	*Excise Taxes as Per Cent of Total Tax Revenue*
Norway	56
Sweden	46
Switzerland	41
United Kingdom	41
Netherlands	32
United States	22[e]

A perennial question asked by Americans is: "Why don't the French pay their taxes?" It can be answered that, in the aggregate, the French do pay their taxes; or, at least, that their tax burden is relatively as large as in other European countries (and larger than in the United States). On the other hand, as will be seen later, tax evasion seems to be relatively high in France. International comparisons are a precarious undertaking, because of differences in the nomenclature and contents of the various fiscal systems and differences in the method and period of reporting, but the following figures are instructive. They show tax receipts in 1952, presented on three different bases: (a) total tax receipts (at all levels of government and including social security and parafiscal revenues) in relation to gross national product; (b) total tax receipts in relation to net national income; and (c) total tax receipts of the central government in relation to net national income. In view of the imprecision of the estimates, the results can best be described as indicating that total tax yields are about the same in France, Great Britain, and Western Germany and substantially higher in these three countries than in Italy and the United States.[3]

	Total Tax Receipts as Per Cent of GNP	*Total Tax Receipts as Per Cent of* NNI	*Total Tax Receipts of Central Government as Per Cent of* NNI
Western Germany	33.0	42.2	24.7
Great Britain	32.7	39.2	36.1
France	31.2	41.3	36.0
Italy	25.6	32.5	28.7
United States	24.7	29.6	23.9

A. PERSONAL INCOME TAX

The personal income tax consists of a proportional income tax and a progressive surtax, which will be described separately since the taxable base and tax rates are different in the two cases.

[e] The United States figure includes customs duties, which are excluded from the figures for the other countries.

TABLE 18

BUDGETARY RECEIPTS OF THE CENTRAL GOVERNMENT IN 1953

(billions of francs)

Category	*Amount*[1]	*Per Cent of total*
1. Income taxes	738.3	25.52
2. Payroll tax[2]	215.0	7.43
3. Excise taxes		
Production tax	872.0	30.14
Transaction tax	218.0	7.55
Specific tax on wines and meat	93.0	3.21
Indirect contributions	57.7	1.99
Customs duties	232.0	8.02
Monopolies and industrial operations	76.0	2.62
Total	1,548.7	53.53
4. Capital taxes		
Sales of property and other assets	43.3	1.50
Inheritance	22.5	0.78
Other registry taxes	64.2	2.22
Stamp tax	27.0	0.93
Stock market operations	3.5	0.12
Total	160.5	5.55
5. Exceptional taxes		
Illegal profits tax	2.0	0.07
National solidarity tax	0.5	0.02
Total	2.5	0.09
6. Revenues of public domain	20.0	0.69
7. Miscellaneous products and exceptional resources	208.1	7.19
8. Grand total	2,893.1[3]	100.00

Source: Ministère des Finances, *Statistiques et études financières, supplément finances comparées* Nos. 19-20, 1953, pp. 314-315.

1 Forecasts in the Finance Law. Incomplete results as of December 31, 1953, which do not differ substantially from the original estimates, can be obtained in the *Journal officiel, Lois et décrets*, March 6, 1954, pp. 2259-2262.

2 Until October 1, 1948, there was a personal income tax on wages and salaries, deducted at the source; it has since been replaced by a compulsory payroll tax amounting to 5 per cent of wages and salaries and paid by the employers. Some sources show it (optionally) as either an income or an excise tax in view of its particular history. An apprenticeship tax of 0.4 per cent of the payroll should also be considered separately, but it was not possible to break it out of the data on income taxes, where it is now shown.

3 Revenues expected to result from new control procedures, estimated at 15 billion francs, are not included in the tabulation.

1. Proportional Tax. As its name implies, the proportional tax is a flat percentage tax. In principle, it is levied on income from all sources, without discrimination as to source or size of income and without any deduction at the base, and is calculated on the basis of a direct evaluation by the taxpayer. These provisions are subject to major exceptions, however, so that in practice both the tax base and the tax rate vary according to the source of income.

a. Tax base. The tax base, or the method of calculating it, depends to an important extent on the source of income. This is most conspicuous in the case of income from wages and salaries, which is totally exempt from the proportional tax (for reasons described below under the payroll tax). Also, small businessmen, artisans, and professional men have the option of substituting a "forfeit" system for a personal assessment and declaration of their profits. Under the forfeit system, taxable income is estimated by the tax authorities on the basis of crude indicators (such as the volume of purchases, gross sales, inventories, number of personnel, number and horsepower of automobiles) submitted by the taxpayer. Various coefficients are applied to these indicators to arrive at an approximation of net income. The presumed advantage of the forfeit system is its ease of calculation, with a minimum of record-keeping and painful contacts between taxpayer and tax authority, and with less likelihood of fraudulent returns. However, in practice the evaluations by forfeit have often been below the real income of the taxpayer.[f]

In the case of unincorporated businesses, the option to use the forfeit system only applies to firms with an annual turnover of sales below a specified amount (currently 10 million francs of goods or 5 million francs of services).[g] Beyond this amount, the unincorporated business must make a direct assessment of income. Most unincorporated businesses are able to use the forfeit, however. In 1952, 1,249,906 taxpayers, with a taxable income of 407 billion francs, used the forfeit system, while only 295,303 taxpayers, with

[f] The estimate is discussed with the taxpayer before it is applied, and in view of the complexities and uncertainties of the forfeitary procedure the final estimate is likely to be a matter of bilateral bargaining. Once established, the estimate can be carried over from year to year unless denounced by either party. During the years 1953-1955, the government's attempt to adjust the forfeits so that they reflected current incomes more closely, and to investigate the bookkeeping records, resulted in the vigorous resistance of shopkeepers and artisans described below. For further details on the forfeit system, consult James L. Houghteling, Jr., "The Income Tax in France," article in *Public Policy*, Vol. v. (Cambridge, Harvard University Press, 1954), pp. 317-319.

[g] In 1955 the ceiling on sales of goods was raised to 15 million francs.

a taxable income of 250 billion, paid a tax based on self-assessed income. In non-commercial occupations, the taxpayer has the option of using the forfeit system except in a limited number of cases.

Farmers enjoy a special kind of "forfeit" system. An estimate of average profit per unit of land and kind of product is made each year by a Committee on Direct Taxes in each *département*, with the individual farmers grouped around the departmental average on the basis of the assessed value of their property. The assessed values of farm property used for estimating the forfeitary tax reflect very imperfectly the actual value of the property, and the departmental committees, in view of their predominantly rural composition, systematically underestimate the average profits per hectare.[h] As a result, the yield of the tax on agricultural income is extremely low and its incidence is very uneven within the agricultural population. The tax on agricultural income has been officially characterized as "the weakest part of our system of income taxes."[4]

What amounts to still another method of arriving at the tax base applies to income from securities. This income is withheld at the source, without the allowance for dependents or the special deduction (described below). Although the proportional tax is part of the "personal" income tax, all distributed income is taxed whether paid out to individuals or to corporations.

In addition to the general distinction among forfeit, self assessment, and assessment and withholding at the source, the tax base may differ for particular sources of income in ways which are sometimes very complicated. Thus, the tax on income from real estate is supposed to be based on a declaration of gross income from property, with permissible deductions for expenses by a combination of forfeitary and direct evaluations. But the tax provisions have deteriorated to a point where the tax is "of extreme complexity for the taxpayer and of minimum return to the Treasury."[5] For rural property, the base of the tax has been limited by an act of Parliament to twice the base used in calculating the 1948 tax, even though the assessed value of the property used in 1948 was entirely obsolete (the last assessment of rural property having taken place in 1912). For certain property, gross receipts used for tax purposes do not include increases in rent subsequent to January 1948 for commercial sites and to September 1948 for residential dwellings. There is also a "temporary" exemption for newly-constructed residential

[h] In the event that the departmental committee cannot agree on the estimate, the problem is shifted to a national committee, where the strong representation of farmer groups is also likely to result in systematic undervaluation.

buildings; the exemption ranges in time from 2 to 30 years depending on the kind of dwelling and date of construction, during which period no proportional tax is paid. These exemptions were intended to counteract some of the pernicious effects of the rent controls which have been kept in force over the past 40 years, resulting in a greatly reduced volume of new construction and inadequate maintenance and repair of existing dwellings. They illustrate how subsidies to one group (and injuries to another) eventually give rise to a complex network of counter-subsidies and counter-injuries.

b. Tax rates. The effective rate of the tax also differs from the nominal rate of 18 per cent according to the source of income. As noted previously, income from wages and salaries is exempt from the proportional tax. The tax is reduced to 9 per cent for incomes below 200,000 francs arising from earnings by artisans, non-commercial enterprises and the small number of wage earners not benefiting from the total exemption.[i] The rate applied to interest income from certain bonds issued prior to December 1948 is only 10 per cent. The tax on capital gains is reduced to 6 per cent under some conditions and if the proceeds are reinvested.

Although the individual taxpayer has no basic exemption, there is a deduction in the amount of tax paid according to the number of dependents. The exemptions for children show an interesting progression:

1 child	– 15%	of the	tax,	but	not	more	than	5,000	francs
2 children	– 30%	"	"	"	"	"	"	10,000	"
3 children	– 75%	"	"	"	"	"	"	25,000	"
4 children	– 100%	"	"	"	"	"	"	40,000	"
5 children	– 100%	"	"	"	"	"	"	55,000	"

In addition, there is a special deduction that introduces a certain measure of progressiveness (in accordance with income) into the proportional tax. If the tax, once calculated, is below 10,500 francs (equivalent to an income of 60,000 francs under the 18 per cent rate or 120,000 francs under the 9 per cent rate) it is not paid at all. Between 10,500 francs and 43,200 francs (equivalent to an income of 240,000 francs under the 18 per cent rate) the tax is paid only in part, through the application of the special deduction.[j]

[i] Two changes enacted in 1954 raised the ceiling on the 9 per cent rate from 200,000 francs to 440,000 francs for artisans and applied the 9 per cent rate to income below 220,000 from small businesses, non-commercial occupations, agriculture and managerial activities. In 1955, small businesses were permitted a lower rate (of 5 per cent) on imputed salaries of up to 300,000 francs.

[j] The deduction is equal to one-third of the difference between the tax as originally calculated and 43,200 francs.

Beyond 43,200 francs, however, the tax is paid in full, with no deduction for the portion of income below 240,000 francs.

2. *Progressive Surtax.* A progressive surtax is superimposed on the proportional income tax. The method of estimating net income subject to tax is generally the same as for the proportional tax, with a number of exceptions of varying degrees of importance. The most important is that income from wages, salaries, and pensions is included in the surtax, on the basis of declarations made by the employer.[k] Other differences are: new construction is not exempt from the taxation of real estate income; certain forms of income from securities excluded from the proportional tax are included in the surtax; and the upper limit on income from rural property of an amount double the 1948 base applies only to owners who farm their own land. On the other hand, certain forms of income which are subject to the proportional tax are exempt from the surtax (for example, interest on treasury bonds of more than 5 years maturity, profits on sales of capital assets taxed at 6 per cent under the proportional tax).[l]

A basic deduction is provided, after which the nominal tax rates rise steeply from 10 to 60 per cent, as can be seen from the following schedule:

Segments of income included between:

0 and 180,000 francs	exempted
181,000 and 350,000 francs	10%[m]
351,000 and 600,000 francs	15%
601,000 and 900,000 francs	20%
901,000 and 1,500,000 francs	30%
1,501,000 and 3,000,000 francs	40%
3,001,000 and 6,000,000 francs	50%
Beyond 6,000,000 francs	60%[n]

k On the grounds that wage earners bore too large a share of the burden under the progressive surtax, the tax reform of April 1954 provided for a deduction of 10 per cent on income from wages, salaries, pensions and annuities before calculation of the tax. There is also a standard deduction for "professional expenses" in connection with wages and salaries, which was at 10 per cent in 1954 and at 15 per cent in 1955.

l As a means of "encouraging" savings, the tax reform of April 1954 authorized a special allowance for savings which were invested in acceptable forms of economic activity. How this provision will be administered so as to avoid the total exemption of the wealthier classes able to save and invest their current "income" is still not clear. So far the Ministry of Finance has only permitted its application to treasury bonds and securities issued by public enterprises.

m This is a considerable simplification of the actual system applied to taxes below 260,000, in view of the supplementary deduction which is allowed. After the theoretical tax on the segment between 181,000 and 350,000 francs has been calculated, it is not paid at all if less than 4,000 francs. If the theoretical tax is between 4,000 francs and 8,000 francs, a deduction is made in the tax by an amount equal to the difference between the tax and 8,000 francs. If the theoretical

However, the effective rate of the progressive tax is reduced—in some cases very appreciably—by the fact that income-splitting is based on the total number of dependents, rather than on the marital status of the taxpayer (that is, splitting only between husband and wife) as in the United States. Thus the net income is divided into a number of "parts" in accordance with the family situation of the taxpayer.[o] After the net taxable income has been divided by the corresponding number of parts in accordance with the family status, the schedule of rates listed above is applied to each segment of income. The taxes calculated under each segment are added to obtain the total tax for one part. This sum is then multiplied by the number of parts to obtain the total tax.

B. CORPORATE PROFIT TAX

The tax on corporate profits is imposed on virtually all business firms organized in the legal form of corporations. With minor exceptions, the taxable base is the same as for the profits of unincorporated businesses which adopt the system of direct assessment of their income under the proportional tax.

The corporate profit tax was applied in 1953 at a uniform rate of 34 per cent.[p] It should be noted that the present system of income taxes involves a multiple taxation of distributed corporation profits. They are taxed at 34 per cent when earned by the corporation. They are taxed again (at 18 per cent) under the proportional tax when distributed to individuals or corporations, and (at a percentage depending on the total income of the taxpayer) under the progressive surtax when distributed to individuals.[q]

---

tax is above 8,000 francs, no deduction is allowed and the 10 per cent rate applies throughout the segment between 181,000 and 350,000 francs. The net result is to exempt all income below 220,000 francs and to apply a 20 per cent rate on the segment between 221,000 and 260,000 francs. The tax reform of April 1954 abolished the supplementary deduction at the same time as it raised the basic exemption from 180,000 to 220,000 francs and applied a 10 per cent rate to the portion between 221,000 and 350,000 francs. The principal effect of this change is to reduce from 20 to 10 per cent the tax on the segment between 221,000 and 260,000 francs.

[n] Taxpayers with no dependents pay a higher rate of 55 per cent on income between 3,001,000 and 6,000,000 francs and of 70 per cent on income beyond 6,000,000 francs.

[o] The division works as follows: Bachelor, divorced person, or childless widow 1 part; Childless married couple, or bachelor or widow with dependent child 2 parts; Married couple or widow with dependent child, or bachelor or divorced person with 2 dependent children 2.5 parts; Bachelor or divorced person with 3 dependent children 3 parts; etc.

[p] The rate was raised to 36 per cent in 1954 and 38 per cent in 1955.

[q] This does not take into account the possibility that part of the corporate income tax may be shifted by the corporation (cf. the discussion under tax equity below).

C. PAYROLL TAX

Until 1948, income from wages and salaries was subject to a "schedular" income tax (the forerunner of the proportional tax), which was withheld by the employer at the source. In order to forestall a demand for further wage increases, the government, as a "temporary" measure, elected in October of that year to shift the burden of the tax to the employer by replacing it with a 5 per cent "payroll" tax on wages and salaries. Wages were not to be reduced as a result of the payroll tax. The temporary measure has proven (like so many other "acquired rights") to be irreversible; it can be questioned, however, whether the burden of the tax has in fact been shifted (see the discussion below under tax equity).

D. PRODUCTION TAX

The tax on the production of goods and services has been the keystone of the French tax system. As a result of its broad base and high rates, it was expected in 1953 to provide larger yields than the personal and corporate income taxes combined. Broadly speaking, it resembles a tax on value added (that is, on sales minus cost of materials) at each stage of the production process. While an endless series of legislative and administrative revisions has moved the tax fairly close to this point, there are a large number of singularly complicated and varied exceptions and special provisions that cannot be adequately dealt with here. The tax on the production of goods is substantially different from that on the provision of services, so these two components will be described separately.

The production tax on goods covers the processes of extraction, production, transformation, and importation (of goods which are subject to the tax if produced in France); it does not (as of 1953) extend to wholesale or retail trade. The tax is levied at each stage of the production process, on the basis of the gross value of sales. The taxpayer may deduct the production tax already paid by his suppliers on a list of inputs which has been gradually extended. In principle, the production tax already paid may be deducted on raw materials or intermediate products that enter physically (in whole or in part) into the product or that are normally destroyed or lose their specific qualities during a single manufacturing operation. Under this tax principle it has been possible to deduct the tax paid on raw materials and some semi-finished goods and some (but not all) forms of energy. Prior to 1953, it was not possible to deduct the taxes already paid on capital goods, on general operating expenses, and on services, and these inputs have been subject to multiple or cumulative taxation rather than to single taxation by "value added."[r]

There is a basic tax rate, together with a multitude of reduced rates, total exemptions, and surtaxes. The basic rate of the tax is 14.5 per cent, to which is added a supplementary rate of 0.85 per cent.[s] These rates apply to the sales price of the merchandise, including the production tax itself. The effective rate of the tax is therefore somewhat higher, about 18 per cent.[t] A reduced rate of 6.35 per cent applies to a list of products of "social interest," such as coal and livestock feed. Wholly exempt from the tax are some twenty-three articles, many of them considered to be basic necessities (such as bread, milk, newspapers, tobacco and matches, gas and electricity provided by public enterprises).[u] A surtax, at rates ranging from 4 to 26 per cent, applies to a small number of heterogeneous products (mineral waters, beer, vinegar, playing cards, vanilla).

In addition to the exempted commodities, various activities are exempted from the production tax on goods. The tax does not cover most of the activities of farmers, farm cooperatives, professional men, and artisans.[v] Credit cooperatives and aircraft and ship con-

[r] A decree of September 20, 1953 made possible the deduction of half of the tax paid on capital goods. A major feature of the tax reform of April 1954, was the replacement of the production tax on goods by one officially labelled a "tax on value added." The new tax comes closer to a bona fide tax on value added, through a series of steps spread out over time. As of July 1, 1954, it was possible to deduct in full the tax paid on capital goods and on general operating expenses. An increasing number of services paid for by the producer were made deductible in 1954 and 1955. These measures were combined with other changes in the production tax and the transaction tax, as explained in succeeding footnotes. It remains to be seen how these measures will be administered in practice; the tax authorities, for example, have the power of withdrawing the deduction of capital goods if the investments in question are not deemed to be in the "national interest."

[s] Of the supplementary rate of 0.85 per cent, 0.55 per cent is allocated to the annexed budget for family allowances to farmers and 0.30 per cent to the special treasury account which provides funds for private school education. This is one of a number of instances where the structure of particular taxes has been distorted to provide funds for totally unrelated purposes.

[t] The tax reform of April 1954 raised the rate on the production tax on goods (now the "tax on value added") from 15.35 per cent to 16.85 per cent. By July 1955, with the transaction tax incorporated into the "tax on value added," the basic rate was 19.50 per cent, with an effective rate of close to 25 per cent (24.22 per cent).

[u] The rate of 6.35 per cent was raised to 7.5 per cent in 1954 and to 10.0 per cent in 1955, and another intermediate rate of 12 per cent introduced for products which had benefited from special deductions or exemptions under the transaction tax. Also, the computed tax was reduced by 25 per cent in the case of fertilizers and by 39 per cent in the case of housing construction. A number of commodities (tea, coffee) were added to the list of total exemptions.

[v] Farm products are exempt from the tax if they are consumed in their natural

struction are favored by exemption from the tax, while exporters are reimbursed for their payments in connection with the export subsidy program described in Chapter 4.

The tax on the sale of services is applied at a lower basic rate of 5.5 per cent, plus a supplementary tax of 0.3 per cent. However, the tax is cumulative; that is, it is levied at the time of each transaction or service without allowance for taxes already paid on raw materials, services, etc. The final rate paid for the service may therefore be a multiple of the basic rate. A number of elaborate special systems apply to certain activities which are joint operations involving the sale of both goods and services, such as those of carpenters and locksmiths.[w]

E. TRANSACTION TAX

The rate and method of calculation of the transaction tax do not vary as widely for different articles or kinds of activities as in the case of the production tax. The basic rate of the tax is 1 per cent, but its yield is considerable since, like the services tax, it is on total sales price rather than on "value added" and may be imposed a number of times before the goods or services reach the consumer; the effective rate of the tax therefore varies from item to item depending on the amount of processing and reselling. The base of the tax is broader than that of the production tax, since it covers sales taking place over the entire cycle of production and distribution. Products made by artisans are subject to the tax, as are farm products (except wheat), both when purchased by a commercial distributor and again at the time of sale to the consumer.[x]

There are, needless to say, some special provisions. Integrated firms and chain stores pay a penalty rate of 1.8 per cent.[y] A number

state; farm cooperatives are exempt if they engage in the same kind of activities as individual farmers; artisans are exempt if their activities are primarily of a manual character, if the artisans do not possess a large stock of machine tools, and if they are assisted only by members of their family in a direct line and by no more than one associate and one apprentice under the age of 18 years.

[w] The tax reform of April 1954 sets up the tax on services as separate from the new tax on value added, which only replaced the production tax on goods. The rate of the tax has since been raised to 8.5 per cent.

[x] The transaction tax was officially abolished in 1955, at the same time as the rate of the tax on value added was raised. The tax on value added was in principle extended to cover wholesale operations, but in practice wholesalers may choose between the tax on value added and a local sales tax (which is technically not part of the tax system of the central government). At the retail level, only the local sales tax, ranging from 2.2 per cent to 2.75 per cent, applies.

[y] Integrated stores (which sell at both wholesale and retail) pay the higher rate if their wholesale activities amount to more than one-third of total sales; the higher tax on chain stores applies, on sales of all stores except the main branch,

of commodities are exempt (bread, milk, newspapers, etc.) as well as certain activities (such as stock market transactions) subject to other taxes. Some farm cooperatives are exempt under specified conditions, as are exporters. Temporary exemptions have also been granted to certain commodities in the course of price reduction campaigns.

It might be added that a "single tax," which substitutes for both the production tax and the transaction tax, is applied to wine, meat, and gasoline. There are also a host of specific taxes (called "indirect contributions") levied on alcoholic beverages, precious metals, bicycles, flour milling, new wine shops, explosives used in mining and hunting, and other items.

F. CAPITAL TAXES

Taxes on the transfer of capital are among the oldest elements of the French system. Their main features have survived relatively intact, although their share in overall tax collections has fallen sharply over the past 40 years as a result of tax evasion, the longer life span of the population, and changes in the tax base and rates. The principal techniques for the taxation of capital are the inheritance and gift taxes and taxes on sales of capital assets. A number of other activities are classified as capital transactions for tax purposes.

1. Inheritance and Gift Taxes. The tax provisions are essentially the same for both inheritances and gifts. The rate varies with the family relationship between donor and recipient, the number of children of the donor, and the family situation of the recipient. It is therefore a highly personalized tax, the yield from which depends in large measure upon the family relationship of the various parties involved. The tax base is estimated by direct assessment. Once the value of the transfer has been fixed, a deduction of 5 million francs is applied to all of the wealth transferred in a direct line between husband and wife, plus 3 million francs for each child or parent under the charge of the donor. The tax rates that are then applied are progressive according to the size of the transfer, but there is an upper limit on the effective rate in accordance with the various family relationships at issue.

2. Other Capital Taxes. Commercial transactions in capital assets

---

to firms with more than two retail outlets. The new tax on value added reinstates this discrimination, in a more complicated fashion which need not be described here. (Cf. *Le Monde*, July 6, 1955, p. 10.)

are subject to a variety of registry taxes. All are at a proportional rate, which differs according to the nature of the transaction. In many cases, the rates finally applied are very high, although the difficulties in estimating the value of the assets transferred mitigate some of their effect. Sales of personal property are taxed at 10.4 per cent, of real estate at 10.8 per cent, of inventories at 2.8 per cent, and of business assets other than real estate and inventories at 10.8 per cent. In addition, the first transfer of buildings bears a supplementary tax of 4.8 per cent. Taking into account the local taxes also levied on these transactions and accessory charges for legal fees and commissions, the total charges on the sale of a capital asset are frequently in excess of 20-25 per cent.

A number of other legal acts are subject to a registry or stamp tax, at widely varying rates. These include stock market operations, insurance policies, passports, marriage contracts, acts of incorporation, increases in corporation capital, and corporate mergers.

G. TAX EVASION

The impression is widespread that tax evasion is higher in France than in most other countries, notably Great Britain and the United States. Part of the impression is undoubtedly due to the fact that evasion, if and when practiced, is more openly admitted in France than in other countries. But there is some evidence that whatever its relative standing may be, tax evasion in France is very extensive. Former Premier Pinay is reported to have placed tax evasion at 600 billion francs in 1951;[6] it is possible, therefore, that tax evasion amounts to 20-25 per cent of tax receipts. The Loriot Report, without citing specific figures, refers to evasion as "the principal weakness of our tax system."[7] A government committee estimated the level of fraud among industrial and commercial enterprises in 1949 at 20 per cent of the taxable base in industry, transportation, and public works, and 28 per cent of the taxable base in commerce, services, and liberal professions. There was considerable variation according to the kind of industrial or commercial enterprise, and also according to the size of the enterprise.[8]

Many factors serve to explain the prevalence of tax evasion in France. Although it has a long tradition, evasion was undoubtedly accentuated by habits formed during the occupation. The decline in the sense of public spirit[9] has also been influenced by the labyrinthine complexity of the tax system, which makes evasion the path of least resistance, and by the numerous legal privileges and exemptions of special groups that are matters of universal complaint. The high rates of many of the taxes are also cited as a cause of fraud. In a vicious circle, the government is obliged to raise rates in order to maintain tax yields in the face of widespread fraud, but the higher rates, in turn, make tax evasion more necessary, more profitable, or more socially acceptable.

These problems are heightened by the inadequate procedures for enforcement of the tax laws. Enforcement officials are relatively few in number and, until recently, organized along lines more appropriate to the eighteenth than to the twentieth century. The measures of fiscal amnesty against prosecution for past violations to which the government has occasionally resorted seem more likely to assure the taxpayer of his freedom from prosecution in the future than to encourage him to settle his accounts during the period of amnesty. There are vigorous and widely publicized campaigns of tax enforcement, but generally of a sporadic nature. Penalties have been low; it has been contended that the prevalence of fraud makes it unfair to penalize severely the few persons who have the bad luck to get caught. In recent years, the Ministry of Finance attempted to crack down on tax evasion by the application of higher penalties and the use of "polyvalent brigades" of officials grouped from the various tax bureaus to study all of the taxes bearing on a single industry or business. The attempt encountered the systematic opposition of small businessmen and artisans organized into the *Union de Défense des Commerçants et Artisans* of Pierre Poujade. The obstructionist tactics of the UDCA, amounting sometimes to physical violence, made it impossible for tax officials to carry out their investigations without local police support, which was rarely forthcoming. Under the strong political pressure of Poujade and his large following, the Faure government abandoned what promised to be the most effective campaign against tax evasion of the postwar period.[10]

The unequal opportunity of various groups to practice fraud is quite marked, depending on the nature of the tax, the source of income, the kind and size of enterprise, and the method of tax declaration. Within the tax on income, there is virtually no fraud in the progressive tax on income from wages and salaries, since the income is declared by the employer. On the other hand, fraud is possible in other elements of the progressive surtax, which are based on a declaration by the taxpayer. No evasion is possible in the proportional tax on income from securities, which is withheld at the source. In general, there is more fraud in taxes subject to direct evaluation than in those under the forfeit system. There is considerable fraud, however, among small businesses operating under the forfeit system, the counterpart of the evasion of the transaction tax by these enterprises. Small firms are generally better able to conceal their income than large ones, and the profits of large firms (e.g., those coming under the corporate profit tax) are being verified with increasing accuracy.

The production tax has a built-in safeguard against evasion, since the deduction for taxes already paid must be based on purchase vouchers on which the taxes are shown separately.[z] The possibilities of verification also make it difficult for employers to evade the 5 per cent payroll tax. On the other hand, the 1 per cent sales tax on all transactions, when it was in effect, was probably the most evaded of the major taxes. It is generally believed that retailers, and to a lesser extent wholesalers, incorporated the tax into their selling prices but frequently did not report the receipts for tax purposes. Evasion of the transaction tax by retailers has been estimated at as high as 40 per cent.[11]

Evasion of the gift and inheritance taxes is also widespread; it has been described as "almost a social habit, extending to the whole population without regard to background or occupation."[12] Fraud is encouraged by the high nominal rates, and facilitated by the difficulties of identifying and evaluating accurately the property donated or inherited. For the same reasons, there is considerable evasion of the taxes on commercial transactions, in the form of "under-the-table" payments.

III EQUITY: EQUAL TREATMENT OF EQUALS

As mentioned earlier, it is usually regarded as inequitable to accord different treatment to persons in similar circumstances. Admittedly what constitutes either equal treatment or equal circumstances is difficult to define precisely. Most persons can nevertheless agree in identifying marked deviations from the notion of treating equals equally. The tax system of any country will, of course, exhibit deviations, that of the United States being no exception. But the preceding description has brought out some especially pronounced instances that are built into the French tax

[z] The safeguard on the production tax does not apply to small producers, who may apply a forfeit system if their sales are below a specified sum (15 million francs in 1955).

system. In Professor Shoup's opinion, the French tax system has been infiltrated by special tax provisions or exemptions to a far greater degree than that of Great Britain or the United States.[13]

It has been seen that the personal income taxes contain a number of major differences in the tax base or the tax rate according to the source of income (rather than to the wealth or income of the taxpayer). Conspicuous examples are the exclusion of wages and salaries from the proportional tax; the different kinds of forfeit systems used and the unequal opportunity to apply them; the withholding of income from securities but not from other sources; and the tax rates of 0, 5, 6, 9, and 18 per cent that are applied to different sources of income. Also, although not officially part of the system, the unequal opportunity to evade taxes results in harsher treatment for the scrupulous or the unlucky.

The deviations with respect to tax rates and the taxable base are due to a number of factors, such as the discrimination between "earned" and "unearned" income and the desire to encourage certain kinds of economic activity for one reason or another. Some reflect an effort to compensate particular groups for the "excessive" burden which would be imposed if taxes were applied at uniform rates, given the existing structure of taxes and the unequal opportunity to evade them. But the existence of these deviations is in itself an invitation to other groups to practice fraud in order to avoid being discriminated against. There is no reason to believe that these special exemptions, advantages, and opportunities offset each other so as to produce an equitable situation. And the resultant complexity of the system contributes to fraud, to popular discontent over real or fancied discrimination, and to the breakdown of public authority.

Data on income reported for tax purposes under the personal income tax are given, by source of income, in Table 19. One point is worth stressing. Agriculture, which occupies one-third of the gainfully employed population and contributes one-sixth of the GNP,[aa] accounts for only a trifling proportion of the income reported for personal income tax purposes. Without entering into questions of tax incidence (discussed below) or the personal distribution of income from various sources, it can be doubted that the French farmer pays the same income tax as that of other taxpayers in the same income class.

As for the corporate profits tax, one of its effects, in France as in

[aa] See the discussion in Chapter 11.

TABLE 19

INCOME REPORTED BY SOURCE FOR PERSONAL INCOME TAX OF 1952 (ON 1951 INCOME)

(values in millions of francs)

Source of Income	Proportional Tax: Actual	Proportional Tax: Per Cent of Total	Progressive Surtax: Actual	Progressive Surtax: Per Cent of Total
Real estate income	10,212	0.93	17,068	0.93
Industrial and commercial profits	657,453	59.65	354,981	19.40
Agricultural profits	82,472	7.49	12,975	0.71
Wages, salaries, pensions, annuities	2,309	0.21	1,241,612	67.87
Profits of non-commercial professions	93,494	8.48	77,443	4.23
Income from securities	(a)200,000	18.15	71,696	3.92
Remuneration of managers	56,097	5.09	47,858	2.62
Miscellaneous	136	0.01	5,888	0.32
Total	(a)1,102,173	100.01	1,829,521	100.00

Source: The data in the columns headed "Proportional Tax" and "Progressive Surtax" are taken directly from Ministère des Finances, *Statistiques et études financières* No. 57, September 1953, pp. 808-811, with the exception of the figures marked (a). The income from securities subject to the proportional tax has been estimated by the author. Most income from securities is deducted at the source. There are no published data on the amount of such income subject to tax. Total receipts in 1952 from securities subject to the proportional tax were 35 billion francs (unpublished data of the Ministry of Finance); from this, the total income subject to the tax was estimated by assuming that the standard tax rate of 18 per cent applied since family deductions are not taken when the tax is withheld at the source. The taxable income is nevertheless somewhat underestimated, because of a number of minor exceptions provided by law to the 18 per cent rate.

other countries, is to apply an additional rate to one source of income regardless of the situation of the ultimate recipient. Thus, two persons who receive the same income and own about the same amount of wealth may be taxed quite differently. Although it was intended that the payroll tax on wages and salaries should be borne by the employer, the incidence of the tax is in fact likely to be shifted back to the wage earner in large part.[bb] To the extent that this occurs, it tends to counteract the initial advantage given to wage earners by their exemption from the proportional income tax.

The production and transaction taxes contain a considerable

[bb] See the discussion below under progressiveness.

number of special provisions, differential rates, or exemptions. Some of these are intended to achieve some measure of progressiveness in these excise taxes, and will be discussed below in that light. Others have an important effect on economic efficiency, and can best be considered under that heading. With respect to the capital taxes, the principal cases of unequal treatment are considered to be due to the "unequal" status of the recipient (for example, to differences in the degree of relationship to the donor or in the number of dependents of the recipient).

IV EQUITY: PROGRESSIVENESS

Some degree of progressiveness is usually regarded as equitable; that is, the higher one's income, the greater the proportion that should be taxed. How progressive the tax system should be is in large part a question of ethics. We shall be content here with what can be said about the degree of progression that in fact exists.

Only a limited group is subject legally to the personal income tax. Although the basic exemption on the proportional tax is trifling (60,000 francs or $170), considerably over half of the potentially taxable income escapes the proportional tax because income from wages, salaries, and pensions is exempt. The generous allowances for family dependents, in the case of the surtax, exempt a large number of persons who would otherwise be liable for the tax. For example, a family consisting of man, wife, and two children (a "3-part" family) would have to have an income of about 700,000 francs to be liable for the surtax—the basic exemption is 220,000 francs per part, to which must be added other exemptions such as the deduction for professional expenses in the case of wage earners. In 1951 (the year for which taxable income is analyzed in this chapter), this meant that a large number—roughly about half—of the potential taxpayers were legally exempt from the surtax. Thus the class of taxpayers liable under the personal income tax consists in the main of those whose principal source of income arises from independent, entrepreneurial, and cultural activities, together with those wage and salary earners and pensioners in the higher income groups or with small families.

Of the income subject to the proportional tax, about 15 per cent is taken by the tax (Table 20). Despite its name, the proportional tax shows considerable progressiveness in the very low income groups, as a result of the family allowances and the basic deductions. The effective rate of progressiveness of the surtax is sub-

TABLE 20

PROPORTIONAL INCOME TAX OF 1952
(ON 1951 INCOME)[1]

Income Class (thousands of francs)	*Number of Taxpayers*	*Income Before Tax (millions of francs)*	*Net Tax (millions of francs)*	*Tax as Per Cent of Income*
1 to 60	–	–	–	–
61 to 80	193,267	13,662	428	3.13
81 to 120	260,003	25,973	2,115	8.14
121 to 200	431,556	70,182	6,911	9.85
201 to 500	836,869	274,757	38,199	13.90
501 to 800	252,539	160,312	25,880	16.14
801 to 1,200	121,417	117,833	19,788	16.79
1,201 to 2,000	71,103	107,627	18,478	17.17
2,001 to 5,000	33,679	95,737	16,801	17.55
5,001 to 10,000	3,845	25,156	4,482	17.82
Beyond 10,000	873	15,075	2,707	17.96
Total	2,205,151	906,314	135,789	14.98

Source: Data from Ministère des Finances, *Statistiques et études financières* No. 57, September 1953, pp. 810-811. Tax as per cent of income computed by the author.

[1] Does not include tax on income from securities, which is deducted at the source (approximately 35 billion francs in 1952 on an income of about 200 billion francs, see Table 19).

stantially reduced by the system of income-splitting according to the total number of dependents. Thus the average rate in the highest income group is only about 38 per cent, and the surtax as a whole takes only 8 per cent of the income subject to the tax (Table 21).

Estimates of the combined effect of the proportional and progressive taxes are presented in Table 22. The results are only approximate, since the two taxes have different sources of income liable to the tax and different methods of estimating taxable income, while different categories of income are used in publishing the returns.[cc] The rate of tax is largely independent of the size of income for incomes of less than 900,000 francs, a category that includes three-fourths (compare Tables 20 and 21) of the taxable incomes reported. The tax absorbs only 13 per cent of taxable in-

[cc] The higher rate of tax in the first two income brackets than in the third is attributable to the fact that the third income bracket, unlike the first two, includes income from wages, salaries, pensions, and annuities (liable only to the progressive surtax) taxed at a rate of only 3 per cent, a rate one-third to one-fourth the rate of tax in the first two brackets.

TABLE 21

PROGRESSIVE INCOME SURTAX OF 1952
(ON 1951 INCOME)

Income Class (thousands of francs)	*Number of Taxpayers*	*Income Before Tax (millions of francs)*	*Net Tax (millions of francs)*	*Tax as Per Cent of Income*
1 to 220[1]	–	–	–	–
221 to 350	670,859	184,023	5,574	3.03
351 to 600	803,009	391,365	14,422	3.69
601 to 900	636,287	462,016	21,805	4.72
901 to 1,500	311,327	346,512	25,908	7.48
1,501 to 3,000	101,662	201,339	25,351	12.59
3,001 to 6,000	22,403	89,124	19,180	21.52
Beyond 6,000	6,320	67,245	25,369	37.73
Total	2,551,867	1,741,624	137,609	7.90

Source: Data from Ministère des Finances, *Statistiques et études financières* No. 57, September 1953, pp. 812-813. Tax as per cent of income computed by the author.

[1] Does not include 79 taxpayers who contributed 5.3 million of taxes for *rémunérations occultes.*

come, and the rate of tax applicable to the highest income group, a group that includes less than 10,000 taxpayers, is only 50.5 per cent. Because the amount of the tax is fairly small, and because the rate of tax is not strongly progressive, the personal income tax as a whole has little effect on the distribution of income reported for tax, as shown by the last two columns of Table 22.

If we consider all income, rather than that part reported for tax, the effect of the income tax appears to be such as to decrease income disparities slightly, but not markedly. First, wage and salary earners and those living on pensions escape the personal income tax altogether if their incomes are not relatively large. Second, among the groups that pay the tax, the rates are only mildly progressive. However, the whole question of the progressiveness of the income tax is clouded by the prevalence but uneven distribution of tax evasion. The total 1951 income reported for tax in 1952 was around 2,300 billion francs, of which 1,200 billion francs were wages, salaries, pensions, and annuities, thus leaving a remainder of 1,100 billion francs for all other sources of income. Total personal income in 1951 has been estimated at 9,500 billion francs,[14] of which somewhat over 40 per cent, or 4,000 billion

TABLE 22. ADJUSTED DATA ON PERSONAL INCOME TAX (PROPORTIONAL AND PROGRESSIVE) OF 1952 (ON INCOME)[1]

Income Class (thousands of francs)	*Income Before Tax (millions of francs)*	*Net Tax (millions of francs)*	*Tax as Per Cent of Income*	*Per Cent of Total Tax Yield*	*Income After Tax (millions of francs)*	*Cumulative Per Cent of Income Before Tax*	*Cumulative Per Cent of Income After Tax*
1 to 120	48,132	4,073[1]	8.46	1.32	44,059	2.06	2.17
121 to 220	108,074	12,892[1]	11.93	4.18	95,182	6.67	6.85
221 to 350	316,848	26,723	8.43	8.67	290,125	20.20	21.11
351 to 600	561,416	49,513	8.82	16.05	511,903	44.17	46.29
601 to 900	519,804	49,265	9.48	15.98	470,539	66.37	69.42
901 to 1,500	383,954	52,648	13.71	17.07	331,306	82.76	85.72
1,501 to 3,000	218,984	46,329	21.16	15.02	172,655	92.11	94.21
3,001 to 6,000	119,423	33,934	28.41	11.00	85,489	97.21	98.41
Beyond 6,000	65,367	33,022	50.52	10.71	32,345	100.00	100.00
Total	2,342,002	308,399	13.17	100.00	2,033,603	–	–

Source: *Income Before Tax.* This column is the sum of the following data from Ministère des Finances, *Statistiques et études financières* No. 57, September 1953, pp. 808-813:

(1) Income from wages, salaries, pensions, and annuities reported for the progressive surtax;

(2) Estimated income from securities (see Tables 19 and 20) distributed by income class in the same proportion as income reported for the proportional tax;

(3) For other sources of income, income reported for the proportional tax, converted by the author by freehand methods to the income classes of Table 22.

Remark: For wages and salaries, the data on income were derived from the progressive surtax, since income from this source is not subject to or reported for the proportional tax. For income from securities, the total income was derived from data on the proportional tax withheld on income from this source. For all other sources of income, it was assumed that the same income was reported for both taxes, and the data for the proportional tax were used since they cover a wider range of income groups. This assumption is liable to considerable error, as is evident from an inspection of the basic data, but appears to be the most reasonable which can be made under the circumstances.

Net Tax. This column is the sum of the following: (1) The net tax of Table 21; (2) The net tax of Table 20, converted by the author to the income classes of Table 21 or Table 22; (3) Tax on securities (see Tables 19 and 20) distributed by income classes in the same proportion as the proportional tax.

Remaining columns computed by the author.

[1] Does not include 5.3 million of progressive surtax on *rémunérations occultes.*

francs, is attributable to sources of income other than wages, etc. While not all of this income is legally liable to the (proportional) tax, it is not possible to account for the great disparity between the distributed income of 4,000 billion francs and the income declared for tax purposes of 1,100 billion francs other than in terms of the combined effect of fraud and tax privileges. It has already been argued (section III of this chapter) that farmers fail to pay the income tax; it now seems that they are not alone in this regard.

The ultimate progressiveness of a tax is, of course, affected by the possibility that it may be shifted from the one who pays the tax initially to some other person or persons. It is generally assumed that the personal income tax (except on the profits of unincorporated businesses) is not shifted. In the corporate profits tax, as in that on unincorporated businesses, there is a greater possibility that part of the tax will be shifted. If the entrepreneur is seeking to maximize profits both before and after the imposition of a fixed percentage tax on net income, the equilibrium price and output should not be changed by the tax, at least until the amount of investment by various entrepreneurs can be altered. Thus, in the short run at least, the taxes on business profits would not be passed on. In practice, however, business price policies are influenced by a host of factors other than profit maximization, which make it possible that some of the taxes are passed on through higher prices than would otherwise be charged. In some studies it has been assumed that the corporate income tax in the United States is passed on in part (e.g., 50 per cent) while in other studies it has been assumed that it is borne entirely by the corporate shareholders.[dd] The likelihood that part of the tax is passed increases, in the case of small unincorporated businesses in France, by virtue of the forfeit system. Since the forfeit relies heavily on gross sales as a means of approximating net income, it encourages firms to maximize their profits (after tax) through a policy of high prices and high profit margins on a low turnover.

To the extent that the taxes on business profits are shifted

[dd] In his study of the distribution of U. S. taxes, Rufus Tucker assumed that 50 per cent of the corporate income tax was passed on to consumers. (Rufus S. Tucker, "The Distribution of Government Burdens and Benefits," *American Economic Review*, Vol. XLIII, May 1953, No. 2, Papers and Proceedings of the Sixty-fifth Annual Meeting of the American Economic Association, pp. 518-534.) On the other hand, the Colm-Tarasov study, while admitting that in exceptional cases it might be passed on, attributed all of the corporate income tax to the stockholders. (Temporary National Economic Committee, Monograph No. 3, *Who Pays the Taxes* [Washington, 1941], pp. 16, 23.) For a recent discussion of incidence theory see Earl Rolph, *The Theory of Fiscal Economics* (University of California Press, 1954), especially pp. 123-171, 246-252.

forward, the effect is likely to be proportional for all consumers of the products of business firms, without regard to their income position. In the case of corporate profits, the tax, if not shifted, is borne by all shareholders in proportion to their incomes from corporate securities. Since the payroll tax is a tax on a single factor of production (labor), it is probably shifted back to the wage earners, who bear the tax burden in proportion to their earnings. The proportionality of a substantial part of the business profits and payroll taxes goes a long way toward counteracting the progressiveness of the personal income tax.

The excise taxes (production tax, transaction tax, single taxes, and "indirect contributions") are the most important for the study of progressiveness. Unfortunately, not much can be said with confidence concerning the final incidence of this large group of taxes. It appears to be the well-nigh universal opinion, not only of the French layman but also of tax officials, that the excise taxes are eventually passed on to, and borne by, the consumer. Such would appear, in fact, to have been the intention or expectation of the legislators, and changes in the basic rates have often been accompanied by government directives specifying how the ensuing price adjustments should take place.[ee] Such discussion of the incidence of the excise taxes as can be found in French economic literature also appears to reflect this opinion, although it is indicated that the possibility of passing on the tax in the short run may occasionally be limited by market demand.[15]

In fact, however, the incidence of the French excise taxes is likely to be much more complicated. It will be recalled that some excise taxes are on "specific" products (wine, meat); others are more general (the production and transaction taxes) but are applied at a multitude of effective rates and contain numerous exemptions. Some factors of production are taxed more heavily than others under the production and transaction taxes. Competitive conditions, the elasticity of supply of factors of production, and price behavior (including government policy) are likely to vary from market to market or product to product. On the basis of present tax theory, all that can be stated a priori is that some consumer prices are higher than they would be otherwise and some consumer prices are lower, that the composition of production has been altered in many complex ways, and that the real returns

[ee] See, for example, the decree issued by the Ministry of Finance when the rate of the production tax was raised as a result of the adoption of the "tax on value added" (*Agence économique et financière*, July 2, 1954, p. 4).

of some or all of the factors of production have been reduced. Part of the tax is probably borne by French consumers in the form of higher prices (in the aggregate) and part by factors of production in the form of lower real returns. A more precise analysis would first require a fairly exhaustive classification of the taxes according to individual products, kinds of markets, and factors of production. Such a study has never been published in France and cannot be undertaken here.[ff]

Conclusions with respect to the progressiveness or regressiveness of the excise taxes are no firmer than the assumptions about incidence on which they rest. To the extent that the excise taxes are passed on to the consumer, the reduced rates, or total exemption, of some "basic necessities" (which occupy a larger proportion of the family budget in the lower income groups) might be expected to introduce a certain measure of progressiveness. This effect is partly offset, however, by the imposition of a number of basic products under other excise taxes, such as the single taxes on wine, meat, and gasoline and the various "indirect contributions." Moreover, the surtax covers a very limited list of commodities and cannot be compared with the extensive taxes on "luxury" goods in the United States or, more particularly, in Great Britain. At first glance it appears doubtful that the rate discrimination is systematic or extensive enough to introduce a substantial degree of progressiveness into the excise taxes (*assuming* that they are borne by the consumer). Also, rate discrimination is an inefficient way of seeking "progressiveness," since the benefits apply to all consumers of basic products, rich and poor alike; selective changes in the income tax structure could achieve the same equity goal more effectively.

To the extent that the excise taxes are passed backwards to owners of productive resources (including wage earners), the reduction in their real income would be roughly proportional. It would not be exactly proportional, since various factors of production are in effect taxed at different rates under the excise taxes. There is no reason to believe that the effect would be progressive.

Capital taxes are not likely to be shifted, but widespread evasion makes it difficult to ascertain the actual progressiveness. Although the generous allowances for dependents modify the steepness of the rates on gifts and inheritances, some progression undoubtedly

[ff] Insofar as I have been able to determine, the Ministry of Finance has not undertaken any comprehensive studies of the incidence of the excise tax system for its internal use.

remains for the relatively small sums reported for and subject to the taxes.

With respect to the tax system as a whole, the exact degree of progressiveness (if any) is virtually impossible to ascertain. But it is at least clear that the progressiveness of the tax system is not especially marked. Some government officials consider that a high degree of uncertainty as to the eventual tax burden has certain practical (and political) advantages. On the other hand, if it may be granted that a necessary condition for an equitable tax system is at least an approximate knowledge of how the tax burden is shared, then the French tax system can hardly be judged equitable. And, even in terms of immediate political advantage, it appears that uncertainty may be a two-edged sword, as will be indicated below.

V ECONOMIC EFFICIENCY

The tax system, through its impact on the structure of prices, may also affect the efficiency of resource use. A necessary condition for an "efficient" use of resources is that prices of goods and services reflect the sacrifices entailed by their being used in a particular way. If prices do reflect these sacrifices, no one will put goods or services to a particular use unless the result is worth at least as much as devoting them to alternative uses.

An example may help to clarify this point. Suppose that a factory manager or homeowner can accomplish the same task with either a ton of coal or 50 gallons of gasoline. Suppose further that a ton of coal is priced at $10 and 50 gallons of gasoline at $15—the prices reflecting the values of these items in other uses. The manager or homeowner will not use either one unless the job he has in mind is worth at least $10 to him—that is, at least the value of the coal in other uses. If the task is worth more than $10, then the prices will induce him to make a decision that results in an improved allocation of the economy's resources, a decision to put one of the fuels to this use. Moreover, the relative prices induce him to pick the particular fuel that is less valuable elsewhere; to pick the coal and leave the 50 gallons of gasoline to some use where it is more valuable than the coal. Thus if relative prices function properly, they help the economy to make the most out of its resources. Conversely, if relative prices get distorted, they may give rise to a misallocation of resources.

It is probably inevitable that the tax system should change the pattern of resource use. Some of the changes may be designed to advance particular social (i.e., non-economic) objectives or to encourage the development of particular forms of economic activity. It is nevertheless pertinent to inquire what economic costs are involved. Perhaps the most valid generalization is that the French tax system has obliged producers and consumers to make choices based on relative prices which bear an unknown relation to the economic sacrifices which are entailed. The net effect of the distortions is impossible to assess,[16] but it is clear that the tax system introduces many promiscuous impacts on prices and on the allocation of the nation's resources.

Thus, particular products and services are made more (or less) attractive than their relative costs of production would warrant as a result of the complicated provisions of the tax system. The problems of determining the base of the production tax, and of calculating the various deductions for taxes already paid, have given rise to endless litigation. The result has been a system of extreme complexity, with special arrangements for many products (products of rapid consumption, special tools, imputed deliveries, self-destroyed products, etc.) and a substantial, if unintentional, discrimination in the effective rates applied to different products or services.

In the past, the production tax was based on a fundamental distinction between goods that were incorporated physically into the production process and goods that were not. Since only raw materials qualified as fully deductible because of their physical disappearance, and since the services tax was a cumulative one, there was a double taxing of intermediate goods and services. Expenditures on research and prototypes, transportation, interest, and capital goods were taxed once when the goods and services were procured and again when the manufactured goods into which they were (financially) incorporated were sold. The double taxation of investments has been considered to have had particularly serious effects; since the effective cost of capital goods was increased by 18 per cent, the possibilities of their profitable use were correspondingly reduced. The discriminatory tax rates tended to encourage the use of labor and raw materials, and made it advantageous to cut down on the use of capital. The low productivity of much of French industry and the inadequate state of mechanization are frequently attributed, at least in part, to the apparent discrimination against the use of capital.[gg] The heavy registry

[gg] The first report of the Committee on Productivity and the Tax System, reprinted in *Statistiques et études financières* No. 42, June 1952, remarks (p. 525): "The production tax is currently imposed exactly as though the legislator had

taxes on capital transactions have probably acted as a further deterrent to the use of capital.

The same product may be taxed differently when put to different uses, thus encouraging its use for some purposes not justified by differences in productivity. Thus, electricity is taxed only once under the production tax and is totally exempt when sold to domestic consumers. Coal is taxed once if "destroyed" in the production process, not at all if sold to consumers, and double-taxed when used for industrial heating.[17] The transaction tax, when it was in force, also had the effect of discriminating between products or services, and thereby of distorting the amount of various inputs that was devoted to the production of different items.[hh]

In addition, some methods of organizing production, kinds of economic activity, or particular products or services receive tax advantages which make them appear less costly than they actually are. Most conspicuous are the advantages of "artisans." In addition to the use of the forfeit system of assessing personal income, artisans are subjected to the proportional income tax at a reduced rate and are exempt from the production and transaction taxes. Persons wishing to qualify as "artisans" for tax purposes must conform to certain standards (little trained personnel, a low state of mechanization, no "commercial" procedures of sale) admirably suited to ensure their low productivity.[ii] Artisans are also exempt from two taxes not discussed here (the apprenticeship tax and the local licensing tax, *patente*).

Small business firms receive a competitive advantage over large ones, insofar as the forfeit system, which small firms may adopt, has frequently resulted in an underassessment of business income relative to that of large firms or corporations, which must declare their income and find it more difficult to evade the income taxes.

---

given himself the objective of surtaxing all the factors of productivity . . . and consequently of preventing their utilization." For evidence of low productivity and inadequate mechanization, including some indication of the other factors involved, see Chapter 9.

[hh] There has been a gradual but important trend in the direction of a conversion of the production and transaction taxes into a single tax on "value added," which would eliminate most of the discrimination between products and services noted above. Thus, tax reform measures of 1954 and 1955 made it possible, in principle, to deduct in full the taxes already paid on capital goods, general expenses, and most services.

[ii] The *Loriot Report* (p. 122) observes "If it were necessary to define the enterprises of which one might say a priori that their productivity must be bad, the formula which would be used would no doubt be little different from the definition of artisans in the General Tax Code." For similar comments, see Maurice Lauré, *Impôts et productivité* (Paris, 1953) p. 40.

Small firms are also able to reduce their payments on the production and transaction taxes through the application of a forfeit system. The fraud of small firms on the transaction tax was particularly great, and the illegal retention of the proceeds constituted an important source of income for many small shopkeepers.[18] For many firms, tax avoidance is probably a more important source of profit than the laborious efforts at cost reduction or quality improvement. Small-size firms may also be encouraged by the differential taxation of incorporated and unincorporated businesses. Individual firms are subject to the personal income tax (under the forfeit system for small firms, by income declaration for large ones); corporate profits (which generally apply to large firms) are taxed under the corporate income tax at a rate of 34 per cent (later raised to 38 per cent) and again under the personal income tax (with no allowance for exemptions under the proportional tax) when distributed. On the other hand, corporations can accumulate undistributed reserves that are free from income tax payments, while the net profits of unincorporated businesses are taxed whether distributed or not. There are also certain tax advantages (such as accelerated depreciation of investments, reevaluation of inventories to take account of price fluctuations) that large firms are presumably in a better position to benefit from. Whether these advantages offset the heavier taxation of corporations cannot readily be ascertained, although relatively few corporations in fact make use of them in calculating their tax.

The tax system thus appears to provide a handicap in favor of the smallest (and generally least efficient) enterprises and forms of business organization. The survival and proliferation of a large number of small enterprises using archaic methods of production and distribution have undoubtedly been favored by the protection and disguised subsidies received via the tax system. (The tax system is not the only element involved in the protection of small enterprises, however, as will be evident from the discussion in Chapter 9.)

The tax system also affects the organization of production in other ways. Since the tax paid on services is not deductible from the production tax, the entrepreneur has a considerable tax incentive to provide his own services (e.g., trucking) even if these would otherwise be less efficient. The transaction tax penalized repeated sales of goods or services, and thus provided an artificial encouragement to integrated methods of production.

Farming activities as a whole are also made to appear more

attractive. The obsolete method of assessing farm income results in very low payments on the income tax, while the exemption of agricultural products from the production tax is an important benefit to the extent that the burden of this tax is shifted backwards to the owners of productive resources. These advantages are among the factors which help to explain the heavy concentration of French manpower resources in agricultural activities despite the relatively low productivity of this sector of the economy (see Chapter 11).

VI AGITATION AND TAX REFORM

With a unanimity of opinion remarkable for France, the tax system is regarded as basically inequitable. This opinion may be presented with classical understatement ("our tax system is not in fact very just"), with forthright bluntness ("our tax system is bad"), or with some passion ("our tax system is scandalously inefficient and unjust").[19] A Parliamentary committee has referred to the "execrable injustice" of the tax system.[20] As a result of the agitation for tax reform, the tax system is undergoing almost continuous revision. However, most of the changes are essentially minor, the obstacles to a real tax "reform" appearing well-nigh insuperable.

A. TAX AGITATION

One would expect that the inequities of the tax system and the multiple discriminations that it contains would give rise to pressure for tax reform. It is an unwelcome tribute to the complexity of the tax system, and its uncertain incidence, that each economic and social group can point to the special benefits or advantages of others and assert, with a reasonably straight face, that it is the most heavily taxed. In France, as in the United States, popular reaction against the inequities of the tax system has played an important role in early revolutionary history. While it is unlikely that history will repeat itself in France, the present tax system still serves to embitter relations between the state and its citizens, to undermine the authority of the state, and to weaken the moral fabric of society.

These points were abundantly illustrated in the tax agitation which coalesced in 1954-1955 around the *Union de Défense des Commerçants et Artisans* led by Pierre Poujade. Mobs of up to five thousand persons, organized by the UDCA, physically obstructed the process of tax investigation and tax enforcement, despite the presence of local police. Public auctions of seized businesses were systematically obstructed, so that the businesses could be returned to their original owners for nominal sums (e.g., 97 francs in one instance). Tax officials and their families were subjected to intimidation and threats of reprisals. The UDCA menaced the government with the refusal to subscribe to treasury securities and with the withdrawal of personal savings from public banking establishments. Taxpayers were encouraged to boycott the government by refusing to pay their taxes;[jj] in at least five or six *départements* this advice was widely followed, resulting in what Premier Faure described as a "state of semi-anarchy" in the relations between certain categories of taxpayers and the administration.[21]

The agitation reached a climax in a stormy Parliamentary session in March 1955, during which Poujade and his followers openly threatened members of the Parliament from seats in the gallery. Without accepting their demands for a complete tax amnesty, the suppression of all controls, and the abrogation of the enforcement procedures adopted in 1954, the government agreed to modify the procedures, to raise the forfeit level above which they apply, and to provide further relief for merchants and artisans through a hastily-organized tax reform law. Observing that the session constituted "a sign of the decomposition of the State," the political analyst of *Le Monde* wrote: "This is not the first time that an organization, in order to obtain satisfaction, has exerted pressure on certain deputies, but we have never seen the latter yield so easily without considering either the situation of other taxpayers equally unfavored or the other duties of the government."[22]

B. PROPOSALS FOR TAX REFORM

Tax reform has been a perennial activity of French governments. One or several proposals for a revision of the tax system has been on the docket of all postwar Parliaments, as was the case with most of their predecessors of the Third Republic. Projects for a thoroughgoing "reform" of the tax system have vied with those for more modest "improvements" (*aménagements*). The adoption, by executive decree or vote of Parliament, of particular reform proposals has provided only a brief respite; the effects of the reforms almost

[jj] In order to avoid prosecution, the UDCA did not openly or explicitly advocate the tax strike, resorting instead to such readily understood directives as "turn off the spigot." According to one source, the tax strike was 50-70 per cent effective in thirteen *départements* in the first quarter of 1955 (*L'Express* March 5, 1955, pp. 8-9).

invariably proving to be less profound than anticipated, the continuing process of piecemeal revision has shortly been resumed.

In 1948, Parliament gave the Executive special powers to carry out a tax reform by decree. However, the 1948 decrees proved to be more a reorganization than a "reform"; the government's powers were limited by the prescription that the aggregate tax burden should not be increased, nor the bases of the taxes modified. Some of the more important changes, such as those in the forfeit system, were subsequently adulterated by Parliamentary action or executive inaction. During the past few years, therefore, "tax reform" has once more been on the agenda, culminating in the legislation enacted on April 10, 1954.

The latest round of activity on the tax front dates from the spring of 1952, following the elections of 1951 during which most political parties had pledged a vigorous tax reform. When his cabinet was formed, Pinay indicated his intention to carry out a thorough-going reform. The introduction of specific legislation was delayed for a considerable period, during which a Committee on Tax Reform (the "Loriot Committee") was appointed to hold public sessions and prepare a detailed report for the use of the government.

The Loriot report contained a penetrating analysis and criticism of the existing tax system. But the proposals for reform rejected the notion of a "revolutionary" change in the tax system; they started instead from the premise that the "equilibrium" between the three broad categories of taxes (excise, income, capital) should be maintained. The principal objective of the limited reform was a widening of the tax base, so that the tax yield could be increased despite reductions in rates. This was to be accomplished by a combination of four elements: a better method of evaluating the taxable base, a lowering of excessive rates, reinforcement of the campaign against fraud, and increased efficiency in the tax administration services.

The tax reform bill submitted by Pinay followed the general spirit of the Loriot report. The limited scope of the proposed reform is indicated by the fact that the government imposed upon itself two major constraints: there should be no new taxes, and the level of tax receipts should not be changed.

Despite, and in part because of, the modest character of the Pinay proposals, they encountered a storm of Parliamentary opposition. The Finance Committee of the National Assembly refused to consider such minor proposals in a separate bill and invited the government to submit "a proposal for tax reform capable of serving as a basis for useful discussion." The government maintained its position, and the Finance Committee refused a second time to examine the reform bill. The project was finally incorporated into the Finance Law, in which form it did not escape the criticism of the Committee. When the Pinay government fell, the immediate issues were closely related to the tax question.

The Mayer government, which succeeded Pinay, displayed even greater prudence in its tax proposals. The less assuming title of "tax improvements" was given to the bill, and some of the more controversial of Pinay's proposals were withdrawn. Most of the Mayer proposals were rejected by the Finance Committee of the National Assembly. The government fell before the bill was brought to a vote by Parliament.

The Laniel government promised a "real" reform, and the bill deposited in Parliament in November 1953 once more bore the title of "tax reform." The bill was extensively rewritten by the Finance Committee. Even then the revised bill was almost rejected by the Committee, and a "rectified" count showed only a one vote majority.[kk] After a very confused Parliamentary debate, a final version of the tax reform law was adopted on April 10, 1954. Its principal contents were:

(1) On the personal income taxes, an exemption of "invested" savings from the progressive surtax, a 10 per cent reduction in the surtax imposed on wages and salaries, and a change in the calculation of the basic exemption on the surtax in order to avoid the higher rate of taxation previously applied on the lowest category of taxable income;

(2) on the corporate income tax, an increase in the rate from 34 to 36 per cent (later raised to 38 per cent); and

(3) on the excise taxes, the adoption of a "tax on value added" to replace the production tax on goods, with a rate increase from 15.35 to 16.85 per cent. Provision was made for the deduction of taxes paid on capital goods, general expenses, and services, on a schedule associated with increases in the basic rates. (By July 1955 the tax on value added had been extended to wholesale trade and the transaction tax abolished.)

Two features of the various reform proposals (both successful and rejected) might be stressed. One is their limited scope. This has

[kk] The first vote was 19 for the revised bill, 19 against and 5 abstentions, which would have resulted in a rejection of the bill. On a recount, the vote was shifted to 20-19-4.

been most evident in the case of the income taxes. The various measures start from the premise that the income tax in France cannot attain the proportions that it was originally expected to, or that it does in Great Britain and the United States. The more constructive proposals have therefore been directed towards a simplification of the income tax structure and a reduction of the possibilities of fraud. In practice, a selective reduction in income tax rates has been the outstanding feature. The proposed changes in the excise taxes have been somewhat more significant, but directed primarily at making the (now defunct) production tax into one closer to a tax fully on "value added."

A second feature of the reform proposals is their fragmentary nature. The Ministry of Finance appears to have an unlimited reserve of minor and uncoordinated proposals to replace those which annually fall victim to Parliamentary opposition. A considerable number of these revisions, some ostensibly for a "provisional" period, are eventually adopted in the Finance Law or by executive decree. As a result of this incessant tinkering with the legislation, the underlying principles of the tax system have disintegrated and it has become increasingly a patchwork of unrelated or contradictory provisions.

The limited and fragmentary nature of efforts at tax reform has many explanations. One of the more important is the small margin within which tax reformers are constrained to operate. The need to maintain a constant and high level of receipts in order to finance the heavy budgetary commitments of the government greatly reduces freedom of action in tax matters and discourages experimentation with new taxes of uncertain yield. Conversely, there is the danger that reform measures may increase the direct or indirect burden of the tax system, particularly on the lower income groups, beyond the "peril point" of political and social instability. Ministry of Finance officials have discovered that the path which leads to reduced tax burdens without reduced tax yields is exceedingly straight and narrow.

A second major factor impeding a drastic reform of the tax system is the resistance of the economic interest groups involved. These interest groups are quick to detect, or at least to suspect, new measures that would shift some of the tax burden in their direction. The coalitions of mutual interest that have been formed in opposition to attempts to alter the existing tax structure, sometimes composed of strange bedfellows, have been particularly effective because of the slim and unstable Parliamentary majority of most postwar governments.

The effective pressure of economic groups is conspicuous in proposals to reform the income tax, where their interests are most easily identified. Since there are few things more difficult politically than to attack "acquired rights," efforts to achieve a greater equality take the form of an ever-lengthening list of selective privileges and exemptions. A wave of labor unrest results in a reduction of the income taxes imposed on wages and salaries; organized resistance of artisans and shopkeepers obliges the government and Parliament to modify the forfeits applied to them. The tendency is to reduce the income taxes to the lowest common denominator of the most privileged groups,[11] with the result that the relative share of income taxes in total tax collections is even further reduced.

The area of agreement on the need for reform is substantially greater than on the appropriate direction of any reform proposal. Those who favor a drastic reform are themselves divided into several different camps. Against them must be set those who argue that the main outlines of the present system should be preserved, either because the three forms of taxes are supposed to provide a harmonious equilibrium or because the present system has the undeniable virtue of being in existence. A Committee on Tax Reform, consisting of representatives of the government, trade unions, government workers, tax officials and technicians, and different categories of taxpayers held sessions in 1946 and 1947 without being able to produce a majority report.

VII SUMMARY

The problem confronting the French government has been to create a tax structure that would yield the large amounts of revenue desired while causing as little inequity or inefficiency as possible.

The French tax system, in the aggregate, collects about as much revenue—on a relative basis—as that of Great Britain or West Germany and more than the United States tax system does. Outstanding features of the French tax structure are: the heavy reliance on excise rather than income taxes; the widespread use of indirect measures of estimating taxable income instead of direct assessment by the taxpayer; the extreme complexity of the tax

[11] This process is reminiscent of a sequence in the film, "A Night at the Opera," in which one of the Marx Brothers, acting as a barber, accidently cuts "one snip too much" off alternate sides of his customer's moustache until eventually it is removed completely.

system, apparently guided by the general principle of raising revenue as unobtrusively as possible; and the prevalence of fraud and special privileges, which go hand in hand and reinforce each other.

The tax system shows marked departures from generally accepted notions of equity. With respect to the "equal treatment of equals," the income taxes are honeycombed with special rates and exemptions that provide differential advantages to one group or another, while the opportunity to evade taxes is also unevenly distributed among the various classes of taxpayers. There is no reason to believe that these advantages and opportunities offset each other so as to provide an equitable outcome. The "progressiveness" of the tax system is also in doubt. While the income taxes show some progressiveness over certain income ranges, most Frenchmen pay little or no income tax as a result of fraud, legal exemptions, or provisions for income-splitting. Capital taxes also show some progression; however, these taxes are quantitatively of only minor importance. An attempt has been made to build some progressiveness into part of the excise taxes, but their incidence is uncertain and some of the burden of these and other taxes (on business profits and payrolls) is borne at a proportional rate.

The efficiency with which the economy uses its resources has been adversely affected by provisions of the tax system. Relative prices have been distorted so that producers and consumers make decisions with respect to the allocation of resources without knowing the real costs that are entailed. Generally speaking, the tax system provides a handicap in favor of smaller and less efficient firms and forms of business organization. Particular products and services are also made to appear more or less attractive than their relative costs of production would warrant; the discrimination against the use of capital has been especially serious in the past.

Popular dissatisfaction with the tax system has been reflected in agitation of varying degrees of violence which has sapped the authority of the state. Under this pressure the tax system undergoes frequent changes. These changes have essentially been of a limited and fragmentary character and not directed towards enhancing the role of the income tax. One reason is that there is more agreement on the need for than on the direction of change; another is that tax reforms must operate within narrow limits since revenues must be kept high and steady. In the last analysis, however, the most serious obstacle to tax reform is the concerted resistance of interest groups protecting their "acquired rights."

PART III

THE STATE AS ENTREPRENEUR

CHAPTER 7

THE DEVELOPMENT OF PUBLIC OWNERSHIP

THE intervention of the state in French economic affairs, arising as it has in response to many different circumstances, has taken an almost bewildering variety of forms. Of these many forms, perhaps the most direct and striking is public ownership and management of individual enterprises and whole sectors of industry.

The French state owns a full or controlling share of so long and diversified a list of enterprises that simply to catalogue them is a formidable task. Publicly-owned enterprises run the gamut from stud farms for horses to the nationalized coal mines. The government is the largest single producer of automobiles in France; it has a monopoly of the sale of alcohol, tobacco and matches; it directs enterprises as geographically dispersed as cotton and rice growing in Niger, public transportation in Paris, steel mills in the Saar, and potash mines in Alsace. It owns a majority share of the national railway system, and controls the major companies of sea and air transportation and aircraft manufacture. The Bank of France, the four largest deposit banks, and the principal insurance companies have been nationalized, as have the production and distribution of gas and electricity. The government owns the national radio and television corporation, two large news agencies, the National Opera and *Comédie Française*, and several movie production and distribution companies. It directs some petroleum research and nitrogen extraction through public corporations. The field of public enterprises also includes the ports of Le Havre, Bordeaux and Strasbourg, and the railway systems of some of the colonial areas.

How large a proportion of economic activity in France is now under public ownership, and how does this compare with the proportion in other countries? Unfortunately, the extent of public ownership in France is difficult to measure accurately on the basis of available data, and no reliable estimate has yet been published.[a] With the principal energy resources (coal, gas and hydroelec-

[a] The principal problems of measurement arise from the need to obtain data (on number of employees or value of sales or payroll) at least at the level of the individual industry, and, in the case of mixed industries, at the level of the individual firm. In addition, there are serious conceptual problems in defining a "public" enterprise.

tricity), the railways, part of sea and air transportation, and the major institutions of banking and insurance under state ownership, it is clear that public control now embraces a large and vital sector of the nation's economic life. Perhaps some indication of the order of magnitude of the public sector is given by an estimate, stated to come from the Ministry of Finance, that nationalized enterprises account for 20 per cent of French industrial capacity[b].[1]

After the last war Great Britain experienced a wave of nationalizations paralleling that of France. In Britain perhaps a larger sector of industry—the Bank of England, coal, transportation, electricity, gas, and iron and steel—was transferred to the public domain. The wave has since receded in Britain, with the denationalization of the steel industry and part of road transportation, while the postwar nationalizations in France have been kept virtually intact. In other Western European countries the nationalization movement after the war was much less extensive. The reader need hardly be reminded that in the United States utilities have commonly been subjected to public regulation rather than ownership. Within the basic industries and transportation, the sector of public ownership has been confined, except in special cases, to water power. The French economy is now possibly the most highly nationalized of any industrial country this side of the iron curtain.

This and the following chapter deal with the role of the state as entrepreneur of the publicly-owned establishments. The present chapter reviews briefly the development of public ownership in France, particularly the reasons why enterprises have come under public control. Attempts to define a new structure for the enterprises, and the struggle of various groups for control of decision-making functions, are also examined. The next chapter looks into the performance record of state ownership in action.

[b] The precise meaning of "industrial" capacity is unfortunately not indicated. It is not clear whether this estimate includes or excludes the "mixed companies" such as the national railways which, as will be indicated later, are a legally different form of public enterprise from the nationalized coal, gas, and electrical industries. It is also not known whether it takes into account the subsidiaries and affiliates of public enterprises, which in some cases are very numerous. Another source has estimated that the nationalized industries and mixed companies in which the state holds a majority share account for 20 per cent of the employed persons in the fields of industry and transportation (Pierre Hoüel, "Comment fonctionne, en France, le secteur nationalisé?", *La Tribune des peuples*, No. 4, September-October 1953, p. 86). This estimate apparently does not include some mixed companies in which the state holds a minority share but may nevertheless exercise a significant, if not dominant, voice in management decisions.

I NATIONALIZATION BEFORE THE SECOND WORLD WAR

The origins of public ownership lie far back in French history. The first prototypes of state ownership date from Colbert's ministry, under the reign of Louis XIV. One feature of the Mercantilist doctrine was the restriction of imports and the stimulation of national industries as a means of achieving economic self-sufficiency and gold-producing exports. The *Manufactures des Gobelins*, *de Sèvres*, and *de Beauvais* were formed as pilot plants to develop the manufacture of tapestry, furniture, and other articles of quality. Alongside these royal establishments were privately owned enterprises which were closely regulated by the Crown. Most of these arrangements, however, did not long survive their chief protagonist.[2]

There were no important movements toward public ownership during most of the nineteenth century. Thus, the statutes of 1800, 1803, and 1806, which established the Bank of France and gave it monopoly power over the issue of currency, and the mining law of 1810, which granted to private groups the right to develop mineral deposits, did not include participation of the government either in the management of the companies or in their profits.

Those activities which the government did take over during this period were ones in which public ownership has been the rule rather than the exception in most countries. This would appear to be the case of the postal system, which was established as a public service by the laws of 1839 and 1851, of the mint (established in 1879), and of the government printing office (in 1902). A somewhat different case was the public monopoly of tobacco, established in 1811, and of matches, in 1872; these actions were motivated primarily by revenue considerations.

The railways are also a field in which extensive public regulation, sometimes combined with public ownership, is commonplace. In France the organization of the railway system initially involved only a limited degree of state participation. In 1842, the concession over the existing network was granted to private companies. The state retained some administrative responsibilities over the construction and management of the lines, and progressively found itself involved more deeply, first in the provision of financial aid and guarantees of various kinds and eventually in the detailed direction of the system.[3]

The first impulse towards state ownership sufficiently extensive to be called a "wave" came at the conclusion of the first World War. The operation of the potash resources of Alsace, returned to France under the Treaty of Versailles, was confided to a "national industrial office," *Les Mines Domaniales de Potasse d'Alsace*, administered directly by a government agency. The *Office National Industriel de l'Azote* was also established under a government agency to take over from a German firm the patent for the Haber process of manufacturing synthetic ammonium. This practice was not consistently followed, however, since the operation of the Lorraine coal mines transferred under the Treaty was given to private companies.

Another development during this period was the participation of the French government, along with private interests, in two "mixed companies" (*sociétés d'économie mixte*), formed in 1924 in the reacquired territory of Alsace; the *Compagnie de Navigation du Rhin* and the *Chantiers et Ateliers du Rhin*. The government owned a minority share in both enterprises and participated in their management along with representatives of private stockholders. These were early instances of a particular form of mixed enterprise that enjoyed considerable vogue in the following decade.

The next group of enterprises coming under public ownership were victims of the financial crisis of the 1930's. The state was called upon to provide support for several companies in financial distress. In the refinancing process, the state, in return for its financial assistance, received a portion of the capital stock, thus transforming the firms into mixed companies. It was in this manner, for example, that the state acquired a share of the steamship company *Compagnie Générale Transatlantique*.

An unusual experiment in public ownership undertaken at this time was the *Compagnie Nationale du Rhône*, organized to develop the hydroelectric energy potential of the Rhone river. It was established as a "mixed company" on the grounds that the full development of the economic potentialities of the river could not be undertaken by private means. Capital was subscribed by the city of Paris (a consumer of electricity from the region), public bodies at the departmental and municipal levels, the *Paris-Lyon-Méditerranée* railroad (later the SNCF), and private corporations or individual consumers of electricity and water. The government did not contribute any of the capital stock, but received two-fifths of the positions on the board of directors in return for its grant of concession and for the guarantee that it provided for the public loan floated by the company.[4]

With the advent of the Popular Front government of 1936, new ideological considerations were added to those that had guided the intervention of the state in the past. Nationalization of key industries had long been a part of the political platform of the French Socialist party. In 1919, the trade union *Confédération Générale du Travail* (CGT) introduced a program for "industrial nationalization," with tripartite direction of the public enterprises by representatives of the state, the personnel, and the consuming public. Proposals for nationalizing the mines, the railways, and "industrial monopolies" were placed before Parliament during succeding years.

The economic crisis of the 1930's heightened the pressure for industrial nationalization. During the electoral campaign that preceded the establishment of the Popular Front government, the nationalization issue was widely debated. The actual proposals adopted by the new government were considerably more modest in scope than the earlier programs demanded by the parties of the left. Nor was the formula of "industrial nationalization" adopted. Instead, the legislators continued to show a preference for the mixed company.[5]

The principal measures adopted by the Popular Front were the reform of the Bank of France in July 1936, the nationalization of the munitions and aircraft industries in August 1936, and the nationalization of the railways in August 1937. The term "nationalization" was not applied to the reorganization of the Bank of France. The principal change in its structure was the acquisition by the government of a preponderant voice in the direction of the Bank. Private stockholders were not displaced, but their representation on the board of directors was reduced to a minority by the addition of representatives of the state, the larger interest groups (agriculture, trade unions, etc.) and Bank personnel.

The munitions industry was a primary target of the leftist parties during the 1930's. An important plank of their legislative programs called for nationalization of armament production to eliminate the "illicit profits" of the "war merchants." It was publicly questioned whether national security interests were compatible with a private monopoly; the anomalous position of the state as virtually the sole customer of these industries was also adduced as a reason for nationalization.

The law of 1936 authorized the three defense ministries to nationalize enterprises in the munitions industry. This authority was exercised in varying degrees. The Naval Ministry requisitioned only two small torpedo plants; the Army took over a total of ten small and specialized establishments; the Air Ministry, on the other hand, proceeded to nationalize almost the entire aircraft construction industry. The enterprises taken over by the Army and Navy were placed directly under the operation of the responsible ministry. The nationalized aircraft construction industry, however, was reorganized into six, subsequently reduced to four, mixed companies in each of which the state possessed at least two-thirds of the capital. Subsequent increases in the capital of the companies expanded the share of the government to over 90 per cent.[6]

The nationalization of the railways marked the close of a long period during which public regulation had gradually been extended. The increased state responsibility for the management of the private railway system during the 19th century has already been mentioned. Before the first World War, the government acquired certain rail lines in Western France as a consequence of the financial difficulties of the private companies. Rail lines in Alsace-Lorraine were added to the public system after the war. The deficits of the public and private railway systems in the late 1920's and early 1930's gave added impulse to state intervention. In August 1937, an agreement between the state and private lines provided for a new organization to be called the *Société Nationale des Chemins de Fer Français* (SNCF). The private companies ceded to the SNCF the franchises previously granted by the state, in return for a share of the capital of the new company. The state received 51 per cent of the capital of the new mixed company, and the private concerns 49 per cent.

II POSTWAR NATIONALIZATIONS

A. THE SENTIMENTS

"In 1944, the great majority of Frenchmen were convinced of the economic, social and political superiority of nationalized industry over private industry."[7] This statement, though somewhat categorical, may nevertheless describe accurately the consensus of publicly voiced opinion prevailing at the time of liberation.

A concerted drive for widespread economic and social reform, including further nationalization of industry, was an integral part of the resistance and liberation movements. As early as May 1942, General de Gaulle, whose support of the reform program undoubtedly contributed to its popular appeal, had said from London: "For France, where the disaster and betrayal have disqualified most of the owners and men of privilege and where the great mass of people have, on the contrary, remained most valiant and faithful, it would be unacceptable for this terrible trial to leave standing a social and moral order which has worked against the nation."[8]

In March 1944 the National Resistance Council, which grouped together the principal elements of the resistance movement, called for "the return to the nation of the great means of monopolized production, fruits of common labor, of the sources of energy, the wealth underground, the insurance companies, and the large banks." A doctrine of public ownership was incorporated into the preamble of the Constitution of 1946 by the statement that "every good, every enterprise, whose use has or acquires the characteristics of a national public service or of a *de facto* monopoly must become the property of the community."

By the time that the Provisional Government was established in Paris, the resistance organizations, the three principal political parties, and the leading trade unions were actively endorsing a broad program for nationalizing the basic sectors of the economy. Only a few conservatives openly opposed the program, and their influence was negligible.[9]

It has frequently been observed that the postwar French nationalizations were as much a psychological as an economic or political movement. For many Frenchmen the word itself has a mythical quality with strong emotional content, originating in its association with the dramatic events of the resistance and liberation. As an article of faith, it has meant different things to different people. Many of the forces which in combination accounted for its popularity were not primarily economic in origin. With these provisos in mind, several factors can be distinguished, in each of which there is an important economic element, that contributed to the strength of the movement: the distrust of private enterprise; the need for rapid reconstruction; and the desire for better labor conditions.

Private enterprise in France had been castigated by leftist groups during the 1930's for its alleged responsibilities in bringing about the Great Depression. A "trustophobia" had developed against the private monopolies or "trusts" personified in the "200 families" said to control the economic and political life of France. The defeat of 1940 urgently required an explanation, if not a scapegoat; the behavior of some industrialists during the occupation reinforced the views of those who believed that the military conquest was facilitated by the failures or "betrayals" of private capital.

The postwar Parliament, made up predominantly of parties traditionally seated on the left side of the Chamber, displayed little confidence in the ability of private enterprise to serve the public interest. "The national economy, at the stage at which it has arrived, can no longer accommodate enterprises which, like the insurance companies, give a higher priority to immediate profit than to the collective interest," declared the deputy reporting on the bill to nationalize the insurance companies.[10]

Dissolution of the power of "private monopolies" did not, of course, necessitate nationalization of industry. Alternative forms of public regulation were at least conceivable which would have been compatible with the preservation of private enterprise. In the climate of the liberation, such alternatives received little consideration. Moreover, a counterpart of the distrust of private enterprise was the strong urge for national economic planning, mentioned in Chapter 2. Public ownership of the "key" industries and of credit was considered necessary to enable the state to direct the whole economy of France in the public interest. The public enterprises were to be the "levers of command" (an expression frequently used) in the process of national planning.

A special case of the general distrust of private enterprise was the desire to impose sanctions on businessmen who had collaborated with the enemy. In the case of the Renault automobile works, deliveries to the French Army before the war were stated to be "notoriously insufficient," while deliveries to the Germans during the occupation were large enough to be an important factor, being limited only by repeated bombing of the plants by the Allies. The government also asserted that a national enterprise, organized in the interests of maximum efficiency, could serve as a pilot plant for the rest of this important industry.[11] The use of nationalization as a means of imposing economic sanctions also figured in the case of the *Société des Moteurs Gnôme et Rhône*, which was transformed into the *Société Nationale d'Etudes et de Construction de Moteurs d'Aviation*. The *Berliet* company was also sequestered by the government on grounds of collaboration, but later restored to its owners.

A second argument advanced in behalf of nationalization was the urgency of economic reconstruction throughout the country. Evidence has been presented earlier of the prostration of the economy immediately after liberation. Many influential Frenchmen doubted that the enormous tasks of reconstruction could be left in the hands of private industry. The poor record of private investment before the war (it will be recalled that there was little or no net capital investment during the 1930's) was taken as evidence that economic reconstruction could only be achieved through extensive public controls. The further step from public control to nationalization was an easy one to take in 1944 and 1945.

Thus the ordinance nationalizing the coal mines of the Nord and Pas de Calais regions referred to the serious condition of the coal mining industry and concluded that structural reforms were essential to perform the task of reconstruction. "Only the State today possesses sufficient authority to assume such a task, the accomplishment of which is so important for the interest of the country as a whole; only the State can, in effect, following an overall plan, bring, in the most favorable and rapid conditions, the coal mines to bear on the recovery of French industry."

A third argument was that nationalization would better the conditions of the working classes. It was expected that elimination of the profits of private monopolies would benefit laborers in two ways: as workers, through higher wages; and as consumers, through lower prices. The spirit of social reform was particularly strong during the period shortly after liberation. The 1945 ordinance which established a new system of plant committees (*comités d'entreprise*) through which labor was to participate in the activities of business firms declared that "the great popular movement which liberated France from the enemy was not only a movement of national liberation, but also one of social liberation."

The nationalization of the Northern coal mines illustrates the general way in which this social reform was to take place. The ordinance declared that "the legitimate aspirations of the working classes" would be met by increased labor participation at all points. The plant committees would give workers the opportunity to participate in various activities. Permanent representation on the board of directors would also enable workers to exercise their voice in the "industrial and social improvements" that would be the principal tasks of the nationalized mines. However, the precise ways in which labor participation was expected to change the direction of the nationalized enterprises were seldom, if ever, spelled out in detail.

No brief list can do justice to the complex forces, economic and non-economic, behind the nationalization movement. The unanimity of opinion in France was reflected in the voting of the nationalization measures. The law nationalizing the Bank of France and the four largest banks was approved by a vote of 521 to 35; the gas and electricity bill was passed 512 to 64 and the insurance bill 487 to 63. The coal mine nationalization bill was approved unanimously. It is difficult to recapture, in retrospect, the spirit of the early liberation period. Whatever their reasons, an overwhelming majority of Frenchmen saw in nationalization the basis for a structural reform which would usher in a new era of economic and social democracy.

B. THE EVENTS

The postwar measures can conveniently be divided into two periods: an emergency period in 1944 and 1945 when certain urgent reforms were undertaken; and the period of the major nationalizations in late 1945 and 1946 after the Constituent Assembly had been formed. After 1946 the movement came virtually to a halt, and the measures adopted since then have been of a somewhat different character.

Labor unrest in the Northern coal mines was acute immediately after the liberation, with miners refusing to work under the wartime management. In October 1944 the directors of the Northern mines were suspended and arrangements made for the appointment of a temporary administration. A provisional ordinance of December 1944 combined the 18 mining companies of the region into a single public enterprise, *Houillères du Nord et du Pas de Calais*. The coal basins in several other areas were also requisitioned in the autumn of 1944 and temporary administrators appointed.

The holdings of Louis Renault were sequestered in October 1944 and the *Régie Nationale des Usines Renault* established in January 1945. The nationalization of the *Société des Moteurs Gnôme et Rhône* was accomplished in May 1945. Among information media, the state confiscated a news agency, a broadcasting company, and several movie companies that had been used for propaganda purposes by the Germans, and replaced them with public enterprises. In air transportation, a provisional nationalization was undertaken in June 1945 by transferring to the state the holdings of *Air France*.

The Constituent Assembly, formed after the elections of November 1945, undertook the major nationalizations in late 1945 and 1946. The first of these was the nationalization of the Bank of

France and of the four largest credit institutions. Participation of private interests in the Bank of France, which had been reduced to a minority status by earlier reforms, was completely eliminated. The number of private banks to be nationalized was the subject of some debate. It was finally decided to nationalize "those institutions which, by the total of their deposits and the extension of their branches throughout the French territory, constitute some sort of public service already almost national in character."[12] Why four banks were chosen and why the particular four fitted this description better than some others, are not entirely clear.

The next step was the nationalization of gas and electricity. The law envisaged separate companies for gas and for electricity, but six weeks later the government approved an agreement between the two companies whereby *Electricité de France* assumed, for all practical purposes, the management of *Gaz de France*. The question of which insurance companies to nationalize was debated with considerable animation. Thirty-four insurance companies were eventually selected. Although the predominant consideration was size, the "political influence" of the companies was also taken into account. The proportion of total insurance activity taken over by the state has been variously estimated at between 50 and 62 per cent.[13] The last of the major laws, passed in May 1946, nationalized the remainder of the coal mining basins and established a national enterprise, *Charbonnages de France*.

By the end of the first Constituent Assembly, about half of the programs of the resistance groups and major political parties had passed into law. The programs had also called for nationalization of the iron and steel industry, the merchant marine, light metals and chemicals, and cement. No major nationalizations were considered by the second Constituent Assembly, however, which sat from June to October 1946. The Paris transport network was subsequently nationalized (in March 1948), but in a different administrative form from the public enterprises established in coal, electricity and gas. Similarly, when the government reorganized two maritime shipping companies (*Compagnie Générale Transatlantique* and *Compagnie des Messageries Maritimes*) in 1948, it maintained their original structure of mixed companies and rejected the proposals of communists and socialists for full nationalization. In adopting a new statute for *Air France* in 1948, the Assembly reverted from the position of the state as sole shareholder in favor of a new mixed company. The communist's bill for nationalizing the steel industry was never brought to a vote.

The summer of 1946 was thus the high water mark of the nationalization movement. No significant proposal for further nationalization has been seriously considered since 1948, and it can safely be said that the movement has come to at least a temporary halt. On the other hand, there has been no serious attempt to reverse any of the established nationalizations.

III STRUCTURE OF THE ENTERPRISES

The postwar nationalization laws were debated in great haste, with four major laws adopted during a short Parliamentary session. Each industry and nationalization bill was treated as a separate case, and in each a somewhat different set of compromises was worked out. The attention of the legislators was devoted more to organizational questions than to the establishment of standards of public performance, as will be evident from the next chapter. One organizational problem which received considerable attention was that of determining the legal and administrative structure of the new public enterprises.

In the search for a new structure, the earlier experiences were mainly of negative benefit. The "national industrial offices" administered directly by government ministries (*Mines Domaniales de Potasse d'Alsace*, *Office National Industriel de l'Azote*) had been criticized as excessively bureaucratic, and their ability to draw readily on Treasury funds was believed to be dangerous. The mixed companies appeared to have too many of the trappings of capitalist enterprise; nor could "the return to the nation of the great means of monopolized production" be made compatible with the continuation of private capital and a private corporate structure. The experiments with mixed companies had also demonstrated that the flexibility of financial operations, believed to be their principal advantage, was more apparent than real. Private capital had generally shown itself reluctant to advance additional funds in cases where the state held a substantial proportion of the shares, and the major responsibility for financial management remained with the government.[14]

The principal innovation of the postwar nationalizations was the creation of the new legal concept of a "public establishment of an industrial and commercial character, provided with a civil personality and with financial autonomy." This concept represented a hybrid mixture of public and private law of a kind previously unknown to France. It was intended to safeguard the legal principles of public ownership while providing an industrial and commercial framework designed for efficient management. The new structure was first applied to the Northern coal mines in 1944. *Electricité de France*, *Gaz de France* and *Charbonnages de France* were subsequently organized as "industrial and commercial" public enterprises. All of the private firms taken over by the state were abolished, and the industries reorganized under the parent public enterprises.

For the banks and insurance companies, a somewhat different system was adopted. Whereas new enterprises had been created in coal, gas, and electricity by reorganizing the existing industries, the government was careful to maintain the original banks and insurance companies. The companies also preserved their existing legal forms, with the important difference that the state was now the only shareholder. The treatment of the Renault company differed from both of these solutions. The old private corporation was abolished, and in its stead was substituted a new public enterprise of industrial and commercial character. But the *Régie Nationale des Usines Renault* was simply the original Renault company under a new name, and no reorganization of the structure of the enterprise accompanied the alteration of its legal status.

Once the crest of the wave of postwar nationalizations had passed, the earlier formula of mixed companies returned to fashion as a means of enlisting private capital. Private investors were invited to participate in the two reorganized maritime companies, and in the *Compagnie Nationale Air France*; the state, however, retained a substantial majority of the shares.

IV CONTROL OF DECISION-MAKING FUNCTIONS

A dominant theme of the postwar nationalization movement was mistrust, not only of private enterprise, but also of excessive government authority. *Nationaliser n'est pas étatiser* ("nationalization does not mean state control") was a slogan on which the major groups were united in 1944-1945. Elimination of private enterprise from the direction of key industries was to be followed by the return of these resources to the "nation," but not to the "state." This position was not paradoxical, according to its adherents, for the industries were to be managed in the interests of all by a combination of groups—not by the government alone.

This deepseated mistrust of the state, so familiar in French society, was based on more than a concern that the bureaucratic inefficiencies believed to be associated with state control would be spread over so large a sector of the economy. It has philosophical roots in the traditional doctrines of the French labor movement. The early syndicalist slogan of "the mines to the miners" was superseded, at the end of the first World War, by the CGT formula of "industrial nationalization" involving the direction of the nationalized enterprises by a tripartite group representing personnel, consumers, and government.

This formula of tripartite management was adopted in the composition of the boards of directors of the major industries nationalized after the war. It constituted a unique and radical reform of the organization of public enterprises. By way of comparison, the British solution to the bureaucratic problem has been the establishment of public corporations enjoying a substantial measure of administrative autonomy, but with representatives of workers and consumers assisting only in an advisory capacity.[15]

While remaining faithful to the principle of tripartite management, the various laws permit substantial variations in the composition of the boards from case to case. The variations appear to be haphazard, resulting from the haste with which the legislation was prepared. Worker representation is based on the principle of the "most representative" unions. Members chosen to represent the consumers are appointed by the responsible ministry on the basis of recommendations by the interest groups involved. All of the board members serve in a part-time capacity and without salary. The statutes also provide for a position of general manager, with variable functions sometimes merged with those of the chairman of the board. The general manager is a full-time official with a high salary (for government employment). In most instances, the men chosen for the position of general manager and for the senior administrative posts are considered to be of high caliber.[c]

The tripartite arrangement quickly proved to be unworkable. The initial shortcomings of the boards were brought about in large part by the introduction of politics into their operations, mostly at the instigation of the communists.[16] As the largest single party in France, the communists held such key posts as the Minister of Armaments and the Minister of Industrial Production until they left the government in 1947. The communist-dominated CGT was also the largest trade union federation. The opportunity was taken

[c] Perhaps the two outstanding persons have been Louis Armand, general manager of SNCF, and the late Pierre Lefaucheux, general manager and chairman of the board of Renault until 1955.

to pack the boards with communists, acting in the guise not only of trade unionists but also of consumer and government representatives. A majority of the positions on the board of *Charbonnages de France*, for example, was given to members of the CGT serving in one capacity or another. One result of this process of using administrative posts as political plums was that announcements of job openings were placed only in communist newspapers. Another was that top staff members were fired as "collaborators" and replaced by loyal party members.

The early introduction of politics created situations which served seriously to discredit the boards. An extreme case of the conflict between special and public interests was the coal strike of 1948, when several directors of *Charbonnages de France*, all CGT members, ordered union members to abandon even the security measures necessary for protection of the mines. Even in the absence of this political interference, however, there is evidence that the tripartite principle, based on the representation of conflicting interest groups, would not have produced the desired results. Thus, the government accounting office (*Commission de Vérification des Comptes des Entreprises Publiques*) reported in 1952 as follows:

> The organization of the enterprises nationalized since 1944 rests on the principle of a tripartite management: the personnel and the consumers share with the State the seats on the Board of Directors which, for the most part, elect their own chairmen. Without entering into a theoretical criticism of this conception it appears possible to observe that the experiment has not yielded the anticipated results. The conflict of interests, as previous reports have indicated, has been manifested in precarious delays and ineffective compromises. The equilibrium expected by the law has not been realized by the facts: the appointment of consumers, most often arbitrarily, almost always reinforces the representation of one of the two other parties. Moreover, political or trade union vicissitudes have prevented the settlement of the legal questions on the composition of the boards of directors required for the respect of public authority and the defense of the interests of the enterprises.[17]

Some of these abuses have since been rectified. The board of *Charbonnages de France*, for example, was reconstituted, with *de facto* labor representation reduced to the point intended by the legislators. To some extent, however, the influence formerly enjoyed by the communists in the selection of key personnel has simply been transferred to the parties now in power. And no permanent solution has been found for the potential conflict, now recognized as inherent in the tripartite formula, between special interest groups and the national interest.

As a result of the failure of the boards, their powers over the management of the public enterprises have been progressively transferred to the general manager and his staff, on the one hand, and to the various ministries of the government, on the other. The responsibilities which the general managers now exercise, with only limited supervision from the boards, relate primarily to the more technical features of the operation of the enterprises, such as the implementation of production and investment programs and the handling of labor relations within the enterprise. More significant is the process through which basic policy decisions have been transferred to government ministries, and frequently to the Cabinet. This has been described either as a "usurpation" or an "abdication" of the responsibilities originally assigned to the boards, depending on the point of view of the critic; that it is a fact is uncontested. The postwar period has witnessed the adoption of a series of measures designed to strengthen the financial and accounting control by Parliament and government agencies. Since there were general price and wage controls during the early postwar inflation, it was inevitable that price and wage decisions in the nationalized industries should be centrally controlled. The large deficits of many of the nationalized enterprises after the war were both a cause and an effect of increased government control, as shall be seen later. The need to finance large-scale investments with public funds made the industries more dependent on the Executive and the Parliament for the review and approval of investment programs and for the voting of appropriations.

The extent of government responsibility is revealed by a statement of the chairman of the board of *Electricité de France* (in 1948):

> The task of our board of directors has become difficult by virtue of the fact that the financial autonomy explicitly conferred on *Electricité de France* by the law has thus far remained only on paper. The board is not really master either of wages, or of sales prices, or of borrowing; in these three fields, it can only propose and the decision belongs to the Government, which is thus the sole master and, consequently, the only one responsible for its policies.[18]

The centralization in the hands of the government of decisions with respect to prices, wages, scale of investments, and personnel statutes was at one time almost complete. With the general relaxation of direct economic controls after 1948, some modifications appeared. When it became possible for the enterprises to earn a profit, they were able to enjoy somewhat greater financial autonomy and independence of management. This has only been a limited development, however. Thus, a new step in the direction of centralized government control was attempted through a series of executive decrees in 1953. The decrees strengthened the supervisory powers of the government in the form of "control missions" with the right to attend meetings of the boards and to suspend their decisions under specified conditions. Parliament objected strongly and subsequently abrogated the decrees.

Within the government, responsibility for key policy decisions concerning the public enterprises has been diffused among a considerable number of ministries and interministerial committees. No single ministry has had final responsibility and, because of their different areas of competence, the points of view of the Ministries of Finance, Industry and Commerce, Labor and Transportation, and of the *Commissariat Général au Plan* have frequently been in conflict. This diffusion of decision-making responsibility may be at the root of some of the uncoordinated or inconsistent policies with respect to different enterprises or different problems noted in the next chapter.

The boards have thus found their influence over policy gradually dissipated to the advantage either of the professional staff or of government agencies. As a symbol of the spirit which animated the nationalization movement, however, the boards appear still to play an important role. Parliamentary reversal of the executive decrees instituting "control missions" has already been mentioned. When the government attempted in 1953 to reorganize the boards of directors of some of the enterprises—by reducing the number of members and introducing a fourth component of "persons known for their industrial or financial competence"—a storm of protests arose. The unions, protesting that this represented a "sabotage" of the nationalizations, elected to boycott the meetings of the board of *Charbonnages*, and in some cases submitted their resignations. In Parliament, the socialists introduced a bill to abrogate the decrees. In the face of this opposition, the government subsequently raised the number of board members and withdrew the fourth component.

V SUMMARY

Many factors explain why a large sector of the French economy has come under public ownership. Some activities, such as the postal system, have traditionally been under public control. State ownership of nascent industry was undertaken during the reign of Louis XIV as part of the Mercantilist doctrine of promoting domestic industry. Following the first World War, several activities transferred to France under the Treaty of Versailles were administered as public enterprises. During the crisis of the 1930's, public assistance to private firms in financial distress sometimes resulted in the creation of a "mixed company" containing both public and private shareholdings. Public ownership was also adopted during this period as a means of developing certain hydroelectric power resources not considered profitable for private enterprise.

The nationalizations occurring over the past twenty years have had a stronger ideological flavor. The parties of the left came into power with the Popular Front government of 1936, and brought about the nationalization of parts of the munitions industry. The railways were also nationalized and the Bank of France reorganized, but these were the culmination of a long process of close state regulation. A strong sentiment in favor of widespread economic and social reform, including further nationalization of industry, was part of the resistance and liberation movements. Nationalization was viewed as a means of "despoiling" the "trusts" of their monopoly powers and of directing the basic industries in the public rather than the private interest. It was widely felt that private enterprise had been discredited by the events of the depression, the defeat, and the occupation, and that the urgent tasks of reconstruction could not be left in private hands. State ownership of key industries and financial institutions was believed necessary for national economic planning to be fully effective. The desire to improve the economic and social status of labor also contributed to the nationalization movement, which embraced the principal banks and insurance companies and the coal, gas, and electricity industries before it came to a halt in 1946.

The nationalization statutes were prepared in considerable haste. One structural problem which preoccupied the legislators was the search for a new legal and administrative formula to safeguard the principles of public ownership while providing for efficient management. The firms taken over after the first World War had been administered directly by government agencies. This method was found excessively bureaucratic; the alternative of the "mixed company" had too many elements of private enterprise. The new formula used for the major postwar nationalizations attempted to provide an industrial and commercial "character" and financial autonomy, while maintaining the legal principles of public ownership.

Another and related concern was to avoid excessive state control. The formula chosen for this purpose was the tripartite board of directors, containing representatives of government, labor, and consumers. In practice, the new system broke down under the introduction of politics into the selection of board members, an attempt by the communists to pack the boards, and basic conflicts of interest among the three groups. Some of the more routine powers which the boards were intended to exercise have been transferred to the general managers and their staffs. Basic decisions with respect to prices, costs, investments, etc., have become the responsibility of various government agencies. Within the government, however, decision-making responsibility has been widely diffused among the interested agencies.

CHAPTER 8

PUBLIC OWNERSHIP IN ACTION

I THE PROBLEM

MORE than eight years have elapsed since the last of the major nationalizations was undertaken, and the nationalized industries now appear to have become firmly embedded in the economic structure of France. The moment is therefore opportune for considering the principal results of public ownership in action.

The structural reforms accomplished by the nationalizations of 1945 and 1946 were widely expected to usher in a new era of economic and social progress. That the results have fallen short of these expectations is beyond serious dispute. Starting in 1947, the opponents of nationalization began to assume the offensive with virulent attacks. The nationalized industries were described as machines for losing money. They were held responsible for the continuing inflation and low living standards and accused of being permanent obstacles to the recovery of the country. The financial improvements registered by most of the public enterprises since 1949 have blunted the force of some of these criticisms. The nationalization issue, although it has recently become less a matter of debate, still contains many explosive elements that are touched off in Parliamentary and public discussions. The record of performance has been obscured by the passion of these discussions, with both sides selecting only those aspects best calculated to suit their purposes. Thus, the critics of nationalization have generally contented themselves with a recitation of the large deficits which have resulted, while its friends have emphasized the production accomplishments; in either case, the figures used have not often been given careful interpretation, and important segments of the record have been ignored.

An examination of the performance of the nationalized industries immediately encounters a difficult problem of selectivity. Each of the many public enterprises has its own history and special record, and ignoring this real diversity gives an over simplified and false picture of the experiment as a whole. Conversely, there is perhaps an even greater danger of superficiality in attempting to compress the analysis of a large number of enterprises within the narrow limits of one chapter. The solution offered is, of necessity, a compromise. The discussion is focused on certain key aspects of the operation of the public enterprises: the movement of production; trends of employment and productivity; investment policy; wages and social security; labor relations; and price policy and financial performance. The case material used under these headings is drawn primarily from the coal and electricity industries. The record of the nationalized railways is also introduced into the discussion at places where it is particularly relevant. A few of the highlights of the *Régie Renault* are examined, in view of its unique status as the single public enterprise in an industry marked by considerable competition. Although this picture is incomplete, it will at least provide a cross-sectional view of how the state-owned enterprises have been operated in France.

In evaluating the record of performance, it will be useful to examine some of the principal criticisms that have been raised. These criticisms stem from different conceptions (as expressed by officials, laymen, and economists) of what the state should be doing. The "official" objectives that the government may have set for itself are often far from clear or consistent. The sentiments in favor of nationalization, described in the preceding chapter, are too general to serve as tests of performance. As will be seen, the legislation also provides few clues as to how the enterprises should be run in the "public interest," which is nowhere defined. In practice, government officials have tended to make *ad hoc* decisions on problems as they emerged, but in the context of certain general objectives that can usually be identified. The principal of these have been: the raising of production to meet certain goals; the implementation of a large-scale modernization program to expand capacity and raise productivity; the control of inflation; the lowering of industrial costs; the subsidization of certain economic and social groups; the improvement of working conditions and labor relations; and the achievement of financial balance in the accounts of the enterprises. It is evident that these numerous objectives may sometimes conflict with each other and that at least some of them cannot, by themselves, serve as guides as to how particular operational decisions should be made.

In the popular debate over the nationalization record, various criteria of public performance have been used implicitly or explicitly. Whether or not production has increased, how productivity has moved, whether investments are "high" or "low," and—above all—whether or not the public enterprises have made money appear to be the issues upon which the attention of the layman has centered. As will be seen, some of these yardsticks are subject to severe limitations as indicators of how enterprises should be managed in the public interest.

From the standpoint of economic efficiency—i.e., maximum production for a given distribution of income—the standards of performance are different from those implicit in most statements by officials or laymen. It is possible to define what an efficient investment policy would be, and what an efficient price-output policy would be, in the sense that under efficient conditions no one person in the society could be made better off without making some other person worse off. There are numerous conditions that must prevail before it can definitely be concluded that one price-output or investment situation is better than another, and any final evaluations that may be drawn must give weight to the "non-economic" objectives that the government may be pursuing.

These different conceptions of how the enterprises should be run, together with their limitations as criteria of actual performance, will be referred to during the examination of the record of public ownership that follows. Under each heading the record is first described, and then its significance considered.

II PRODUCTION TRENDS

Of the various natural sources of energy, coal is by far the most important in France; more than two-thirds of energy consumption in 1952 was derived from coal. France is one of the important producers of coal, with production in 1929 (the prewar peak) of about 55 million tons of hard coal and lignite. Coal production was maintained at only slightly below the (depressed) 1938 level during the occupation, largely as a result of the influx of forced labor and the intensive working of the best seams. Shortly after the liberation, however, the mines were in a serious situation. The period of war and occupation had further retarded normal maintenance and re-equipment, which had been slowed down during the prolonged depression of the 1930's. The facilities in the Nord and Pas-de-Calais had been extensively damaged by bombardment. Added to a critical shortage of pit props were difficulties of transportation and shortages of trained manpower. Labor unrest was widespread. When the mines reopened in September 1944 their production was only 25-30 per cent of 1938.[1]

It has been a matter of national pride that the postwar recovery of coal production was more rapid in France than in any other country of Western Europe. In early 1945 the shortage of coal had become the foremost obstacle to economic recovery. What came to be called the "battle of coal" was successfully waged in the mines in 1945 and 1946, with the full cooperation of the miners, including communists, whose leaders had enjoined them to "produce first." Output began to rise appreciably in 1945, and by 1946 had reached 49.3 million tons, a higher level of production than in 1938. In 1947, production fell off somewhat as labor unrest and strikes in the mines reached serious proportions. Sporadic strikes also occurred in the spring of 1948, and in October the most serious postwar coal strike took place. Production for the year was only 45.1 million tons. Despite the falling-off of production in 1947 and 1948, the output of coal, supplemented by large imports, was sufficient to meet the needs considered to be "essential." (Production data for the postwar period and some prewar years can be found in Table 23.)

TABLE 23

COAL AND ELECTRICITY PRODUCTION, 1929, 1938, 1946-1954

	Coal (million tons)				*Electricity*[1] *(billion Kwh)*
	France (excluding Saar)			*Saar*	*France (excluding Saar)*
Year	*Hard Coal*	*Lignite*	*Total*	*Hard Coal*	*Total*
1929	53.8	1.2	55.0	13.6	14.4
1938	46.5	1.1	47.6	14.4	18.6
1946	47.2	2.1	49.3	7.9	22.2
1947	45.2	2.1	47.3	10.5	25.2
1948	43.3	1.8	45.1	12.6	27.7
1949	51.2	1.8	53.0	14.3	28.6
1950	50.8	1.7	52.5	15.1	31.5
1951	53.0	2.0	55.0	16.3	36.0
1952	55.4	2.0	57.4	16.2	38.5
1953	52.6	1.9	54.5	16.4	38.9
1954	54.4	1.9	56.3	16.8	42.8

Source: United States Operations Mission to France, *France Data Book—1954*, Tables H-2 and H-3 for years through 1953. For 1954, coal figure from Charbonnages de France, *Rapport de gestion exercice 1954* (Paris, 1955), p. 38, and electricity figure from the OEEC Statistical Bulletin, *General Statistics*, January 1956, p. 18.

[1] Excludes thermal plants with a capacity of less than 5,000 Kw and hydroelectric plants with a capacity of less than 1,000 Kw. These exclusions account for about 5 per cent of total electricity production.

The year 1949 marked the restoration of (comparative) labor peace, a large increase in the output of coal, and the end of the period of shortages. Since that time, fluctuations in the market situation have had a major impact on the trend of production. Thus, by the end of 1949, a reduction in the demand for coal began to be apparent as a result of the slowing down of industrial activity. The mild recession, which continued into the spring and early summer of 1950, resulted in a piling up of coal stocks.

Coal production again increased in 1951, following the upturn of economic activity as a result of the Korean war. At existing prices, however, the demand for coal quickly exceeded the supply. The coal shortage persisted throughout most of 1951, but did not attain serious proportions—except in the case of coke for the steel industry—owing to a combination of mild weather, heavy rainfall which increased hydroelectric output, and substantial coal imports. Coal production reached 55.0 million tons in 1951, and in 1952 attained an all-time high of 57.4 million tons.

By the end of 1952, the stimulus to the economy from the Korean war and French rearmament had largely spent itself. Coal production in 1953 reached only 54.5 million tons, 5 per cent less than in 1952. Despite the decline in production, record stocks of coal accumulated at the mines. To the slackening industrial demand for energy as a whole were joined the effects of increased competition from fuel oil and hydroelectric power, the latter facilitated by a year of abundant rainfall. Marketing difficulties continued in 1954, although some recovery of foreign demand made it possible to increase production above the 1953 level. Production was still below 1952, however, and 8 million tons of stocks had been piled up by the end of the year.[a] [2]

The first version of the modernization and equipment plan for the coal mines, established in 1946, had set a target for coal production of 65 million tons in 1950. This goal was drawn up under the assumption that a continuation of the balance of payments deficit would justify a policy of national autarchy. By the beginning of 1948, it was evident that the goal was unrealistic in view of the total domestic demand for energy in various forms, the comparative costs of domestic production and of feasible imports of different grades of coal, and the increased availability of substitute forms of energy. In 1948, *Charbonnages* fixed a new goal of 60 million tons for 1952; in 1952, when production was 57.4 million

[a] By way of comparison, stocks amounted to 1.3 million tons at the end of 1951.

tons, the target for the modernization and equipment plan was set at 60 million tons by 1954. The figure of 65 million tons appeared subsequently in OEEC reports, but there is some evidence that the government once more lowered its production sights in the face of the changing market. The second modernization plan apparently did not contemplate an increase in capacity beyond the level of 60 million tons.[3]

The trend of output in the electric power industry is also noteworthy. Electricity is a relatively new source of energy which has been constantly growing in importance in France. The country is well favored by nature in the water power resources of the Alps, Massif Central, and Pyrenees and of the Rhine and Rhone rivers. Thermal electric power output is less than half of total output in seasons of normal rainfall.[4]

The war caused some damage to electric installations, but its more serious consequences were the heavy use and inadequate maintenance of existing equipment and the postponement of new construction, already deferred by the crisis of the 1930's. Production recovered rapidly after the war, reaching 22.2 billion Kwh in 1946, or almost 20 per cent above the 1938 level (see Table 23). It has continued to rise, without interruption, throughout the postwar period. The recession of 1953 led to a slackening of the rate of increase, but production picked up again in 1954. For the year as a whole, electricity production was about 43 million Kwh, or double the 1946 level.[b]

Despite the substantial increases in production, the shortage of electricity was serious during the first five postwar years, necessitating rationing and periodic interruptions of current that handicapped the recovery of industrial production. The drought of 1949 sharply reduced the supply of hydroelectricity and resulted in an intensification of rationing. In 1950, a combination of several circumstances—better rainfall, the completion of new hydro and thermal installations, and a decline in industrial demand—led to the removal of most of the restrictions on domestic and industrial consumption. The remainder of the restrictions was removed in the spring of 1951.

[b] Virtually all electricity is produced by publicly-owned enterprises, but not all by *Electricité de France* (EDF). EDF accounts for 80-90 per cent of hydroelectric production, the remainder coming from the *Compagnie Nationale du Rhône*. With respect to thermal electricity, EDF controls only about 50 per cent of the output of major producers. The coal mines and nationalized railways have been increasingly important producers of thermal electricity, and the thermal plants of EDF have been used primarily to meet peak demands and during years of low rainfall.

The original production goal of the Monnet Plan called for total electricity output of 39.5 billion Kwh by 1951. Actual production was close to the intermediate goals in 1947 and 1948, but fell behind in 1949 and 1950. In December 1949, the *Commissariat Général du Plan* raised the goal to 43 billion Kwh, postponing its realization until 1953. Production fell short of the goal in 1953 as a result of slackening demand, but reached it in 1954. The goals of the second plan called for an increase in production to 70 billion Kwh annually in the period 1960-1962. This was based on the assumption that the general "law" whereby consumption in most industrial countries doubles every ten years would remain approximately valid for France in the next decade as it did in the past one.

What significance may be attached to these production trends? The rapid recovery of coal production during the critical period immediately after the war was a notable achievement. As a general proposition, however, rising production is not necessarily a sign of "good" performance nor declining production a sign of "poor" performance, although in many popular and official discussions they are so considered. Continual increases in output for a particular product sound impressive, but in a properly functioning economy there are industries that decline and others that grow, both at a variety of rates. The most efficient output depends on a number of factors that affect the costs of the industry and the value of its product; also, for defense or social reasons, the government may attach values to some products different from those of consumers. Thus, it is not intuitively clear whether coal or electricity production should have increased more or less rapidly during the postwar period, or whether the most efficient allocation of resources among coal, water power, and fuel would require more or less coal or electricity production at the present time. By the same token, whether or not the production goals fixed by planners were attained is not a satisfactory test of the industry's performance, unless those goals are known to be consistent with an efficient allocation of resources. As indicated in Chapter 2, analyses of comparative efficiency did not usually play an important role in the setting of these goals.

III EMPLOYMENT AND PRODUCTIVITY

The initial increases in coal production were brought about mainly through a massive increase in the number of coal miners and a slight increase in the length of the working day. At the time of liberation, the mine labor force was substantially below prewar; from a total of about 290,000 workers in 1929 and 1930, it had fallen to around 120,000 at the end of 1944. Many of the younger skilled miners had left the mines, and absenteeism was high among those that remained. Unrest was prevalent among the large contingent of foreign workers. A large increase in the mine labor force was achieved in the period through 1947, in part through the employment of about 55,000 German prisoners of war.

With the exception of short-run increases in employment during periods of intensive demand for coal, the trend of employment in the mines has been consistently downwards since the end of 1947, despite the higher levels of production. The reduction in employment in the mines in 1948 was at the outset more a matter of necessity than of planning, arising from the loss of German prisoners of war and the repatriation of Polish miners. Despite efforts to hire additional French or immigrant labor, employment fell below the programmed level. With the termination of the period of coal shortage in 1949-1950, greater stability in the labor force was achieved and an orderly program of reductions undertaken. In 1952, with record coal production, employment was about 15 per cent below the highest prewar level; it fell further in 1953, and by 1954 had dropped to 217,000.[5] Despite these reductions it was necessary for some of the mines to close down periodically in 1953 and 1954 to cut back the production of unmarketable stocks.

The productivity of the coal miners has generally varied inversely with the number employed. The dislocations attendant on the liberation were reflected in the fact that output per worker in 1945 was less than 75 per cent of prewar. Productivity (i.e., output per worker) recovered only slowly in 1946 and 1947, owing to the large turnover of workers, heavy reliance on unskilled labor, and the obsolescence of much mining equipment. The restoration of labor stability in 1949 and 1950 coincided with the first results of the large-scale program of new investment in the mines. By 1954 productivity had increased to a level substantially in excess of the highest prewar year. The following figures reveal the marked increase in productivity in the mines since their nationalization.[6]

Average Coal Output Per Underground Worker Per Shift (in Kilograms)

1930	984	1949	1,099
1938	1,227	1950	1,203
1945	893	1951	1,309
1946	935	1952	1,364
1947	959	1953	1,429
1948	975	1954	1,519

Data compiled by the OEEC suggest that the rise of productivity in the French mines compares favorably with the experience of the other major coal-producing countries of Western Europe.[7]

Labor productivity has little meaning in an industry that is as capital-intensive as the production and distribution of electricity, and no index of productivity is published. While production has doubled since the war, there has been only a slight increase in the number of personnel (8 per cent between 1946 and 1954).[8]

In the case of the national railways, there has been a fairly steady decrease in the number of SNCF employees during the postwar period. There were 427,000 employees on the rolls in 1936 and, as a result of a reduction in the work week, 515,000 in 1938. By 1954 the number of employees had dropped to 383,000.[9] This sizable reduction is due to several factors, among them: a lengthening of the work week; increased mechanization of rail services; and a considerable loss of traffic in recent years to competing forms of transportation. Despite the reductions, there is still some evidence of excessive employment in the railway system.[10] A "productivity index" published by the SNCF shows a spectacular increase, from 48 "traffic-units" per hour worked in 1938 and 59 in 1946 to 81 in 1954.[11]

Once again, it is necessary to be clear on the limited significance of the productivity figures. Changes in productivity may come about through changes in capital equipment, training of workers, or methods of organizing production. With respect to the industrial economy as a whole, higher productivity from these factors can be regarded as evidence of material progress. On the other hand, changes in productivity per worker in a particular industry may merely reflect a change in the scale of output. Thus, if production is reduced by combining existing capital equipment with fewer workers, productivity per worker may rise sharply simply because activity is declining. It is also possible to increase productivity per worker sharply by an intensive investment program, although the level of investment and scale of output may be excessive (in terms of efficiency) for the industry in question. Hence, while it is desirable to increase productivity with a given labor force, it is not desirable to increase productivity in a particular industry in *any* way that this can be accomplished. And the record with respect to productivity, while it is suggestive, may also be misleading unless other aspects of performance are examined in relation to it.

IV INVESTMENTS

It will be recalled that the urgency of the need for reconstruction and modernization of the basic industries was considered a reason for nationalization. Private investment in coal and electricity had been low before the war, and some of the projects were believed to be beyond the financial capacity of private enterprise. A massive investment program has in fact been undertaken in these industries since the war, within the framework of the modernization and equipment plan.

The plan for the modernization of the mines has officially had two closely related objectives: to increase production and to increase labor productivity. The coal investment projects fall under four categories: long-term projects, concerned primarily with the expansion of extractive capacity through new shaft sinkings, modernization and extension of screening and washing facilities, etc.; medium-term projects, directed towards the maintenance of existing production capacity through annual expenditures for the replacement of obsolescent equipment; investments in the auxiliary non-mining industries (thermal power plants located at the mines, cokeries and briquetting plants, and plants for the manufacture of synthetic nitrogen from byproducts); and a housing program, which plays an important part in the efforts to establish a permanent labor force. The relative importance of these categories of projects can be gathered from the data on investment expenditures given in Table 24.[12]

The modernization and equipment plan for electricity has been by far the largest segment of the overall plan. The objectives of the plan are threefold: (a) to bring into production the full hydroelectric potential of the Alps, Pyrenees and Massif Central and of the Rhine and Rhone rivers; (b) to modernize existing thermal power plants and to create new plants for the utilization of waste or byproducts of coal extraction and iron and steel production; and (c) to construct additional installations for the transmission and distribution of electricity. *Electricité de France* has been the principal organization concerned in the first and third of these objectives. The *Compagnie Nationale du Rhône* has also played a part, while the second has involved *Charbonnages de France*, the SNCF, and the steel industry to a larger extent.[13] As indicated in Table 25, hydroelectric construction has been the most important element of the investment program.

TABLE 24

INVESTMENTS REALIZED IN THE NATIONALIZED COAL MINES, 1948-1954
(billions of current francs)

	1948	*1949*	*1950*	*1951*	*1952*	*1953*	*1954*
Long-term projects	12.4	24.9	20.3	20.0	29.3	26.8	23.6
Medium-term projects	12.2	13.7	13.3	13.5	16.6	17.4	18.2
Housing and social activities	13.0	7.7	3.3	2.1	3.8	6.5	7.2
Auxiliary industrial plants[1]	11.8	19.1	25.7	30.0	38.9	33.8	27.3
Total	49.4	65.4	62.6	65.6	88.6	84.5	76.3

Source: Derived from data in the annual *Rapports de gestion* of Charbonnages de France, except for 1953 which was taken from Commissariat Général au Plan, *Rapport annuel sur l'exécution du plan de modernisation et d'équipement de l'Union française* (Paris, 1954), pp. 130, 159, 172, 180.

[1] Electricity, coke and gas, fertilizers.

TABLE 25

INVESTMENTS REALIZED IN ELECTRICITY, 1946-1954
(billions of current francs)

	1946-1948	*1949*	*1950*	*1951*	*1952*	*1953*	*1954*
Electricité de France							
Hydro	73.0	56.6	56.0	52.5	58.1	31.3	22.9
Thermal	15.0	13.6	13.7	10.4	11.1	15.2	19.7
Transmission	13.1	11.3	12.1	12.2	24.2	21.9	15.5
Distribution	23.9 (Distribution and Associated Projects combined)	13.0	14.6	19.7	24.5	24.6	35.9
Associated Projects		11.5	16.0	18.8	19.4	17.3	17.9
Total	125.0	106.0	112.4	113.6	137.3	110.3	111.9
Others[1]	36.6	34.6	39.1	43.4	46.5	28.7	n.a.
Total	161.6	140.6	151.5	157.0	183.8	139.0	n.a.

Sources: Commissariat Général du Plan: *Quatre ans d'exécution du plan de modernisation et d'équipement de l'Union française* (Paris, 1951), p. 92; *Rapport sur la réalisation du plan de modernisation et d'équipement de l'Union française, année 1952* (Paris, 1953), p. 119; *Rapport annuel sur l'exécution du plan de modernisation et d'équipement de l'Union française* (Paris, 1954), p. 173; and Electricité de France, *Rapport d'activité, comptes de gestion, exercice 1954* (Paris, 1955), p. 65.

[1] Includes Compagnie Nationale du Rhône, Charbonnages de France, Société Nationale des Chemins de Fer Français, and the steel industry.

Realization of the investment programs in coal and electricity has been beset with financial difficulties. Inflation discouraged the investment of private savings in the nationalized industries, since private investment in these publicly-owned enterprises was restricted to fixed-interest obligations, the yield of which was highly vulnerable to inflationary price rises. The large deficits incurred in early years, the delays in indemnifying the former stockholders and the somewhat cavalier attitude displayed towards them, also discouraged private investors. The price policies adopted in early years (see below) seriously limited the possibilities of self-financing. As a result, *Charbonnages* and *Electricité de France* were obliged initially to resort heavily to medium-term bank borrowing at high interest rates for financing investments; shortly thereafter, the Treasury, through the Modernization and Equipment Fund, became the principal source of investment funds. These funds were available for longer time periods and at more favorable rates. While government loans have remained the principal method of financing, it has been possible in recent years to rely more heavily on self-financing through depreciation reserves and on borrowing from the public in the form of medium-term bond issues with a built-in guarantee against inflation (for example, by indexing the annual income and the capital value to the wholesale price of coal or the average price of electricity).

The investment programs have thus been largely dependent on an annual vote of public funds by Parliament to the Modernization and Equipment Fund. Delays and reductions in the program have been brought about by the blockage or curtailment of investment appropriations in the interests of budgetary economy, the control of inflation, and (later) national defense. The effect on actual investment expenditures (in real terms) is particularly noticeable after 1949. The planning and realization of long-range projects have also been handicapped by the need for annual appropriations.

Despite errors in programming judgment, some false starts, and cutbacks in available funds, an extensive investment program has been carried out in both coal and electricity. Some financial measure of the size of the coal investment program is given by the fact that during the period 1949-1951 investment expenditures were about one-third of gross receipts.[14] Investments by *Electricité de France* between 1947 and 1953 represented 70 per cent of the value of sales over this period.[15] In comparison with the prewar situation, the hydroelectric installations brought into service between 1946 and 1953 represent a production potential six times greater than that of new installations during the years 1933-1940; in thermal electric capacity, the postwar effort is ten times greater.[16]

Officials of the nationalized enterprises have pointed with satisfaction to the large investment effort that has been realized, and to the increases in capacity and in labor productivity that have followed from it. In turn, critics have asserted that the investment effort was achieved only at the cost of prolonged inflation and the sacrifice of more worthwhile investments in other (private) sectors of the economy. The relationship of the investment program (in which the nationalized industries occupied a major role) to the inflationary problem has been discussed in a previous chapter. With respect to the second criticism, it is obvious that the goal of public policy must be something other than to maximize the volume of investments in nationalized enterprises. The economist's test of "efficient" performance is that investment in each industry should be expanded until the value of additional investment is equal to its cost (i.e., to its value in other uses). If investment is not expanded to this point, resources are being misallocated, since additional investments would yield a higher return in this industry than in other uses. Conversely, if investment is expanded beyond this point, resources are also being misallocated, since they would yield higher returns in other uses than the one in question.

This is a crude and vastly oversimplified description of the criterion of efficiency, and there are many difficulties attached to its practical application. But, in any case, about all that can be said with respect to the investment decisions of the nationalized industries is that such a criterion was not applied in any comprehensive or systematic fashion. The key decisions on the allocation of investment resources to the "basic sectors" were made at a time when the imperative was considered to be "produce (and invest) at any price," and estimates of alternative costs and returns did not play a major part.[c]

In a few instances where the choice was between alternative investments that would produce the same physical output, more can be said. Thus, the fundamental choice with respect to the relative emphasis on thermal power plants and hydroelectric installations

[c] Cf. the discussion in Chapter 2 above. The coal modernization committee, for example, observed simply that the modernization program would reduce costs by 18 per cent and that "such a result. . .would amply suffice to justify the investments demanded by the Modernization Plan." (Quoted by Pierre Maillet, "Politique de l'énergie et expansion économique," *Les Cahiers économiques*, May 1954, pp. 6-7.)

was made on the assumption that the coal shortage would be chronic. This assumption proved incorrect, at least with respect to the first postwar decade, and it appears that more investment in thermal power and less in water power could probably have produced the same amount of electricity at lower cost and with greater regularity. As a result of some study of alternative costs and returns, the second plan was intended to redress the balance in favor of thermal electricity.[17] The second plan also contained the more auspicious comment that "it is no longer a question of producing energy at any price, but of selling it at the best price."[18]

V WAGES AND SOCIAL SECURITY

The principal change in labor remuneration brought about through nationalization has been a broad extension of social benefits rather than a modification of relative wage rates. A possible exception is the coal industry where, at least in the early post-nationalization period, wage rates were considerably higher than in the Paris metallurgical industries or in French industry as a whole. The disparity has been attributed by *Charbonnages de France* to the hazardous conditions of mine work and the difficulties of labor recruitment. There is inadequate evidence to determine whether the higher wage policy has been altered now that there is a surplus of mine labor in some areas. The personnel statutes established for *Electricité de France* and *Gaz de France* fixed approximately the same schedule of wages as then prevailed in private mechanical industries. It does not appear that wage rates are higher in these nationalized industries, or in the SNCF, than in comparable private employment. Some differential in favor of the nationalized industries may have been achieved, however, through the reclassification of workers.[19]

A new development in the wage field has been the establishment of wage incentive schemes or productivity bonuses of some sort in most of the public enterprises. As a result both of successive increases in the schedule of payments and of increases in productivity, bonus payments by *Charbonnages* rose from 2.3 per cent of direct wages in 1949 to 9 per cent in 1954. In the case of the *Renault* company, the workers also share in the net (distributed) profits of the automotive firm.

One of the major gains of labor in the nationalized industries was the adoption of personnel statutes that, in most instances, substantially enlarged the systems of social security and allied benefits relative to the programs previously in existence or to those applicable to private enterprise. These gains have been jealously guarded by the trade unions, and (unsuccessful) efforts by the government to reduce their scale have figured in a number of postwar strikes. Although this reliance on non-wage rather than wage benefits has been an important postwar development throughout French industry, it is particularly pronounced in the nationalized sector.

In the case of the coal mines, non-wage payments related to labor amounted to over 82 per cent of wage payments in 1954, as indicated by the following figures. The comparable percentage is about 42 per cent for private and public industries combined.

Non-wage Payments as a Per Cent of Wage Payments[20]

Family allowances	15.5
Old age insurance	8.2
Sickness and maternity insurance	5.5
Workmen's compensation	7.2
Vocational training	2.6
Paid vacations[d]	12.1
Payroll tax[d]	5.0
Housing	14.2
Heating	7.3
Transportation	1.9
Miscellaneous indemnities	2.8
	82.3

The fringe benefits of personnel of *Electricité de France* and *Gaz de France* include such favorable features as: one month's paid vacation each year; two months' wages in case of marriage; full wages while on military service for fathers and 20 per cent of wages for bachelors; up to three years of full wages in case of illness; and one month's wages for the first child, one and one-half months' for the second and third, and two months' for the fourth. The age of retirement was set at 55 years for active workers and 60 years for sedentary workers, with the result that pension payments are among the highest in France. In 1949, total benefits under these various programs amounted to 64 per cent of direct wage payments. Employees of EDF also receive special benefits in the form of electricity, gas, coke and coal provided free or at reduced rates. A fund for social activities of the employees has been

[d] Vacation pay is frequently shown as part of the direct wage bill in other countries. The payroll tax is not, of course, a social benefit to the employee (in fact, as indicated in Chapter 6, he probably bears the burden of this tax).

established, and is generously endowed by a 1 per cent levy on gross sales.[21]

Railway employees benefit from a special system of social security, some features of which are over forty years old. One of the more unusual benefits is fare concessions to parents, grandparents, and in-laws of permanent personnel. Family allowances are considerably higher than under the regular social security system. The most significant feature from the standpoint of the financial solvency of the SNCF, however, is the pension system. Locomotive engineers and other active employees retire at the age of 50, while sedentary employees retire at 55. Since these provisions have been in force for a long period, the number of pensioned employees is now very high. In 1954, it was expected that the number of persons receiving pension benefits would be greater than the number of current employees. Total payments from the retirement fund in 1954 were expected to reach the imposing figure of 84 billion francs, of which only 8 billion would be covered by current employee contributions. The sum of all social payments, including pensions, amounted to 108 per cent of direct wage payments in 1954.[22]

The *Régie Renault* has attempted to fulfill, at least in part, the responsibility conferred upon it by the legislators to act as a "model enterprise" within the automobile industry by instituting an extensive program of social benefits (as well as incentive schemes and higher overtime pay rates). More liberal benefits than those provided by private competitors are given in case of death, old age, or marriage.

In the aggregate these policies have led to a higher rate of labor remuneration (through higher wage rates and/or social security payments) in the nationalized industries. Also, to some extent these policies may have established a pattern that has resulted in an increase in social payments to labor elsewhere in the economy. Whether the real income or aggregate "welfare" of the working class as a whole has been increased as a result of these measures—in accordance with one of the announced goals of nationalization—is less clear. It depends on the effect of increases in the rate of labor remuneration on the demand for labor in these and other industries, an effect which is difficult to determine empirically. However, the policy of enlarged benefits—to the extent that it has not been followed in private enterprise—has probably impaired the usefulness of the price system in allocating resources in several ways. It may attract more labor, or perhaps higher quality labor, into industries where it is not necessarily more valuable. For example, a worker with a large family might be drawn to a nationalized industry on account of the higher family allowances even if he were a highly skilled and more productive worker in some other industry. This practice also has dissociated still more labor payments from productivity, presumably with some impairment of incentives. The emphasis on early retirement is particularly significant; a country that has great need for a larger total output can ill afford to retire its workers at the age of 50 or 55.

VI LABOR RELATIONS

There is perhaps no phase of the nationalization experience in which the gap between expectations and realizations is as great as in the field of labor relations. The nationalization of industry was to be the leading, but not the only, element in the "social liberation" expected to follow after the war. The failure of the tripartite principle which was to assure effective labor participation through the boards of directors of the nationalized enterprises has already been alluded to. As has been seen, the position of labor in the public industries is more favorable than in the private sector with respect to wages and non-wage benefits combined. Despite this advantage, there appears to have been little change in the climate of labor relations in France as a result of the nationalizations.[23]

Labor-management relations in the coal industry were already strained before the war. The war and occupation accentuated the problem, and the wholesale purging of managers and engineers following the liberation helped to create an atmosphere of indiscipline and lack of authority in the mines. Several waves of strikes broke out in 1947 and early 1948; the climax was reached with the coal strike of October and November 1948. The 1948 strike had numerous and varied origins, and changed in character as it evolved. The immediate and official cause was a decree which strengthened the disciplinary features of the Miner's Code and provided for a reduction in the number of surface workers and a minor reorganization of the social security system. Also involved was a political test of strength on issues not directly related to the mines themselves. The strike, marked with violence from the outset, assumed the appearance of open political warfare between the government and the communist-dominated CGT when the latter gave instructions to withdraw the mine security personnel and the socialist Minister of Interior ordered the troops into the mines. The strike effort had petered out, and many workers had returned to the mines, when the CGT officially terminated it on November 28, almost eight weeks after its start. The close of the 1948 strike introduced a period of comparative labor peace in the mines, which has continued without serious interruption although there have been a number of lesser strike activities.[24]

Labor-management relations in the electrical industry have not been marked by strikes of the violence and intensity witnessed in the coal mines, whère the trade-union movement was more developed at the outset. More limited strikes, related to grievances in the field of wages and social security benefits, have been a comparatively frequent occurrence. Also, the trade unions of all of the nationalized enterprises have participated jointly in nation-wide strikes throughout the public sector or in union-wide strikes in public and private enterprises.

The "general strike" of August 1953 in the public sector (including some parts of the civil service) illustrated how wide the breach is between government and labor in the public enterprises. The immediate cause of the strike was a series of "economy" decrees, which in their original version provided for: (a) a reduction in the number of state employees (by cancelling vacancies) and a limitation on new recruitment; (b) an extension of the age of normal retirement by two years; and (c) a reclassification of the categories of active and sedentary workers for retirement purposes. Workers in the nationalized industries were included in the retirement provisions "in principle" but with some exceptions, such as miners and railway engineers.

The non-communist unions took the initiative at the outset of the strike, accusing the government of going back on the nationalization statutes and "attacking acquired rights."[25] At its height, the walkout was almost complete in the postal, telephone, and telegraph services, gas and electricity, the SNCF, the banks, the coal mines, and many categories of municipal employees. Despite the government's attempts to provide emergency services, a substantial part of the activity of the country was brought almost to a halt. The workers' enthusiasm for the strike movement apparently surprised even the union leaders, who have been described as "following their troops" into the field. That the economy decrees were not the only factor is indicated by a Catholic trade union spokesman who said:

> There are two reasons for the success of the movement: the decrees, the terms of which have been felt very strongly by the workers, and also the growing dissatisfaction of the workers with regard to the social policy of the present Government and of those which have preceded it. This policy attacks the social gains of labor and does not have the effect of bringing about the economic recovery of the country. The workers no longer have confidence in the men in power.[e] [26]

The strike had no precise objective and ended, as it had begun, in an atmosphere of confusion. The government abandoned the decree to reclassify active and sedentary workers before it was issued; it subsequently indicated that it would give a "liberal" interpretation to the exceptions to be granted in the nationalized industries and that the interested trade unions would be consulted before the retirement decrees were applied.[f] Other government concessions were granted in the fields of collective bargaining and the determination of the minimum wage.

In this and similar nation-wide strikes, French labor has been pitted not against the management of the individual enterprises, but directly against the government, which has had the final responsibility in wage and related matters. The government has therefore been unable to act as an independent mediator, and strikes in the nationalized industries have assumed the regrettable character of challenges to the sovereignty and authority of the state.

The layman, the government official, and the economist are likely to agree that "good" labor relations (somehow defined) are an important objective of public policy in the nationalized industries. Even without a more precise definition, it is reasonably clear that this goal has not been attained in France. But labor discontent in the public sector is only a chapter in the larger record of the "social liberation" which did not attain its objectives, and this discontent is not solely a function of the operation of the nationalized enterprises as such.

[e] Professor Ellul, commenting on the strike shortly after it ended, concluded: "Only a profound discontent can explain the adherence to these strikes. And not a discontent on a specific point of wages or decrees, but general, latent, constant, permanent. The strikes have been followed . . . because they permitted an explosion of this generalized discontent. They have been a sort of protest against everything." (*Le Monde*, September 9, 1953, p. 5).

[f] This somewhat vague agreement seems to indicate that the retirement decrees would not be applied automatically. The government has apparently decided subsequently not to attempt to implement any of the retirement decrees.

VII PRICE POLICIES AND FINANCIAL RESULTS

A. LEGISLATIVE BACKGROUND

Since some of the chief differences between "public" and "private" interests are believed to center upon the earning of profits, it might be expected that the legislation would be explicit about the financial results that the nationalized enterprises should seek and hence the price policies that they should adopt. In fact the postwar legislation is somewhat ambiguous, though there is some evidence that the management was expected to earn profits, or at least to break even financially.

The enabling legislation of *Charbonnages de France* and the *houillères de bassin* (nine regional units, organized according to the principal coal basins) specifies that these enterprises of an "industrial and commercial character" must observe, in matters of financial and accounting management, the customary rules of business concerns. As has been mentioned, the emphasis on this characteristic apparently reflects the view that business concerns are efficiently managed while public agencies suffer from excessive bureaucratization. The word "profit" does not appear in the statute of *Charbonnages.* On the other hand, each basin is responsible for assuring the financial equilibrium of its operations, taking into account all costs relating to it, including interest and depreciation. The meaning of this provision is somewhat confused by the fact that *Charbonnages* is authorized to operate a compensating fund among basins to provide for their financial equilibrium.[g] One article contains the interesting provision that, in case the operations of a fiscal year should end in a deficit, the continuance in office of the responsible administrators requires the express approval of a body charged with the auditing review. A further clue to the expectations of the legislators is contained in a subsequent decree that defines the net operating profit of the *houillères* and specifies the uses to which this profit can be put. First priority is assigned to the amortization of the obligations paid as indemnities to the former stockholders.[h] The remaining surplus is to be divided three ways: up to one-fifth may be given to social services for the personnel; the balance may be used for the creation of reserve funds to finance

[g] This compensation fund has been used in practice as a means of reducing the bookkeeping deficits of some of the mines by levies on the more profitable ones. The amount of such compensations has been around 1.5 or 2 billion francs annually during the postwar period.

[h] As a matter of bookkeeping practice, the indemnities now appear to be deducted as a cost before arriving at the profit to be distributed.

investments or paid to the state in its capacity as owner of the mines. Essentially similar provisions are found in the gas and electricity statutes. None of the statutes specifies the price or output policies which might be expected to yield these profits.

In the case of the SNCF, the agreement of 1937 indicated that, as a general principle, the company was expected to achieve and maintain financial equilibrium by adjustments in its prices (i.e., rates). If rate increases were required to restore balance, they were to be proposed by the SNCF and to become effective unless opposed by the government. If the government, for reasons presumably connected with the public interest, objected to a justifiable increase it had to pay the SNCF a "compensating indemnity" in an amount equal to the estimated additional receipts from the proposed increase. The government could also request a rate reduction, provided that it paid an indemnity for the resulting loss of revenue. The government was to provide reimbursable, interest-bearing treasury advances to cover any operating deficits that might remain at the end of a fiscal year, but in the long run the SNCF was expected to be in equilibrium through an appropriate rate policy, together with the indemnities paid by the state for enforced departures from that policy.

The indemnity features of the original SNCF statutes still remain in force, but subsequent modifications of other provisions have enlarged the financial assistance provided by the government on a regular basis. The principal modifications were introduced in July 1952, when a major reform of the 1937 agreement was undertaken. The government contributes 60 per cent of the cost of maintenance of the railroad infrastructure (stations, signals, roadbeds, etc.) and 50 per cent of the expenses for control stations at grade crossings over the national highways. The SNCF is obliged in turn to pay a "duty" to the government, which began at 2 per cent in 1952 and is to reach 5 per cent of total receipts by 1958. The government has also taken over a portion of the heavy pension payments of the SNCF, those resulting from the retirement after January 1, 1949 of SNCF employees who are not replaced. Finally, if the SNCF accounts remain in deficit despite all economy efforts and feasible rate adjustments, the government provides an "equilibrating subsidy" to be reimbursed from future surpluses (if any).

In the case of *Renault*, it has apparently been considered that the company should be operated along normal commercial lines and for maximum profit with, however, labor benefiting from participation in the management and in the profits of the firm. The unique status of the company has necessitated the working out of a modus vivendi between it and the government, which differs from the practices generally followed in other public enterprises. In order to keep *Renault*'s competitors on an equal footing, the company does not receive financial support from the state, either for the financing of its current operations (or of any deficits in which they might result) or for its modernization and equipment program. This should not be surprising in a firm that enjoyed considerable profits before the war, but it is in marked contrast with the situation in the "key" nationalized industries.

B. ACTUAL POLICIES

What in fact did the nationalized industries do about adjusting their prices in order to achieve these or other financial objectives? In practice, policies appear to have evolved in a highly pragmatic fashion with each decision determined largely by immediate political, economic, and social factors. Broadly speaking, however, the price policies of the nationalized industries appear to have gone through two main stages. During the first years following nationalization, a policy of low prices was more or less systematically pursued. The application of price increases followed cost increases with a considerable time lag, and the companies had large operating deficits. Instead of frequent, slight increases in prices in the face of continually mounting costs, price adjustments were made infrequently and in large amounts. A realignment of many industrial prices took place on each occasion.

The disparity between costs and prices is illustrated by the fact that the average cost of a ton of merchant coal was 1,987 francs in 1947 while the average price was 1,461 francs.[27] Moreover, the costs included only very inadequate allowances for depreciation. In view of the critical coal shortage and the high price of imports, it would have been possible to market coal at considerably higher prices if the government had chosen to do so. The most celebrated, although somewhat extreme, example of the kind of price decisions that were made in the early years occurred in July 1946. The board of *Charbonnages*, largely controlled by the trade unions and particularly by the CGT, voted a 25 per cent increase in wages but stated that no increase in prices would be required, an opinion in which the communist Minister of Industrial Production subsequently concurred.

In the case of electricity, a highly complex maze of industrial and domestic rates, inherited from the pre-nationalization period, was carried over by the nationalization statute. The basic rate procedure applied by the government to electric utilities during the 1930's was the use of an "economic index" whereby changes in the price of electricity were made in accordance with a composite index which included wages, the price of coal, and indices of general prices. There were many individual variations in applying the formula, however, and the base period was different for different enterprises. Although the "economic index" procedure was still largely followed after nationalization, the prices actually charged were deliberately set below those that would have resulted from its automatic application.

The explanation of this low-price policy is several-fold. The government reportedly did not wish one of the first results of nationalization to be a sharp increase in prices. Of the more strictly economic considerations, perhaps the most important was the attempt to control the mounting inflation by keeping down the prices of basic materials and services (though this simultaneously entailed the injection of additional purchasing power via extra government subsidies). Of less importance, there was a feeling that the management of the public enterprises would grow lax if the financial situation were too favorable, and that the earning of profits would encourage the trade unions to demand higher wages. These considerations outweighed any interest which the government might have had in raising the price of energy and transportation as a means of rationing their use during the period of shortages.

The first important modifications of this policy were made at the end of 1948. A realignment of coal prices in October 1948 brought about a more favorable cost-price relationship, but the new prices still did not permit an adequate allowance for depreciation. Coal prices were not increased in 1949 and 1950; in 1951 they were raised on three occasions as a result of increases in wages and other costs. This time the price increases occurred more promptly, and the third increase was expressly made large enough to create a wider margin for depreciation and self-financing of investment. In 1951, the average level of coal prices was above average costs for the first time, a situation reflected in the improved financial position of the coal enterprises. Similarly, the economic index formula used for electricity rate-making was adjusted in 1951, apparently so that it would be followed more closely in the future and would allow a more adequate margin for self-financed investment. The rates charged by the national railways also followed these general trends.

Among the principal reasons for this gradual shift was the end of the first postwar period of inflation which, combined with a gradual rightward movement of successive coalition governments, resulted in some relaxation of price and other direct controls. Also, the large deficits of the nationalized enterprises, taken by critics as prima facie evidence of failures of management, had caused unfavorable public reactions. At the same time, the government found it difficult to resist the pressure of consumers (mostly industrial) who objected to the notion that the public enterprises should earn a profit at their "expense." A situation of "no-profit, no-loss" apparently became the *summum bonum* of government action; that is, the one which would minimize adverse criticism of the public management. A final factor that helped swing the government to the no-profit, no-loss objective was that improvements in productivity made it easier to equilibrate the accounts of the public enterprises without sharp price increases.

Price policies thus evolved to the stage where the most general objective that appears to be pursued is that of equating average prices to average costs (including depreciation) so that the enterprises are in financial equilibrium. In the case of coal, conversations with officials of *Charbonnages* indicate that this is the general policy, with each coal basin treated as a unit for pricing purposes. Several studies have been undertaken at the request of *Charbonnages* to consider the feasibility of adopting a policy of pricing in accordance with marginal cost (i.e., the incremental cost of producing an additional unit of coal) rather than average cost. The conclusion of the principal of these studies was that pricing in accordance with marginal costs would result in a substantial increase in the level of coal prices (on the average about 35 per cent). The policy has been rejected, apparently on the grounds that a price increase of this magnitude would adversely affect coal-consuming industries and would cause a shift to imported coal (requiring additional foreign exchange) or to other domestic energy resources. Such a shift, it is argued, would not be justified unless other producers (foreign and domestic) also uniformly followed a marginal-cost pricing policy.[28]

In the case of electricity, the official policies of EDF in the establishment of rates are currently two-fold: non-discrimination among consumers of the same "kind" of electricity in the same region; and price discrimination among consumers of different "kinds" of electricity on the basis of differences in the cost of service. Among the numerous cost factors that are involved in the determination of differential rates are the kind of electricity (thermal or hydro), the distance of transmission, distribution voltage, the duration of use, and the season, day, and hour. Each kind of service is in principle sold to the consumer at a rate that covers all long-run costs of production and distribution, including interest and depreciation necessary for an "adequate" level of maintenance and new investment. To the extent that this differential-cost principle has been applied, it appears to have been based largely on some approximate measure of the average cost of production. An experiment in the use of marginal cost as the basis of differentiating electrical rates has been under way since 1952 in connection with some of the high-tension rates for industrial users. The experiment is still at too early a stage for definitive results to be known. It should be noted, however, that the "economic index" procedure, from which EDF has only been able to extricate itself in part, gives, at best, an imperfect measure of the average or marginal cost of providing electricity.[29]

The structure of railroad rates is also currently based on the broad principle that rates should vary in accordance with costs so that financial equilibrium is attained. Maximum and minimum prices are fixed by the government, within which the SNCF is free to adjust rates without prior approval in accordance with actual costs of transportation. It is often not clear in the legislation to which category of "costs" prices or rates are, in principle, to be related. Some research has been devoted by the SNCF to the question of determining how economic and social welfare can be maximized in an industry subjected to decreasing costs (so that pricing in accordance with marginal cost would result in deficits), which is expected to equilibrate its budget. An elaborate theoretical solution has been worked out,[30] but is far from the stage of practical application. It appears in practice that the "costs" to which the recent legislation refers, or on which price calculations are based, are some general concept of average cost. The adjustment of prices to average costs, whether or not it would achieve the optimum of economic welfare, is considered by the SNCF to have the concrete advantage of avoiding the political and financial hazards of large operating deficits.

C. EXCEPTIONS

There are a number of exceptions, some of major importance, to the general rule of no-profits, no-losses through average-cost pricing. Some of the higher cost coal mines have been unable, over protracted periods of time, to market their coal at prices that would cover average costs because of competition from other basins and foreign sources. This problem became more general in the French mines during the crisis in the European coal market of 1953-1954, and many of the basins were obliged to quote prices below costs. Conversely, some of the more favorably situated coal basins have, at least on occasion, been permitted to take advantage of the market situation in order to earn profits. Competition from fuel oil has also compelled the mines to lower their prices on some occasions, although the preferred solution of *Charbonnages* is to "coordinate" relations between fuel oil and coal so as to reduce the competition.[1]

The rates actually charged by the SNCF also deviate from average costs in some cases, because of the market situation. Inroads into rail traffic made by the trucking companies have necessitated a system of "defensive" rates designed to maintain output in the face of this competition. These rates, while below average costs, more than cover the variable (out-of-pocket) costs of handling the freight. As long as a part of the rail network must operate below cost, the incentive to reduce rates on other traffic on which the SNCF can more than cover its costs is weakened.[31] An answer to the problem of road competition is also being sought through a program for the "coordination of transportation," which has been the subject of lively Parliamentary debate but little concrete action for more than two decades. To the SNCF, coordination of transportation apparently means either agreement on non-competitive rate schedules or, if competition must be maintained, "equalization of costs" (that is, raising the cost of trucking services) by compelling trucking companies to observe the same kinds of published schedules, fixed itineraries, standards of public comfort, and infrastructure costs as the railways.[32] (The SNCF proposals do not, of course, include an "equalization" of the heavy tax on petroleum products which trucking companies pay.)

[1] This "coordination" has taken the form of an agreement, approved by the government, to limit the domestic sales of fuel oil in 1954. *Charbonnages* has also been able to persuade the government to raise the price of fuel oil, and has attempted to have the government impose higher taxes on petroleum products on the grounds that coal is taxed more heavily. (Cf. *Le Monde*, November 13, 1954,

Another series of exceptions arises from the continuance, although on a somewhat reduced scale, of the government's preoccupation with the level of costs and prices in industry as a whole. Thus, in 1952, the mines were obliged to lower their prices by 4 per cent as part of the price-reduction program of the Pinay government, despite their precarious financial position at the time. During 1953 and 1954, government pressures were frequently exerted on *Charbonnages* and EDF to reduce their prices in order to lower the industrial costs of energy, and a number of selective price reductions were carried out. More generally, the price ceilings which have been continuously in effect since August 1952 have curtailed the flexibility of the nationalized enterprises in adjusting prices to changes in costs.[33]

A third set of exceptions to the general principle of average-cost pricing has been due to the government's desire to subsidize particular business or consumer groups. Thus, beginning in December 1947, EDF was obliged to sell electricity to a list of "protected" industries (nitrogenous fertilizers, zinc, sodium, chlorine, aluminum, magnesium, cement) at specially reduced prices. Several industries were still on the "protected" list in 1952, although the number has been gradually reduced. Similarly, the electricity rate increases instituted early in 1948 included the imposition of an "equalization" tax in favor of gas, the price of which was kept lower on the grounds that gas was a more "democratic" form of energy.[j] Electricity consumers have thus paid a tax for the benefit of consumers of gas. Rural consumers of electricity have also benefited from a departure from avowed pricing principles; the narrow spread between rates to rural and urban consumers does not reflect the appreciable differences in the cost of providing services. Since 1953 or 1954, this particular policy has found a new rationalization in the government's program to promote regional decentralization.

The SNCF rate structure is riddled with special rates designed to subsidize some group in the population. The use of what the

---

p. 14.) The fuel industry argues in return that the tax system discriminates against it through the heavy tax and customs duty on petroleum products.

[j] Presumably because most gas consumption is in the form of domestic cooking. (See *Le Monde*, February 18, 1948, p. 4.) In May 1952, gas rates were only eight times the 1938 level, while wholesale prices had increased twenty-sevenfold. A special gas rate for paupers (*économiquement faible*) was instituted in May 1954. One result of this policy of using the gas rate as a means of subsidizing certain economic and social classes has been that the deficits of *Gaz de France* have been among the largest, on a relative basis, of any of the nationalized industries.

SNCF sometimes refers to as "public interest" rates is particularly widespread in the case of passenger traffic, as evidenced by the fact that in 1951 only 47.5 per cent of the total passenger traffic paid the full fare. The proportion has been declining slowly but steadily each year. Some of the groups receiving reduced fares are suburban workers, employees on paid vacations, large families, soldiers, wounded veterans, artisans, farmers, and paupers.[34]

There are also numerous subsidies provided through modifications of the freight rates from those based on the costs of providing transportation for the goods in question. The use of railroad rates as a means of protecting uneconomically-located industries is sufficiently widespread to have been described as "an internal network of invisible customs duties" designed to preserve the *status quo*.[35] Agricultural products coming from regions distant from consuming centers are also not charged fully in accordance with the costs of transportation, and reduced rates are provided on "surplus" agricultural products as a means of lowering their delivered price. In a gesture towards a sister public enterprise, coal from certain regions receives a reduced rate in order to make its price more competitive with fuel oil or foreign coal. This list is by no means exhaustive.[36]

D. FINANCIAL RESULTS

In view of this diversity of price policies (together with the diversity of investment programs and the shifts in the market situation), it is not surprising to find a variety of profit-and-loss records in the nationalized industries. On the whole, however, deficits seem to have been the order of the day. For each of the major public enterprises, a composite picture of the financial record over the whole postwar period shows at least a small deficit, and in some (*Charbonnages*, *Gaz de France*, and the SNCF), the deficit is appreciable.

Table 26 presents the financial operating statements of the nationalized mines for the years 1947-1954. The first full year (1947) following nationalization, like the several which preceded it, was marked by a large operating deficit. The net losses of 1947 and 1948 are substantially understated by virtue of the inadequate allowances for depreciation. The fixed installations taken over from the private companies were evaluated on the new books at their 1945 prices, despite the large increases in prices subsequently. The *Commission de Vérification* described the depreciation

TABLE 26. FINANCIAL OPERATING STATEMENTS OF CHARBONNAGES DE FRANCE, 1947-1954
(billions of current francs)

	1947	*1948*	*1949*	*1950*	*1951*	*1952*	*1953*	*1954*
Net receipts								
Sales of coal	n.a.	n.a.	157.5	157.8	208.4	241.1	224.3	228.3
Sales of by-products, electricity, synthetics	n.a.	n.a.	13.1	13.6	19.2	23.9	29.0	34.0
Miscellaneous receipts and increases in stocks	n.a.	n.a.	8.3	6.9	10.2	20.8	13.4	17.2
Total	n.a.	n.a.	178.9	178.3	237.8	285.8	266.7	279.5
Expenses								
Personnel and related costs	n.a.	n.a.	106.2	110.8	139.0	164.3	155.5	156.4
Raw materials and supplies	n.a.	n.a.	44.5	41.7	50.6	72.1	69.0	60.0
Financial expenses	n.a.	n.a.	7.1	5.4	6.6	9.3	13.0	15.8
General and miscellaneous expenses	n.a.	n.a.	6.9	5.3	13.2	14.6	15.3	17.3
Total	n.a.	n.a.	164.7	163.2	209.4	260.3	252.8	249.5
Gross operating results	n.a.	–0.1	+14.2	+15.1	+28.4	+25.5	+13.9	+30.0
Ordinary depreciation	n.a.	5.1	13.5	16.3	20.2	30.8	36.8[2]	37.4
Net operating balance	–4.8	–5.2	+0.7	–1.2	+8.2	–5.3	–22.9	–7.4
Special depreciation[1]	–	–	–	1.3	8.7	1.0	[2]	1.5
Carryover and special profits and losses	0.7	n.a.	+0.5	–	+1.4	+1.6	+0.1	–0.5
Net surplus or deficit	–4.1	n.a.	+1.2	–2.5	+0.9	–4.7	–22.8	–9.4

Source: Derived from Charbonnages de France, *Rapports de gestion*, for the years 1947-1954.

[1] Consisting of accelerated depreciation of plant and equipment, writing-off of projects which could not be completed because of lack of funds, some depreciation allowance for new long-term projects, and creation of miscellaneous funds.

[2] Special depreciation included with ordinary depreciation.

allowances of 1946-1948 as "notoriously insufficient."[37] A slight surplus was registered in the accounts of the nationalized mines in 1949, following the change in price policy described previously. This result was the more "remarkable" (to use the term applied to the year's operations by the annual report of *Charbonnages*) because of the substantial increase in depreciation allowances arising from the re-evaluation of fixed installations on the basis of new coefficients prescribed by the government. Since 1950, depreciation provisions have been sufficient to permit the financing of all medium-term investment projects, which provide for the normal replacement of existing equipment, from internal funds. Although the "extra" depreciation rates applied to projects that had been halted for lack of funds resulted in a slight net deficit in 1950, the finances of the nationalized mines could be characterized as "healthy" in official reports. In 1951, substantial operating profits were registered. In addition to the full allowance for normal depreciation of existing facilities, it was possible to finance 3.7 billion francs of long-term investment projects.[k]

The figures for 1952, 1953, and 1954 indicate net financial losses for *Charbonnages* of 4.7, 22.8, and 9.4 billion francs respectively. In addition to the sharp decline in demand to which production was only slowly adapted, the mines suffered from the combined effect of the wage increases provided in 1952 and 1954 and the reductions in prices which the mines have been obliged ("voluntarily") to adopt as part of price reduction campaigns. A re-evaluation of the fixed installations of the mines also added appreciably to the depreciation charges in these years. As a result of the losses in these years, the cumulative financial position of *Charbonnages de France* since its inception now shows a substantial deficit.

The financial accounts of *Electricité de France* are mingled with those of *Gaz de France* during the first several years. Numerous retroactive and "exceptional" adjustments and settlements enter into the accounts, the form of which has also been modified. There were deficits in 1946 and 1947. A surplus was registered for the first time in 1948, but wiped out in the following year. Small profits were earned in 1950 and 1951; since then, the accounts have been very close to balance, with only minuscule profits or losses, as indicated by the following figures.[38]

[k] This figure is included as part of the 8.7 billion francs of "special" depreciation shown in Table 26.

Year	Net Profit (+) or Loss (—) in billions of francs
1946-1947 (19 months)	—7.4
1948	+5.5
1949	—5.5
1950	+3.1
1951	+4.4
1952	—0.3
1953	—0.1
1954	+0.4

This simplified description does not depict the financial results of EDF with full accuracy since the deficits of *Gaz de France* were a burden on the common treasury accounts until the end of 1951, when the financial relationship between the two enterprises was finally severed. On the other hand and more important, the depreciation allowances, which are particularly significant in view of the extensive fixed installations of EDF, were undoubtedly underestimated in 1950 and 1951 since these installations were carried on the books of the enterprise at their replacement cost in 1948 prices. On balance, it seems probable that a complete and accurate picture of the financial position of EDF during the period 1946-1954, if one could be drawn up, would show at least a slight deficit.

In 1938, the first full year following its establishment as a mixed company, the SNCF had a deficit of 2.5 billion francs. In 1939 equilibrium was achieved and some of the treasury advances of the preceding year repaid. During the postwar period, the deficits have been very substantial, as indicated by the following figures, which include in the "deficit" all the payments made by the government because of compulsory rate reductions or of rate increases that it refused to grant, as well as the net contributions made by the government to infrastructure and pension costs.[39]

Year	Net Deficit (Including Government Payments to SNCF)[1] (billions of francs)
1946	11.3
1947	14.6
1948	37.2
1949	71.8
1950	99.3
1951	104.3
1952	116.7
1953	142.6
1954	150.1

[1] Government postal subsidies (about 3 billion francs yearly) are included, but payments to the SNCF under the reconstruction program are not.

Early in 1950, Parliament endeavored to keep the mounting deficit within bounds by stipulating that the deficit for that year, arising from all sources, could not exceed 50 billion francs. Government payments to the SNCF within this ceiling were to be made in installments depending on the efforts and progress towards financial recovery. When it became clear that the deficit would far exceed the ceiling however, it was raised to 75 billion francs. Ceilings were similarly adopted by Parliament in 1951 and 1952, but in both cases they were exceeded. The SNCF management was able to find some consolation in the fact that the deficit, in comparison with total receipts and expenses, was relatively smaller in 1951 than in 1950. In 1952-1954 even this consolation was denied it.

According to a government spokesman, the avowed purpose of the new category of government contributions introduced in 1952[m] was to spur the SNCF on to greater productivity (and therefore reduced deficits). "If a man is asked to lift a weight of 500 kilograms, he does not even try; if this weight is reduced to 70 kilograms he tries to raise it."[40] In bookkeeping terms, the weight-reducing exercise resulted in a diminution of the "official" deficit of the SNCF in 1952 by 56.1 billion francs, broken down as follows: net government contribution to infrastructure and level crossings (less "duty")—44.1 billion francs; government payments of pensions—12.0 billion francs. The SNCF was undoubtedly mindful of its problems in public relations in seeking to have its apparent deficit reduced through these accounting adjustments, which do not, of course, in themselves affect the real magnitude of the cost to the government of financing SNCF operations.[n] Whether or not these adjustments inspire the management to greater productivity, it is clear that the main sources of the SNCF's difficulties lie elsewhere.

The *Renault* company has earned a slight "profit"[o] in all years except 1947, as indicated by the following data. The profits have been only a small fraction (less than 2.5 per cent) of sales.[41]

[m] See Section VII A of this chapter.

[n] Although the SNCF has attempted to redefine its "deficit" to eliminate the new contributions, Parliamentarians persist in discussing the full costs of SNCF to the government along the traditional lines. On the other hand, the accounting records have now become so complicated that few persons outside of the SNCF can hope to decipher them. Cf. the widely divergent figures for the 1953 and 1954 deficits discussed at the time of the 1954 budget hearings. (*Le Monde* of October 25, 1953, p. 14, November 5, p. 14, November 6, p. 14, and December 15, p. 14; and *Agence économique et financière*, October 23, 1953, p. 4, December 8, p. 2, and December 14, p. 2.)

[o] As will be noted in the pages immediately following, *Renault* makes a practice of deducting self-financed investments before reporting profits.

Year	*Net Profit (+) or Loss (—) (millions of francs)*
1945	+47 (after distribution of 110 to employees)
1946	+68
1947	—46
1948	+762
1949	+696
1950	+84
1951	+896
1952	+490
1953	+2,311

E. EVALUATION

1. Popular Tests of Performance. There has been a marked tendency in popular (and, frequently, Parliamentary) discussions of the nationalization issue to equate financial losses with "bad" management and profits with "good" management. Data on the size and trend of profits must be used with caution, however. Such data will usually, in the absence of monopolistic practices, suggest whether the industry's investment should be expanded or contracted, but they may reveal little about the correctness of price policies and of the ensuing financial results. For, as will be seen below, in one market situation and with existing facilities, the appropriate policy may be to operate at a loss, while in another situation it may be to operate at a profit. There may in fact be market situations where no firm, however well managed, can avoid losses and other situations where any firm would be hard put not to earn a profit. Similarly, an improvement over last year's position need not indicate that price-output decisions are more correct.

Another popular test of performance might be mentioned. The losses that have been incurred since nationalization are sometimes compared with the profits or losses of previous years under private ownership. By itself this comparison has very little meaning, however. As just noted, comparisons over time are hazardous because the cost-demand situation differs from one time period to another. Also the transfer from private to public ownership significantly altered the financial structure of the enterprises in at least two respects: (a) indemnification of the stockholders has introduced a new set of fixed costs in lieu of the earlier return on invested capital, which depended on the profitability of the private enterprises; (b) the public enterprises, being precluded from augmenting their capital stock as a means of financing new investments, have been obliged to resort to external borrowing (with a corresponding increase in fixed interest and amortization payments) or to enlarging depreciation reserves. Finally, under private ownership some of these industries were organized as cartels and/or regulated by the state rather than being governed by competition; these are not the institutional arrangements with which the efficiency of the nationalized industries should be compared.

The presence of the *Renault* company in an industry marked by considerable competition might appear to afford an opportunity for a direct comparison of the efficiency of public and private ownership. Most of *Renault's* competitors have enjoyed relatively larger profits during the postwar period. Once again, however, the comparison must be carefully qualified. The assimilation of *Renault* to the position of a private enterprise is far from complete. One important handicap from which *Renault* suffers is the fact that it cannot augment its capital by stock flotations. The company has therefore been obliged to finance the largest part (about 65 per cent) of its extensive investment operations from reserves set aside before the calculation of profits to be distributed. Also, as a "model enterprise," it has tried to improve social relations through higher wages and fringe benefits than other automotive firms provide. Another point, of less importance, is that the recorded profits must be shared with employees and the government. Some observers believe that this has led *Renault* to allocate more of its funds to special reserves, before estimating net profits, than would otherwise be the case.

2. *The "Low Price" Policy.* Whether the low-price policy of the early period achieved its official anti-inflationary objective is a moot point. Its initial effect was certainly to keep *particular* prices lower than they would otherwise have been. But the policy resulted in larger operating deficits for the enterprises, which in turn had to be met by increased subsidies from the government and larger government deficits. As has been indicated in Chapter 3, the government's deficits fed the inflation by increasing aggregate demand, especially insofar as they were financed by the creation of new money. As far as resource allocation is concerned, this distortion of particular prices made it more difficult for the price mechanism to assign resources correctly to their different uses.

3. *Average-Versus Marginal-Cost Pricing.* Although official policies are far from clear-cut, average-cost pricing and the no-profit, no-loss rule appear to have gained considerable favor. While the no-

profit, no-loss objective has merit for the purpose of adjusting investment in the nationalized industries, for the purpose of adjusting prices and output with existing capital it may have serious drawbacks. There will be situations in which price should be above average cost and others in which price should be below average cost. For, from the point of view of an efficient use of resources, prices should be equal to marginal rather than to average costs. According to this economic standard, output should be expanded until the value of an additional unit (that is, the price that the user is prepared to pay for it) equals the incremental or marginal cost of producing the unit. If the price at which an additional ton of coal can be sold is greater than its incremental cost, it is efficient for the economy to devote resources to the production of the extra ton; if the price is lower than the cost, the extra unit should not be produced since resources could be employed to greater advantage elsewhere. With the existing capital equipment of the industry, this may imply either profits or losses.[p]

Again, this description is crude and oversimplified. But the discussion has shown that this test was not applied for the most part, and that performance was apparently inefficient with respect to it. Rail services were probably priced above the cost of additional output, so that additional units would have been worth more to users (and to the economy) than they cost. Competition has probably had the salutary effect of forcing rail prices closer to marginal costs. Coal, on the other hand, was apparently priced below the cost of additional output, so that some units that were used were worth less than they cost. Pricing in accordance with marginal cost would have resulted in higher coal prices and reduced output, but also in higher profits (or lower losses) for the mines and a more efficient use of resources with respect to the economy as a whole.[q]

Admittedly, it is not always easy to measure marginal cost, and average-cost pricing may sometimes be a reasonable rule of thumb that approximates the policy of pricing at marginal cost. But setting price equal to average cost is not a good rule of thumb if it is

[p] If there are profits (losses), presumably investment should be increased (decreased), unless only large "indivisible" chunks of capital can be invested (disinvested) for technological reasons or as a matter of government policy. The government may insist, for example, on maintaining some enterprises for purposes of national defense or of furthering some "social" objective. If indivisibilities are present, it may be better to have the investment, even though it must run at a loss, than to eliminate it altogether.

[q] This assumes *inter alia* that the resources liberated by the reduction in output could move relatively freely to find employment elsewhere in the economy.

applied in a deliberate effort to avoid either profits or losses. For this will allow the rule to be used when average costs and marginal costs are far apart. Unfortunately, from the standpoint of economic efficiency, this seems to have been the way in which the rule has sometimes been applied in the nationalized industries.

4. Below-Cost Pricing. Even though in later years the no-profit, no-loss policy gained fairly wide acceptance, a number of cases have been noted of prices set below cost in order to subsidize some producer or consumer group. It is possible that this practice may have achieved some of its desired effects. However, these advantages generate counter-claims for similar advantages, and the provision of subsidies (in one form or another) has become so widespread that their net effect is in considerable doubt. Since the subsidies provided by public enterprises tend to create financial deficits, which must eventually be covered somehow by public funds, their final incidence becomes even more uncertain, and the advantages more dubious. There is little doubt, though, that this practice distorts the price mechanism in its function of allocating resources, and that it contributes to the proliferation of pressure groups attempting to acquire or preserve "rights."

VIII SUMMARY

The performance record of the nationalized industries has been the subject of lively controversy, with government official, Parliamentarian, layman or economist attacking or defending it on the basis of concepts, often not clearly defined, of how enterprises should be run in the public interest. In practice the record is a highly complex one and defies simple description or evaluation.

Output of coal and electricity increased rapidly after the war, helping to alleviate the serious shortage of energy resources that was handicapping industrial production. The longer-run trend of coal output has fluctuated with changes in market demand. Electricity output has risen continuously since the war, at rates that have also been influenced by the market situation. Production in both industries has fallen short of the targets, but little significance can be attached to the movement of production as such.

Employment has declined steadily in the coal mines and national railways over most of the postwar period, and has increased only slightly in the case of electricity. These movements have been attended by substantial increases in the productivity of the mines and the railways, which compare favorably with the trends in other countries. Changes in productivity may come about for various reasons, however, and the increases cannot be taken by themselves as evidence of "good" performance.

A massive investment program has taken place in those nationalized industries located in the "basic sectors," despite cutbacks in the public funds on which the enterprises have primarily had to rely as a result of their status and of the price policies that have been adopted. Investment levels have been considerably higher than in the prewar period of private management. To the economist, however, the appropriate size and composition of an investment program should be determined by considerations of efficiency of resource use, and these considerations have not figured prominently in investment decisions in the publicly-owned industries.

The remuneration of labor in the nationalized enterprises has probably been raised, relative to labor in the private sector, principally as a result of enlarged programs of social benefits. Whether this policy has increased the welfare of the working class as a whole is doubtful. Special remuneration in these enterprises would tend to reward equal productivity unequally, pull resources into less efficient uses, and possibly affect incentives unfavorably. Despite the added benefits, labor relations have not improved noticeably as a result of nationalization and a wide breach exists between labor and management in these industries.

As for price policies and financial results, the original legislation seemingly favored policies that would lead at least to financial equilibrium. Popular criticism of the early deficits and also of the notion that the government should make a profit has led the government, at least in recent years, to aim at a goal of having neither profits nor losses. This is to be accomplished by setting the price at which the output is to be sold at its average cost of production. Actual results, however, are still characterized mostly by deficits. *Electricité de France* has had a slight deficit in its financial accounts during the postwar period; the deficit is more sizable in the case of the coal mines and the gas industry, and has reached prodigious proportions in the national railways.

The no-profit, no-loss rule has certain practical and political advantages, but it can lead to an inefficient use of resources. A government enterprise may make profits, or losses, not because the consuming public is being exploited or because the enterprise is being poorly run, but because price should be higher or lower than average cost in view of the market situation and the existing capital equipment. There have been departures from this no-profit, no-loss rule in order to make the best of the situation in the face of competition, in order to restrain the upward movement of "key" prices, or in order to subsidize some producer or consumer group. In the last case, these price-output decisions have probably put resources to incorrect uses and encouraged the development of pressure groups, while it is doubtful that the intended effects (e.g., subsidies to low-income groups) have been realized to a significant degree.

PART IV

THE STATE AS REGULATOR OF BUSINESS

CHAPTER 9

IMPACT OF THE STATE ON THE EFFICIENCY OF FIRMS

I THE PROBLEM

DIRECT government intervention in French business affairs has been a frequent, if not regular, occurrence throughout their long history. The problems which have led to state regulation of private business are numerous. Intervention has been aimed at controlling economic fluctuations, redistributing income, increasing the dignity and importance of labor's role, promoting industrial growth, increasing productivity, protecting and encouraging family-size enterprise, and so forth. The impulse toward state intervention has sometimes come from those who wished the government to exercise a large degree of centralized direction and control over the whole of the economic process. But state assistance has also been invoked by groups that have vociferously deplored the general movement toward increased intervention.

In this Part, attention is focussed on the role of the government in the regulation of business, with particular reference to the implications for productivity and for economic efficiency.[a] Some of the government's actions have been intended to influence directly the productivity and efficiency of private business, while other actions have indirectly had such an influence whether anticipated or not. Both direct and indirect types of actions will be considered, with emphasis on the programs (e.g., to promote competition or to shelter particular industries) in the former category.

In the next chapter, some of the ways that state action has affected the market mechanism, and the efficiency of its functioning to allocate resources among business uses, will be taken up. The present chapter considers some of the ways that state action has influenced the level of efficiency within firms.

II THE SETTING

The existing estimates of the comparative productivity of business in different countries, while very rough, are nonetheless highly

[a] It should be kept in mind that these are different concepts: productivity means output per unit of one particular input, e.g., output per worker; economic efficiency means maximum output for a given combination of resources (or production of

suggestive. According to some measurements, average output per industrial worker in France is approximately one-fourth of that in the United States. Within Europe, France ranked with Holland and Germany, but below the United Kingdom and the Scandinavian countries in 1950, as indicated by the following data:

	Net Value of Production per Industrial Worker (United States as base)[1]	
	1938	*1950*
United States	100	100
Sweden	57	52
United Kingdom	53	50
Norway	51	37
Germany	47	28[b]
Holland	46	29
France	33	27
Italy	26	21

Even with their limitations, the data indicate that industrial productivity is relatively low in France. There is also some evidence that productivity is relatively low in the sector of distribution. A higher proportion of the population is engaged in commercial activities in France than in any of the other leading European countries. The title "a nation of shopkeepers," once derisively applied to England by Napoleon, has reverted to France. In 1949, 54 persons per thousand of population were employed in distribution; the comparable figure is 46 for Great Britain (in 1948), Belgium (in 1947) and Western Germany (in 1950).[2] Similarly, there is one retail store for every 48 inhabitants in France, one for every 68 in Italy, and one for every 87 in Great Britain.[3] A partial explanation of the larger number of retail outlets in France can be found in the geographical dispersion of the population. On the other hand, and contrary to the experience in industry where many firms believe that their stability is enhanced by producing a wide range of products and models, there is extreme specialization in French retail stores. A separate establishment is often involved in the sale of beef, pork, poultry, fish, dairy products, fresh vegetables, and bread and pastry; the American "general store" or supermarket has few French counterparts. This specialization is not matched with any rationalization of distributive methods, which generally remain

a specified output at minimum cost). But productivity figures, even if they are not conclusive evidence, may strongly suggest whether or not resources are being used efficiently.

[b] The low figure for Germany in 1950 is probably due primarily to the effect of wartime devastation.

on a relatively primitive level. An indication of the high costs of distribution in France is given by the following statistics:

	Share of Retail and Wholesale Trades in the National Income in 1949[4]
France	16.0
Netherlands	14.2
Great Britain	13.2
Italy	10.4
Western Germany	8.5

If not fully deserving the title of "the paradise of the inefficient,"[5] the French private economy, it seems reasonably clear, suffers from relatively low productivity. This situation has many complex causes. Two of them, which will be described here and discussed in this chapter in the light of the relevant government policies, are the small size of most firms and the low degree of mechanization. Another important factor contributing to low productivity—the sluggish adaptation of the market process—is discussed in the next chapter.

A. SIZE OF FIRMS AND EFFICIENCY

There is no simple relationship between the size of a firm and its efficiency, but clearly the firm can be either too big or too small for the optimum combination of factors of production. American experience suggests that efficiency increases with size over a considerable range. The full economies of scale can be enjoyed by firms of medium size in most industries, however, and the largest establishments in an industry are not necessarily the most efficient. In France, while there are a few large firms, most are very small—probably not large enough for the most efficient scale of operations.

It is a standard observation that the typical French firm is small.[6] The notion of the "typical" firm, however, does not do justice to the real diversity that exists in industry and (to a lesser extent) trade with respect to the size and economic importance of firms. There is, of course, no sharp line of demarcation between "small," "medium," and "large" firms, nor is there any wholly satisfactory unit with which the relative size of firms can be measured. Data are presented below on the size of establishments and firms, and on the value of payrolls, in industry and commerce. Data also exist on the value of sales and on earned profits; these do not alter the general picture, and are believed to be less reliable since they are based on tax estimates and declarations.

1. Size of Establishments. Table 27 presents a frequency distribution of establishments in private industry and commerce (trade) in 1950, measured in accordance with the number of employees. The concept of an establishment is a geographical one; one or more establishments may belong to a single firm, which is essentially a legal concept. It will be noted that there were 2,071,911 private business establishments in France (excluding the liberal professions) of which 46 per cent were in industry and 54 per cent in commerce.

TABLE 27

DISTRIBUTION OF PRIVATE INDUSTRIAL AND COMMERCIAL ESTABLISHMENTS ACCORDING TO THE NUMBER OF EMPLOYEES IN 1950[1]

Number of Employees per Establishment	*Number of Industrial Establishments*	*Number of Commercial Establishments*
0	468,257	706,065
1	168,668	185,037
2	82,989	83,611
3	37,437	30,743
4	23,458	16,992
5	16,062	10,163
6-10	41,556	22,089
11-20	31,267	13,249
21-50	25,117	6,818
51-100	8,864	2,846
101-200	4,445	524
201-500	2,536	254
More than 500	1,081	88
Unspecified	34,307	47,388
TOTAL	946,044	1,125,867

Source: INSEE, *Bulletin mensuel de statistique*, supplement April-June 1952, p. 41.

[1] An establishment is defined as a group of one or more persons working in the same geographical location for the same management. The table does not include liberal professions and public establishments in coal, gas, electricity, and transportation.

The small scale of most of French industry is suggested by the fact that of a total of almost one million establishments, about half employed no salaried workers and almost 85 per cent employed no more than five workers in 1950. Only 1,081 establishments, or 0.1 per cent of the total, had more than 500 employees. The number of small firms gives an exaggerated impression of their economic importance, however. Thus, while it is not possible to measure exactly the proportion of the total labor force employed by establishments of different size, it can be roughly calculated from the data in Table 27 that the 1.78 per cent of total firms with more than 50 employees accounted for slightly less than half of the total industrial labor force (including proprietors as well as employees).

If all establishments are taken into account, the average French industrial establishment contained about five employees in 1950. The "typical" or modal establishment, however, had no employees.

The small shop is even more characteristic of the wholesale and retail trades. Of the total of 1.1 million establishments, 63 per cent had no salaried employees and 92 per cent had no more than five employees. Only 88 establishments had more than 500 employees in 1950. Unlike the situation in industry, the small establishments also account for the majority of the labor force in the distribution sector; almost 60 per cent of the proprietors and employees are in establishments with five or fewer employees. According to another source, the more modern forms of distribution (department stores, chain stores, consumer cooperatives) occupied only about 15 per cent of the employed labor force and less than 1 per cent of all persons (proprietors and employees) engaged in commercial activities in 1949.[7]

The most striking feature of the commercial sector is the importance of the small shop operated by a single proprietor assisted by members of his family but with no, or at most one, salaried employee. Thus, according to a different source from that shown in Table 27, there were 1,290,000 proprietors to 960,000 salaried employees in 1949. The average commercial establishment has therefore less than one (0.74) salaried worker.[8]

2. *Size of Firms.* The overwhelming majority of French firms consist of only one establishment. Data from INSEE reveal a total of 2,160,348 firms, of which only 40,949 had more than one establishment in 1951.[9] It may therefore be expected that the statistics with regard to the size of firms will not differ appreciably from those observed for single establishments. In the case of firms, however, it is possible to obtain additional information from data on the frequency distribution of payrolls.

No studies have been found for employment, by firm, in industry. A separate study of employment, by firm, in the commercial sector in 1951 shows results almost identical with those above for commercial establishments in 1950. Thus, 60 per cent of the firms employ no salaried personnel, and 95 per cent of the firms employ between one and five workers. Firms with more than 100 employees represent 0.1 per cent of the total.[10]

The data given in Table 28 for distributed payrolls in 1951 also demonstrate the numerical preponderance of the small firm and the economic importance of the large. The precision of the results, but not their general magnitude, is affected by the fact that the INSEE data sometimes confuse establishments with firms, and do not take account of indemnities, family allowances, or payments in kind.[11] At the lower end of the scale, 65.8 per cent of the industrial firms had payrolls (per firm) of less than 1 million francs (about $2,860); these payrolls represented only 3.9 per cent of distributed wages and salaries in industry in 1951. At the other end of the scale, more than half (55.4 per cent) of the total payrolls were accounted for by only 1.7 per cent of the total number of firms. In the distributive trades, 78.8 per cent of the firms had an annual payroll of less than 1 million francs, representing 15.6 per cent of total payrolls in 1951. Conversely, 1.9 per cent of the firms, with payrolls of more than 10 million francs, accounted for 46.8 per cent of total payrolls.

TABLE 28

PERCENTAGE DISTRIBUTION OF NUMBER OF FIRMS AND OF TOTAL PAYROLL IN INDUSTRY AND COMMERCE BY SIZE OF PAYROLL PER FIRM IN 1951

	INDUSTRY		COMMERCE	
Size of Payroll per Firm (millions of francs)	*Per Cent of number of firms*	*Per Cent of total payroll*	*Per Cent of number of firms*	*Per Cent of total payroll*
Less than 0.5	52.3	2.0	65.2	8.7
0.5 to less than 1	13.5	1.9	13.6	6.9
1 to less than 2	11.0	3.1	9.6	9.7
2 to less than 5	10.4	6.5	7.1	15.6
5 to less than 10	5.4	7.5	2.6	12.3
10 to less than 20	3.4	9.5	1.2	11.7
20 to less than 50	2.3	14.1	0.6	12.8
50 to less than 100	0.9	11.6	0.1	6.3
100 to less than 200	0.4	11.8	–	4.6
200 to less than 500	0.2	14.0	–	5.3
500 to less than 1,000	}	7.1	–	4.1
1,000 to less than 2,000	}	5.9	–	1.3
2,000 to less than 5,000	} 0.2	2.5	–	0.7
5,000 to less than 10,000	}	1.3	–	–
Above 10,000	}	1.2	–	–
TOTAL	100.0	100.0	100.0	100.0

SOURCE: INSEE, *Bulletin mensuel de statistique*, supplement October-December 1953, pp. 46-47.

Despite the uncertainty attached to any measurement of business concentration, certain points stand out clearly. French commerce and, to a somewhat lesser extent, French industry are characterized by a multitude of very small enterprises. The typical commercial establishment is likely to be family owned, with no, or at most one, outside employee. In industry, the great majority of firms have fewer than five employees.

As a sociological phenomenon, and as a political force, the many small, family-owned French firms are of great significance. In considering their economic consequences, it should be recalled that a limited number of larger firms account for a major share of economic activity. An essential characteristic of French business is therefore its duality; in most market situations, a host of small firms, presumably of low efficiency, is mixed with a few larger ones. In practice, this mixture of small and big business has proved to be a stable one. The structure of costs and prices, as modified by actions of business groups and the government, is such that the least efficient firms are able to survive, as will be indicated in this and the following chapters.

It should be emphasized that "small" and "large" have been used here as a means of grouping businesses within France. In terms of efficiency, it is equally significant that the "large" French firm, in many instances, is smaller than its foreign counterpart, not only in the United States but in Germany and some other European countries. Thus, the average industrial (i.e., manufacturing) firm in the United States contains 59 employees, as against five per establishment in France. Three German enterprises account for 23 per cent of chemical production, while the ten largest firms manufacture only 18 per cent of French production. Numerous other examples could be cited.[12]

B. LACK OF MODERNIZATION AND MECHANIZATION

The small scale of operations in most French industries is accompanied by a low level of mechanization. The available statistical evidence is fragmentary. Consumption of energy per worker in industry (excluding steel) in 1951 was 7.8 tons of coal-equivalent in France, as against 9.8 in Germany, 8.8 in the United Kingdom, and 15.2 in Sweden.[13] In 1938, the stock of machine tools in France had an average age of twenty years, as against seven in Germany and five in the United States. West German industry is stated to have twice the stock of machine tools of France.[14]

There are, of course, many exceptions which modify, but do not invalidate, these general observations. Certain French industries, such as automobile production, compare favorably in terms of overall mechanization and productivity with their European or American competitors. In some branches of industry, large firms that are highly mechanized can be found, sometimes in appreciable numbers. Within a single enterprise, modern machines may exist side by side with their more obsolete predecessors, which the prudence of the French businessman has led him to conserve. It is nevertheless true that a substantial part of French industry is characterized by archaic production methods, high costs, and low productivity.

III THE POLICIES

Two contradictory tendencies dominate the policies of the state in its relations with private business. On the one hand, the state has attempted to promote economic progress through the modernization of private industries, the development of new production methods, and the encouragement of competition. The origin of this attitude may be traced as far back as the support for the establishment of the silk industry provided by Louis XI in the fifteenth century and the "royal factories" of Colbert in the seventeenth century. On the other hand, and over equally long a period, the state has intervened in order to preserve the *status quo* and to protect economic and social groups from exposure to the effects of economic progress. How these contradictory tendencies have affected the functioning of the market place is examined in the next chapter. This chapter considers how these actions have affected the efficiency of operations within firms.

A. MEASURES THAT ENCOURAGE EFFICIENCY WITHIN FIRMS

Although both are aimed at higher efficiency, a distinction can be drawn between policies directed towards increasing the size of firms and those directed towards "modernizing" firms (that is, raising the level of mechanization).

1. Increased Size. Some of the recent governments—most notably those of Pinay and Laniel—announced their intention to achieve a further concentration of business activity. Witness the following statement by M. Louvel, Minister of Industry and Commerce in both cabinets: "It is necessary first of all that the industrial sector become adapted to a modern economy. The number of firms is much too high. Only concentrations of firms will be able to bring about an appreciable reduction of prices. The Government must facilitate merger operations—this concentration presupposes that certain marginal firms will disappear. This disappearance is not an evil, quite the contrary, but public and business authorities must concern themselves with the great social problems which such disappearance will engender."[15] In view of the large number of small firms this policy need not be inconsistent with another avowed objective, that of increasing competition. Government measures to this end have included tax and credit incentives and a special program to "streamline" (*assainir*) the distribution system.

Prior to 1920, the tax legislation imposed severe penalties on business mergers, ownership of subsidiaries, and increases in capital. Profits earned by a subsidiary and distributed to the parent company were double taxed, and high rates were applied to the capital gains resulting from mergers. Since that date the tax laws have been modified in a direction increasingly favorable to business concentration. A law of July 1920, undertook to eliminate double taxation by permitting the parent company to redistribute the income received from its affiliate without payment of the "cedular" income tax (forerunner of the proportional tax). The special taxes applied to business mergers were reduced for the first time in 1926; in 1948 the reductions were extended to partial mergers approved by the *Commissariat Général du Plan*. Further exemptions to the taxation of mergers were introduced in the tax reform of 1948. Finally, a decree of June 1952, expanded the exemptions relating to ownership of subsidiaries, capital increases, mergers and similar operations. The decree provisions, originally for a period of one year, have since been renewed on several occasions.[c] [16]

[c] Under the 1952 decree, the dividends of the parent company are exempt from the proportional tax to the full amount of its net receipts from subsidiary companies, while its own profit tax is also reduced by 75 per cent of the value of these net receipts, provided that the parent company holds at least 20 per cent of the shares of the subsidiary. As concerns increases in capital by the incorporation of reserves, the 1952 decree suppressed the additional taxes (generally at 12 per cent) imposed on these transactions, while increasing slightly the smaller contributions tax (*droit d'apport*) to which these capital increases are also subject.

Equally favorable changes with respect to mergers were made by the decree. The additional tax on capital gains (*plus values*) arising from mergers was permanently abolished, the contributions tax being unchanged except on the gains on assets in excess of the nominal capital value. Moreover, a special system was invoked in behalf of partial or complete mergers taking place prior to December 31, 1953; the contributions tax was reduced to 0.25 per cent or 3 per cent, depending on the nature of the transaction, and the tax on the first transfer of fixed property and other business assets was postponed until the following transfer.

In 1954, a new tax incentive was provided to firms reaching specialization agreements designed to encourage mass production of a more limited number of articles. "Crossed sales" (of components, supplies, etc.) of independent firms involved in specialization agreements were exempted from the transaction tax.

It has frequently been contended that the credit policies adopted by the banking system, and condoned by the government in its role as supervisor of the distribution of credit, have tended to favor large firms at the expense of small and medium-size ones. The fragmentary evidence that has been advanced is inconclusive.[17] One particular credit provision designed to encourage larger-sized firms or larger-scale operations might be noted. In connection with the Industrial Conversion Fund (described below), special credit arrangements and loan guarantees may be obtained by firms engaging in concentration or specialization agreements.

Despite the frequent references to the excessive number of persons engaged in distributive activities, the action of the state to achieve a concentration and/or rationalization of the commercial structure of France has, until recently, been most conspicuous by its absence. Active interest in government intervention dates essentially from 1952, when it appeared that the Pinay campaign to roll back prices was being impeded by the inflexibility of wholesale and retail prices. In the fall of 1952, Louvel drew up a "plan to reform distribution"; using its special decree powers, the Laniel government adopted in 1953 a host of measures officially directed towards "streamlining" or "cleaning up" the distribution system.

The Laniel decrees relating to distribution were a heterogeneous mixture. The government indicated that its major objective was to eliminate "marginal" or "parasitic" merchants (i.e., those able to survive only through tax fraud and other illegal practices). The measures adopted to this end included: a revision of the system of inscriptions in the commercial register (designed to disclose enterprises not recorded with tax officials and to permit a more up-to-date census of the number of commercial establishments); greater surveillance of itinerant vendors; and an increase in the minimum capitalization of limited liability companies (intended in part to make it more difficult to establish fictitious firms). One decree was designed to modernize the distribution system through the estab-

(The deadline was twice extended, to December 31, 1955.) Specific measures were also taken to facilitate the reorganization of corporations.

lishment of a network of national food markets, including a reorganization of the major Parisian market (*Les Halles Centrales*).

As in the case of so many "reform" programs in France, governmental interest has waned with the demise of the particular ministries responsible for their adoption. Thus little progress has been made towards the use of the national markets in the face of the opposition of the powerfully organized groups of merchants (the celebrated *mandataires*) of *Les Halles*.

2. *Modernization.* As has previously been indicated, a major facet of postwar government policy has been the stimulation of investment in order to achieve a modernization of the French economy. The primary emphasis of the first modernization and equipment plan was on the development of the "basic" sectors of the economy, which were mainly under public ownership. The revised list of basic sectors did include such private industries as steel, cement, and tourism. Also some of the firms in the energy and transportation sectors were privately owned (most of the firms in the petroleum industry, some firms in inland transportation or the merchant marine). The housing industry was a major recipient of investment funds through the reconstruction program. More than 25 per cent of the investments actually made during the period 1947-1952 were in private firms in industry and commerce and in the fields of energy and transportation. Another 25 per cent was devoted to housing construction and reconstruction (primarily residential but including some reconstruction of industrial facilities).[18]

As a result of the special emphasis of the modernization and equipment plan, however, many other private industries obtained only a small proportion of their investment funds from public sources. These industries, more numerous and (in aggregate value) more important than the private industries included in the plan, have been discriminated against as a result of the distortion of the structure of interest rates through the provision of public funds at artificial rates. Although the private industries that have been the principal beneficiaries of public funds are of obvious importance, there is little evidence that the scale of investment priorities applied (in effect) to private industry reflected a carefully developed set of economic criteria or a rational plan for the development of the private sector as a whole.

Several activities directed towards modernizing the private economy fall under what has been called a "productivity drive." Productivity-consciousness is of comparatively recent origin in

France. Interest in this range of problems appears to have been stimulated, if not awakened, by the productivity programs initiated by the OEEC and the ECA. Although the National Association of French Employers (*Conseil National du Patronat Français*) was quick to appreciate the advantages of higher productivity, the support of individual businessmen, as well as of some parts of the government, has developed more slowly. The trade unions were, at least at the outset, deeply suspicious of the program, which Communist propaganda has associated with labor exploitation and technological unemployment. In the past few years a considerable number of productivity programs have nevertheless been embarked upon, financed in large part with funds provided by the United States under the foreign aid programs.

One aspect of the productivity drive has been a burgeoning of organizations dealing with productivity matters. A *Comité National de la Productivité* (CNP) was formed in June 1950, consisting of representatives of businessmen, technicians and supervisory employees (*cadres*), workers, farmers and merchants as well as of the interested government agencies. The operating arm of the CNP, the *Association Française pour l'Accroissement de la Productivité*, arranged study teams, exchanges of technical information, etc. More recently a *Commissariat Général à la Productivité* has been established, primarily to coordinate and direct the use of funds provided by the United States under the so-called "Moody Amendment" (section 115 k) to the Mutual Security Act of 1953. The *Conseil National du Patronat Français* has a standing committee on productivity questions, and productivity groups have been formed by trade associations in a number of industries.[19]

Among the manifold activities which form part of the "productivity drive," the most important to date has been the sending of study missions or teams to foreign countries. The teams are made up of persons from all branches of economic activity and all steps of the economic hierarchy. In addition, French employers, workers, and farmers have participated in international missions sponsored by the OEEC. Other parts of the program include visits of American experts to French plants, collection and dissemination of technical documents, and a campaign of public information which involves discussion groups, expositions and the publication of a monthly review.

Another productivity program, still getting under way, is financed by the $30 million which France received in 1953 under the Moody Amendment. The bulk of the funds (5.1 billion francs or $14.6 million) has been devoted to a National Productivity Fund, which extends loans on favorable terms (an interest rate of 5 per cent for a maximum period of seven years) to private firms desirous of increasing their productivity. Principal recipients of the loans are to be small and medium-size enterprises that wish to modernize their equipment. Certain conditions are attached to the loans, such as the establishment of a general productivity plan by the enterprise, including an indication of how the benefits of increased productivity are to be shared with the personnel. The funds may also be used to guarantee private bank loans, and the government is attempting to mobilize private bank credit to support part of the operation. The fund is apparently being used selectively on behalf of projects that have a maximum appeal for demonstration purposes.[d] The remainder of the Moody Amendment funds are being used for the French contribution to the European Productivity Agency and for the financing of a number of separate projects (consumer education, housing construction, agricultural extension, productivity research, technical films, etc.).[20]

Some achievements are already claimed in connection with the productivity program. Representatives of the textile industry signed an agreement in June 1953 with the three leading non-communist trade unions for "the renovation and expansion of the textile industry in the common interest of the workers, the firms, and the country." A plan for an increase in real wages has been adopted within the framework of the agreement; in the cotton branch of the industry, reconversion of unprofitable plants is being undertaken under the program. A labor-management productivity agreement has also been signed by twelve shoe companies, while production methods throughout the industry are stated to have been revised as a result of team visits to the United States. A standardization program is under way in the men's ready-made clothing industry, where a productivity center has been established and a pilot plant selected for experimental purposes. In the electrical construction industry, a center has been established for the exchange of technical information; worker-management discussion groups have been formed, and detailed operational studies undertaken. The use of

[d] As of February 5, 1955, 374 requests for funds had been received, totalling 9.2 billion francs. 149 requests were rejected, postponed, or directed to other means of financing. 131 requests were officially "considered," totalling 3.0 billion; of these, 35 had resulted in loans totalling 796 million francs. (*L'Economie* February 10, 1955, p. 10.)

pilot plants and productivity groups has been reported in the foundry and leather industries.

These isolated episodes cannot give an accurate impression of the progress of the program as a whole, on which it is too early to pass judgment. In the long run, the development of productivity will depend more on the climate of business enterprise than on specific productivity experiments, and this climate is more likely to be affected by government policies in taxation, credit, trade, cartel and other fields than in those which fall within the sphere of influence of the productivity program as such.

In addition to the Modernization and Equipment Fund and the National Productivity Fund, the government established in 1954 a trio of funds for the the "readaptation of the productive forces of the economy."[21] The funds in question, established by a decree of the Mendès-France government, are a reconversion fund for outmoded industrial concerns, a retraining fund for displaced workers, and a fund to promote industrial decentralization as part of the readaptation program.[e]

The Industrial Conversion Fund is intended to facilitate not only the conversion of obsolete firms but also the concentration of producing units on the part of one or several firms and the realization of "specialization" agreements among independent firms to produce a more limited number of (non-competing) products. Three forms of assistance may be provided by the state: long-term loans (for a maximum period of 20 years) at an interest rate of 6 per cent; government-subsidized reductions in the interest rates charged on regular borrowing by the firm for these purposes; and state guarantees of loans contracted by the firm for these purposes. It is expected that the principal form of assistance will be the interest-rate reduction, to amount to 3 or 4 points. Total funds for these purposes in 1955 (5 billion francs) were very small relative to the dimensions of the problem.

The initial reaction of businessmen to the new fund was basically hostile. A suspicion that the government was going to determine by administrative decision which firms in an industry should be permitted to survive was engendered by some overzealous bureaucratic pronouncements. The coordinating committee in charge of these funds later sought to allay these fears by indicating that the government's role would be passive; requests for funds would have

[e] The three funds were combined, along with the Productivity Fund, into a Fund for Economic and Social Development in July 1955.

to come from business itself, and state help would only be used on a selective basis to supplement private initiative. Early indications are that few businesses have been beating a path to the government's door, but this may be due in part to the currently prevailing prosperity.

An additional 5 billion francs was provided in the 1955 budget for a companion fund to facilitate the retraining or transfer of workers affected by the conversion, concentration, and specialization operations. The fund is expected to provide two forms of assistance: subsidies to firms that establish special worker training programs as part of the readaptation process, the subsidy to cover the wages of workers and instructors engaged in the program; and indemnities to individual workers who move to a new location, covering transportation and moving costs and "reinstallation." Worker relocation is to be kept at a minimum. The non-communist labor unions, participating in the program on an advisory basis, are openly suspicious that the readaptation program will be based on technical and financial factors without due regard for "human" considerations (such as the social cost of moving a worker from his home).[22]

A special treasury account bearing the imposing title National Fund for Regional Improvement has been in existence for a number of years, with funds devoted to a variety of isolated projects of industrial relocation on the part of public establishments and local communities. There has been growing concern in recent years over what is considered to be the excessive centralization of industry in urban areas, especially in Northern and Eastern France, taken to be a primary cause of the marked disparities in the economic wealth of different regions. Thus, between 1949 and 1953 two-thirds of all new industrial installations were in the Paris area, prompting the government to contemplate a ban on new industrial construction in the area.[23]

The Mendès-France program hoped to combine industrial conversion (and concentration/specialization) with regional decentralization. To this end a small (one billion franc) fund was added as a part of the National Fund for Regional Improvement. The fund is to provide assistance to firms that relocate, extend their activities, or establish new plants in areas approved by the government. The assistance takes the three forms used for the conversion fund (20-year loans at 6 per cent, reduced interest rates, or state guarantees). Although the program has scarcely been launched, no fund of this size can be expected to offset the presumed advantages of industrial location in certain urban areas.

It should be noted that the programs for concentration, rationalization, and modernization have been designed to increase the size and technical efficiency of business units, without altering the structure of market relations. Such measures alone cannot ensure that the process of technological change will be continuous, or that its benefits will be passed on to the consumer in the form of lower prices and improved products. In a dynamic, competitive economy these results might be expected to follow from the operation of market forces; in the absence of such forces, the outcome is much less certain. The extent of competition and the effects of government policies with respect thereto (discussed in the next chapter) are thus likely to be of crucial importance in determining the eventual results.

B. MEASURES THAT DISCOURAGE EFFICIENCY WITHIN FIRMS

Despite the apparent belief that larger-scale operations would often be more efficient and despite the occasional measures intended to encourage larger establishments, the fundamental bias of government policy in favor of family-size enterprise has not been removed. As noted in the chapter on the tax system, the artisan and small establishment are highly favored—by the tax rates, by the method of calculating the tax base, even by the comparative opportunities for evasion. These are significant advantages and must exercise considerable influence on the relative attractiveness of employment in large industry versus self-employment in a small shop and hence on the cost of labor to large firms and on the number of small establishments.

In addition to the special advantages given to small businesses, various government policies have the effect of providing shelter for the inefficient in general, presumably blunting the incentives to adopt efficient methods and technological advances. Public funds have been used on occasion to subsidize businesses suffering from a competitive disadvantage at home or abroad. The working of many of the public "subsidy" funds included in the general budget or the special treasury accounts[f] is very complex, and the lack of documentary evidence makes it difficult to ascertain to what extent they may be used in practice to make possible the survival of obso-

[f] A partial list of the economic subsidy funds has been given in Chapter 5.

lete firms (as distinct, for example, from their avowed purpose of promoting research and development throughout an industry). There is scattered evidence that some of the funds have been employed, at least occasionally, to provide financial resources to unprofitable business undertakings. Thus, the Textile Production Fund has frequently been criticized for the "compensatory subsidies" that it gives to inefficient domestic producers of textile raw materials. Some 2,000 silkworm growers, for example, receive a subsidy of 550 million francs a year; this amounts to about 5,000 francs per kilogram of cocoons, which sells for only 4,000 francs.[24] Similarly, a high cost domestic producer of sulphur received subsidies from the government, over a number of years, in order to enable it to compete with foreign producers. When the domestic mine was finally closed down under pressure from the sulphur transformation industry, the government indicated that the cost of the subsidy was more than double the cost of procuring the same quantity of sulphur abroad.[25] Parliamentary pressures on the government to continue the subsidy of a domestic gold mine, which produced gold at a cost of 700 francs per gram at a time that the world price was 430 francs, led Finance Minister Faure to observe that "There is an increasing tendency to make the state the protector of bad businesses. . . . Is this an expansion policy?"[26]

Certain features of public price policy have also apparently served to subsidize individual firms or to protect them from the rigors of the competitive process. In the application of direct price controls, the government's policy is stated to be the alignment of prices on the basis of the costs of the least efficient firm, to ensure survival of all firms in the industry (and substantial profits for the more efficient).[27] Distortions in the price or rate structure of some of the nationalized industries in order to assist firms or industries which would find it difficult to survive without such advantages have already been noted. Mention should be made of the various price compensation and equalization funds operating under the "parafiscal" system (described in the next chapter) which are designed to achieve uniform prices for all users of a product despite differences in costs. Twenty-four separate funds of this kind were identified in 1950. In the case of coal, for example, the equalization fund has been used to eliminate the disparity between imported and domestic coal prices. This disparity would otherwise have given a competitive advantage to certain industrial coal consumers at the expense of others.

Thus, while some steps have been taken to stimulate modernization and larger-scale operations, there has been a contradictory tendency to preserve inefficient technologies within firms by various restraints on the competitive process through which such inefficiencies would otherwise be eliminated. This is not to condemn the provision of shelter as being wholly bad, for the objectives of the French state or of any government are manifold. But the sheltering process entails some cost or sacrifice in terms of one objective—that of economic efficiency and the expansion of total output. Commenting on policies of this kind, two reports of the Finance Committee of the National Assembly have noted with approval this statement of Léon Blum: "While the law of American capitalism, for example, is: 'to allow young firms to be born,' it seems that the law of French capitalism is: 'to allow old firms not to die!' But French capitalism cannot obtain this result, which is against nature, without the toleration or even the active intervention of the State. That is what must change."[28]

In this chapter, one aspect of the restraints on competition—the sheltering of inferior technologies within firms—has been stressed. Such restraints also affect the market process and the resulting allocation of resources among alternative business uses. These effects will be taken up in the next chapter, and in this connection certain policies that promote or thwart competition will be described in greater detail.

IV SUMMARY

State regulation of private business has been inspired by many considerations, one of which is the desire to increase efficiency. Productivity is relatively low in comparison with the United States and the industrialized countries of Western Europe, both in French industry and in the distributive trades. Two factors which probably account for some of this low productivity are the very small size of most French firms and their low state of mechanization.

In recent years, the government has attempted to increase both the size and the mechanization of French business. Larger-size firms have been encouraged by more favorable tax provisions with respect to business mergers, ownership of subsidiaries, and increases in capital. Some credit provisions appear designed to encourage larger firms or large-scale operations within firms. Measures have recently been taken in an effort to reduce the number of firms engaged in distribution activities.

Increased mechanization or modernization of private business has been selectively encouraged through the modernization and equipment plans, which have provided funds at reduced interest rates for certain private activities (but at the expense of others in which investments might have equal or greater efficiency). A several-pronged "productivity drive" is being undertaken, and three funds have been established for the reconversion of obsolete businesses, the retraining of displaced workers, and the decentralization of business activity. The resources of the funds are limited, however.

At the same time, the built-in bias in favor of artisans and small businesses, and the sheltering of the *status quo* in general, have not been changed much. Measures in the tax, price, wage and other fields continue to protect small and inefficient firms; one effect is to dull incentives to mechanize or modernize or to adopt the most efficient scale of operations within business firms.

CHAPTER 10

IMPACT OF THE STATE ON BUSINESS MARKETS

I THE PROBLEM

As indicated in the preceding chapter, the objectives or problems that have led to state intervention in private business affairs are varied, but attention is directed here at the consequences for one objective—that of increasing efficiency. In this chapter, the impact of intervention on the way in which the private market economy allocates resources is considered. Two types of government actions are examined: those affecting the extent of competition and those directly affecting prices and costs.

Before getting into these matters, it may help to review briefly why they are important. In order to get the most out of existing resources (that is, to be most "efficient") an economy should assign each resource to its best uses. Whatever the mechanism that directs resources, a condition that would exist if they were correctly apportioned among uses is equality between the value and the cost of an additional increment of each product.

If we accept the price that consumers will pay as the appropriate measure of the value of extra output, the market process can be a remarkably good mechanism for allocating resources, stimulating innovations, and directing growth (at least in comparison with alternative mechanisms). Several conditions must be satisfied, however. Some of these conditions, although important, will not be considered here.[a] Attention will be focussed on government actions which influence two of the necessary conditions—freely moving prices and vigorous competition—which are vital to the healthy functioning of the market mechanism.

[a] These conditions include the existence of an acceptable distribution of income, of a considerable degree of consumer knowledge, and of a close relationship between private and "social" costs (or gains). If the distribution of income is regarded as "bad," the decisions evoked by the market process will reflect this fact. Thus, if some groups have greater wealth than others, and this disparity is not considered to be justified, resources will nonetheless be channeled into the production of the commodities demanded by the favored groups (e.g., Cadillacs instead of baby carriages). Also, quite apart from income distribution, if consumers have little knowledge about the properties of the products offered for sale, they cannot choose wisely. Or if private costs or gains differ markedly from "social" costs or gains (if one firm's costs do not reflect the way its operations pollute the water supplies of other firms), the market mechanism may result in the production of items that cost the economy more than they are worth.

If relative prices are distorted, or are prevented from reflecting shifts in demand and in costs, the distortions will draw goods and services into the wrong uses. If relative prices cannot change easily, they will keep resources in their present uses even if changes (innovations, investments, shifts in demand) warrant reshuffling.

There must also be a high degree of competition if the market is to allocate resources correctly. If resources can enter various industries freely in search of higher incomes or profits, monopolistic restraints on competition will usually be temporary. But if owners of capital cannot or do not consider using their factories and equipment to compete with those who seem to enjoy abnormal profits, monopoly power may persist. Also if laborers, for one reason or another, do not compete (that is, do not consider entering occupations in which other laborers are getting higher rewards), the price mechanism will not have the desired allocative effect. These influences may also hamper growth and development, failing to stimulate innovations in the places where they would be most valuable and preventing the reshuffling of resources so as to reap the full fruit of innovation and investment.

In practice, of course, no price system is fully flexible, nor can any economy be entirely free from monopolistic forces if only for reasons of technology. All economies fall far short of perfection in these respects. And in practically all economies, some distortions are created in efforts to control fluctuations, redistribute income, affect the balance of payments, and influence investment. But if the price system is particularly rigid or distorted, and if the functioning of the market process is particularly impeded because of restraints on competition, the resultant misallocation of resources is likely to be serious and must be weighed against the advantages (if any) of the interventions.

II THE SETTING

Both price distortions and restraints on competition are so extensive in France that the market mechanism is said to suffer from what is called "sclerosis."[1] Reference has already been made to the relatively low level of productivity, the marked differences in the productivity of industry and commerce in different regions, and the apparent underemployment of resources in some sectors of industry and commerce (e.g., the proliferation of shopkeepers). All of the evidence suggests considerable impairment of the mechanism through which resources should get assigned to their most productive uses. Referring to the "extraordinary rigidity of the French economy" one government report observes:

> The state of mind of individuals, action of business groups, attitude of banks, interventions of public powers, everything in France, by giving priority to the concern for security and to the conservation of acquired positions, has in effect contributed for a number of years to a structural sclerosis that can only result in the prevention of all adaptation of firms, as well as of the general [market] mechanism, both to technological progress and to the development of consumer wants.[2]

Explanations of this rigidity or sclerosis of the French market system are manifold. Such factors are involved as labor immobility (between regions or between occupations within a region) for reasons of habit or social choice. Two important elements are the distortion of particular cost and price relationships and the weakness of competitive pressures.

A. COST-PRICE DISTORTIONS

An impression that distortions or inflexibilities of the cost-price structure are very extensive becomes almost inescapable as one examines the state interventions affecting individual costs and prices. In advance of such an examination here, it may again be helpful to fall back on the observations of a government report:

> Each Frenchman senses obscurely that there are numerous cases where the market mechanisms are distorted, either by regulations or by the behavior of producers. But the multiplicity of texts and practices (sometimes useful or well-intentioned, as we shall see) is such that there are probably no more than a few persons in France who retain an overall view of the rules of the real functioning of the economy.
>
> Liberalism, planning, and even coherent direction [*dirigisme*] leave a few simple criteria that permit an economic calculation. The proliferation of regulations, of avowed and hidden protectionism, results in a state of affairs where the price of each product no longer is based on economic laws, but must be justified by a monographic description taking into account not only the technological structure of the industry but also the number of producers, their political influence, and their sociological solidarity.[3]

B. COMPETITIVE RESTRAINTS

In describing the extent of restraints on competition, it is again necessary to rely on qualitative impressions drawn from a catalogue of individual practices. In view of the magnitude and significance of these restraints, the background setting will be described in some detail before considering the impact of government policies. Four separate kinds of competitive restraints are identified: the actions of trade associations; cartel agreements; collective business attitudes; and external protectionism through tariffs and quantitative restrictions. The composite picture that emerges is that French business affairs are highly organized into something resembling a private corporate state, with uniformity of behavior and common action replacing competition in many markets.

1. Trade Associations. Over the past twenty years, trade associations have become a prominent feature of French economic life. These organizations can now be found in all fields of economic activity, carrying on functions so varied that they are difficult to enumerate. Their effect has been to substitute collective action with respect to key elements of costs, prices, investments, and market behavior for the individual action of the businessman attempting to increase his profits at the expense of his competitors.

Trade associations are particularly active in the field of foreign trade. Special import associations (*groupement d'importation et de répartition* and *groupement national d'achat*) have responsibilities of varying degrees of importance. Some have the prerogative of processing requests for import licenses, while others have the power to distribute import quotas by themselves or to collect funds under programs to equalize imported and domestic prices for a particular product. The influence of trade associations in the import field is further enhanced by technical committees, comprising a majority of the members of an industry, which give advisory opinions to government agencies on the granting of import licenses on products that concern them.

Corporate organizations are also active in exporting. The Federation of Small and Medium-Size Businesses (*Confédération des Petites et Moyennes Entreprises*) has established an export association that provides a number of information and prospecting services to small businesses and assists them in obtaining the benefits granted by the state to exporters. The association also holds a global insurance policy for its members and enjoys special credit arrangements.[4] A parallel organization is being considered for artisans.

In addition, trade associations also manage some of the foreign currencies placed at the disposal of business firms under export promotion schemes. In the textile industry, for example, a portion of the foreign exchange is placed in a common fund where it is used by the trade associations to purchase equipment for the industry, in agreement with the Ministry of Industry and Commerce.

Trade associations also flourish in the domestic market, where they may be found carrying on highly diversified economic activities in almost every branch of industry and trade. The most important of these activities are the ones conferred upon business organizations to administer, in the "general interest," the numerous "parafiscal" taxes authorized by the state. The "parafiscal" taxes are special purpose taxes, generally levied on specific products, which do not pass through the general budget but are used to finance a wide range of specified activities. Some of the taxes are administered by government agencies or by public or semi-public organizations, while others are administered by duly authorized trade associations. The official list for 1954 contained 143 different parafiscal taxes, administered by 122 separate organizations.[b] [5]

Among the functions carried out by private trade associations under the parafiscal system as a whole are technical research, quality control, vocational training, and publicity. Other associations have the more sensitive tasks of operating price regulation or price equalization schemes on domestic products or of administering public subsidy funds for development purposes. In some cases, such important operations as the maintenance and replacement of plant and equipment throughout an industry are controlled financially by trade associations that administer, with the approval of the Ministry of Industry and Commerce, funds for "technical amortization." Various schemes of social insurance that do not form part of the general social security system are also collectively administered by trade associations on behalf of the industries which they represent.[6]

Not all of the activities of trade associations in the domestic market arise in connection with the parafiscal system. One of the more recent developments has been the use of associations to finance

[b] The list does not include taxes to finance any of the social security systems or to cover "parafiscal" expenditures administered by the government through the special treasury accounts.

investments throughout an industry by the floating of public loans. Thus, a private corporation comprising 17 of the largest steel companies was activated at the end of 1953 to issue a public loan of 8 billion francs. The loan was guaranteed by the member companies, and its proceeds were divided among them on an agreed basis. The apparent success of the steel companies' venture, repeated in 1954 with a loan of 18.5 billion, led the electrical construction industry to establish a comparable association.[7]

2. *Cartel agreements*. The official functions of the trade associations merge, in some cases almost indistinguishably, with restrictive activities of a more clandestine variety. Despite their generally secret nature, cartel agreements or *ententes* are so widespread that considerable information, albeit somewhat superficial, is available on them.

How extensive a share of French business is covered by restrictive agreements of some sort can only be a matter of conjecture. Although these agreements operate so close to the surface of normal business activity that even the most perfunctory investigation produces a wealth of material,[8] no systematic enquiry into either their extent or their effects has been undertaken by any public body.

Some branches of industry and broad areas of commerce are comparatively free from restrictive agreements. In some industries with a large number of small firms and little effective concentration (such as wool and cotton weaving), there is considerable competition in price and quality in normal times. The automobile industry, in spite of its high concentration, has also proved to be highly competitive.[9] At the other extreme, in some branches of industry one firm may enjoy a near monopoly, or so dominate the market that identity of behavior is achieved without agreement. In the intermediate zone, in which the largest proportion of French industrial markets are found, some form of restrictive agreement is likely to exist among the various independent firms. Some clue as to the extent of these agreements is given by the statement of an SNCF official that 80 per cent of the purchases of the company encounter either cartel agreements or *de facto* monopolies (which may themselves be the result of an agreement).[10] According to a reliable private informant, there are 112 separate cartel agreements in the electrical equipment industry.

The character of the agreements varies widely from industry to industry on the basis of several factors, one of the most important of which is the structure of the market (and notably the degree of concentration). In oligopolistic industries, cartel policy is likely to be aimed at joint profit maximization through market sharing in the form of production quotas, common sales organizations or product specialization. In industries with a considerable number of small or medium-size firms, approximating the standard classification of "monopolistic competition," the agreements generally attempt to fix a common price that will assure a "reasonable" profit to the majority of firms. Most market situations are of a mixed type; a nucleus of large firms is surrounded by a fringe of numerous small firms. In this case, the most common type of agreement is intended to guarantee the survival of all firms and, consequently, substantial profits to the more efficient. Prices are likely to be fixed on the basis of the costs of the least efficient firm, with some scheme of market sharing also being observed in the case of the stronger cartels.[11]

While the economic provisions of the agreements may thus vary, their ultimate objective is essentially the same: to eliminate competition and share the market by specifying prices and conditions of production and sale. The differences in specific content presumably arise less from divergences of opinion on the objective than from differences in the feasible limits of market control.

The legal form of the agreement also varies widely. A simplified version is the informal understanding or "gentleman's agreement," often reached at meetings of a trade association but not necessarily involving the association. Such an agreement is likely to rely for its enforcement on moral suasion, backed by the economic influence of its participants. Other agreements may be in writing and may contain clauses that seek to make their terms legally binding on the contracting parties. The more complicated agreements usually require the participation of a separate administrative organization, which may be either the trade association or another group formed for this purpose and having its own legal status.

The written cartel agreements frequently contain provisions concerning their enforcement, with specific sanctions or penalty clauses to be applied by the association. An agreement in the non-ferrous metals industry provides that "the members pledge themselves to furnish to the designated comptrollers all the means of verification, notably by making available at their headquarters, factories, or warehouses, their order books, shipment books, copies, bills, and in general all documents of whatever nature that the comptrollers shall judge necessary for the accomplishment of their mission."[12] Infractors are subject to fines, with the ultimate penalty of removal from the association, perhaps combined with a boycott organized around sales orders or supplies of raw materials.

3. Business attitudes. The collective organization of business life would not have reached its present magnitude if it did not reflect the underlying attitudes of a majority of French businessmen. These attitudes deserve brief mention, since they contribute to uniformity of behavior and the absence of competition even without a formal or informal association or agreement.

In an interesting study of French businessmen, Landes has pointed out: "The whole thing simply boiled down to this: given the same machines and the same funds as an American, the French businessman will not use them in the same way or for the same ends."[13] The family structure of many firms and the deep respect for the virtues of conservatism and thrift, combined with the individualistic tastes and low purchasing power of the French consumer, tend to limit the economic horizon of business enterprises and to encourage the search for stability at the expense of progress. The emphasis on stability and security, rather than profit maximization, greatly facilitates the establishment of a modus vivendi between potentially competing firms. Underlying these attitudes is a conception of business as a way of life, a family and social institution, which is substantially different from that of the American businessman. Landes quotes one business executive as follows: "Do you mean to tell me that you can respect a man who has become wealthy through the ruin of a dozen or more competitors? Such a man is a menace to society."[14] These and other sentiments also help to explain the survival of the host of small and inefficient firms. As another commentator has observed: "Anxious to maintain around them a screen of small firms which can justify for their industry the solicitude of public authorities and the indulgence of popular opinion, the owners of large and perfectly equipped firms devote as much care to keeping alive their infirm competitors as they formerly expended energy to eliminate them."[15]

4. External Restraints. The internal restraints on competition in the market place are matched by practices designed to reduce or eliminate competitive pressures from foreign sources. Since the practices in question—most notably tariffs and import quotas—are directly matters of government policy, their description will be deferred until later in the chapter. Some indication of their magnitude can be gathered from the statement in an OEEC report that external protection in France "surpasses that of any other member countries."[16]

We turn now to a discussion of government policies as they have affected the structure of costs and prices and the extent of competition. The latter policies will be dealt with first, since they are perhaps the more important.

III THE POLICIES—ACTIONS AFFECTING THE EXTENT OF COMPETITION

The government's attitude towards the desirability of competition has been marked by many inconsistencies. "Anti-trust" legislation has been on the statute books for more than a century, and recent efforts to revive and enforce it have been coupled with other measures designed to promote the freer play of competitive forces at home or abroad. On the other hand, the government has frequently encouraged the development of cartels and trade associations and has itself indulged in restrictive practices in both the domestic and foreign fields. On balance, the net result of government policy has almost certainly been to strengthen the forces, formidable enough in their own right, tending to restrict or eliminate competition. We will begin by examining policies directed towards the promotion of competition from domestic or foreign sources.

A. PROMOTION OF COMPETITION

1. Anti-trust Legislation. French anti-trust legislation antedates the industrial revolution and has survived remarkably intact (largely, perhaps, by virtue of its lack of application) despite the economic changes which have occurred in the intervening years. The basic statutes are articles 419 and 420 of the Penal Code, adopted in 1810. The purpose of these articles was to prevent individuals or groups from interfering with the "natural and free competition of the market." Accordingly, they prohibit fraudulent actions by individuals, or coalitions and associations, with the object of cornering the market in a given commodity and thereby raising its price above the normal level. The language of the articles reflects public concern over efforts by combines to corner the market in scarce commodities (such as wheat) during periods of shortage or famine.

Despite the economic evolution of the nineteenth century, the basic provisions of the criminal code underwent no modification prior to 1926. In the intervening century, the severe if imprecise language of articles 419 and 420 resulted in a liberal interpretation of their spirit by the courts, particularly with respect to market situations which the original legislators could not have envisaged. Only a few cases resulted in convictions in the courts, which insisted upon evidence of the influence of the suspected actions upon prices and market conditions that was, by the nature of the situation, difficult to obtain. By 1926, a long series of judicial interpretations had established a distinction between "good" and "bad," or "defensive" and "offensive," cartels. "Good" or "defensive" cartels, which appear to have been in the great majority, were those that assured the "legitimate" interests of business groups by "regularizing" the conditions of production and sale and avoiding the unfavorable effects of "uncoordinated" or "ruinous" free competition. In one of the most celebrated cases (*Comptoir Longwy* in 1902) the Court found that a cartel which controlled over half of total steel production in France, fixed sales prices and production quotas, arranged for common procurement of raw materials, and imposed penalties for infractions was not in violation of the law since the principal objective was "to regulate the particular operations of its associates according to an overall plan and in the general interests of production in a great industry."[17]

Articles 419 and 420 were modified in 1926. Slightly greater linguistic precision was introduced but the law did not substantially alter, or attempt to modernize, the principal features. Successful prosecutions in the courts were almost as infrequent after the passage of the new language as before; the rare applications of the Code were to speculative activities.

Following the second World War and the period of shortages and extensive direct controls, the reappearance of cartels in 1948 and 1949 led to a recrudescence of activity on the Parliamentary front. A number of bills bearing the "anti-trust" label were introduced into Parliament by the government and various political parties between 1947 and 1952. Only one of these was debated by Parliament. Approved by the National Assembly in July 1952, it was rejected by the Council of the Republic; an impasse has resulted from which no compromise bill has any immediate prospects of emerging.

Despite the stalemate on the Parliamentary front, two measures have been adopted that provide the government with a potential weapon for an "anti-trust" campaign. The first is a law of July 1952, prohibiting resale price maintenance. The 1952 law formed part of the Pinay government's price reduction campaign. Although the language was somewhat ambiguous, the government indicated that the law was intended to prohibit the fixing of minimum prices by cartel agreement or the action of a trade association; trade-marked goods (broadly defined to include any product the price of which is fixed by an individual producer or distributor) were specifically exempted. In December 1952, Pinay announced that 21 cartels had been "abolished" under the July law. By the spring of 1953, some 40-odd cartels had entered into discussions with the Ministry of Economic Affairs concerning their pricing practices, with the avowed intention of conforming to the new legislation.[18]

The 1952 law was intended as a temporary measure, pending the voting of a definitive law to control *ententes*. When it became apparent that no such law would be forthcoming, the Laniel government, in August 1953, used its special powers to adopt a decree for the "maintenance or reestablishment of free competition" which *inter alia* replaced the 1952 law. The Laniel decree, which has been euphemistically referred to as the "Sherman Act of the IVth Republic,"[19] prohibits, in sweeping language, "all concerted actions, agreements, explicit or tacit cartels, or collusive actions of any form or for any reason which have the purpose or may have the effect of interfering with the free play of competition by opposing the reduction of costs or prices or by favoring an artificial increase in prices." The notion of "good" cartels is reinstated, however, by a subsequent article that declares that the decree does not apply to concerted action, agreements, or cartels, "the authors of which shall be able to justify that they have the effect of improving and extending production outlets or of assuring the development of economic progress through rationalization and specialization." It thus appears that a "bad" cartel is one that raises costs or prices above the otherwise prevailing level, while a "good" cartel presumably lowers costs and prices through a rationalization of production and sales methods. Other articles of the decree include a prohibition against refusals to sell, against fixing of minimum prices or mark-ups either by price schedules or by cartel agreements, and against discriminatory price increases.

There are many difficulties in applying the distinction between "good" and "bad" cartels laid down by the legislation and by court decisions. If rationalization and specialization are achieved by an agreement that allocates markets among producers, is it not likely to be accompanied by some agreement (explicit or tacit) on prices?

Is it not also likely that the favored way to expand production outlets will be through agreements that ensure markets and therefore "regularize" production by curtailing competition? The dynamic aspects of the problem are particularly important. If a rationalization and specialization agreement confers a monopoly upon a business firm, is it not probable that, in the long run, prices will be higher and output lower than if competition had existed? Is the "quiet life" of a monopoly the most suitable atmosphere in which technological change and economic growth can be pursued?[c] What reliable yardsticks, either theoretical or practical, can demonstrate that production has been increased, or made more efficient, or that prices have been lowered as a result of the existence of the cartel?

Such questions raise serious doubts about the utility of the distinction currently employed. These doubts are strongly reinforced by the long experience with cartels in France. The tendency appears to be for the cartel progressively to assume as extensive a control as possible over the activities of the industry. The opinion of the general purchasing agent of the SNCF, based on wide experience, is worth recording: "In the long run, there are no good cartels."[20] Also, despite the considerable weight of evidence on the existence of "bad" cartels by the government's own standard, there is remarkably little record of enforcement of the anti-trust legislation.

The Laniel decree established a *Commission Technique des Ententes* to review possible infractions of the law and deliver advisory opinions, usually at the request of the Ministry of Economic Affairs, for use by the government or the courts. These opinions are not legally binding. The Commission therefore serves essentially as a group of "experts" to give advice on the extent to which various restrictive business practices may be considered to obstruct the free play of competition. More than a year elapsed before all of the members of the Commission were appointed, and the issue has again virtually disappeared from the public eye without any evidence that the new decree is being enforced.

2. *Exposure to Foreign Competition.* The programs of economic integration and trade liberalization may also be viewed as efforts to promote competition and thereby to help get French resources into the "right" uses (that is, where they would have a comparative advantage). Official support for these programs has been based

[c] As J. R. Hicks has observed, "The best of all monopoly profits is a quiet life." *Value and Capital* (Oxford, 2nd edition, 1946), p. 265.

on the proposition that the "fresh air" of foreign competition would have a beneficial effect on the congested French economy.

The vicissitudes of French policy with respect to the liberalization of restrictions on imports from other OEEC countries have been described in an earlier chapter. It will be recalled that, as of the spring of 1955, the program was only aproaching the "hard core" of restrictions designed to protect domestic industry and agriculture.

In the postwar history of European economic integration, a special place must be accorded to France as the leader, on occasion, and the most recalcitrant member, on other occasions. As a committee of the French National Assembly has observed, "Always in the forefront of international initiatives on an ideological plane since the end of the war, France has also not ceased to be the last to be able to put into practice the ideas which she has launched."[21]

A project for the integration of agricultural production among interested European countries (the "Green Pool") has been initiated by the French government. If it is premature to pronounce a verdict of "still born" upon the project, it is at least clear that the period of gestation has been so prolonged as to raise serious doubts about the eventual outcome. The fate of a French plan for a sort of economic union among France, Italy, Belgium, Luxembourg, and the Netherlands is less ambiguous, the project having been abandoned before a better name had been found for it than Benefit, Finebel, or Fritalux. Despite a longer and more intensive period of negotiation among diplomats and business and farmer groups, which permitted the raising of higher hopes, the proposal for a Franco-Italian Customs Union has also passed on into history without either Parliament having voted on the Treaty signed by the two governments. The European Coal and Steel Community (the "Schuman Plan") therefore stands as the most important, if not the only plan for economic integration which has advanced beyond the prospectus stage.[22]

The objectives of the Coal and Steel Community, and the influence of Frenchmen such as Jean Monnet and Robert Schuman in bringing about its realization, need not be repeated here. Nor is this the place to enquire into the extent to which the goal of a common market may have become a reality during the first years of the Community's existence. It may be of interest, however, to consider briefly the attitude of French business groups and of the French government towards the Community.

The position of a number of important French officials, industrialists and labor leaders towards the Community has been, at best, one of lukewarm support and, at worst, of scepticism or strong opposition. The proposal was essentially the product of a small number of influential persons in the Monnet Plan group and the Ministry of Foreign Affairs. Some American observers attribute its ratification to the highly favorable reaction of international public opinion that caught the opposition by surprise. Considerable effort was expended by French business associations in order to obtain its defeat by Parliament.[23] Since the inception of the Community, the mixed support of French participants has been invidiously compared to the strong "team play" of the German delegates, and the French government has been characterized as the most "reticent" members of the Community.[24]

Parliamentary ratification of the treaty instituting the Community was made conditional upon several commitments made by the French government to provide assistance to strengthen the French coal and steel industries and to improve their competitive position. These commitments pledged the government to regulate the status of the Saar, to negotiate the canalization of the Moselle River (of particular interest to the Lorraine steel industry), to carry out investment programs necessary for the modernization of the coal and steel industries, to "realign" all of the loans made to the steel industry between January 11, 1947 and the date of ratification of the treaty on the borrowing terms enjoyed by the nationalized industries, and to eliminate international differences in the cost and price structure by the "harmonization" of social payments, indirect taxes and transportation costs in the member countries. Some action has been initiated in connection with each of these commitments, but progress has been slow, particularly on those issues which require international negotiation.

The common markets in coal and steel were opened on schedule; that in special steel products was twice postponed because of problems presented by the French steel industry and the French government. When the market in special steels was opened after three months' delay, France was permitted to maintain for an additional three months its export subsidies on special steel products (considered to be in violation of the treaty) and the High Authority of the Community had to agree to invoke the "safety" clauses of the treaty at the earliest signs of distress in the French industry.[d]

[d] The French steel industry was reluctant to remove its external protective measures (particularly the 15 per cent "compensatory" tax on imports) on the grounds that French costs and prices were substantially above the level of other

The coal and steel markets were opened at a time of financial difficulties for these industries in France, and the claim was quickly advanced that these difficulties were due to the functioning of the Community.[25] Towards the end of 1954, more prosperous conditions returned to these industries and they began to share in the general economic expansion at home and abroad. But if the prophecies of doom emanating from French business circles were momentarily stilled, official enthusiasm for economic integration as a general economic prescription waned perceptibly during the early years of the Community. Most revealing was the position of former Foreign Minister Schuman: "Our economic situation is so unsatisfactory, in present circumstances, that we cannot submit to a supranational authority in other fields than coal and steel. We cannot institute any new steps in the immediate future. I am very categorical on this point. It is necessary beforehand to reorganize, rationalize, adapt French enterprises, arm them and prepare them so that they may confront foreign competition. . . ."[26] These words of the nominal father of the Coal and Steel Community were reflected in the hostile positions towards further measures of economic integration that the French government adopted in international negotiations. The European movement for economic integration thus came temporarily aground on the sands of the French economy.

B. RESTRAINT ON COMPETITION

Government policies in favor of increased competition currently occupy the center of the stage. But action in the contrary direction, if less openly proclaimed, is nonetheless vigorously pursued. It is exercised on many fronts. Those to be considered here are internal restraints on competition through the encouragement of trade associations and cartels and external restraints through tariffs, quotas, and import procedures.

1. Internal Restraints. It has been seen that the French trade associations take collective action on a wide variety of important business policies that, in the United States at least, have customarily been left to the initiative of the individual businessman. In the United States such collective action, with its corresponding reduc-

members of the Community. A part of the cost-price disparity was attributed to the fact that the steel industry was obliged to procure its raw materials from within the French Union. Thus the world price for nickel (mostly Canadian) was 463 francs per kilogram at a time that the price of New Caledonian nickel, landed in France, was 775 francs per kilogram. (*Le Monde*, July 27, 1954, p. 10; *L'Economie*, July 1, 1954, p. 8.)

tion in the scope of private competition, would certainly run afoul of the anti-trust legislation. In France, however, public policy has generally been to encourage the development of such associations; indeed, many of their activities would not be possible without the authority and support given by the state.

The trade associations owe much of their present influence to the extensive responsibilities conferred upon them by the government during the wartime and immediate postwar periods. Parafiscal taxes flourished during the Vichy régime, and were indispensable tools in the operations of the trade associations which directed many of the price fixing, material allocating, and other economic activities of the government. Most were carried over into the early post-liberation period of extensive government controls. Since then, there has been a gradual elimination of some of the taxes as parts of the complicated machinery of direct control have been dismantled. Many of the taxes have survived into the current period, however, and new ones have been authorized. The present trend is to submit the parafiscal system to closer government control rather than to abolish it, and in 1950 the Minister of Industry and Commerce still referred to it as "an essential method of operation of the state in economic affairs."[27]

The principal functions performed by the trade associations under the authority or with the approval of the state (promoting exports, allocating imports, directing funds for research, price equalization, investment, social welfare, etc.) have already been mentioned. In addition, the associations have been assigned an important role vis-à-vis the Administration through their participation in a host of government-sponsored councils and committees. Although these councils and committees are nominally only advisory, in some instances they have exercised a considerable influence over government policy; the relations between the trade associations and the government have at times been so close that some of the leading associations have found it desirable to pattern their internal organization upon that of the executive agencies with which they deal.[28]

Where the existing structure of the trade associations was not adequate for the accomplishment of their economic duties, the government has sometimes stepped in to help establish a new one. The government assisted in the organization of artisans for purposes of export promotion and pledged its financial assistance (in the form of loans on favorable terms) to the "commercial organization" of export operations. The government has also indicated its desire to encourage the formation of investment associations to float bond issues before the general public and gave its approval to the bond issues of associations in the steel and electrical construction industries.[29]

Heavy reliance was placed on business organizations in the price reduction campaigns of Pinay and Laniel. Commenting on the Pinay program, Alfred Sauvy concluded: "In order to help a policy considered to be favorable, the producers have agreed to place their protective apparatus (cartels, etc.) at the service of the price reduction campaign. This apparatus therefore emerges from the adventure more reinforced than compromised."[30] Similarly, the key element in the Laniel experiment—a reduction in the retail price of meat—was achieved through the "voluntary" cooperation of the butchers' trade association, following intensive negotiations with the government. The various trade associations involved were described by Finance Minister Faure as the "shock troops" of the price campaign.[31] This use of trade associations is only a logical extension of the practice, followed in connection with price controls, of permitting the members of an industry to agree (in their trade association) on common prices and mark-ups to be approved by the government.

Pronouncements of the conservative governments of 1952-1954 confirm the vital part that trade associations have been expected to play in the direction of economic affairs. Premier Laniel stated that "The State, when it is not totalitarian, can only gain by relying on organized business, but could only lose by wishing to substitute itself for that organization." In a similar vein, M. Boisdé (secretary of state for economic affairs in the Laniel cabinet) spoke of a "new social economy," preferable to the "arbitrariness" of both the liberal and totalitarian economies. This economic order was to be based on "free contracts" among interested parties, which would be guaranteed by the state.[32] This corporate organization of economic activity on the part of private business groups, enjoying special favors and the open support of the government, is much closer to reality than the somewhat hypothetical flavor of M. Boisdé's remarks might suggest.

With respect to cartel agreements, against the lukewarm efforts at anti-trust enforcement must be set the fact that the government has frequently given its support to these *ententes* and has even participated in them on occasion. Perhaps the most striking example of a government-sponsored cartel can be found in the steel industry during the years 1947-1952. The central organization in the steel cartel structure was the *Comptoir Français des Produits Sidérurgiques*, a private corporation with a capital distributed among 99 firms. The functions of the *Comptoir* were set forth in a government decree of July 4, 1947 issued by the Ministry of Industrial Production. The decree gave the *Comptoir* general responsibility for applying the decisions and programs reached by the *Chambre Syndicale de la Sidérurgie Française* (the principal trade association of the industry) in agreement with the Ministry.

The principal duties of the *Comptoir* were to assure that orders and deliveries conformed to the decisions of the government and the *Chambre Syndicale*. Execution of the orders was closely supervised. The *Comptoir* also administered a fund for equalizing profits and losses among firms in their export activities, as well as those funds, collected from the sales of steel products, that did not revert to the individual producers (i.e., parafiscal receipts for depreciation/reequipment, vocational training, scientific research). During the period of the *Comptoir*, the price of steel products was fixed by the government in close consultation with industry representatives. The decisions of the *Comptoir* were binding in all matters under its jurisdiction. Its activities covered all iron and crude steel products, castings, and non-specialized steels. The *Comptoir* acted as direct sales agent for 20 per cent of the commercial sales, which were made to "reserved clients" and used to "equilibrate" production in the various plants. The remainder of the sales were made by the individual enterprises under terms supervised by the *Comptoir*.

The *Comptoir* was abolished by the steel industry with considerable fanfare in 1952 because of the establishment of the European Coal and Steel Community, with whose provisions its activities were in direct violation. There is no reason to believe, however, that the centralized control over French steel operations once exercised by the *Comptoir* with the government's approval has disappeared with the abandonment of the *Comptoir* itself, and some evidence exists that its functions may in fact have been taken over by the *Chambre Syndicale*.[33]

The government has also participated in cartels through the intermediary of public enterprises in branches of industry containing both public and privately-owned firms. The *Office National Industriel de l'Azote* is a member of the *Comptoir Français de l'Azote* which engages in technical research, information activities, and measures to "make uniform" the conditions of sale of nitrogen. Similarly, *Mines Domaniales de Potasse d'Alsace* is a member of the sales agency *Société Commerciale des Potasses d'Alsace*, which before the war was used to divide the domestic market between *Mines Domaniales* and its Alsatian competitor, *Kali Sainte Thérèse*. The common sales agency has the official status of a public enterprise, with duties defined by a law of 1937.[e] [34]

An interesting and important case of a cartel agreement both sponsored by the government and participated in by a nationalized industry is the 1954 agreement between *Charbonnages de France* and the principal trade association of the petroleum industry (*Union des Chambres Syndicales des Industries Pétrolières*). The agreement, requested by the Ministry of Industry and Commerce (under the Mendès-France government), specified the maximum amount of fuel oil which might be sold in France in 1955 in order to "limit the current competition between fuel oil and coal."[35]

2. *External Restraints.* The principal restraints on foreign competition take the form of tariffs and quantitative restrictions. French foreign trade policy has traditionally been marked with a strong flavor of protectionism; tariffs are in fact among the more venerable of French institutions, dating from the end of the thirteenth century. While there is little reason to believe that the protectionist spirit has diminished appreciably in recent years, its identification has been made more difficult by the persistent balance of payments problem, which has served as the public justification for most foreign trade activities of the French government.

Many of the prewar tariff duties were specific. As a result of the rise in prices and the depreciation of the value of the franc, the specific duties no longer gave sufficient protection to domestic producers after the war. The French tariff was therefore overhauled and a new tariff devised with ad valorem rates and a complete revision of the nomenclature. The new ad valorem rates were stated to give only the same measure of protection as had existed before the war under the specific duties. While comparison of the rates is made difficult by changes in nomenclature, it has since been admitted that some of the new tariff rates were higher than the old, the rates having been raised in order to provide domestic industry and agriculture with sufficient protection to make possible the eventual removal of quantitative import restrictions.[36]

[e] The agency still functions, although since the war *Mines Domaniales* has been officially responsible for the operation of *Kali Sainte Thérèse* as well.

The postwar tariff was officially put into affect on January 1, 1948. Like the prewar tariff, it consists of a general tariff and a minimum tariff, with the duties of the former about four times those of the latter. Since France has accorded "most favored nation" treatment to all the signatories of the General Agreement on Tariffs and Trade (GATT), in effect only the minimum tariffs are applied. The protection of industrial products (taken as a whole), while substantial, is probably less than that provided to agricultural products. Industrial raw materials are, in principle, not subject to duty, while the rate of the ad valorem duties increases with the degree of fabrication. Duties average 5 to 15 per cent for semi-finished products and 15 to 25 per cent for finished products; they may be as high as 30 to 35 per cent on specific articles (e.g., automobiles, plastics).

In early postwar years the French tariff was suspended, since the primary need was to increase import supplies and the import quota system could be used to give protection to domestic producers if required. As some quota restrictions were lifted the tariff was gradually put into effect; in some cases the new tariff was found to be a more serious limitation than the previous quotas had been.[37] Other OEEC countries complained that the French action violated the members' pledge not to raise tariffs when removing quota restrictions, but the French government insisted upon a logical distinction between "raising" and "applying" a tariff.

A substantial relaxation of the import quota system has taken place only with respect to trade with other OEEC countries and their associated monetary areas, and even here it seems doubtful that the more "protectionist" of the restrictions (e.g., those on industrial products competing with domestic industry) have been liberalized. Also, the advantages (in terms of the introduction of competitive pressures) that might have been derived from the trade liberalization program have been mitigated, at least in part, by the application of disguised tariff increases in the form of temporary compensatory taxes.[f]

How important is the protection afforded by the system of tariffs and quotas? The Nathan report refers to the "restrictive tradition of France with respect to foreign imports." It concludes that: "The French market, except for short periods, has largely been isolated from foreign markets for the past 20 years. . . . The economic cloistering has, in effect, permitted our country to develop, purely

[f] See Chapter 4 above.

on the basis of internal exigencies, practices or policies which could not fail to have consequences on the structure of national costs. . . ."[38] A report of the Commission on National Accounts contains similar views: "In effect, in the shelter of our frontier which foreign merchandise finds it difficult to cross . . . a structure is developed which is no longer oriented towards the most profitable activities, which is no longer incited to maximum productivity. . . . It is in the structure which it has established that the almost complete cloistering of the French market must be judged. The true long-term cost of abusive protectionism is the low productivity of the economy."[39]

The administrative procedures established by the government in the import field may also have acted, perhaps unintentionally in some instances, to limit the degree of competition among domestic firms. The granting of import licenses has generally been on the basis of the level of activity during some earlier reference period, tending to freeze established market positions and to prevent the expansion of firms or the entry of new ones. Perhaps more important is the key role given to trade associations which, as has been seen, may monopolize the import of certain products or advise the government on the allocation of import quotas among member firms. There is at least a presumption that this corporate organization of importing procedures has restricted the competitive search of individual firms for cheaper or superior sources of procurement abroad.[40]

IV THE POLICIES—ACTIONS AFFECTING THE COST-PRICE STRUCTURE

While state interventions that affect particular costs and prices sometimes seek to improve the way in which the market process performs its allocative task, they are often aimed at accomplishing other ends (such as the control of business fluctuations, improvement in the balance of payments, a better income distribution). The success of public interventions in achieving these other ends will not be discussed at this point, although it may be recalled that a good many reservations were expressed earlier in connection with them. At issue here is their impact on the functioning of the market system. The overall impression that emerges is one of extreme government intervention with respect to particular costs and prices, with the consequences of a considerable rigidity of key elements of the cost-price structure, multiple distortions of prices, and much added complexity and confusion.

The following discussion deals separately with the costs to the businessman of the various factors of production and with the prices of business products.

A. COSTS

Most attention is given to wages and social benefits, which are by far the most important elements in the cost structure; for other costs, the discussion seeks primarily to identify the ways in which state intervention appears to exercise a significant influence.

1. Wages and Social Benefits. Government activities in the wage field affect the general level and structure of wages to a major extent, presumably altering the relative attractiveness of employment in different industries and/or forcibly shunting part of the labor force into "under-employment." In part as a result of state intervention, the wage structure has tended to become monolithic, with only limited adaptability of wage payments to variations in productivity at the plant level.

All wages were blocked, and collective bargaining suspended, in November 1939. Wages were tightly controlled throughout the Vichy period; the controls were not relaxed during the immediate postwar years, and functioned more effectively than the government's price controls. Collective bargaining, with which there had been little experience before the war,[41] was nominally restored in 1946, but the exclusion of wage questions from these negotiations deprived the bargaining of much of its significance.

The relaxation of price controls in 1948 and 1949 created strong pressures for the abandonment of governmental wage fixing in favor of free wage determination through collective bargaining. Following a nationwide strike, a law was adopted (on February 11, 1950) providing for the freeing of wages. Wages were henceforth to be determined by employer-worker understandings taking the form of full collective bargaining agreements or (originally as an interim measure) simpler contractual agreements concerned only with wages.[42]

The 1950 legislation appears to have had more of an effect on the character than on the extent of government influence over wage determination. The government retained the power to fix and adjust a guaranteed minimum wage, which in practice has proven to be the key element in the movement of the wage structure as a whole.

The 1950 law established a High Commission on Collective Bargaining comprising representatives of employers, unions, family associations, and government agencies, to advise the government in fixing the minimum wage. This advice, which the government was not committed to accept, was to be based on a study of the "typical budget" of a Parisian unmarried, unskilled laborer. After three and a half years of dissension, a budget was finally voted by a "majority" of the Commission, but with the employer representatives boycotting the meeting and the government representatives abstaining from the vote.

During the initial deadlock of the High Commission, the government proceeded to fix the minimum wage independently. Subsequent increases in the minimum have taken place by executive action, with or without the advice of the Commission and without reference to the typical budget. In 1952, a step was taken to link the guaranteed minimum wage automatically to (upward) movements in the price level by establishing a sliding scale for the minimum wage. The government is obliged to increase the minimum wage (on a proportional basis) if the index of the cost of living rises by 5 per cent beyond a reference point.[g] The cost of living index not having reached the fatal point, there has not been (as of 1955) any occasion to apply the sliding scale.[43]

Experience since 1952 indicates that the movement of the wage structure as a whole closely follows changes in the government-determined minimum wage.[44] Thus, according to Edgar Faure, the minimum wage was increased by 28 per cent between January 1, 1950 and the beginning of 1954, while the general level of wages increased by 26 per cent over this period.[45] Changes in the minimum wage have particular relevance by virtue of the fact that a substantial number of wage earners actually receive close to the minimum. Moreover, the law of February 1950 built the minimum wage into collective bargaining agreements by requiring that these agreements contain provisions with respect to the hierarchy of wages according to skills, starting from the wage rate of an unskilled worker, which cannot be below the legal minimum. Some collective bargaining agreements go further and specify that wages must be increased each time that there is a rise in the legal minimum. Increases in labor remuneration can, and in numerous

[g] The index in question is the monthly index of prices of 213 articles, entering into family consumption, published by INSEE. The law provides that the minimum wage can only be increased once every four months in the absence of "exceptional circumstances."

individual cases do, take place through collective bargaining or through action by employers to raise wages, to provide thinly disguised wage increases in the form of special bonuses of one sort or another, or to reclassify personnel. But for the most part there have not been substantial increases in the wage level except through government action on the minimum wage.

It was apparently not the original expectation of the government that the minimum wage would have this decisive influence on private wage behavior.[46] Among the factors which explain its influence is the fact that wage determination through private collective bargaining has not been as effective as was envisaged in 1950. A substantial weakening of the position of organized labor had taken place since labor's heyday at the time of liberation. The initial negotiations revealed a marked disparity in the bargaining positions of employer and employee. Moderate Premier Bidault was impelled to observe that "the freedom of bargaining is not the freedom not to bargain."[47] The CNPF was able to impose a remarkable degree of discipline upon its employer-members, and in most instances the first round of collective bargaining resulted in labor's acceptance, after some unsuccessful strikes, of the terms "recommended" in advance by the CNPF. The disciplined behavior of the rank and file of French business in following the advice of the CNPF has also been demonstrated on subsequent occasions.[h]

The trade unions have consequently tended to pin their hopes on negotiations at the national level on the minimum wage and related government responsibilities, their premise being that their influence over wage policies is greatest in direct dealings with the government. Heads of private business organizations have also often looked to the government for leadership in wage matters.[i] The government's influence has been enhanced by the fact that it is the largest employer in France. (Over one-fourth of non-agricultural wage earners are on the government payroll in the administrative services and the nationalized enterprises, according to one estimate.)[48] There has thus been a tendency to "nationalize" wage policies, with the wage structure as a whole following the outcome of government decisions (in response to business and labor pressures) with respect to the minimum wage.

[h] The president of the CNPF has claimed that only 10 per cent of business firms failed to carry out a wage recommendation made by it in September 1953. (*Le Monde*, January 8, 1954, p. 5.)

[i] In September 1953, for example, the president of the CNPF stated "We will not be able to choose a formula for increasing wages in the private sector until the Government has decided on its policy." (Quoted in *Le Monde*, September 17, 1953, p. 1.)

In 1954 the government devised an ingenious strategy in order to increase minimal wages without officially raising the minimum wage (which would automatically entail some increases throughout the wage hierarchy). A "bonus" to be added to the minimum wage was invented, with the provision that no wage could be below the (unchanged) hourly minimum plus the bonus. The bonus was raised again in October 1954, and April 1955, and a legal phrase coined ("minimum social remuneration") to cover the new *de facto* minimum wage. The process of adjusting the bonus was formalized by Mendès-France, who instituted a semi-annual rendezvous with labor representatives to reach a decision on the feasible increase in wages, taking into account changes in production, productivity, and prices. The institution was carried over by his successor; on both occasions, however, the rendezvous was largely an empty formality, the government making a unilateral decision with little consultation of organized labor.

While the legal fiction of the "bonus" may reduce the magnitude of the wage increases following automatically upon government decisions to raise the *de facto* minimum, it does not prevent these decisions from exercising an important influence on the movement of the level of wages and costs. And the process of semi-annual consultations has increased the uniformity of wage behavior at the expense of the adjustment of wages to changes in productivity. The sliding wage scale adds a further element of rigidity to wage and price policy. The fatal index number, like the sword of Damocles, hangs over the economy, inhibiting government action, desirable for other reasons, that might bring about an increase in the domestic price level.

The flexibility of employer policy with respect to labor remuneration and the effectiveness of wage incentives have been further reduced by the growing importance of social or fringe benefits, the magnitude and character of which are fixed by the state on the basis of "social need" rather than individual productivity. The foundations of the system (or systems) of social security were laid in the decade before the start of the second World War. An expansion of the social security system, together with the establishment of plant committees and the nationalization of basic industries, were the three major "conquests" of labor after the liberation. The most important postwar development has been an increase in the rate of payments under the various programs. Some overhauling was undertaken, but the term social security "system" still applies loosely to the three component programs of family allowances, social insurance, and workmen's compensation. Unemployment insurance, never appreciable in France because of the low rate of nominal unemployment, is separate from any of these systems. Various groups (farmers, miners, railroad employees, civil servants) with special (and usually more favorable) programs for social insurance have been able to maintain their separate identities. Attempts to broaden the coverage of social insurance by extending it to non-wage earners have made little progress.

On the whole, the French programs of social security appear to be about equal to the average for Western European countries in terms of risks covered and proportion of the population benefiting from the program. Family allowances are considerably higher than the European average, reflecting the government's concern with the demographic problem, but widows and unemployed persons receive relatively less.[49]

A distinctive feature of the French social security system is that the programs are expected to be self-financing (largely through employers' contributions) without public assistance from the state or from local communities. In practice, the state regularly contributes to some of the special funds and has been obliged to make up a substantial deficit in the general system in a number of years. The family allowances to farmers are administered as an "annexed budget" that receives the proceeds of a special tax on agricultural products and a part of the production tax. Despite these exceptions, the French system relies more heavily on contributions from employers and employees than is the case in any other country. As a result of the present method of financing, about three-fourths of the receipts of the social security system are paid in by the employer.[50]

Some indication of the cost (and extensiveness) of the social security system is given by the fact that total social charges (i.e., employers' payments) for firms in the private sector of the economy represented 33.7 per cent of the wage bill in 1952.[j] [51] The total is composed of social insurance (8.2 per cent), family allowances (13.8 per cent), work accidents (2.1 per cent), and private social welfare programs instituted by the employer (2.0 per cent); a small percentage is attributable to the apprenticeship tax and special retirement funds, while the remainder—about 7 per cent—is for paid vacations.

[j] This figure does not include the 5 per cent payroll tax on wages or the transportation bonus to Paris workers, which some sources include in a broader definition of "social" charges.

The ratio of social charges to wages more than doubled between 1938 and 1952.[52] The expansion of the social security system since the war and the reliance on employer financing do not necessarily mean, however, that the real income position of the worker has increased correspondingly. Measurement of changes in the real income of labor over time is extremely imprecise. It is probably safest to conclude, in qualitative terms, that the real income position of French labor increased slightly during the period 1938-1954, primarily in the last two years.[53] The principal effect of the substantial increase in social transfers since the war has therefore been a massive redistribution of income within the laboring class. This "immense and permanent transfer of real income"[54] has gone from the young to the aged, from the healthy to the sick, and from bachelors to parents of large families.

2. *Management Decisions.* Government policy has at times been directed towards giving labor a greater voice in management. This policy, if implemented, would no doubt have affected business costs (in such ways, for example, as subordinating efficiency to other aims). But it has not had much success, and labor in fact plays little role in the conduct of business operations.

The establishment of labor-management plant committees (*comités d'entreprise*) was expected to be a key element in the "social liberation." The preamble to the 1946 Constitution declared that "Every worker may participate through his delegates in the collective determination of working conditions and in the management of the enterprise." The Parliamentary debates on the proposal to establish plant committees revealed, however, a sharp ideological difference between the extreme left, which regarded the plant committees as a prelude to social revolution, and the groups that considered them to be an organ of collaboration between workers and management within the framework of private capitalism. The crucial decision was in favor of evolution rather than revolution, with management retaining its decision-making powers in the important areas of business policy.

The legislation of 1945 and 1946 provided for the establishment of plant committees in firms of more than 50 employees. The functions of the committees are most extensive in the social field, where they may direct, or participate in the direction, or simply supervise the direction of social welfare programs established and financed by the management (canteens, sports activities, etc.). Their technical functions include the study of suggestions made by personnel or management for increasing production and productivity. The committees may also give opinions on general organizational matters. The economic and financial functions assigned to the committees are primarily consultative. The head of the concern must give a general report on the situation and activity of the business at least annually. He must inform the committee of his profits, and the committee may make suggestions as to their disposal. The committee may also be represented in a consultative role on the board of directors of corporations. It may discuss wage questions in the specific context of the economic and financial position of the firm.

The consensus of most observers is that the effectiveness of the committees has largely been confined to the area of social programs. In very few cases have the committees exercised a significant measure of influence or control over the financial or technical management of the firm, although some use has been made of the committees to develop suggestions for improving production methods. The consultations with employers over matters of financial policy have frequently been reduced to the legal minimum of hollow gestures. Although a considerable number of employers have made a genuine effort to have the experiment succeed, a larger number have attempted to whittle away the influence of the committees through a combination of inertia and more-or-less open resistance. On the labor side, the CGT has adopted an uncompromising and revolutionary attitude towards the committees, which a communist deputy and former Minister of Labor described as a "weapon in the class struggle."[55] In instances where both labor and management have been prepared to cooperate, the lack of financial or management training on the part of worker representatives has made it difficult for them to carry out their intended functions. Also, divided responsibility, where there is some conflict of interest, makes for slow and sometimes inconsistent decision-making.

3. Raw Materials. The purchase of raw materials is influenced by public action by virtue of the fact that a substantial proportion of industrial raw materials must be obtained from abroad. The price at which these materials can be procured and the quantities which are available therefore depend on government policies (discussed previously) with respect to exchange rates, tariffs, and quantitative restrictions.

On some imported raw materials (nickel, zinc, tungsten), subsidies are provided by the Treasury in order to reduce the price to domestic industrial users. The prices of a number of imported raw materials are also influenced by equalization or compensation funds which the government has instituted. In some cases (sulphur), the imported price is raised through the compensation scheme, while in others (coal, hides and skins) it is reduced to the lower price of domestic production. In either case, the price of domestic and imported materials is made identical for all industrial consumers. In the absence of an equalization fund, the prevalence of import monopolies—in the form either of state trading agencies or of private associations of importers acting under the state's authority—also contributes to price (and cost) uniformity.

4. Excise Taxes. The various excise taxes constitute a major element of the cost structure of the firm. A measure of their importance is given by the Ministry of Industry and Commerce which has estimated that tax payments represented 22.3 per cent of industrial costs in 1953.[56] How the structure of excise taxes may influence the cost behavior of the firm has been indicated in the chapter on tax policy.

5. Cost of Borrowing. The cost to the firm of its external borrowing bears the influence of government policy, both directly and indirectly. The interest charges on short-term borrowing are very closely related to the discount rate fixed by the Bank of France. On longer-term borrowing through the private capital market, the state may be considered to share responsibility for the high prevailing rates on security issues and medium-term bank loans because of its failure to check the postwar inflations of 1945-1948 and 1950-1951, which contributed to the popular reluctance to place funds in the capital market.

Government policy on the use of public funds or public guarantees has led to differential costs of borrowing for different investment purposes, in accordance with criteria, not always clearly defined, of relative importance. Some public funds are provided in the form of grants, at no expense to the private investors (who may, however, have been obliged to borrow in order to make the payments which the state later reimburses, as in the case of reconstruction grants). Bond issues, or loans by private credit institutions, that are eligible for a guarantee by the state are floated at rates lower than those which normally prevail. The same is true for medium-term bank credits extended with the cooperation of public authorities, and probably also for loans extended by public and semi-public institutions (the rate on the latter being generally

6 per cent to 8 per cent). Loans from the Modernization and Equipment Fund were in principle to be made at the prevailing market rate, since to do otherwise would subsidize the borrowers and therefore discourage investment by other firms. Nevertheless, in the period up to 1950, 90 per cent of the long-term loans were extended at rates well below the market level.[57]

6. *Rent.* The rental of business premises has been the subject of elaborate legislation since 1914. As a practical matter, the legislation is chiefly concerned with the situation of small firms, particularly small shopkeepers in the distribution trades, since the larger industrial and commercial buildings are generally erected on a site owned by the firm. Two related problems have been dealt with by the legislation: the right of the lessor to terminate the lease or at least not to renew it when it expires; and the determination of business rents. Not surprisingly, the legislation appears to be inspired by the desire to prevent the landlord from utilizing his economic position to the full; the economic consequences have probably been some loss of resource mobility and of flexibility of costs and prices.

During both world wars and for several years thereafter, leases were extended automatically by law to protect the lessee against eviction. Legislation immediately after the second war suppressed the "right of recovery," which had allowed the lessor to expel the lessee in order to convert the business premises into a private dwelling for personal use. Since September 1953, eviction of business tenants has again been made possible, but substantial "due compensation" (e.g., three times the annual rent) must be provided for the loss incurred. The lessee thus receives considerable protection against a refusal by the lessor to renew the contract. It seems likely, therefore, that this aspect of rent legislation has distorted the apportionment of sites and structures among different uses.

As concerns the amount of business rents, this is determined, unlike rents on dwelling units, by free negotiation. Government regulations nevertheless specify the conditions under which rents may be revised (e.g., when the lease is renewed, three years after the lease has been renewed or entered upon). Some leases contain a provision for automatic "sliding-scale" increases in rents with changes in the economic situation; a decree of September 1953 has protected tenants from frequent increases in rents under this clause by stipulating that it can only be invoked when the adjustment exceeds 25 per cent. The same decree also introduced some measure of business rent control by providing that when a rent is renewed or revised, the value must correspond to a "fair rental" of the premises. The legislation lists some criteria for determining this fair value; in the event that the contracting parties cannot agree, a court ruling is obtained.

B. PRICES

The price decisions of the firm are influenced by a multitude of government interventions (tariff policy, credit controls, tax measures, etc.) that affect the market situation for its products. In addition, the state has exercised a more direct control over price policies through a variety of measures generally aimed at curbing inflation or subsidizing particular groups. The combined effects of government action in all its forms have been to deprive the entrepreneur of a large measure of individual responsibility over one of his principal decisions, to introduce a considerable degree of price rigidity, and (by applying different kinds of controls to different products) to distort the structure of relative prices.

A complete system of price controls was introduced during 1940-1944 and continued during the early postwar years. There has since been a progressive relaxation of price controls on specific products, with the establishment of an intermediate zone of "controlled freedom" through which products may pass on the road to "freedom." The trend has been reversed on occasion, however, and general price freezes have frequently been applied.[58]

When prices of specific products are fixed by administrative action, it is the maximum price or margin which is prescribed; in practice, however, prices are set at the maximum level in almost all cases. The fixed price or margin is based, in principle, on a study of the production costs of a group of at least three "representative" firms (one large, one medium, and one small), weighted according to their relative importance in the industry. In practice, it is customary to base the price or margin on the costs (plus minimum profit) of the least efficient firm. The price is therefore adequate to permit the survival of all firms and, consequently, substantial profits to the more efficient.[59]

A notable exception is that of house rents, which have been controlled since 1914 at extremely low levels. (Housing rents are considered here as a source of business income to the lessor, as distinct from the earlier discussion of commercial rents as a business cost.) As a result, the share of consumer income devoted to housing, which was 16 per cent in 1914, was 7.3 per cent in 1938 and 2 or 3 per cent in 1951.[60] A law of September 1948 attempted to rectify this situation by authorizing rent increases in successive stages and linking subsequent increases in rents to the movement of wages. The latter provision has not been applied, since the nominal wage used for reference purposes has deliberately not been increased since 1948, while the permissible increases in rents were wiped out, in large part, by the rise in prices. As a result, the "average" French family spends about the same proportion of its income on rent as on tobacco products, and less than half (40 per cent) of what it spends on alcoholic beverages.[61] While the artificial level of rents has undoubtedly conferred some benefits on the tenants in place, it has resulted in a diversion of resources from the upkeep of existing houses and the construction of new ones. Among the many unfortunate economic consequences of the ensuing housing shortage has been a sharp reduction in the mobility of labor.

The system of "controlled freedom" differs from that of fixed prices primarily in that the role of the government is reduced to the occasional exercise of its right to veto the proposals for maximum prices submitted by trade associations. The practical effect of this difference should not be exaggerated, however, since the trade associations play an extensive ("advisory") role in determining the level of fixed prices. The greater ease with which prices can be changed is probably the distinguishing characteristic of the system of "controlled freedom."

The difference between the system of "free" prices and the two examined above is often more a matter of degree than of kind. As has been seen, prices not controlled by the government may be fixed privately, either by cartel agreement or by the joint action of a trade association. In addition, the "free" sector of prices has been the object of considerable government activity. In February 1948, a law was enacted to oppose "unjustified" price increases on fully freed articles, apparently to serve as a warning against massive increases. In October of the same year, the addition of a number of articles to the free list was made conditional upon the agreement of employer representatives to reduce prices voluntarily on a list of "essential" products. A decree of January 1949 prohibited the incorporation of an increase in excise taxes into prices charged in the free sector. The price reduction campaigns of Pinay and Laniel were initially based on agreements negotiated with trade associations for specific reductions in "free" prices.

The significance of these several categories of price regulation may be sharply reduced by action taken by the government on the level of prices as a whole (regardless of the price zone in which they may be found). A celebrated campaign to reduce all prices by 5 per cent was undertaken by Premier Blum in January 1947. In October 1950, a government decree blocked all prices in order to limit and spread out the effects of an increase in raw material prices. In September 1952, Pinay blocked prices at the level of August 30. In February 1954, the Laniel government consolidated the general reduction in the price level that had since taken place, largely through the economic recession, by freezing prices and markups (except for imports, agricultural products at the production level, and fishery products) at the level of February 8. By the end of 1955, therefore, all prices except those exempted by the original government order or subsequent administrative decision had been blocked for a period of over three years.

The tendency of such freezes, insofar as they are effective, to make the price mechanism more sluggish is easy to understand. Whatever their efficacy in checking inflationary expectations and pressures may be, they are hardly the medicine for "sclerosis."

V SUMMARY

The French economy suffers from an impairment of the market process through which resources are put to different uses. Two symptoms of this impairment are the rigidity and distortions of major elements of the cost-price structure and the pronounced weakness of competitive pressures. Some government measures have been aimed at correcting these problems, but the present magnitude of the afflictions is due in considerable part to the aggravating effect of public policies in these and related fields.

The government has attempted to strengthen competitive forces through legislation against agreements or practices which restrain competition. The legislation embodies a dubious distinction between "good" and "bad" cartels, and there is little record of enforcement against even so-called "bad" cartels. Foreign competition has been encouraged by the international programs for economic integration, of which France was once the leader but later became the most recalcitrant member. Trade liberalization has also been directed towards this end, but has not yet broken into the core of protectionist quotas.

On the other hand, the government has given important encouragement and assistance to the extensive activities of trade associations, which have resulted in a collective organization of large elements of business operations. It has also authorized the activities of some cartels and participated in others through the intermediary of public enterprises. A combination of tariffs and import quotas still provides considerable protection from foreign competition. On balance, the net effect of government action appears to have been to strengthen the forces, formidable enough in their own right, that restrain the competitive process and reduce its effectiveness in allocating resources or promoting growth.

State intervention has given rise to multiple distortions of costs and prices. Labor costs, a key element of the cost-price structure, have become less adaptable to changes in productivity at the plant level as a result of government fixing of the minimum wage and increased reliance on non-wage payments based on social need. Excise taxes, interest charges, the costs of raw materials, and business rents are also extensively influenced, in a variety of directions, through public action. The needed flexibility of prices has been sharply reduced by specific price controls and general price freezes. In the case of house rents, the low level of controlled prices has created a major housing shortage with serious economic and social consequences. None of these policies is well suited to cure the sclerosis of the market or to promote rapid economic growth.

PART V

THE STATE AS REGULATOR OF AGRICULTURE

CHAPTER 11

STATE ACTION ON THE EFFICIENCY OF FARMS

I THE PROBLEM AND ITS SETTING

As IN the preceding discussion of private business, government regulation is divided here into two chapters dealing, respectively, with actions affecting the efficiency of individual farms—the subject of this chapter—and actions affecting the functioning of the market process. These are both aspects of the broader question of the efficiency of resource use within agriculture and between agriculture and other parts of the economy.

In its approach to farm problems, the government has frequently been torn between two objectives: the protection of agriculture against economic change, particularly in the form of preserving the *status quo* of small, family farms; and the modernization and expansion of farm operations by measures to increase the size or efficiency of farm units. The "golden rule" of agricultural policy, according to a spokesman of an influential farm organization, is "the safeguarding of the maximum number of family farms."[1] This strong ideological preference for a high farm population, organized into a large number of small farms that are owner-operated and where the only labor is provided by the farmer and his family, is voiced not only by farm organizations but also by deputies and senators and by government officials. Premier Mendès-France asserted that "No prejudice against small, family farming exists in the government's thinking. We still consider it to be the basic unit of the agricultural economy."[2] This sentiment is reflected in a host of protective measures that influence both the structure of farm operations and the marketing system of farm products. On the other hand, the theme of agricultural expansion has found some supporters, and was officially consecrated in the first and second modernization plans. A variety of measures have been adopted with the aim of modernizing French agriculture, mostly under the aegis of the plans.

Another striking contrast in French agriculture is that between the rich endowments of nature and the meager uses to which man has put his inheritance. If, unlike the prodigal son, the French farmer cannot be accused of having wasted his substance in riotous living, he can be said, like the cautious servant, to have used unwisely the talent of silver placed at his disposal.

While nature, in France as elsewhere, has been capricious in the short run, her permanent gifts have included an excellent geographical location, a mild but varied climate suitable to the growing of a diversity of crops, numerous rivers, and a terrain unbroken by deserts, swamps, or flooded lands. Natural conditions are somewhat less favorable in Central and Southern France, particularly in the mountainous regions; except on the plains where irrigation is possible and in the areas where vineyards are the main farm activity, only the more extensive types of farming can be carried on. The total land area available for farming is larger in France than in almost any other European country this side of the Iron Curtain. The area of arable land and orchards is largest in France, while the area of permanent pasture is second only to Spain. The arable land per inhabitant is higher in France than in countries other than Denmark, Finland, Spain, and Sweden.[3]

Despite these advantages, and taking into account the marked disparities among regions, the dominant impression is that the productivity of French agriculture is very low. A report of the *Commissariat Général au Plan* observes:

> The facts are obvious: while French agriculture occupies a third of the employed population, it contributes only a fifth of the national production. For the same cultivated surface, the French soil produces half as much as the Danish soil and one-third as much as the Belgian or Dutch soil. A flagrant contrast exists between the richness of this soil, which could nourish 70 million inhabitants, and the poverty of the farmers in certain regions of France. These disparities are inadmissible, and hardly worthy of an economically developed country.[4]

How this situation has come about will be more apparent when the farm population, size of farms, state of equipment, and attitude of farmers have been examined.

A. POPULATION IN AGRICULTURE

A relatively high proportion of the population lives by means of agriculture—roughly 25 per cent of the total, according to the 1946 population census. The proportion of old and young people who remain actively employed (on a part- or full-time basis) is higher in agriculture than in non-agricultural pursuits; the number of persons employed in agriculture (7.3 million in 1946) is therefore a higher proportion—about 36 per cent—of the total active population.[5] Some of the older and younger persons and many of the wives of farm operators classified by the census as actively employed were only part-time workers. If a correction is made to convert the data into full-time adult equivalent persons, it appears that agriculture accounts for about 30 per cent of the actively employed population.[6]

Agriculture is relatively a more important source of employment in France than in many European countries and in the United States. As can be seen from the following figures, the proportion of the total active population employed in agriculture is appreciably lower in the countries of Northwestern and Central Europe; the countries in which the French proportion is exceeded are in the less industrialized regions of Southern Europe.[7]

Country	*Year of estimate or census*	*Per cent of total active population engaged in agriculture*
Spain	1940	52
Portugal	1950	49
Italy	1952	39
France	1946	36
Western Germany	1950	23
Denmark	1952	23
Switzerland	1941	20
Netherlands	1947	19
Sweden	1950	17
Belgium	1947	12
United States	1952	11
United Kingdom	1952	5

Because of the high proportion of the population engaged in agriculture, the amount of land per farmer is only about equal to the European average. France ranks below the United Kingdom, Sweden, Ireland, and Denmark, and above Western Germany, the Netherlands, Norway, Switzerland, and Italy in terms of "arable equivalent" land per active person in agriculture.[8] If grouped according to the number of *male* active persons, the ranking would be changed only slightly.[9] Thus, the advantages to productivity arising from a large land area have been partly offset by the high proportion of the population engaging in farming.

B. SIZE OF FARM UNITS

Another offsetting factor is the organization of landholdings into many small operating units, most commonly owned by the farmer and operated by him and his family with no hired labor.

The land area is divided into a large number of farms, about 2.3 million in 1946 if one counts those which provided the main employment for their operators; the total is raised to 2.5 million if farms providing only a secondary source of employment are included.[10] From crude data it appears that the average size of a French farm does not differ substantially from that of neighboring countries. As in some other countries, however, a single French farm (as a unit of ownership) may be broken up into a large number of discontinuous parcels or strips. This parcelling, which is one of the most widely discussed problems of French agriculture, is a serious obstacle to the adoption of efficient farming techniques, and may result in the farm unit being operated (in some respects) as several farms.

A very rough impression of the relative size of farms within France can be obtained from their classification according to the value of output. Table 29 presents data drawn from two different sources. They do not agree precisely, but nonetheless the data

TABLE 29

DISTRIBUTION OF FARMS BY VALUE OF GROSS FINAL PRODUCTION IN 1950-1951

Gross Final Production (thousands of francs)	*Number of Farms (in thousands)*	*Per Cent of Total Farms*	*Per Cent of Total Gross Final Production*
Source A:			
Less than 500	1,100	46.0	13.0
500 to 750	450	19.0	11.0
750 to 1,500	550	23.0	27.0
1,500 to 3,000	200	8.0	25.0
More than 3,000	100	4.0	24.0
Source B:			
Less than 300	1,000	40.0	–
300 to 450	400	16.0	–
450 to 750	500	20.0	–
750 to 1,500	400	16.0	–
1,500 to 3,000	160	6.4	–
More than 3,000	40	1.6	–

Source A: Data from *Les Services Economiques et Financiers*, January 17, 1953, reproduced in La Documentation Française, *Problèmes économiques*, February 24, 1953.

Source B: Ministère des Finances *Rapports sur les comptes provisoires de la nation des années 1951 et 1952 et sur le budget économique de l'année 1953* (Paris, 1953), p. 75.

show the existence of a large number of small farms with a low value of production and a comparatively small number of larger farms that account for a substantial proportion of the total value of farm production. Thus, 8-12 per cent of the farms account for under (but probably close to) half of the total gross output; at the other extreme, some 67-75 per cent of the farms, with annual gross production of less than 750,000 francs in 1950-1951, produce about one-fourth of the total. The disparity is even greater in terms of cash receipts, since small farmers consume a greater share of their own production.

Most French farms are small enough to be operated only by family labor, without outside help. Salaried workers are relatively unimportant in agriculture (representing only one-sixth or 1.2 million of the 7.3 million persons actively employed in farming in 1946), and are concentrated in a relatively small number of large farming operations in certain regions. Again according to the 1946 census, one-third of the farms employed only the operator and his wife, and 78 per cent of the farms used only family labor and no permanent hired labor. The large-scale farms with more than two permanent salaried workers represented only 3.4 per cent of the total. About two-thirds of the farms were owner-operated in 1946; of the remainder, considerably more were operated by cash tenants than by share tenants.

C. FARM BUILDINGS, MACHINERY, FERTILIZERS

The dilapidated condition of many farm buildings, the absence of basic comforts and utilities, the low mechanization of farm operations, and the limited use of fertilizers also contribute, directly or indirectly, to the low productivity of French agriculture.

As for rural housing, "it is still characterized by antiquity, discomfort, lack of elementary equipment, and in certain regions by overpopulation," observed a draft report of the *Conseil Economique*.[11] The average age of farm buildings is over 100 years and reaches 137 years in Normandy.[12] Traveling through France, one is struck by the large number of abandoned farm buildings and the poor maintenance of those still standing. Only their solid construction enables these farm buildings to survive despite the small amount of resources devoted to maintenance. In the area west of a line Cotentin-Nevers-La Rochelle, 60 per cent of the farm houses consist of only one room; in some regions, such as Brittany, 45 per cent of these rooms have dirt floors.[13]

The electrification of rural areas (farm and village) has proceeded slowly. An estimated 3 million rural inhabitants did not have electricity in 1951, while a further 6 million were supplied with only a small amount of power; 10 million rural inhabitants, or slightly more than half of the total, had "adequate" electricity.[14] The situation with regard to water supply is considerably worse. Only 10,503 communes of less than 5,000 inhabitants (out of a total of 37,077) had satisfactory water distribution systems. In all, only about one-third of the rural population received water (and not always in adequate supply).[15] The proportion of farms receiving both water and electricity has been estimated to range between 1 per cent (in Brittany) and 18 per cent (in Southeastern France).[16]

The prewar stock of modern types of agricultural machinery was extremely low, and deteriorated during the war through the inability to provide normal maintenance and replacement. There has since been a rapid and encouraging increase in the use of machinery; the number of tractors, for example, has risen from a prewar 30,000 to 275,000 at the beginning of 1955.[17] In comparison with agriculturally developed countries, however, the French tractor supply is still low. Thus, there was one tractor for each 77 hectares of cultivated land in France at the beginning of 1955, as against 1 for 44 in the United States, 18 in Great Britain, 24 in Western Germany, and 33 in Sweden.[a] In Italy the proportion was 1 for 109.[18] There were 2.2 times as many tractors per active male engaged in agriculture in Denmark than in France, 8.1 times as many in the United Kingdom, and 2.3 times as many in Western Germany in 1953 or 1952-1953. Wide regional differences in the use of tractors within France can be noted; the number of tractors per employed male in agriculture in Southeastern France is only half that of Northern France, while in Brittany it is only a third.[19]

The consumption of fertilizers has also increased since the war, but, until recent years, in much smaller proportions. There appears to have been a promising increase in the use of fertilizers in the last few years; consumption of nitrogen, phosphoric acid, and potash was 32 per cent, 43 per cent and 40 per cent higher (respectively) in 1954-1955 than in 1952-1953.[20] In comparison with other European countries, however, French use of fertilizers is still low, as can readily be seen from the data in Table 30. More recent but less complete data indicate that consumption of ferti-

[a] A hectare is equivalent to 2.47 acres.

lizers per hectare of agricultural area in Denmark and Western Germany is about triple, and in the United Kingdom almost double, that of France.[b] [21] Regional differences in the application of fertilizers are striking. In the North, fertilizer consumption compares favorably with that in other European countries, while

TABLE 30

CONSUMPTION OF FERTILIZER IN VARIOUS EUROPEAN COUNTRIES, 1950-1951

	Fertilizer use in kilograms per hectare[1]			
Country	*Nitrogen (N)*	*Phosphoric Acid (P_2O_5)*	*Potash (K_2O)*	*Total*
Netherlands	71	52	66	189
Belgium	42	44	83	169
Norway	31	34	40	105
Germany	26	31	48	105
Denmark	23	27	33	83
United Kingdom	18	34	18	70
Switzerland	7	29	15	51
Sweden	15	23	11	49
France	11	15	14	40
Austria	8	13	8	29
Portugal	8	17	1	26
Italy	8	15	1	24
Ireland	2	13	4	19
Greece	6	6	1	13

Source: Data from the OEEC, cited in INSEE, *Etudes et conjoncture*, August 1953, p. 873.

[1] The area used to measure fertilizer application per hectare includes all agricultural land, except rough pasture and waste land.

in Brittany it is only one-half, and in Southeastern France one-ninth of consumption in the North.[22] The disparity has been increasing with time, and in some of the poorer regions fertilizer consumption is now below the prewar figure.[23]

D. FARMER ATTITUDES

The attitudes of farmers and farm groups are another important element in the setting. Except in some areas where specialization, and therefore commercialization, are widespread, the small farmer

[b] The indices (France = 100) were 292 in Denmark, 341 in Western Germany, 177 in the United Kingdom, and 76 in Italy, in 1953 or 1952-1953.

or peasant has a noticeable distrust of the market mechanism. He may consequently attempt to avoid the market by recourse to diversification of production and autoconsumption, sometimes through the use of highly backward techniques. The small farmer is said to resist strongly technological changes that would increase the measure of his dependence on the outside world, and is likely to feel that he knows his land better than any outside "expert," particularly one hired by the "state," of which he has the deepest suspicion. Pride in land ownership and in the independence that comes from lack of indebtedness discourages recourse to outside borrowing as a means of financing farm equipment.

Farmers are organized into a number of active and vocal groups. The principal farm organization is the *Fédération Nationale des Syndicats d'Exploitants Agricoles* (FNSEA), which claims a membership of 1,750,000 farmers.[c] The guiding philosophy of the FNSEA, according to its president, is the defense of "family agriculture," which is the "base of the whole of the French economy."[24] The FNSEA contains a number of affiliates, generally organized on a commodity basis, such as the organization of sugar-beet producers (*Confédération Générale des Planteurs de Betteraves*) and of wheat growers (*Association Générale des Producteurs de Blé*), which have been among the most influential of the Parliamentary lobbies. The efforts of these various organizations have been primarily directed towards market protection and guarantees (discussed in the next chapter) and towards a reduction in agricultural taxation and an increase in social benefits to farmers. Comparable interest has not generally been displayed in programs to increase productivity or to lower production costs.

E. PRODUCTIVITY

These considerations help to explain how the natural advantages enjoyed by French agriculture have been associated with a low level of productivity. A United Nations study of 14 European countries in 1950 showed that France had the largest gross output of agricultural products, but ranked tenth in terms of output per unit of arable land. The results of the study (shown in Table 31) are at best very approximate, especially in view of the problem of comparing agricultural output in a common unit of value. A more

[c] The FNSEA was (until 1954) part of a larger organization, the *Confédération Générale de l'Agriculture*, which included groups representative of cooperatives, credit systems, farm workers, etc.

TABLE 31

GROSS OUTPUT PER HECTARE OF "ARABLE EQUIVALENT" LAND IN SELECTED EUROPEAN COUNTRIES, 1950[1]

Country	*Gross output per hectare of arable equivalent land (in dollars)*
Belgium	561
Netherlands	497
Switzerland	489
Luxembourg	318
Denmark	285
Western Germany	273
Norway	236
United Kingdom	221
Italy	194
France	160
Sweden	151
Finland	143
Greece	125
Ireland	101
Weighted average 14 countries	204

Source: U.N. Economic Commission for Europe and Food and Agriculture Organization, *Output and Expenses of Agriculture in Some European Countries* (Geneva, January 31, 1953) Table 5, p. 16.

[1] The source of these data emphasizes that they should be considered as "very approximate."

recent study, referring to averages for the period 1950-1953, also reveals the relatively low yield of French farming:[25]

	Production per active male engaged in agriculture (France = 100)	*Production per hectare of agricultural area* (France = 100)
Denmark	203	200
United Kingdom	207	117
Western Germany	120	170
Italy	47	110

As might be expected, there are marked regional differences within France, the yield of some regions being more than double that of others.

The long-run growth of productivity in French agriculture also appears to have been relatively slow, as suggested by the following data of Colin Clark:[26]

	Period	*Rate of growth of output per man year*
Austria	1901-1951	2.3%
Belgium	1910-1953	2.2
Denmark	1880-1952	2.0
France	1870-1920	0.4
	1920-1952	1.9
Germany	1882-1938	0.9
Ireland	1867-1952	1.3
Netherlands	1934-1950	0.9
Norway	1890-1951	2.9
Sweden	1860-1925	2.1
	1925-1952	4.0
Switzerland	1890-1950	0.7
United Kingdom	1870-1930	0.5
	1930-1951	3.7

It may be efficient for different countries to apply different combinations of labor, fertilizers, and capital to the land, thus obtaining different results in terms of output per worker or per hectare. But the markedly low ranking of France by the various measures of productivity does suggest an inefficient use of farm resources, with substantial opportunities for raising productivity by substituting capital for farmers.

II POLICIES TENDING TO INCREASE THE EFFICIENCY OF FARMS

In considering the ways in which state action has affected agricultural productivity through its impact on the size and efficiency of farm operations, it is useful to examine separately the various factors of production. The results that can be observed are very uneven, with notable progress in some sectors and very little in others.

A. CAPITAL

The Modernization and Equipment plans have been the focal point of government efforts to raise efficiency by lowering the cost or improving the use of factors of farm production. Action on specific factors is discussed below. With respect to the plans as a whole, it will be recalled that the original version, drawn up in 1946-1947, placed relatively little emphasis on agriculture. It was not included in the "basic sectors" of the economy, although the farm machinery and nitrogenous fertilizer industries were included. It was only in September 1948, when the plan was revised to take into account the objectives of the OEEC long-term program (particularly balance of payments viability), that agriculture was placed in the privileged category that entitled it to receive low-interest loans from the Modernization and Equipment Fund.

The planning authorities seriously overestimated the amount of private financing that would take place. It was widely believed, for example, that the mattresses and washtubs of French peasants were filled with the profits of black-market operations during the wartime and early postwar periods. But such funds as existed were unevenly distributed, and small farmers were not inclined to place whatever cash they had into new techniques (though they might have felt differently, had there been educational programs and/or state financial assistance). By the time that the investment program was well under way, inflation had wiped out a substantial part of the value of accumulated savings. For these and other reasons, the amount of self-financing was far below expectations. Public assistance was originally conceived as serving primarily a "pump-priming" function; even in 1948-1949, by which time the expected share of public investments had been increased on several occasions, the estimates called for self-financing of more than 60 per cent of total agricultural investments. In practice, self-financing accounted for only 45 per cent through the end of 1952. The government has therefore played a major role in the realization of postwar investments in agriculture, as evidenced by the fact that the bulk of agricultural investments have been financed through public funds (broadly defined). Of the public funds, loans or grants from the administrative budget and the Modernization and Equipment Fund amounted to 30 per cent of the total. The remainder (25 per cent) came from semi-public credit institutions, notably the mutual farm credit system of the *Crédit Agricole*.[27] Although some of the *Crédit Agricole* loans were based on funds derived from member deposits and from bonds floated on the money market, the long-term loans can be regarded as at least semi-public in character since: a) the *Caisse Nationale de Crédit Agricole* operates under the authority of the Ministry of Agriculture; and b) state assistance, rediscount facilities, and guarantees have been provided in connection with the loans.

Agriculture officially occupied a more prominent position in the second plan. Public financing was expected to be required for a high proportion of the investments; in the case of "basic" investment projects for utilities and land improvement, public financing (broadly defined) was estimated at close to 90 per cent of the total.[28]

1. Basic Utilities. Investments to improve rural utilities and farm buildings received a high proportion of the public funds invested in agriculture during the life of the first plan, as can be seen from the data in Table 32.[d] These have undeniable social and economic

TABLE 32. INVESTMENTS IN AGRICULTURE, 1947-1952
(Values in billions of 1952 francs)

Item	*Total Invest-ments*	*Per Cent of total Invest-ments*	*Public Funds Invested*[1]	*Per Cent of Public Funds*	*Public Funds as per cer of total*
Factors of Production used by agriculture:					
Farm machinery industry	17	2	3	1	17
Nitrogenous fertilizers	28	3	24	9	85
Potash fertilizers	26	3	0	0	0
Sub-total	71	8	27	10	38
Agriculture:					
Electrification	66	7	53	19	80
Water supply	71	8	57	21	80
Buildings	38	4	25	9	65
Land improvements	38	4	25	9	65
Purchases of farm machinery	470	51	56[2]	20	11
Other	51	6			
Sub-total	734	80	216	78	29
Storage and Processing	113	12	34	12	30
Grand total	918	100	277	100	30

Source: Derived from Commissariat Général au Plan: *Rapport sur la réalisation du plan de moder sation et d'équipement de l'Union française, année 1952* (Paris, 1953), pp. 80 and 198-216; a *Rapport annuel sur l'exécution du plan de modernisation et d'équipement de l'Union fronça* (Paris, 1954), pp. 128-146.

[1] These funds relate to public investments narrowly defined (i.e. excluding loans from se public agencies, for which data are not available in this form). It should be noted that public fur are only given by the source as rough percentages (e.g. 85%) and therefore must be taken o as approximations.

[2] This figure is obtained by subtraction (from the total of 277 billion francs) and applies to b farm machinery and "other."

[d] A comparable breakdown by category of project is not available for the investments financed by semi-public credit institutions. It cannot be emphasized too strongly that the investment data in Table 32 are only rough approximations. Some investment figures are likely to be net, while others are gross. Some investments financed without state participation undoubtedly escape from the official enumerations. Data on the share of public financing have been computed on the basis of rough percentages given in the plan report and may have a wide margin of error.

utility, especially in view of the depressed living conditions on many French farms. But most (although not all) of the projects in this category only contribute to higher productivity in a roundabout fashion and over the long run.

Rural electrification and water supply are expensive operations. While progress in both fields as a result of the public loans and subsidies provided under the first plan can be noted, the second plan confirmed that "an immense task remains to be accomplished."[29] Although 1.8 million rural inhabitants benefited from new or improved water services under the first plan, it is estimated that more than 60 years would be required, at the rate of expenditure under the first plan, to complete the supply of water to the 13 million inhabitants who were still without it in 1954.[30] The situation with respect to electricity, while less serious, is also viewed as unsatisfactory. The second plan projected a rate of expenditure for water and electricity about double that of the first plan.[31]

Improvements in farm buildings (barns, silos) and housing have taken place under the plans, but it is difficult to obtain meaningful (and consistent) figures on the amount or importance of expenditures for this purpose. New farm housing is eligible for assistance under the various state subsidy programs for housing of all kinds. As pointed out in the second plan report, this legislation was conceived in terms of urban dwellings, and is not always well adapted to agriculture where the need may be more for remodeling and improved sanitation than for new construction.

2. *Farm Machinery*. The government has attempted to develop the use of farm machinery by action in three directions: a) investments in the farm machinery industry; b) financial assistance to purchasers of farm machinery; and c) encouragement of machinery cooperatives.

The farm machinery industry was placed among the "basic sectors" at the outset of the first plan. MEF loans for the construction of new plants or the enlargement of existing facilities represented 15-20 per cent of the funds invested in the industry between 1947 and 1952. The production of tractors has shown a striking increase from the prewar level of about 1,700 yearly:[32]

1950	14,200
1951	16,000
1952	26,100
1953	28,200
1954	39,800

The 1952 goal of the first plan, 41,000 tractors annually, was thus approximately reached in 1954.

Despite these investments in the industry, the cost of French tractors is high in comparison with that of other countries, in part because of the large number of producers and the lack of standardization of models. Between 1947 and 1953, 45 per cent of the tractors purchased in France were produced abroad, mostly in the United Kingdom and Germany.[33] The proportion of foreign tractors has been declining, in part because the heavy duties imposed on imports of tractors have reduced their share in the French market and have also raised their price to French consumers. The high costs of French production are indicated by the fact that, despite the duties, comparable French tractors sell for about the same price as imported German tractors and 15-35 per cent higher than imported British ones.[e] [34]

Farmers have been eligible for public loans for the purchase of farm machinery. These loans have presumably helped to make possible the remarkable increase in the stock of tractors since before the war. The extent of the contribution is not clear, however, since loans by the *Crédit Agricole* from its own funds for the purchase of farm machinery are not included in the data in Table 32. Financial assistance to machinery purchasers is also provided through a significant measure adopted by the government in 1954 that reduces by 15 per cent the price of specified types of new machinery sold to farmers. In practice, sales of tractors are conducted at the regular factory price, and the farmer receives a subsidy or rebate from the government equal to 15 per cent of the purchase price. Ten billion francs were appropriated for this purpose in 1954.

In the past the government has also promoted the establishment of cooperatives for the better use of farm machinery. These cooperatives help to spread the fixed cost of farm machinery over several farms, and make the use of tractors more economical for small farmers. In the years when farm machinery, especially tractors, was in short supply and allocations were in force, machinery cooperatives had priority over individual farmers.[35]

B. FERTILIZERS AND FUEL

The low average rate of fertilizer consumption on French farms has already been mentioned. Since the war, the government has

[e] The farm price of the British Ferguson TEA 29 CV tractor is 632,000 francs in France, 552,000 in Belgium, and 338,000 in Great Britain. The German Allgaier A III (12 CV diesel) costs 641,000 francs in France, 552,000 in Belgium, and 440,000 in Germany (Data for 1954).

endeavored both to increase the supply of fertilizers and to control their price.[86]

The nitrogenous fertilizer industry was one of the basic sectors of the first plan. For the 1947-1952 period, investments reached the sizable total of 21 billion (current) francs, of which 85 per cent were financed by loans from the MEF. Nitrogen production capacity was substantially increased, from 226,000 tons in 1946 to 333,000 tons in 1952.[87] No state funds were provided directly for potash or phosphates, although the expansion of the steel industry under the plan increased the production of basic slag, a phosphorous-bearing material.

The price of fertilizers has been fixed by the government continuously since the war. Industry representatives maintain that the government has allowed only narrow profit margins in order to keep down the cost of fertilizers to the farmers. Fertilizers were in short supply at least during the early postwar years—the situation more recently is less clear—and prices would undoubtedly have risen in the short run in the absence of controls. Whether supply would have increased more rapidly without controls and whether the present price of fertilizer would be higher or lower under a system of complete price freedom are debatable points. On the other hand, the price of fertilizers has undoubtedly been lowered by the inclusion, since 1952, of fertilizers among the products benefiting from the reduced rate (7.50 per cent instead of 16.85 per cent since the 1954 tax reform) under the tax on value added.

Despite the efforts of the government to control the price of fertilizers, an international comparison shows French prices to have been among the highest in Europe in 1951-1952. Of the 13 European countries studied by the OEEC, French prices for nitrogen were the highest, for phosphoric acid the third highest, and for potash the fifth highest.[f] [88]

Although consumption of fertilizers has risen relative to prewar levels, the 1953-1954 consumption was nevertheless below the targets of the first plan.[89] The limited use of fertilizers still constitutes one of the major weaknesses of French agriculture. Despite present price relationships, officials in the Ministry of Agriculture believe that there are few cases where the marginal productivity of fertilizers does not exceed their cost. Lack of technical knowl-

[f] The data for France may not incorporate the effects of the reduction in the rate applicable under the production tax (now the tax on value added), which took place in August 1952. This could conceivably alter somewhat the international ranking of France.

edge and lack of credit are important causes of the low utilization of fertilizers; it is probable, however, that a reduction in their cost would also favorably affect consumption.

It is commonly believed that the high price of tractor fuel, for which the state is largely responsible, has inhibited the use of machinery on at least some farms. Very heavy excise taxes are imposed by the government on gasoline and other fuels. In 1952, the wholesale price of gasoline was 15 francs per liter and the commercial margin 7.79 francs, while taxes amounted to 37.21 francs or more than 60 per cent of the retail price of 60 francs per liter.[40]

Since 1950 farm consumption of gasoline and other fuels has been subject to a special rebate that, while substantial, amounts to less than the excise taxes. The rebate in 1953 was 21 francs per liter of gasoline, 15 francs per liter of diesel oil, and 12 francs per liter of kerosene. This resulted in a one-third reduction (from 64 to 43 francs per liter) in the price of gasoline and a similar reduction (from 46 to 31 francs) in that of diesel oil. Each farmer obtains rebate coupons based on the acreage of his farm, the type of farming, the type of tractor, and the number of draught animals. If the tractor is used intensively, the rebate coupons do not cover all fuel purchases. Appropriations for the fuel rebate were 8.5 billion francs in 1952 and 8.75 billion francs in 1953; this compares with about 40 billion francs of fuel consumption by farmers in these years.[41]

Despite this significant reduction in the farmers' fuel bill, the price of French fuel remains high in comparison with other countries, as evidenced by the following figures of the price of tractor fuel, in francs per liter, which appear to relate to 1952 or early 1953.[42]

	Gasoline	*Kerosene*	*Diesel Oil*
United States	20	17	–
United Kingdom*	37.7	13.5	32
Germany	46	–	30
Belgium	–	–	17
Netherlands	32	–	14
Sweden	29	–	17
France (net of rebate)	44	30	32

* A study by the International Federation of Agricultural Producers (mimeo report 2/54, January 1954, Table IX) shows much lower prices for diesel oil in the United Kingdom.

C. LAND

Reclamation of waste land and creation of new farm land from deserts, swamps, or the sea have been accepted in many countries as responsibilities of the state. Some action in this direction was taken under the first plan; the second plan devoted more attention to the question of major land improvement, including long-run projects for regional development through new irrigation schemes, etc. The government has also been concerned with the problem of inferior use of land as a result of excessive parcelling. These interventions have been motivated by a desire both to raise overall production and productivity and to create new farms for socio-political reasons. The second consideration is acquiring more importance with the pressure of "farmers without land" in more densely populated areas.

1. Large-scale Land Improvements. Large-scale projects for irrigation or drainage cannot be undertaken by individual landowners because of the lack of capital resources or the need to enlist the joint action of numerous owners. State help may take the form of direct administration of the improvement project or, more commonly, of assistance in the form of technical advice, subsidies, and loans to compulsory or voluntary organizations of landowners, known as *associations syndicales*. Free technical advice is provided by the Ministry of Agriculture. It generally deals with the planning and development of the project, but does not extend to fixing the details, for which engineering consultants must be hired. The maximum rate of subsidization of approved projects ranges from 33 per cent to 60 per cent depending on the extent of the project. Half of the subsidy is paid upon approval of the project and half in 15 annual instalments. The local *association syndicale* must therefore provide the necessary funds in anticipation of subsequent subsidy payments. Long-term loans are available for these projects, however, from the MEF.

The total cost of land improvements through irrigation and drainage undertaken between 1947 and 1952 was 14.1 billion (current) francs.[43] Another source indicates that 5.5 billion of subsidies and 7.3 billion of MEF loans were granted from July 1948 to the end of 1952.[44] On the generous assumption that these two sources are consistent, these improvements were therefore financed almost entirely by state subsidies and loans. The data publicly available are not adequate to permit an economic evaluation of the results of these projects.[g] To date they do not appear to have been of major importance.

2. *Land Reorganization.* The excessive fragmentation of farmlands is one of the major structural defects of French agriculture and has served to lower appreciably the efficiency of farm operations. The working of a number of discontinuous strips by the same farmer entails substantial waste of transportation, complicates the processes of crop rotation and land improvement, and, above all, makes it difficult to use farm machinery efficiently.[45] It has been estimated that the increase in crop yields as a result of land reorganization could be at least 15 per cent and that the savings of labor and equipment could amount to 20-30 per cent.[46] The government has been involved in several efforts to reorganize landholdings, but the programs have not been pushed vigorously and the progress to date has been disappointingly slow.

Historically there has been a gradual process of concentration of land operations into a reduced number of farms, which has led to some reorganizing of scattered land parcels. Also, in areas where cash tenancy is common, informal exchanges of land use among tenant farmers may sometimes occur. Under the 1946 tenancy laws, these informal exchanges cannot be opposed by the landowners. Exchanges of land among owners have been made exempt from the taxes on capital transactions. In the Paris area, many cash tenants rent from several small owners and can operate their machines on large fields even though the individual parcels may be small. The concentration process has been slow, however, and voluntary exchanges among tenants or owners have been limited. The government has therefore relied primarily upon a process of wholesale land reorganization, involving a considerable number of farmers and some degree of compulsion, known as *remembrement.*

Remembrement is now carried out under the procedures set forth in laws of 1941 and 1945. The initiative for a *remembrement* project may come either from individual farmers or farm associations in an area, or from the government. In either case, the decision to proceed with *remembrement* is taken by communal or intercommunal commissions made up of government representatives and farmers. Once a decision to undertake *remembrement* has been made, it is irrevocable. Under the law, the owner is to receive an

[g] The plan report for 1952 indicates that 350,000 hectares were involved in operations for the removal of excess water and 110,000 with irrigation operations. For much of this area, however, the projects involved improvement of existing drainage or irrigation systems rather than creation of new ones; as a result, the figures have little meaning.

equivalent acreage of land, of the same quality as before; the land is to be regrouped in the minimum number of strips, located the minimum distance from roads and farm buildings. The government initially covers all of the costs of the project—for surveying, land assessment, etc.—in the form of subsidies. Twenty per cent of the costs are eventually borne by the landowners involved, who reimburse the government.

From 1941 to the end of 1952 (but in practice almost entirely after 1947 since early accomplishments were slight) *remembrement* was officially completed on 1,112,000 hectares and almost completed on an additional 250,000 hectares.[47] This was far below the objectives of the first plan, which called for the *remembrement* of 500,000 hectares during the first year and 1 million yearly thereafter. How slow the movement has been is revealed by the second plan report, which estimated the amount of land still in need of reorganization at 14 million hectares: 10 million hectares of plowed land (or more than half of the plowed land area of France); 2.5 million hectares of permanent grass; and 1.5 million hectares of uncultivated land (which could be brought into use through *remembrement*). At the 1953 rate (313,000 hectares), completion of the *remembrement* program would require almost fifty years.

Most farmers now support the principle of *remembrement*, and the number of project applications exceeds the financial resources of the program. In practice, however, *remembrement* generally proves to be a protracted operation—the average time for completion of a project is two years—and a delicate one, during which the antagonism of some farmers is bound to be aroused. In early years, technical difficulties and a lack of trained surveyors seriously delayed the program. At present, however, the principal obstacle to more rapid activity is apparently bureaucratic inertia. For the civil servant *remembrement* is likely to be a thankless task, while for his superior it appears to entail more political risks than advantages. Appropriations dropped from 2.8 billion francs in 1949 to 2 billion in 1950 and 1.8 billion in 1954, while the overall budget of the Ministry of Agriculture tended to increase slightly. Mendès-France placed new emphasis on the program, and raised the 1955 appropriation to 4.8 billion francs.

D. TECHNICAL KNOWLEDGE

It is generally accepted that improving the technical knowledge of the farmer is an activity where public assistance is both indispensable and highly productive. Efforts in this direction have been very inadequate in France, with the result that the technical backwardness of farmers is a serious obstacle to modernization. The final report of the first plan described the programs in this area as "clearly insufficient." In view of the low cost of these activities and the high returns generally obtained in other countries, curtailing public expenditures for these programs is very shortsighted. Perhaps the most that can be said is that some progress can be discerned in the form of somewhat higher appropriations for research and extension.

1. Research. The 1952 plan report observed that the national research center for French agriculture (*Institut National de la Recherche Agronomique* or INRA) suffered from inadequate funds and insufficient personnel. Thus the operating budget of INRA amounted to about 1 billion francs in 1953, or about 0.7 francs per thousand of agricultural income in France. The corresponding proportions for state-financed research in other countries are: Netherlands—5 per thousand; Sweden—4.5 per thousand; United Kingdom—4 per thousand; Belgium—3 per thousand; United States (in 1950)—3 per thousand; Switzerland—2.4 per thousand.[48]

The neglect of research in France is commonly attributed to its lack of electoral appeal. The INRA component of the budget of the Ministry of Agriculture has regularly proven to be highly vulnerable to "economy" drives. On the other hand, some progress can be noted since before the war, when the research staff was at one-third and budgetary expenditures at about one-fourth of present levels.

2. Agricultural Education. The situation is even less satisfactory with respect to the teaching of future farmers. Before the war, it was asserted in Parliament that there were more agricultural schools in Germany than agricultural students in France.[49] The second plan report called for a quadrupling of the number of young farmers receiving vocational training, at the same time recognizing that this would still not bring France up to the level of other European countries. According to a recent study, both public and private agricultural instruction at the secondary level (*second degré*) do not reach even 2 per cent of the possible number of male students; this proportion is of the order of 25 per cent in Denmark and the Low Countries. At the higher level (*enseignement supérieur*), there are about 1,400 students in agricultural colleges in France (excluding veterinary schools); in Denmark there are about 1,000 students, while the Netherlands, with a male farm population one-eighth that of France, has more than 1,000.[50]

For courses at the lower level (*premier degré*) aimed at future farmers who have completed grade school and cannot go to regular agricultural schools, the inadequacies of the educational system are even more apparent. There are only a handful of itinerant school teachers; the *département* of Ille-et-Vilaine has one itinerant school teacher for 49,000 farms.[51] In the Netherlands, there were 1,300 itinerant teachers, as against 648 in France in 1953.[52]

The future course of public education for farmers is tied up with the clerical dispute. Private agricultural schools (usually Catholic) help to remedy some of the deficiencies of the public educational system. In 1954 and 1955, the possibility of giving legal status to the private school system, including the provision of state subsidies, or of incorporating it into the public school system was under intense Parliamentary debate. The granting of subsidies to private schools was vigorously opposed in some quarters. Linked to this issue was a dispute between the Ministry of Education—a stronghold of religious neutrality—and the Ministry of Agriculture—more susceptible to religious influences—for control over the public schools. With Parliament sharply divided, no majority has yet been able to resolve the religious problems involved in structural reforms of the educational system.

3. *Extension Services*. In the short run, extension is possibly the most important of the three means of increasing the technical skill and thereby the productivity of farmers. The manpower involved in the extension services of the Ministry of Agriculture is very limited. Excluding the time of extension workers devoted to other duties, the time devoted to extension services is equivalent to about one full-time agent per 6,000 farmers. The customary invidious comparison with other European countries and the United States gives the following results:[53]

	Number of Farmers Per Extension Agent
Netherlands	240
Denmark	360
Germany	420
Great Britain	800
Switzerland	1,000
Belgium	1,000
United States	1,000
Italy	2,700
France	6,000

The public funds available for operating the extension services, including some funds not in the general budget, amounted to about 1,500 million francs in 1953 and 1,400 million in 1954; the 1955 program is projected at an increase to 1,700 or 1,800 million francs. By way of comparison, expenditures in the Netherlands in 1949 were equal to about 1,200 million French francs.[h] [54]

In addition to the defects arising from a shortage of personnel and money, the extension services suffer from poor organization, which was highlighted in the critical report of an OEEC survey team in 1950.[55] The survey also suggested that the operation of the extension services probably acted to widen the gap between progressive and backward areas by giving most advice to those farmers who (relatively) needed it least.

A favorable development in the extension service has been the use of model villages (*villages témoins*) and model regions (*zones témoins*). The model villages were organized in 1947-1948 by a farm organization of wheat producers. They involve intensive use of extension services in underdeveloped areas, combined with small subsidies and particularly favorable borrowing terms from the *Crédit Agricole*. The dramatic results of some of these experiments (doubling of yields in some villages within a few years' time) have demonstrated the large returns which can be obtained from relatively small investments of this type. Following the success of the model villages, the government has started a more ambitious scheme of model regions. The principles are the same—intensive use of agents and instructors, subsidies, and credit on favorable terms—although the financial arrangements are more advantageous and the area involved in the experiment is larger.

III POLICIES TENDING TO REDUCE THE EFFICIENCY OF FARMS

The defense of the small, family farm is one of the major leitmotifs of French agricultural policy and the stock-in-trade of almost every politician or Sunday orator. Among the arguments made in its behalf are demographic considerations: small farms are associated with a high farm population and, since the birth rate in rural areas is about one-third higher than in large cities, a larger number of children.[56] Another argument is that small farms are

[h] The dividing line between extension and other activities is difficult to draw, and there has been some use of other French funds (under the productivity program) for extension work. The general orders of magnitude probably remain valid, however.

believed to "feed the country" better, since the land is used more intensively on small farms. For social reasons, some Frenchmen consider it better to have individualistic farmers, working as family units, than the agricultural "proletariat" of large-scale farming. Many large-scale farmers approve of the sentiment in favor of small farms, believing that their own profits are increased by the price supports and other measures adopted by the state to keep the small farmers in existence (even though the financing of these measures may bear more heavily on the large producer). The population pressure arising from small farms is also believed to result in increased farm rents to landlords and lower wage rates for employers of farm labor.

Whether the small, family farm has the social and political advantages commonly attributed to it can be debated, but not here. As far as economic efficiency is concerned, there are a priori reasons for believing that the small farm in France has serious disadvantages. Although cost of production data are not available with which to make a systematic comparison, somewhat larger farm units appear to be appropriate for the efficient utilization of modern developments—e.g., farm equipment, fertilizers, technical advances. If this is correct, the policies favoring small farms are seriously at odds with the government's efforts to raise farm productivity.

A. LABOR POLICY

As in most other European countries, there has been a continuous secular decline both in the proportion of the active population engaged in agriculture and in the total number of persons so engaged. The number of male farm workers has declined as follows:[57]

Number of Male Farm Workers
1896-1946 (in thousands)

1896	5,670	87 départements
1901	5,520	
1906	5,450	
1911	5,270	
1921	4,990	90 départements
1926	4,740	
1931	4,450	
1936	4,220	
1946	4,019	

Despite this decline, most observers believe that there is still excessive manpower in agriculture, due in part to the special benefits to small farms that keep labor attached to them and prevent the substitution of capital for labor.

The Monnet plan advocated raising farm productivity by moving farmers out of areas of low productivity (i.e., where there was a very high ratio of labor to capital) into industry and commerce. The original plan recommended that 900,000 employed persons leave agriculture; in an earlier press conference Monnet had mentioned a figure of 1,500,000 persons. However, French agricultural thinking has traditionally been preoccupied with the agricultural "vocation" of France and the virtues of a high farm population. This "back to the land" sentiment was encouraged by the Vichy régime, since it coincided with the interest of Germany in expanding its own industrial markets and converting France into a primarily agrarian economy. The notion of an orderly exodus from the land, associated with rising productivity, was therefore regarded as somewhat heretical, and farm pressures forced the official abandonment of this objective in the 1948 revision of the plan. The second plan rested on the assumption, which appears to be as much a matter of dogma as of economic analysis, that there would be no decrease in the number of persons engaged in agriculture. Popular or official sentiments to the contrary notwithstanding, the rural exodus has continued (though perhaps not rapidly enough from the standpoint of overall efficiency). Preliminary figures from the general population census of 1954 indicate that rural communes lost 800,000 inhabitants between 1946 and 1954, at the same time as the total population increased.[58]

While opposing a reduction in the overall size of the farm population, the government has sought, with little success, to facilitate the relocation of farmers within agriculture. One of the weaknesses of the family farm system is the rigidity of the farm as a unit of land in the face of changes in the size and average age of the family. In areas of high farm population, farmers' children often have difficulty in finding employment as farm operators. A decree of October 1949 attempted to promote "rural migrations" to less populated farming areas. Until 1954, the encouragement took the form of a subsidy to cover part of the costs of moving. Two small funds (a 600 million franc fund for equipment loans and a 100 million franc fund for equipment grants) were added in 1954. The "cost of moving" subsidy (which has averaged 77,000 francs per family) is of limited effect, since it does not overcome the uncertainty of future income in a new location. The results of the program to date appear to have been slight.

B. SPECIAL BENEFITS TO SMALL FARMS

A number of special advantages have been conferred on small farms. In contrast to the measures aimed at increasing concentration (mentioned above) there has been direct intervention intended to prevent farm concentration. The state has also attempted to prevent the excessive fragmentation of small holdings, on the grounds that such fragmentation may eventually result in further concentration. Special credit terms have been provided, and marketing regulations organized in their behalf. The establishment of farm cooperatives has been encouraged as a means of strengthening the bargaining position of the small farmer.

1. Legislation Against Concentration. Under the terms of postwar legislation no longer in effect, farmers operating several neighboring farms that were operated as separate units before the war and that exceeded a certain limit of total acreage could be forced to rent the farms thus operated in excess of the minimum (if they were owners) or to give the lease to another tenant (if they were tenants). In each *département* the prefect was to fix the local minimum acreage above which the law applied. The law did not operate automatically, but only in instances where some qualified person (an evicted tenant or a young farmer looking for a farm) entered a claim. In practice the law was never of any consequence. Most prefects did not fix the legal minimum necessary to make the law applicable to their *département*. In the 28 *départements* where the minimum was announced, only a small number of claims were entered, not all of which were successful. The law ceased to be in effect after 1950. Its principal interest is therefore as an indication of government intent.

2. Legislation on Inheritance. One of the basic principles of the Civil Code is that inheritances should be divided equally among direct heirs.[1] Dividing a farm inheritance among several heirs results in increased fragmentation of farm holdings, which may lead eventually to their disappearance and the sale of parcels to larger landowners. To defend the small family farm against these dangers, several laws were passed between 1938 and 1943 to permit undivided transfer of the family farm to a single heir.

Under the legislation, one heir can take over the farm by buying out the others within five years' time. If in the past he has furnished

[1] When there is no will, the inheritance must be so divided. In case of a will, a limit is placed on the proportion of the inheritance which can be disposed of freely. Thus with two children the margin of freedom is one-third of the value of the inheritance; with three or more children, it is one-fourth.

unpaid labor on the farm (as is normally the case), he may receive from the unsettled estate a "postponed salary," which assists in the settlement. The farms to which the laws apply are limited to those below a maximum size and value and above a minimum (below which the farm unit does not appear capable of surviving).[59]

3. *Credit Advantages of Small Farms.* There is a ceiling on the amount of farm credit (presently 5 million francs) that may be provided to an individual farmer. This is intended, in part, to prevent the funds from being concentrated on a few large farms. In addition, the *Crédit Agricole* makes special long-term loans for the acquisition or development of small property that the farmer must cultivate with his family. There is a ceiling on the size of these loans, and farmers with assets above a specified amount are not eligible. By the end of 1954, 194,260 loans, for an appreciable total of 26.7 billion francs, had been granted.[60]

4. *Marketing Regulations.* At several points in the organization of farm markets, described in the next chapter, there is built-in discrimination in favor of small producers. Some examples are: the progressive structure of the tax on wheat growers; the special credit provisions for small winegrowers whose stocks are blocked; the higher-than-proportional quotas on compulsory distillation of wine residues for larger wine producers; the limitation on new vineyard plantings on large farms; and the exemption of small producers from the compulsory distillation of wine surpluses. The right to plant tobacco under the state monopoly is given by preference to small, family farmers. In the aggregate, these add up to sizable advantages for small farms.

5. *Encouragement of Cooperatives.* The avowed objective of state encouragement to farm cooperatives has been to assist the small farmer faced with a competitive disadvantage vis-à-vis the large farmer or merchant. The encouragement takes several forms: technical advice on organizing the cooperative and constructing its buildings; legal exemptions from various income and excise taxes; and subsidies for new plant construction by cooperatives that "serve the general agricultural interest." Thus, between July 1, 1948, and December 31, 1952, cooperatives received a total of 4 billion francs in subsidies for the construction of new plant facilities.[61] To benefit from these privileges the cooperatives must conform to fairly stringent rules with respect to liability, disposal of shares, etc.

"Cooperative" undertakings among farmers antedate the favorable legislation in their behalf, but the several advantages provided by the state have undoubtedly assisted in the extensive development of the movement in France. It should be noted, however, that participation in the cooperative movement is not necessarily confined to the small farmers whose interests are usually invoked in its defense.

C. TENANCY REGULATION

The laws on farm tenancy have been so numerous since the liberation that Parliament appears to have devoted more attention to this than to any other agricultural problem. Since the basic ordinance of October 1945, twenty-three laws have been concerned with the question of farm tenancy.[62] The primary objectives of public policy have been two-fold: to protect tenants against dispossession by landowners and to facilitate the acquisition of land by tenants. Whatever their other consequences, the regulations with respect both to cash and to share tenancy have had the effect of encouraging more rigid land-use patterns.[63]

The laws on cash tenancy rested on the conviction, strongest at the moment of liberation, that owner-operation was "the best form of operation" (these words appear in the 1945 ordinance), an idea presumably inspired by the socialist slogan "The land to him who cultivates it." Added to this ideological motivation was a general awareness of the defects of existing legislation, which provided inadequate safeguards both to tenants and landlords, particularly the former.

The acquisition of farm property is made possible by rules concerned with the "preemptive right" of the tenant to purchase the farm if it is put up for sale. First priority is to the tenant (or to his widow or descendants over the age of sixteen); the second is to any "agricultural person." The preemptive right, in effect, gives the tenant the power to ask a tenancy court to determine the price of land, since he can argue that the price quoted by the landlord is "fictitious" and intended to deprive him of his priority. The extent to which the tenancy courts have replaced the market mechanism in this role has, in practice, been limited. Landlords have largely succeeded in circumventing the preemptive right—which, if fully enforced, would tend to eliminate tenancy in the long run—by various means, including bribery of tenants.[64]

The legislation also provides important protection to the tenant in place. Leases must be for a period of at least nine years. In principle, every tenant has the right to renew his lease. An owner therefore cannot change tenants except under two special circumstances, strictly defined. The first is if the owner intends to operate the farm himself. He must intend to do so for a period of at least nine years; the owner must also live on the farm while he works it or have one of his children operate it directly (the child must be of age and the owner not a farmer elsewhere). Even then, notice can only be given at the end of the nine year lease. The second circumstance is a "grave fault" by the tenant, such as repeated delays in payment or bad farming, which must be recognized as such by the tenancy courts.

While frequent changes in tenants are undesirable, stability can also have disadvantages if it results in excessive rigidity. The owner may be discouraged from making improvements. The tenant in place is sheltered; this may have the effect of preventing the introduction of new methods, the elimination of the unfit (except the very worst), and the accession of young farmers to tenancy. The legislation also tends to be self-defeating. Knowing that the land, once leased, cannot be regained, owners cling to direct operation, even if this results in inefficient farming methods.

The tenancy laws undertook to encourage the adoption of improvements, but with little effect. If the landlord objects to land improvements contemplated by the tenant, approval may be obtained from the tenancy courts. When the tenant leaves, he may obtain an indemnity for the unused portion of his investment, if it is not a "luxury." The owner must also set aside a fixed proportion of the rent in a special fund deposited at the *Crédit Agricole* to be used for housing and building improvements on the farm. This important provision has been almost entirely disregarded.

The laws concerning share tenancy are more drastic, and more frequently transgressed. The objective of the legislators was eventually to eliminate share tenancy as a "reactionary" form of tenancy. Either owners or tenants can demand (unilaterally) that the share tenancy be converted into cash tenancy. After the passage of the legislation, there was a wave of demands by share tenants for conversion of their leases, but the movement has since subsided because few tenants have had enough money to purchase the owner's share of the operating capital. The laws also prescribe sharing arrangements; the tenant is to receive two-thirds of the total production, and the owner one-third. The inflexibility of this rule has been modified, in practice, by the vagueness of the sharing procedures (e.g., concerning the payment of farm expenses) and the local tenancy courts may authorize different sharing methods.

Apparently few changes in sharing methods have been made as a result of the legislation. For share tenancy there are the same rules on duration of leases (although the tenant can give notice at three year intervals), rights of renewal and preemption, and right to an indemnity for the unused share of improvements. The landlord's building fund also exists, and is also ignored.

Share tenancy has frequently-cited defects, notably with respect to the tenant's incentives and opportunities to carry out improvements. But it has the advantage of enabling young farmers with little capital to become farm operators and has often been used as a stepping stone towards ownership. The desirability of abolishing share tenancy is therefore open to question. In any event, as has often proven to be the case with government attempts to legislate away conditions or institutions that have important economic and social reasons for their existence, the attempt has had little success.

IV SUMMARY

Despite the considerable natural advantages enjoyed by French agriculture, the productivity of farming is below that of most countries of Western Europe. A number of efforts have been directed towards raising the efficiency of French agriculture, principally under the aegis of the first and second modernization plans. On the other hand, other government policies reflect the strong ideological preference in favor of preserving a high farm population, organized into a large number of small, family-owned farms.

Considerable public funds have been invested in agriculture under the modernization plans. A large proportion of the funds has been devoted towards an improvement of electrification and water supplies which, while undeniably important, contributes to productivity mainly in a roundabout fashion and over the long run. Investments in the farm machinery industry and financial assistance to farmers have played a part in the impressive increase in the use of tractors during the postwar period. Government assistance has probably also stimulated a greater use of fertilizers, although fertilizer prices remain higher, and fertilizer consumption lower, than in most West European countries. The price of fuel is also high and may have discouraged intensive use of farm machinery; despite the rebates provided to farmers, the heavy excise taxes are a major element in the high price. More efficient land use has been encouraged by large-scale land improvement projects and by a reorganization of land holdings. The latter program, the more important, has not been pushed vigorously, and adequate funds have not been provided for it. Government expenditures for agricultural research, education, and extension services are conspicuously low, and undoubtedly help to explain the survival of backward production techniques.

Measures which tend to reduce the size or efficiency of farms include: the encouragement of a heavy use of labor in agriculture; legislation against concentration; modifications of the inheritance laws; credit advantages to small farms; sundry provisions of the marketing regulations which discriminate against the large farmer; and the encouragement of cooperatives. The numerous tenancy laws have had the effect of encouraging rigid land-use patterns.

On the whole, government efforts to meet the serious problem of low productivity have not shown a great deal of vigor and consistency, while a variety of incentives and benefits to small farmers have tended to keep productivity in agriculture lower than it might otherwise be.

CHAPTER 12

IMPACT OF THE STATE ON THE MARKETING OF FARM PRODUCTS

I THE PROBLEM AND ITS SETTING

How much regulation there should be of the marketing of farm products has been a difficult and controversial question in many countries. The desire to subsidize farmers arises from the special instability of farming and the low income of farmers, who frequently form a large segment of the population. And, when subsidies are granted, there are pressures to bestow them by means of the price mechanism (i.e., in the form of market protection or guarantees of one sort or another) rather than through direct income payments, because the latter might offend the more independent farmers (as well as other parts of the population). These sentiments in behalf of farmers are understandable and widespread. They have led to extensive interventions in the marketing of farm products in the United States and in many other countries.

But satisfying these sentiments entails some economic cost. Most interventions are aimed, directly or indirectly, at supporting the prices of farm products. To the extent that price supports succeed in raising market prices above the level that would otherwise prevail, they tend to draw resources—e.g., land or labor—away from activities in which they would yield a higher return and into the production of agricultural commodities. The result is also a misallocation of productive resources within agriculture if some farm commodities receive more support or shelter than others.

The size of the "surplus" that cannot be marketed at the supported price is (relative to the value of the crop) a rough clue to the extent to which the supported price differs from the "free" market price and to which resources are misused. "Surpluses" may be disposed of abroad by the government at a loss, or else, still worse, they may be destroyed and completely wasted. In either case, consumers pay a higher price for farm products, which figure importantly in family budgets. If production quotas are applied, they act to limit the diversion of resources to the sheltered commodities, but such controls are difficult to enforce so long as the price relationships remain favorable to the sheltered commodities. Supports may also prevent the optimum allocation of resources between production for the domestic and for the foreign market along the familiar lines of comparative advantage.

How the French government has sought to handle these problems is the subject of this chapter. The success of the policies in achieving the desired subsidy effects are not investigated. Instead, as in Chapter 10, attention is directed mainly to the implications of these policies for resource allocation, that is, to the price that is paid for sheltering farmers against the economic process.

The French soil supports a wide variety of crops. As mentioned earlier, France is the leading agricultural producer of Europe. Some crops have been in "surplus" for a considerable number of years (i.e., some quantities could not be sold at the fixed price), while others have been in relatively short supply over much of the postwar period, with prices rising in the absence of government ceilings. Despite the large volume and wide variety of crops produced, Metropolitan France has had a deficit in its agricultural trade with foreign countries and with its overseas possessions throughout the postwar period, as in most prewar years.[a]

Also by way of background, something should be said about the attitudes and activities of farm groups in the marketing area. These groups, in most cases strongly organized and highly influential, have demanded protective controls on individual farm products as soon as prices have fallen and marketing difficulties arisen. The pressure they exert has been expressed in a variety of ways: by strikes of local public officials, non-payment of taxes, barricading of national highways, and even "ultimata" and open threats of violence bordering on insurrection.[1] In some of these manifestations, farmers have been joined by their deputies and senators, united in their common opposition to the "state." Within Parliament, farm interests have been able to count on sympathetic attention, and the existing administration has sometimes been overruled or even overthrown when it has gone too far in opposing the interests of particular farm groups.

II REGULATION OF THE DOMESTIC MARKET

Marketing interventions began, for the most part, during the

[a] By 1954 the deficit on trade in agricultural products (notably food and tobacco) with foreign countries had been reduced to 4.6 billion francs, with imports of 142.7 billion and exports of 138.1 billion. Trade with the overseas territories showed a large deficit (237.2 billion francs), with imports of 328.8 billion and exports of 91.6 billion. Data from Ministère des Finances, Direction Générale des Douanes et Droits Indirects, *Statistique mensuelle du commerce extérieur de la France, année 1954*, No. 12, December, 1954, *passim.*

economic crisis of the 1930's. After hesitant and haphazard beginnings, fairly extensive support programs were set up for wheat, wine, sugar beets, and a few crops of lesser importance. During the 1940's food supplies were largely below prewar, and expansion of the output of most commodities seemed to be desirable. There was no extension of protective supports to new products, and some controls were administered more as ceilings than as floors (as in the case of wheat and meat). The expansion of production resulted in a farm "crisis" during the years 1953-1955, with falling prices and growing concern about overproduction. There was a consequent widening of supports to embrace important new products such as meat and milk. In terms of comprehensive support of fixed farm prices, most French products were still (as of 1955) not heavily protected. But the situation is evolving continually, and in the general direction of more price support.

For purposes of analysis, French farm products can be divided roughly into three groups: "uncontrolled," "partially controlled," and "sheltered." In the first group ("uncontrolled") there has been virtually no government support. In the second group ("partially controlled"), the government has not acted directly to fix a guaranteed minimum price, but has attempted to influence prices through short-run action on supply. To the extent that prices have been raised above the short-run equilibrium, there have been limited programs of surplus disposal. For commodities in the third group ("sheltered"), there are comprehensive programs to fix prices and dispose of surpluses, along with some measures aimed at influencing supply in the short or long run.

Classification of farm products into these three groups is somewhat arbitrary, and the categories do inadequate justice to the variety, complexity, and occasional ingenuity of the particular control mechanisms devised for individual products. Nevertheless, they do show that only a relatively small proportion of total farm production is "sheltered" by the government. The "uncontrolled" group includes poultry and eggs, vegetables and fruit, and potatoes. As can be seen from Table 33, these accounted for about 25 per cent of the value of gross final production of agriculture in 1953-1954. "Partially controlled" commodities are meat and milk, which, in combination, are slightly under 50 per cent of the total. Slightly more than 25 per cent are "sheltered" products, notably wheat, wine, and sugar beets.

While there is no measure of the relative degree of protection in industry and agriculture, it does not appear offhand that the sheltering of farm products has been a major factor in keeping excessive labor in agriculture, at least until recent years. On the other hand, the substantial differences in the amount of protection accorded to different commodities can be expected to result in some misallocation of resources within agriculture. To observe the

TABLE 33

COMMODITY COMPOSITION OF GROSS FINAL PRODUCTION OF AGRICULTURE, 1953-1954 CROP YEAR

Commodity	*Value (billions of fr.)*		*Per Cent of Total*[1]	
Meat	625		29	(28)
Milk[1]	365	(450)	17	(20)
Poultry and eggs	255		12	(11.5)
Wheat	255		12	(11.5)
Wine	200		9.5	(9)
Vegetables	155		7.5	(7.5)
Fruit	70		3.5	(3)
Sugar beets	60		3	(2.5)
Potatoes	58		2.5	(2.5)
Other	110		[2]	[2]
TOTAL	2,155	(2,240)	–	–

Source: INSEE, "Le Revenu de l'agriculture en France en 1953-1954" *Etudes et conjoncture*, December 1954, pp. 1072, 1082-1083.

[1] The figure of 365 billion francs for milk production is from the Ministry of Agriculture. The figure in brackets (450 billion francs) is based on a study of milk production by R. Veisseyre, *Contribution à l'étude de la consommation du lait et des produits laitiers en France*, Conseil Supérieur de l'Agriculture, Paris, 1954. Because of the wide discrepancy, both figures are shown by INSEE. The percentages given by INSEE in brackets are based on the Veisseyre figure.

[2] INSEE does not show a percentage for "other" products. By subtraction, the residual for others is 4.0% and (4.5)%.

situation more closely, particular cases of government controls must be examined. There is no general legislation of importance with respect to agricultural market organization, and no two commodities are subject to the same regulations and procedures. Also, the regulations and procedures in each case change frequently over time. These wide variations reflect the *ad hoc* approach of the government, acting in a crisis atmosphere in response to pressures of farm groups.

There is no need to describe the "uncontrolled" products. The other two groups ("partially controlled" and "sheltered") are discussed separately.

A. PARTIALLY CONTROLLED PRODUCTS

1. Meat. Meat stands first among French agricultural products in value terms, accounting for 28 to 29 per cent of total production. France is the largest meat producer of Europe, and the fourth largest in the world. It has not been an important meat exporter, however. Domestic meat consumption is high, particularly of the better cuts and grades, and only inferior quality meats have generally been offered for export.

Unlike the case of the other farm products studied here, the government's concern throughout almost all of the postwar period has been with expanding supply and limiting increases in the price of meat. "Surpluses" in the domestic market did not appear until 1953-1954, and then were easily handled by an increase in exports without large subsidies. Government intervention to support the meat market has therefore been negligible. Intervention to limit meat price increases, while very extensive, has been singularly ineffective. Commenting on the government's efforts to prevent increases in the price of meat during early postwar years, the *Conseil Economique* observed: "The too numerous plans which have followed each other since the liberation involve various approaches. They all have one point in common: their failure."[2] The fact that price ceilings were relatively less effective for meat than for other farm products during the period of widespread price controls may inadvertently have had the effect of diverting resources to meat production. However, at the consumer level meat supplies increased rather slowly during 1945-1947 owing to the normal length of the production cycle, the shortage of livestock feed, and the need to reconstitute livestock herds.

By 1950 meat production had risen to 116 per cent of the prewar (1934-1938) level. The increase continued, with production at 122 per cent in 1952; by 1954 it had risen to 2,440,000 metric tons or 144 per cent of prewar production. A decline in farm prices in the summer and autumn of 1953 led to vigorous demands for government help from the numerous cattle raisers.

Government intervention took two forms. One was financial assistance for the temporary storage of meat products to reduce seasonal fluctuations in price. A minimum guarantee against losses (through price declines) while in storage was provided. The other measure was surplus disposal through subsidized exports. These activities were financed through a new "Fund for the Improvement of the Meat Market," receiving 10 per cent of the proceeds of the regular excise tax on meat. While subsidies from the Fund made it possible to push exports more vigorously, some export outlets were found without subsidies, since the French meat price in 1954 compared favorably with that of most exporting countries. The Fund was consequently not obliged to use all the resources at its disposal. According to one source, 1954 exports of meat carcasses were 100,000 tons, of which 25 per cent required subsidization; this compares with 2,270 tons in 1938, and 36,600 tons in 1952.[3] The government also resorted to bulk purchases of meat by the Army to support the meat price during the worst seasonal periods. These measures resulted in a substantial increase in prices above the low point reached in 1953.

Meat is thus one of the farm products whose marketing problems have been least serious and one in which substantial amounts of foreign exchange can be earned by pushing exports. An expansion of meat production and exports was one of the major goals of the second modernization plan. In recent years, however, the greater sheltering of other farm products has probably kept some resources out of meat production and prevented it from expanding more rapidly.

2. *Milk (and dairy products).* Milk (and dairy products) have been steadily growing in importance as a source of farm income. From 10-12 per cent of the gross value of farm production before the war, they rose to 17-20 per cent in 1953-1954 and are now the second ranking product of French agriculture. There has been a parallel increase in government interest in the marketing situation, but (at least until prices began to fall with the large production of 1953-1955) the interventions have been neither numerous nor particularly effective.

Milk is produced by a host of farmers—some estimates range as high as 1,700,000—though few have large herds or specialize in milk production. Most farmers produce milk and dairy products under rather primitive conditions; the quality of milk is inferior, and production costs are relatively high. France is the largest milk producer of Europe, but the average yield of 2,000-2,400 liters per cow per year compares unfavorably with the 3,500 liters of Denmark and the Netherlands. The geographical dispersion of producers and the small output of milk per farm also result in high processing and distribution costs.[4]

Most milk is consumed after processing or transformation rather than in the fluid state, and the proportion of the milk output so marketed tends to increase in years of high production. Of the

98 million hectoliters of milk and dairy products sold commercially in 1950, only about 30 million hectoliters were sold for fluid use; 44 million were used for butter and cream, 21 million for cheese, and 3 million for powdered and condensed milk.[5]

As of 1954-1955, the principal methods of government intervention in milk marketing were: a) the fixing of a "benchmark" price for milk at the production level, plus retail price-fixing of fluid milk in each *département* (but no price-fixing for butter and cheese); b) short run action on the price of some dairy products by seasonal storage programs; and c) incipient programs of surplus disposal through campaigns to increase domestic consumption and through subsidized exports.

The government fixes a reference or benchmark price (*prix indicatif*) for milk at the farm level. The benchmark price is not a guaranteed or legally enforceable minimum, however, but simply a statement of the government's intent with respect to the farm price of milk. In principle, it is determined by estimating the average cost of production, based on "typical" inputs for keeping a "typical" herd of cows. The retail price of fluid milk is not fixed by the central government but by the prefect in each *département.*

Prices and marketing margins are therefore not uniform throughout the country. In *départements* of large production, the benchmark price may have little influence on the actual level of retail prices; processors may frequently pay below the benchmark price, and prefects may base the retail price on the actual farm price plus margins. Thus, "the farmer has no certainty that he will really obtain the 'benchmark price.' "[6] In the face of rising milk production, the government has apparently been reducing the benchmark price without reference to changes in the "cost of production." At the same time, it has instructed the prefects to set their retail prices at a level that will ensure that farmers obtain the benchmark price. How well this instruction will be observed remains to be seen.

Apart from the benchmark price for fluid milk, the principal action of the government on the price of milk and dairy products has been a program to reduce seasonal fluctuations in price by controlling movements in the supply of butter and cheese. The government has given financial assistance for the storage or blocking of dairy products, undertaken at the season when butter and cheese supplies are at their height, in the form of a partial guarantee against losses through price changes. At the other end of the season, when butter and cheese prices may rise rapidly, the government has requested handlers to take the commodities out of storage. Only a small proportion (less than 3 per cent) of the butter supplies have been covered by the contractual guarantees, however.

In 1954-1955, the government set floor and ceiling prices for milk at the farm level (in addition to the "benchmark price") as guides for its interventions in the market for milk and dairy products. A "Fund for the Improvement of the Market for Milk and Dairy Products" was established to support the domestic price of milk products and to finance exports. Whether the new Fund, which was given 6 billion francs in 1955, will result in action to support the domestic market other than through financing the carryover of stocks and subsidizing exports is not yet clear.

The principal method considered for disposing of the stocks of butter and cheese kept off the market in 1954-1955 was subsidized exports. There was also under discussion the imposition of uniform standards of quality for milk exports, which could increase the possibilities of finding foreign outlets.[b] Per capita consumption of fluid milk is low in France, most Frenchmen preferring their "little glass" of wine. The Mendès-France government introduced milk into the public schools, where wine is often served.[c] A public information campaign on the nutritive value of milk, of which the French population is largely ignorant, has also been mentioned but not yet undertaken.

Milk is one of the products from which resources may have been shifted by the greater protection given to other commodities, even though these resources may have had a higher yield in milk production. However, in view of the declining price of milk and/or milk surpluses in recent years, the marketing difficulties for milk would have been even greater had these resources remained in milk production (at least with the existing consumption habits and cost structure). If these marketing difficulties continue to spread throughout French agriculture (including the less sheltered commodities) it will suggest a generalized excess of resources in agricultural production.

B. SHELTERED PRODUCTS

These require a lengthy description, since the interventions with respect to them are numerous and complex.

[b] For example, the American military forces stationed in France have been purchasing a large part of their milk supplies in other countries because of the inferior quality and inadequate sanitary standards of French milk.

[c] School milk programs, operated with state subsidies, were in existence from 1932 to 1939 but were not renewed after the war.

1. Wheat. France is the largest wheat producer of Western Europe and ranks fifth in world production (after the United States, Canada, USSR, and India). Within France, wheat ties poultry and eggs for third place in the ranking of French farm products. Wheat is produced by a large number of farmers (one source estimates 1,770,000) on more than 4 million hectares of farm land.[d] [7] The price of wheat is regarded by many farmers as a symbol of agricultural prosperity. The contractual obligations of tenant farmers are frequently fixed on the basis of the price of wheat. To the price-conscious consumer the price of bread has also a symbolic importance far out of proportion to its (declining) share of the average family budget.

While the details of the wheat support program have undergone frequent alterations since it was established in the 1930's, its essential features are: (a) the fixing each year by the government of a national wheat price, using methods which have changed on several occasions; (b) stand-by production controls, most recently in the form of a limitation on the amount of the wheat crop benefiting from the national support price, first invoked for the 1955 harvest; and (c) surplus disposal, mainly in the form of exports subsidized in part by the government and in part by the wheat producers.

a. Price supports. During the 1930's the price set by the government was based on a kind of parity concept. It was computed on the basis of 1911-1913 prices, adjusted by the average of four price indexes (some of them calculated exclusively for this purpose). After 1938 there was also an adjustment to take account of the size of the crop. Between 1947 and 1953, a different price formula, based on the "cost of production," was used. The government set what was called the "price framework"—a list of inputs needed "on the average" to grow wheat on one hectare of land. The inputs used were not the result of a statistical average based on a sizable sample, but a combination of the results of a small number of specialized studies. Each year, the cost of producing one hectare of wheat was computed by applying current prices to the average inputs.

The other features of the "cost of production" method were more novel, and more complicated. It was necessary to divide the average cost of producing a hectare of wheat by the average yield of a hectare in order to obtain the average cost of producing a unit of

[d] This figure may be too high; unpublished data from an official government source show 1.3 million wheat producers.

wheat. Instead of estimating the average yield each year, an "arbitrary theoretical yield" was used. Once calculated, this theoretical yield was increased each year by 3 to 4 per cent. This meant that a farmer whose cost of production was just covered by the price in a given year would operate at a loss in the following year if he did not increase his yield. To compensate for this provision, the average cost of production derived from the list of inputs was increased by the inclusion of a "modernization margin," which was supposed to enable the producers to invest in order to obtain the higher yield. In 1952, the margin was about 4.3 per cent of the price. In addition, bargaining among the interested parties also played an important part. The arbitrary theoretical yield could be adjusted by a factor that took into account the actual yield; the margin of adjustment, within which bargaining could in practice take place, was originally 6 per cent but was later raised to 20 per cent.[8]

The latest pricing procedure, applicable to the period 1954-1957, abandons the cost of production formula in favor of a return to a modified parity concept. The base period is the years 1952 and 1953, when the price of wheat was 3,600 francs per quintal. The indexes used to adjust the base price are those of the prices of selected industrial commodities purchased for use on the farm and of the cost of living. The parity price thus obtained is reduced by 1 per cent the first year, 2 per cent the second, 3 per cent the third, and 4 per cent in 1957 to take account of expected increases in productivity. A "correction factor" of ± 6 per cent makes it possible to adjust the price on the basis of the expected size of the crop and other factors and introduces some margin of flexibility or bargaining.

All of the pricing methods have, in practice, permitted the government some flexibility in fixing the national wheat price each year. This flexibility comes about both through the inclusion of a specific margin of correction or adjustment and through the government's ability to influence the indexes, coefficients, average costs, etc. used in the calculations. (The second influence has been exerted either through direct action, e.g., subsidies and price controls, on some of the key components or through the interpretation and application of some of the statistical results.) During the early postwar period the government exercized these powers in the direction of keeping down the price of wheat (and therefore the price of bread to the consumer). Thus in 1950 the wheat price had increased 13 fold over the 1938 level, while all wholesale prices were at 21.7 times and wholesale food prices at 18.4 times the 1938 level. Between

1951 and 1953, the price of wheat rose relative to the prices of other products; thus, in 1953 the indexes were 1800 for wheat, 2560 for wholesale prices and 2180 for wholesale food prices. With the large surpluses of 1954 and 1955, the government again lowered the price of wheat relative to that of other products.[e]

A common feature of the various pricing methods has been the concept of a national wheat price uniform to all producers. In fact, however, the net return is not the same to all wheat growers. A special "absorption tax" (*taxe de résorption*) is included in the national price in order to finance the disposal of surpluses. The tax, described more fully below, is steeply progressive according to the size of deliveries. Therefore the net return is lower for the large than for the small farmer, providing once again an advantage to small producers.

Wheat handlers must purchase all of the crop offered by the farmer, thus guaranteeing that the national price is in fact obtained by the farmer. Short-term loans from the *Crédit Agricole*, on notes discounted at the Bank of France, are essential to the financing of wheat purchases by the handlers.

b. Production controls. In the absence of price supports, there has been a long-run tendency for the acreage in wheat production to decline as average yields have risen. This movement was accelerated in the early postwar period as a result of the unfavorable price relationship between wheat and other farm products. Marginal wheat land was abandoned, and other land formerly in wheat was converted to more profitable uses, such as pasture land for cattle; in 1950, the wheat acreage was almost 20 per cent below 1934-1938. With the more favorable price relationships prevailing since 1951, however, there has been a gradual increase in the acreage devoted to wheat production, mostly in 1954 and 1955. At the same time, average yields have increased sharply, from

[e] The 1954 indexes were 1700, 2515, and 2170. In 1955 the wheat price was nominally kept at the 1954 level (3400 francs), but in fact reduced since it no longer applied to the whole crop (see the discussion below). In comparing movements of the price of wheat with those of food products, it should be borne in mind that wheat productivity has probably been increasing more rapidly than the average for agriculture as a whole, since mechanization is easier to adopt and there has been considerable progress in improving wheat varieties. The wheat price index numbers have been computed from (unpublished) data on wheat prices supplied by the *Office National Interprofessionel des Céréales.* The index numbers of all wholesale prices and of wholesale food prices are taken directly from or based on the "Annuaires statistiques" and various "Bulletins mensuels de statistique" of INSEE. The 1951-1954 wholesale price indexes in the original are on the base 1949 = 100; these have been converted to the base 1938 = 100 by using the coefficients recommended by INSEE (*Bulletin mensuel de statistique*, quarterly supplement July-September 1951, p. 38).

15.6 quintals per hectare in 1934-1938 to 17.8 quintals in 1950 and 22.5 quintals estimated for 1954.[9] In 1954 there was a record wheat harvest of more than 100 million quintals. After several years of good harvests, the wheat surpluses that could not be marketed at the fixed price had mounted rapidly.

Under a 1939 law, the government was given stand-by authority to set individual producer quotas if the total wheat crop exceeded a specified figure (90 million quintals). This figure was not reached while the law was in force (until 1953), and production quotas have never been applied. When the parity price formula was reinstated in 1953, the government was empowered to influence wheat acreage and production in a more roundabout fashion by limiting the amount of the wheat harvest that could be sold at the guaranteed national price. In the face of the serious problem of surplus disposal, it was decided in 1955 to exercise this power, applying the restrictions to the 1955-1956 marketing season. The government specified the amount of the total wheat crop eligible for purchase by handlers under the guaranteed national price; the remainder of the wheat crop was to be purchased at the "free market" price that it could command (on the domestic or world markets) when sold for livestock feed or as a commercial export. The price eventually received by each wheat producer was to be based on the proportion of the total wheat crop sold at the guaranteed and free prices.

c. Surplus disposal. At the end of the marketing season, the National Wheat Office takes title to wheat that has not been sold by the handlers through commercial channels. Most of the surplus is eventually sold at a loss in export markets. It was originally intended that the funds for storage and eventual export dumping would be provided by the wheat producers themselves, in the form of the "absorption tax." The rates of the tax have increased with the size of the surpluses. The tax is steeply progressive, as indicated by the following figures for the 1953 crop:[10]

Size of deliveries (in quintals)	*Total tax (francs)*	*Net price per quintal* (francs)*	*Average tax per quintal (francs)*
50	0	3,600	0.
75	1,250	3,583	16.55
100	3,750	3,562.5	37.50
200	16,250	3,519	81.25
300	31,250	3,496	104.10
400	46,250	3,484	115.60
500	63,750	3,472.5	127.50

Size of deliveries (in quintals)	*Total tax (francs)*	*Net price per quintal* (francs)*	*Average tax per quintal (francs)*
600	81,250	3,465	135.35
700	101,250	3,455	144.65
800	121,250	3,448	151.55
900	143,750	3,440	159.72
1000	166,250	3,434	166.25
2000	416,250	3,392	208.10

* The net price per quintal does not include sums deducted for the "statistical tax" (25 francs) and the 8 francs subscription to a parafiscal "Fund for Technical Progress."

In recent years, producer contributions under the absorption tax have not been adequate to cover all of the costs of surplus disposal, and the Treasury has been called upon to make up the deficit through export subsidies. From scattered information it appears that the program cost the Treasury the relatively small sum of 2 billion francs for the 1951-1952 season. No state subsidies were required for the 1952 crop (marketed in 1953). A sum of 16 billion francs was provided by the 1954 budget as the state's share of subsidized exports for the 1953-1954 crop. With the large 1954 harvest, surplus disposal has become more costly. The loss on a quintal of wheat sold at the 1954-1955 world price was estimated at about half the domestic price, or 1,700 to 1,800 francs per quintal. (This means that consumers in France had to pay twice as much for wheat as a purchaser on the world market had to pay.) The disposal of the 1954 crop was expected to cost about 40 billion francs, of which 14 billion francs was to be provided by the absorption tax[11] and 26 billion francs by the Treasury. The cost to the public in 1954-1955 of surplus disposal under the wheat program was therefore around 10 per cent of the value of the 1954 wheat crop.

2. *Sugar beets and alcohol.* Sugar beets are among the less important agricultural crops. The gross value of beet output represents only 2.5 per cent to 3 per cent of the total for agriculture, and the growing area concerned is only about 400,000 hectares. However, the state has given extensive assistance to sugar beet producers by supporting the price of sugar beets and by providing an outlet for large quantities of industrial alcohol (and recently sugar) made from excess beets. The sugar beet-alcohol program also deserves consideration here because, with its high costs to the government and the nation, it constitutes, in the words of one economist, "along with the legislation on rents, the most Malthusian

institution of our country.[f]"[12] Alcohol is made from wine, from apples and cider, and from other sources, but beets are by far the principal source.

Regulation of alcohol began during the first World War and underwent various modifications during the interwar period. In its present form, the bare essentials of the alcohol program are as follows: (a) the government fixes the prices paid to growers of sugar beets, apples, pears, and other sources of alcohol as well as the margins allowed to distillers; (b) the fixed prices apply to specified quotas for each of the sources of alcohol; (c) the government also fixes the price paid for sugar beets to be refined into sugar, and may directly control the amount of sugar beets used as sugar rather than as alcohol; (d) the State Alcohol Monopoly (*Service des Alcools*) purchases all of the ethylic alcohol distilled in France (except for certain brandies) and bears the heavy financial losses incurred in the storage and disposal of surplus alcohol; and (e) the government provides subsidies to make possible the export of surplus sugar.

The success of a small group of beet growers and beet distillers in obtaining extensive legislation in its behalf has been due to its skill in joining forces with the legion of small wine growers. As will be indicated later, large wine producers have been compelled to convert a portion of their wine to alcohol, thus reducing the quantity of marketed wine and so helping to raise the price above the disastrous levels that had threatened to wipe out the small growers during the crisis of the 1930's. Cider producers from Western France, where the apple crop varies widely from year to year, also stood to benefit from the alcohol program. To all these producers, the program has been presented as the safety valve, the protection against troublesome surpluses. It was said to constitute "the corner stone of the whole French agricultural structure."[13] As the program has been applied in the postwar period, however, most of its benefits have accrued to the sugar beet producers and to the distilling industry.

a. Price supports. Although the commodity purchased by the alcohol monopoly is pure alcohol, the purchase price varies widely according to the source of the alcohol. In principle, the price relationships are supposed to reflect differences in costs of production. For certain wine producers, however, distillation of specified quantities is imposed as a device for protecting the wine market and

[f] The term "Malthusian" is frequently used in French literature to characterize practices that are considered to restrict production or impede economic progress.

results in losses to the producers since the purchase price of the alcohol is low relative to production costs. For alcohol made from sugar beets, the purchase price is high; in 1953-1954, for example, it was 83 francs per liter, or about 7 times the world price of alcohol.[14]

The key price in the alcohol system is that of beet alcohol, which in turn is derived from the price of sugar beets plus a margin for transportation and distillation. Between 1946 and 1954, the price of sugar beets was based on a "cost of production" method. The calculations were somewhat fictitious and tended to overestimate average costs. This was admitted implicitly in 1954, when it was announced that in the future, for sugar beets and "all other" products whose prices are fixed by the government through the cost of production method, the calculations would be based on a "normally equipped" farm or enterprise.[g] [15]

The experimentation with pricing methods continued in 1955. A parity-price concept was introduced but modified to allow for seasonal variations in the size of the crop (i.e., in average yields) and to incorporate an automatic factor tending to reduce the price each year. Specifically, the sugar beet price for the 1955-1956 crop is to be based on the 1954-1955 price, adjusted for the change in two indexes: that of prices of industrial products necessary for farm operations and that of wholesale prices of manufactured products in the provinces.[h] The resultant price is then reduced by 4 per cent by the application of a "productivity" coefficient, and may be further adjusted by 6 per cent in either direction to take account of annual variations in the yield of a farm with "average" equipment. At the same time, it was announced that the wide distillers' margins would be reduced 5 per cent in 1955-1956 and 7 per cent in 1956-1957. But the new system was no sooner instituted than it was disregarded. According to *Le Monde*, the government decided not to change the 1955 sugar beet price, although application of the new formula would have resulted in more than a 10 per cent reduction. The decision was not publicized because it was a violation of the government's own statutes.[16]

The price of sugar derived from sugar beets is also fixed by the government. In the past, higher processing margins have been allowed for alcohol than for sugar made from sugar beets, with

[g] The estimated cost of fertilizers, for example, was based on the highly optimistic assumption that all farmers used the amount recommended by extension agents.

[h] The latter index appears to be a way of approximating the cost of living in rural areas.

the result that processors have been encouraged to direct the beet crop into alcohol.[17] Since the government suffers a smaller loss in the subsidized export of sugar than in the support of the sugar beet-alcohol program, it has, on several occasions, stated its intention to change the price relationships in order to encourage the production of sugar rather than alcohol. No steps in this direction were taken prior to the 1954 program mentioned below.

b. Production controls. The price paid by the monopoly applies only to specified quotas, fixed separately for each of the sources of alcohol. Before 1953, the quota for alcohol made from sugar beets was 3,845,000 hectoliters of pure alcohol. The quota for alcohol from all sources was about 5,375,000 hectoliters.[1] The quotas were generous to the point of being practically ineffective, and in some years production was far below them. In some cases they could be transferred from year to year, and purchases could thus exceed the yearly quota. The monopoly's purchases between 1948-1949 and 1953-1954 ranged between 3,250,000 and 5,200,-000 hectoliters.[18] The past quotas have therefore had no effect in reducing the excess resources in sugar beet production resulting from the sheltered market of many years duration.

An important exception to the quota system exists for home distillers (the celebrated *bouilleurs de cru*). Farmers are entitled by law to distill for their own use their production of wine, cider, and other fermented fruit juices, up to a limit of 10 liters per year of pure alcohol. The number of such *bouilleurs de cru* has grown steadily and rapidly; it was over 3.5 million in 1954, or more than the total number of farmers in France. The amount of alcohol distillation was well in excess of the maximum; a report to the *Conseil Economique* has placed the amount of illegally-produced alcohol at 200,000 liters annually. For a long period of time, the *bouilleurs de cru* have enjoyed the status of political "untouchables." This privilege has greatly encouraged alcoholism among farmers and established a lively black market in alcohol sales outside of government channels. There is a close correlation between mortality due to alcoholism and the number of *bouilleurs de cru* in different regions of France.[19] The Mendès-France government attempted by decree to reduce the number of *bouilleurs de cru* by 800,000

[1] These figures include about 1,350,000 hectoliters of alcohol made from sugar beets under special contracts to induce new areas to produce beets. These contracts were made in 1944-1945 but have not been rescinded despite the mounting surplus of alcohol.

through a redefinition of their status, but Parliament subsequently postponed its application at least until September 1, 1956.[j]

Using its special decree powers, the Laniel government undertook to reform the alcohol quota system in 1953. The quotas on alcohol purchased at the guaranteed price were to be progressively reduced until they had been almost halved (to 2,775,000 hl.) by 1957-1958, with most of the cutback coming in alcohol from sugar beets. The blow was softened by the provision of substantial "compensations" or subsidies. The difference in the value of alcohol under the new and old quotas was to be placed in a fund to be used to compensate distillers that reduced their operations or closed down, distillers that might be ordered to transfer their sugar beets to sugar factories, refiners who stored or exported sugar, beet producers who shifted voluntarily to other crops, and apple growers who were unable to market their crops after the closing of the apple distilleries.

The 1953 reform got off to a particularly bad start; the 1953-1954 crop of sugar beets was considerably higher than in the preceding year, and the government agreed to an "exceptional" increase in the quota. The following year, the Mendès-France government took more drastic action by ordering that two-thirds of the 1954-1955 sugar beet crop normally destined for distillation into alcohol should be diverted instead into sugar manufacturing. The government covered the additional transportation cost involved, indemnified the distilleries for the loss of business, and agreed to finance the additional exports of sugar.

Although no additional action was taken on the alcohol quotas, a slight reduction in the 1954 sugar beet price and the automatic reduction factor incorporated into the 1955 price formula were considered as warnings to producers to reduce their acreage. The

[j] Mendès-France referred to alcoholism as the "number one national scourge of France" (*Le Monde*, September 12, 1954, Financial and Economic Supplement). A few statistics on the subject may be enlightening. The per capita consumption of alcoholic beverages in France is by far the highest in the world; it is double that of Italy and Switzerland and triple that of Great Britain, Belgium, and the United States. Of the net national income of France, 9 per cent is devoted to alcoholic consumption. Relative to income, this is 10 times the amount in the United States and 5 times that in Great Britain. There is one outlet where drinks are sold for every 34 adults, or 10 times the number of bakeries. A high proportion of the adult population suffers from the effects of alcoholism (as do a considerable number of children). A close correlation has been established between alcoholism and the high rate of mortality in France. The medical costs to the state of alcoholism run over 200 billion francs annually. Data from *Le Monde*, August 15, 1953, p. 7; H. Dijon "Alcool, ou lait et viande?" *Economie et réalités mondiales*, July 1953, p. 64; *L'Express*, January 23, 1954, p. 10; and *Agence économique et financière*, August 3, 1954, p. 4.

closing of distilleries also worked in this direction by depriving some farmers of accessible outlets for their crops. Later, however, Mendès-France assured sugar beet growers that he would not permit the area in sugar beets to fall below 375,000 hectares, without indicating what implications this might have for the future implementation of the alcohol quota system. Some reduction in acreage did take place, from 409,000 hectares (the average of 1950-1953) to 380,000 hectares in 1954 and 376,000 in 1955.[20]

At the urging of the farm bloc in the National Assembly, the Faure government undid some of the work of its predecessor by reopening some distilleries and widening their processing margins. Whether the scheduled reductions in alcohol quotas will be carried out by future governments remains to be seen; it can at least be safely predicted that they will be under strong pressure to modify or ignore the earlier decrees.

c. Surplus disposal. The alcohol monopoly has had increasing difficulty in disposing of its product to conventional users. In the postwar period, there were no serious surpluses of alcohol until after the recovery of beet production around 1948-1949. Since then, the yearly surplus above normal uses has amounted to between 2 and 3 million hectoliters, or between 50 and 60 per cent of all the alcohol acquired by the monopoly. The principal outlet since 1950-1951 has been an exceptional contract to sell 5 million hectoliters to the American government for the manufacture of synthetic rubber; but this was a non-recurring sale, which only postponed temporarily the alcohol crisis. The expedient of requiring that alcohol be mixed with motor fuel was used before the war, and 1 million hectoliters of alcohol were disposed of in this fashion in 1950-1951. With alcohol stocks rising to reach the level of 5,430,000 hectoliters at the end of 1954, the government was again considering this last-resort device. It is necessary to provide heavy subsidies or tax rebates, in one form or another, to the petroleum industry in order to reduce or eliminate the losses that it incurs through this compulsory use of alcohol. In fact, the use of alcohol in motor fuel is so uneconomical that it apparently would cost the government and the economy no more to dump the alcohol in the river.[21]

An appraisal of the financial costs of the program to the state is made difficult by the accounting practices followed by the monopoly and by the complicated conditions surrounding some of the sales. INSEE has estimated that the effective loss to the monopoly and to the state through the operation of the alcohol program during the three-year period 1948-1949 to 1951-1952 amounted to 45-50 billion francs (in 1953 prices). Rough confirmation is given by the fact that Treasury "advances" to the monopoly to cover its operating losses (i.e., the difference between gross receipts and gross payments) between 1950 and 1952 amounted to 48 billion francs. The costs of the program have been rising with the accumulating surpluses; in 1954 the government's loss was estimated at 18 to 20 billion francs.[22]

A substantial part of the benefits of the alcohol program do not go to farmers. Over the period 1948-1949 to 1951-1952, the farmers' share of the expenditures of the monopoly amounted only to about 45 per cent. The margins allowed to distilleries were wide enough to permit extremely obsolete plants to continue in operation. Among farm recipients, most funds spent by the monopoly benefited beet producers, since about three-fourths of the purchases of the monopoly were of beet or molasses alcohol. Of the total income of beet growers, one quarter came from alcohol and the rest from sugar. The use of beets in the manufacture of alcohol, introduced as a safety valve, is becoming a regular and permanent operation, with about 20 per cent of the beet crop regularly going to distilleries. The benefits of the sugar beet-alcohol program are received by a very limited number of farmers (150,000 at most) and a still smaller number of distillers. Most of the farmers are in areas of France that have the best soils, the most regular climate, and the largest farms. On these farms can be grown alternative crops that fit nearly as well into crop rotation and that can be used to increase the output of more readily marketed products such as milk and meat.[23] In the subsidy-ridden economy of France, it can perhaps be said that never has so much been paid to so few for so little.

The benefits afforded to wine growers have, in the past, been of much less importance. According to the *Conseil Economique*, for the period 1948-1949 to 1951-1952 the monopoly only provided 1.3 per cent of the wine growers' gross receipts. The 1953-1954 and 1954-1955 distillation of alcohol made from wine was substantially greater, however, and the alcohol program may assume more importance for wine growers in the future.

The reform measures of 1953 and 1954, if continued along the lines originally laid down, would eventually lighten the financial burden on the state. Unless the area in sugar beets is reduced substantially, an essential feature will be the transfer of part of the beet crop from alcohol to sugar production. The price of French sugar is also far above the world price, and surpluses exist for which export outlets are difficult to find. A shift from alcohol to sugar is still desirable, however, since sugar made with one ton of beets costs 4,200 francs more than the world price, while alcohol made from a ton of beets requires a 7,500 francs subsidy to be exported.[24] There will be no reduction in the costs incurred by the government in the short run, since the projected savings from the reduction in alcohol production will be offset by the added subsidies for sugar exports, the indemnities paid to distilleries, and the transportation costs covered by the government for the transfer of beets from distilleries to refineries.[25]

3. Wine. Wine ranks fifth among French crops, accounting for 9-9.5 per cent of the gross value of production in 1953-1954 (as against about 12 per cent shortly before the war). There are a large number of winegrowers—about 1,700,000 in 1950—most of whom produce a relatively small crop. Wine growing is often a specialized operation; in the Mediterranean border plain, which is the main wine producing region, wine is virtually the only crop produced and the only source of income in the region. In the past, wine depressions have caused serious upheaval and riots in Southern France. In 1953-1955, telephone wires were cut and roads barricaded in the South, the wine farmers being joined at the ramparts by their deputies and senators in vigorous demands upon the government for further action in their behalf.

The interventions of the state in the marketing of wines are particularly complex. The Association of Wine Producers has complained that "the protection granted by the state is far from being as efficacious as that from which sugar beets and wheat benefit."[26] While the "efficaciousness" of the protection may be questioned in all three cases, it has probably been less comprehensive for wine in the past. Additional controls are rapidly being installed or considered, however.

The essential features of the regulation of the wine market are: (a) no direct controls over the price of wine for domestic consumption, although wine prices are fixed for other uses and the market price is indirectly influenced by other features of the regulatory system; (b) short-run action on the supply of wine by compulsory blocking and by compulsory distillation of wine-making residues; (c) long-run action on supply by restrictions on new plantings and by the payment of indemnities for the uprooting of vineyards; and (d) surplus disposal through distillation into alcohol and government subsidies for export dumping. Built into the system at several points is discrimination against large producers in favor of the small.[27]

a. Price supports. The government does not fix directly the price of wine sold as such on the domestic market. Direct price support has been considered but so far has been rejected for a number of reasons, among them the difficulties arising from variations in quality. The price of wine and of wine residues when compulsorily distilled into alcohol is fixed administratively, as is the export price as a result of the subsidies provided for export promotion. In 1955, the government's influence over the wine price was further strengthened by the stipulation that export subsidies would be provided only to wines purchased at or above a specified minimum price. These points will be examined further below.

During early postwar years, wine was in relatively short supply, and the uncontrolled wine price was considerably above the general price level. Thus the 1949-1950 price at retail stood at an index of 2300 (1938 = 100), while the general retail price index for the same period was about 1900.[28] Prices fell sharply with the larger harvest of 1950-1951 and again in 1953-1955, giving rise to farm pressures for government price support through various indirect means.

b. Production controls. Action to control the short-run supply of alcohol takes two forms: seasonal blocking and unblocking of wine stocks and compulsory distillation of wine-making residues. The seasonal blocking of stocks has helped to dampen fluctuations in the market price in the short run. The crop of producers of more than 50 or 100 hectoliters (the figure has varied in recent years) may not be sold freely. Except for a small proportion that may be sold immediately, it is blocked in the cellars of producers. Loans from the *Crédit Agricole* may be extended to growers whose crops are blocked, with special advantages to small growers. Under the recent procedures, blocking only lasts until January 15 at the latest. By that date, crop reports give sufficient information on the size of the crop for decisions to be reached with regard to the amount of "excess" wine. The surplus wine is then removed from commercial channels and diverted to other uses or kept in stock until the next crop; the remainder of the wine may be sold at will.

Compulsory distillation of wine-making residues serves two purposes: improving the quality of wine and reducing the supply of commercial wine. Inferior quality wines may be made by strong-pressing of the grapes, which reduces the residues. This is prevented by compelling wine growers to provide specified quantities of alcohol, which will naturally be made from wine residues and by-products rather than from the better grades of wine. These compulsory deliveries of alcohol made from residues, called *prestations d'alcool vinique*, help to improve the quality of commercial wine. They have a small effect on the wine supply; on the average, about 2 or 3 million hectoliters of potential wine, or 2 to 5 per cent of the crop, are withdrawn in this fashion. Until 1953, the compulsory *prestations d'alcool vinique* only concerned producers of over 200 hectoliters of wine (or about 40 to 50 per cent of the total crop). In 1953, the Laniel government extended the system by decree to all growers regardless of size, but this move was subsequently nullified by Parliament. The Mendès-France government again attempted to extend the system to all growers, with lower rates for smaller growers, but ended by retaining the previous system with a lowering of the minimum crop size, below which distillation did not apply, to 75 hectoliters.

During periods of large wine production and falling prices, there have been some efforts to adjust long-run supply by reducing the area devoted to vineyards. A 1931 law prohibited additional plantings of vineyards on large farms (over 10 hectares in vineyards). No limit was placed on new plantings on small farms, however. The limit was lowered substantially, to one-quarter hectare of vineyards, in 1953. New vineyards for "family" requirements still remain authorized, and these have been extensively planted, often in low quality varieties.

There have also been subsidies, in AAA style, for the voluntary uprooting of vineyards. The prewar program called for the uprooting of 150,000 hectares; from 1934 to the beginning of the war, some 50-70,000 hectares were uprooted. In view of the new plantings on small farms, the net reduction in vineyard acreage was about 40,000 hectares between 1934 and 1938, not all of which was due to the uprooting program. The 40,000 hectares represented about 3 per cent of the vineyard area and a potential output of under 2 million hectoliters.[29]

The area in vineyards has remained roughly constant since the war, at a level about 4 per cent below prewar (1,450,000 hectares in 1952 against 1,510,000 in 1938).[30] The production of wine is particularly susceptible to variations in the weather, however, and the crops in 1950, 1953 and 1954 exceeded the 1934-1938 average. With wine stocks piling up despite the distillation of record quantities of alcohol, the voluntary reduction of vineyard acreage was reinstituted in 1954. The voluntary program, hopefully expected to cover 150,000 hectares or about 10 per cent of the total, is to end in 1958, after which year compulsory uprooting may be applied if the anticipated results have not been forthcoming. The bonuses or indemnities for uprooting range from 250,000 to 400,000 francs per hectare in accordance with an intricate formula purported to be based on the productivity of the soil, the quality of the plants, the age of the vineyard, its condition of maintenance, and so forth. The formula is designed to provide the largest bonuses to vineyards that produce large quantities of inferior quality wines. There has been no rush of farmers to take advantage of the bonuses, since the price support and surplus disposal arrangements make the growing of inferior quality wines profitable to the farmer. So long as winegrowers benefit from market sheltering, voluntary reductions in supply are not likely to occur in large amounts.[31]

c. Surplus disposal. The principal method of disposing of "excess" stocks, which the government elects to keep off the market as a means of supporting the price, has been compulsory distillation. During 1935-1940, about 20 million hectoliters were distilled in addition to the distillation of wine residues or the voluntary distillation of inferior quality wines.[32] It is difficult to obtain precise figures on the amount of wine ordered for distillation in recent years, since the stocks declared as excess may be carried over for several years in the hopes of a small harvest in the future. It appears that about 8-10 million hectoliters were distilled between 1950-1951 and 1953-1954. The "excess" stocks at the end of the 1954-1955 season were 19 million hectoliters, despite the distillation of 11 million hectoliters during the season. By way of comparison, the 1954 crop was 78 million hectoliters.[33]

The compulsory distillation of wine is subject to complicated rules. The smallest producers are exempt completely. For those subject to compulsory distillation, the proportion of the crop that must be distilled increases with its size. Alcohol made from this source has been purchased by the monopoly at what amounts to a "penalty" price, which is only about half that of commercial wine of average quality. The compulsory distillation of wine may thus involve a financial loss to producers on that part of their crop that is subject to it, against which must be set the higher price for the balance of their crop as a result of the removal of this part of the wine supply from the market. This price relationship differs markedly from the case of beets, where the alcohol price is at least as favorable as that of sugar, or that of apples where the apples (or cider) are often purchased at a higher price to make alcohol.

The compulsory distillation applies to a given quantity of alcohol regardless of the quality of the wine used for this purpose. It is possible for the farmer to transfer the distillation obligation to another winegrower (in effect, to purchase a portion of the crop of another farmer and substitute it for his own). This is extensively practiced, with the objective of distilling inferior and low-price wines rather than good ones. These transfers have been encouraged by the government.

A second outlet for "surplus" wines in 1953-1955 was subsidized exports. The government agreed to provide the substantial subsidies necessary to lower the French price for table wines to the price quoted by France's principal competitors in the export trade. By stipulating that these subsidies do not apply to wines purchased from the producer at prices below a specified minimum, the government has attempted further to bolster the sagging price of wine on the commercial market. In addition, free wine is being distributed to paupers, who already benefit, presumably with more salutary effects on their health, from the sugar surplus. French soldiers, who have been drinking up part of the milk surplus, have had their wine ration increased.[34]

According to a newspaper source, the cost of the wine support program in its several forms (loss on the additional production of alcohol, cost of uprooting vineyards, export subsidies, etc.) was expected to amount in 1954 to 30 billion francs.[35] If this figure is correct, the cost of the support program was about 15 per cent of the total value of the crop in 1954. It must be recalled, however, that stocks may be carried over from one year to another, so that some of the cost may be attributable to production of earlier years.

III REGULATION OF THE FOREIGN MARKET

Tariff protection has been the traditional agricultural policy in the foreign market, later followed by the imposition of quotas. Concern over the "anomaly" that France, despite its natural advantages and the large volume of diversified production, regularly had a deficit in its agricultural trade was officially manifested by the Monnet Plan. The (revised) plan called for an improvement in the trade balance from a deficit of $264 million in 1948 to a net surplus of $313 million in 1952-1953 (equivalent to about 110 billion 1953 francs). It is not clear whether these figures refer to the total agricultural trade of Metropolitan France or only to its trade with foreign countries.[36] The second plan reaffirmed the objective of converting France into a substantial net exporter of farm products. Its targets were set at a reduction of 70 billion francs in imports from foreign countries between 1952 and 1957 and an increase of 130 billion francs in exports to foreign countries. These improvements would result in a net surplus in agricultural trade of 120 billion francs.[37] While agricultural trade surpluses are a thing of the future, the accounts with foreign countries had been brought close to balance by 1954.

Despite the import-reduction target, some attention has been given since the war to the problem of liberalizing imports (in the interests of more competition). But progress in this direction has been slow, and the restrictions on free trade in farm products continue to work against the flow of resources to their best uses. On balance, the external protection afforded to domestic producers has probably encouraged resources to remain in particular branches of agriculture even though they would be more productive elsewhere.

A. IMPORT RESTRICTIONS AND LIBERALIZATION

The long-standing tradition of high protection of French agriculture has sometimes been defended on balance of payments grounds, although more commonly the question of the level of French tariffs is ignored in public discussions of trade policy. A comparison of French agricultural tariffs in 1950 with those of several other OEEC countries is presented in Table 34. A statistical comparison of the average tariff levels of the eight countries would be misleading because of the complexity of the underlying data and the differing importance of various products. It is evident from even a casual inspection of the table, however, that French tariffs on important agricultural products were among the highest in Europe. Thus on a considerable number of products (beef, pork, potatoes, rye, wheat flour, and sugar) the French tariff was as high as, or higher than, that of any other country. For butter and wheat, the French tariff was second only to Italy.

Quantitative restrictions have been more important than tariffs in limiting imports into France since the war. Within the OEEC program of trade liberalization, the freeing of agricultural imports by France has been less than that of industrial products. Thus in the 1950-1951 phase, 76 per cent of all private imports from OEEC countries was liberalized, while only 65 per cent of agricultural production was liberalized. In view of the amount of state trading and the small importance of intra-European trade, the liberated

TABLE 34. TARIFF RATES ON CERTAIN FARM PRODUCTS FOR SELECTED EUROPEAN COUNTRIES, 1950

(ad valorem rates or equivalents)

Product	*Benelux*	*Denmark*	*France*	*Italy*	*Norway*	*Portugal*	*United Kingdom*	*Sweden*
Beef	12.0	0	40.0	36.0	26.9	5.4	10.5	4.1
Pork	12.0	0	40.0	40.0	13.9	24.1	0	4.9
Butter	15.0	0	25.0	30.0	n.a.	17.1	4.5	5.1
Eggs in shell	5.0	0	20.0	30.0	26.5	2.9	15.5	6.5
Onions	0	7.3	20.0	13.7	21.8	30.3	10.0	8.5
Potatoes	7.5	0	32.0	20.0	7.5	17.6	6.0	5.0
Spinach	15.0	0	18.0	10.0	14.3	30.3	6.0	14.0
Table grapes	49.4	3.1	20.0	10.0	4.1	30.1	7.0	5.7
Eating apples	12.0	4.1	9.0	9.0	35.4	108.2	5.0	8.5
Wheat	0	0	30.0	40.0	0	n.a.	0	7.6
Rye	0	0	50.0	30.0	0	48.4	10.0	6.6
Wheat flour	3.0	0	70.0	60.0	0	n.a.	10.0	11.8
Sugar	50.3	n.a.	130.0	105.0	22.7	72.7	17.0	1.8
Canned tomatoes	20.0	30.0	30.0	15.0	50.0	114.3	10.0	50.0
Canned peas and beans	25.0	28.9	25.0	25.0	41.9	114.3	10.0	75.0
Beer in bulk	32.1	n.a.	35.0	35.0	52.4	140.6	10.0	45.0

Source: Group d'Etudes pour l'Union Douanière Européenne, Comité Douanier, Comité Spécial Restreint de la Nomenclature, *Moyenne des Tarifs basée sur la Nomenclature de Bruxelles de 1949*, Tome I, Brussels, July 1950 (mimeographed). Cited in William Diebold, Jr. *Trade and Payments in Western Europe* (New York, Harper & Bros. 1952), p, 257.

Note: Where specific or compound duties were levied, the ad valorem equivalent has been computed for most countries on the basis of 1948 imports; for Norway and Sweden, 1947 was used. The tariffs are those in effect at the end of 1949, except for Italy, which used the revised tariff put into effect in July 1950. The rates are those applied to ordinary imports from countries receiving most-favored-nation treatment. National tariff classifications have been adjusted to conform to the 1949 nomenclature established by the European Customs Union Study Group. The items shown in the table have the following code numbers in the Study Group's nomenclature, where a more detailed definition of each product can be found: 02.01A, C, 04.04, 04.06A, 07.01E, F, K, 08.04AI, 08.06B, 10.01, 10.02, 11.01A2, 17.01A, 20.02A3, 5,22.02A.

imports represented only 15 per cent of all agricultural imports.[38] In the 1953-1955 phase of trade liberalization, the proportion for agricultural imports was only 62 per cent at the time that the average level attained 75 per cent. On the other hand, most French exports of agricultural products to other European countries were completely free of quotas during 1953 and 1954.

B. EXPORT PROMOTION

During the food shortages of the early postwar period, prohibitions were applied against the export of farm products. With the growing emphasis on improving the balance of payments, the official policy has shifted to that of export promotion. The more intensive prospecting of foreign markets in 1953-1955 revealed that France had "lost the habit"[39] of exporting. Not only was the knowledge of the world market situation deficient, but French producers had often been guilty of exporting sub-standard and inferior products.[40]

Exports of agricultural products are eligible for the subsidies applied to other exports (i.e., reimbursement of taxes and social security charges) under the promotion program described in Chapter 4. Except for wine and meat, where special "single" taxes are applied, these reimbursements are not very important. They apply mainly to processing operations, since crops at the farm level are not subject to the production tax. Because of the limited effect of these measures, special subsidies have been required for exports of wheat, sugar, alcohol, wine, meat, and dairy products, as has been seen. These subsidies have been financed in part by levies on the producers, but mainly from special funds provided directly by the Treasury or by a diversion of the normal proceeds of the taxes on the commodities in question.

The aggregate effect of these subsidies on export prices has not been publicly estimated. Because many exporting countries have adopted similar practices, some subsidies serve only to maintain the original competitive position. While the substantial volume of subsidies provided in 1953-1955 has undoubtedly contributed to the expansion of agricultural exports, this practice tends to encourage resources to go into uses (or to remain in uses) in which France has no comparative advantage.

IV SUMMARY

In view of the instability of farm income, many countries provide some support or protection to farmers against the vagaries of nature, technological change, and shifts in demand. To what extent and in what way support should be provided has been a difficult and controversial problem, since such action is likely to result in a misallocation of resources within agriculture and between agriculture and other sectors of the economy.

The trend of public policy in France has been in the direction of increased state intervention in the marketing process. Some crop support programs were initiated with the crisis of the 1930's. Most food products were in relatively short supply during early postwar years, and market protection was not required; with the large harvests of 1953-1955, however, the number of interventions in the form of price supports, production controls, and surplus disposal programs has been multiplied. Although the majority of farm products were still not subject to comprehensive supports in 1955, the situation is evolving rapidly. Policies have been adopted, pursued, and revised or abandoned in an *ad hoc* fashion, with different procedures in the case of each particular commodity. External protection, through tariffs and quotas, has been of longer standing and has not been substantially weakened by the efforts at trade liberation.

External protection has probably kept resources in some agricultural uses although they would have higher productivity elsewhere. Within agriculture, the widely different degrees of support provided to different commodities have probably shifted resources away from some commodities (meat, milk, fruits, and vegetables) into the production of others that are more sheltered. The case of meat is particularly unfortunate, since export outlets have been available for the earning of foreign exchange. Large surpluses have been piling up recently in the sheltered areas; the government has been able to dispose of these surpluses only at a substantial loss to the economy. This is most striking in the case of sugar beets, and, more recently, wine. It has been less striking in the case of wheat, where some flexibility and concern for consumer interests can be observed.

CHAPTER 13

CONCLUSIONS

THIS chapter recapitulates the main findings of the study and generalizes from them. So far the objectives of the state have been examined one at a time while holding all other objectives constant. There is no generally accepted scale of values with which to weigh the importance of one objective against that of another, but a more meaningful picture of the extent to which the different objectives have been achieved or sacrificed can be gained by juxtaposing the various results. This chapter also pulls together some of the conclusions about certain objectives (growth, economic efficiency) that have been scattered through several chapters.

Some of the qualifications introduced at the beginning of this study should be mentioned again:

(1) Only some of the objectives or ends of state intervention have been considered. Other important ones (personal security, leisure, preservation of traditions) have been given little or no attention;

(2) Success or failure in attaining the various objectives studied here depends on many factors other than state action, but only the effects of state action have been examined;

(3) The "state" has been treated as an entity separate from the people that compose it. The popular pressures giving rise to state action have not been systematically explored, nor has it been asked where the responsibility for the state's performance might lie in some ultimate sense;

(4) Only limited use has been made of international comparisons. The unimpressive record of state performance that has unfolded makes it especially interesting to know to what extent the objectives pursued, and the policies adopted, have been peculiar to France. Certainly many of the tendencies observed here have their counterparts in other countries, although there may be significant differences in degree. But a systematic comparison of the economic roles of government in different nations is beyond the purpose of this book.

I WHY DID THE GOVERNMENT ACT?

In connection with each major activity in which the state engages, the question has been asked: Why did the state intervene? What were the problems and objectives which motivated state action?

In retrospect one cannot fail to be struck by the wide, almost bewildering, variety of problems that the government has tackled and of functions that it has assumed. The objectives that figured in connection with specific problems and functions will not be summarized here. Speaking more generally, it appears that the state has been pursuing the following main objectives:

(1) To promote economic recovery and growth and to raise living standards;
(2) To control fluctuations in the level of employment, production, and prices;
(3) To achieve viability in international trade;
(4) To redistribute income in favor of particular groups or classes;
(5) To expand social security benefits to various parts of the population;
(6) To preserve particular groups or classes against the process of economic change;
(7) To improve the efficiency with which resources are employed and thereby raise living standards;
(8) To improve the pattern of labor-management relations;
(9) To change the ownership structure of basic industries and operate them in the "public interest."

Obviously, these objectives may sometimes conflict with each other, so that more of one cannot be achieved except at the expense of another. The essence of government is choosing among conflicting aims. But the French state at times has not recognized the conflicts, or at least has acted as though they didn't exist by pursuing all of the objectives separately and simultaneously. There is, for example, the separate and simultaneous pursuit of modernization and of protection of the *status quo*. And there are attempts to encourage large firms but at the same time to preserve small ones. Contributing to the difficulty is the fact that one year's policy becomes next year's heritage; broad social and political waves (such as the "social liberation" and the nationalization drive after the war) advance and recede, but the controls and institutions which they bring about remain imbedded in the system.

Thus state action has been inspired by numerous objectives. And a major reason why the state's actions have not been more effective is the failure to perceive the conflicting nature of these aims or, when it is perceived, failure to choose among them or to abandon a set of measures once it is in effect.

II HOW DID THE GOVERNMENT ACT?

Much attention has been devoted to examining how the government has acted; the methods of intervention, the kinds of policies adopted, and the ways in which they were implemented. These descriptive materials were designed primarily to shed light on significant results of state action, but partly to convey some general impressions about methods of intervention themselves.

With respect to the scope of state intervention, it is difficult to find an economic activity of any consequence in which the state does not exercise an important role. The imprint of the state is particularly marked in the control of foreign trade. Also, costs and prices throughout the economy are strongly influenced by state action, as is the process through which goods are sold in the market place. Perhaps the most general index of the extent of intervention—although only a partial one—is the proportion of the national income which the state channels through the public budget in order to finance its various activities. This has risen to the imposing figure of more than 40 per cent. The proportion of industrial activity which is under state ownership (about 20 per cent) is another significant clue to the extent to which the state has become a major force in the economic process.

The methods that the government has adopted cover a very wide range. At one extreme, the government has influenced the economic system in such direct ways as owning and managing key industrial sectors or controlling the use of resources through priorities, licensing arrangements, and allocations. At the other extreme, the government has attempted to exert its influence in indirect ways through moral suasion, bestowing tax advantages, or altering incentives. The ways in which prices are determined illustrate the variety of means employed. Some prices (of products sold by nationalized industries) are set by the government. Others are subject to specific ceilings, while general price freezes may be in effect for several years at a time. In the case of farm commodities, a floor is placed under some prices through action on supply. Still other prices are influenced indirectly through tax favors or penalties, subsidies, compensations, or rebates, and the general level and flexibility of prices are affected by state action on the degree of competition.

Some tendency to shift to less direct methods of influencing economic activity can be observed during the postwar period, no doubt in part because of the unpopularity of direct controls and the consequent difficulties of enforcement. Rationing, allocations, and priorities have been abandoned; the direct use of public funds for investment purposes has been reduced, and tax provisions that encourage private investors have been relied upon more heavily; wage-fixing has been eliminated except for the minimum wage; foreign trade controls have been partially relaxed; no nationalization of industry has taken place since 1948, and private capital has again been invited into some of the public enterprises. On the other hand, a general price freeze was reinstituted late in the postwar period and has been kept in effect, while direct supports of farm products are increasing in importance. And, while the state's influence over economic affairs has partially changed in character, there are no grounds for believing that it has appreciably diminished over the postwar period.

Despite the multiplicity and extensiveness of state controls, it cannot be said that France has a "planned" economy. To be sure, there are plans in profusion: the Monnet plan, the Hirsch plan, the Faure plan, the Louvel plan, *etc.* But there has been little systematic planning in the sense of a set of specific and internally-consistent goals combined with a set of policies and controls to make sure that the goals can be achieved. Planning in France has stopped for the most part at the stage of elaborating goals which are too general and imprecise to serve as guides for practical decisions. (Indeed, the statistical base on which systematic planning would have to rest is still seriously deficient.) There are, of course, some measures which bear on the implementation of the "plans" or goals. Usually they are adopted on an *ad hoc* basis to meet particular problems as they arise. Even at the height of the planning movement (in 1945-1947), there were significant gaps in the array of controls necessary for realization of the plans. To use a French distinction, which is difficult to translate, there has been a great deal of *dirigisme*, but not much *planisme*.

Conversely, it certainly cannot be said that the government's policies have been consistent with the role assigned to it under a "free" economy in the liberal tradition, or in the twentieth century American variant thereof. Despite some efforts in the direction of freer internal or external exchange, most French policies, reflecting attitudes prevalent in business and agriculture, reveal an abiding lack of faith in a competitive market economy.

Thus, as *The Economist* observes, "economic activities are directed neither by the conscious choice of the planners nor by the incentives and penalties of a free price mechanism."[1] In practice, of course, all economic systems lie somewhere in the spectrum between the hypothetical extremes of complete *laissez faire* and complete central planning. France appears to be in the intermediate position of having less "planning" than the planned economies (such as the Soviet Union) yet more controls and intervention than the "free" economies (such as the United States).

Another characteristic of the methods of intervention adopted in France is their great intricacy and complexity. Frenchmen are noted for their propensity to "legislate on everything and for everyone." Closely allied to this propensity are two others: (a) a preference for elaborate regulatory formulae (as in the pricing of electricity or wheat), which are only partially observed in practice; and (b) a mixing-up of unrelated or distantly related subjects in the same regulations (as in the use of a tax on imports and exports to finance farmers' old-age insurance or in the linking of authorized rent increases to the minimum wage). The result is a crazy-quilt of detailed and highly complex regulations of many phases of the economic process. A case in point is that of wages. The government fixes a legal minimum wage, after consulting with an advisory group that does not advise, or whose advice is rarely heeded. The minimum wage proving to be something of a strait-jacket, the government may then add bonuses, of questionable legality, to the minimum in order to raise it *de facto* but not *de jure*. It may also give special bonuses to workers on its payrolls in order to raise their wages without raising the minimum. To circumvent the effects of such legislation, the employers may in turn resort to "black" wages and to a reclassification of workers; these stratagems may prompt further intervention by the government with respect to the wage hierarchy, and so forth and so on.

III RESULTS OF GOVERNMENT ACTION

The implications of public policy have been examined here only in terms of certain selected objectives. As indicated from time to time, various qualifications must be attached to any specific conclusion. There are also extenuating circumstances that should be borne in mind, such as the heavy material and psychological damage inflicted by the war and the continuing need to divert resources to western defense or the campaign in Indochina. Still, after all the reservations have been entered, one cannot escape feeling that not much progress has been made in the postwar period towards the achievement of the main objectives of state intervention.

Some measures may have promoted equity, but discouraged growth. Some stimulated growth, but impaired stability. Some worked in the direction of stability at the expense of efficiency. Some actions, while perhaps helping one distressed group, contributed to a network of inequitable privileges and adversely affected political behavior. When all measures bearing upon any one objective are examined, it seems doubtful that the objective has been furthered very much. Perhaps the most general conclusion is that the state has undertaken a great many economic tasks in France, but has done none of them particularly well. Considerable distance separates the French experience from that model of "good" government laid down by Messrs. Gilbert and Sullivan in *Iolanthe*:

> When Wellington thrashed Bonaparte,
> As every child can tell,
> The House of Peers, throughout the war,
> Did nothing in particular,
> And did it very well;
> Yet Britain set the world ablaze
> In good King George's glorious days!

A. GROWTH

Although a major objective of certain policies has been to encourage the growth of the French economy, it is clear that other policies—inspired by the instinct for security and the preservation of the *status quo*—work in the opposite direction. The net results of state intervention are not impressive except for the rapid recovery of production achieved immediately after the war. Over the first decade of the postwar period, as well as over a longer time span, economic growth took place more slowly in France than in most other Western countries. (During the prewar period this was due in part to the slower rate of population growth.) The lack of dynamism of the French economy relative to that of Germany has undoubtedly been an important factor in postwar relations between the two countries, and indeed in the postwar history of Western Europe as a whole. Production has been expanding more rapidly in recent years (from a relatively low starting point), but this expansion, while encouraging, has not yet been sufficiently extensive to modify the above findings.

1. Investment. The principal method of promoting growth has been to expand the volume and alter the composition of investments. Under the first and second modernization plans, a large share of the public budget was devoted to investments. Whether or not the level of total investments was raised as a result of government action in all its forms is uncertain. Government financing probably had the immediate effect of increasing the total of investment. On the other hand, the prolonged inflation, which the government had little success in curbing, undoubtedly discouraged some forms of private investment. By European standards, the actual level of investments during the postwar period as a whole was not high. The composition of investments was altered both by the plans and by the impact of other policies on investment choices, but without much careful thought. Investments in the nationalized industries were not based on a systematic effort to compare the prospective gains and costs of alternative projects. Similarly, investments by private industry were affected, either directly under the plans or indirectly through the impact of price, wage, and tax policies on the comparative profitability of different ventures, again without much attention being given to possible criteria of desirable investments. It is likely that neglect of these considerations has led to a more haphazard set of investment decisions than would have resulted from either consistent use of relevant criteria or from the working of a predominantly market economy.

Several of the more specific influences on investment deserve to be mentioned again. At least until recently, the production tax, the heart of the French tax system, discriminated seriously against the use of capital goods and undoubtedly acted to discourage investments. A form of investment which has proven to be highly profitable in some nations—education and training, or investment in the human agent—has been relatively neglected by French policy. In agricultural policy this neglect is especially marked, for the dissemination of technical knowledge has received surprisingly little support.

2. *Shelter for the Status Quo.* Growth and development require the appearance of new resources (through innovations, new investments) and then a reshuffling of resources in response to their appearance. Actions which shelter the *status quo* may affect this growth process by impeding either the development of new resources and techniques or the subsequent reorganization of production necessary to take advantage of them.

There exist in France a large number of measures that tend to preserve the *status quo*. Numerous tax and subsidy provisions shelter existing firms, small businesses, certain occupations, and particular ways of organizing production. Price controls have been designed to ensure the survival of the least efficient firms and farms. There are acts of commission and omission that discourage competition, both from abroad and from within. A complex network of transfer payments and special compensations is intended to protect various groups from injury. All of these measures, plus the prospects of compensation for any who might be injured and of high tax burdens for any who might gain, probably discourage innovation and change. And, even when new ideas and methods are developed, the forces just mentioned retard their adoption and the movement of resources (out of small shops, small farms, and the establishments of artisans) that are prerequisite to significant gains from the standpoint of the whole economy.

Many of the measures to preserve the existing way of life are motivated by an understandable quest for security. Unfortunately, security may prove to be most elusive to those who search for it most arduously. The French government, in its search for security, has adopted a kind of Maginot-line approach. As a result, such security as has been attained for the artisan, the peasant, and the shopkeeper has been at a near-subsistence standard of living. It may well be asked whether greater security would not be found in the continuously expanding opportunities of a dynamic economy.

B. STABILITY

It cannot be said that the consequences of state intervention have been very favorable with respect to the stability of the economy.

1. Control of Inflation. Over a large part of the first postwar decade, both the balance of payments gap and the domestic situation called for vigorous anti-inflationary policies. Such policies were rarely adopted. Inability to decide what demands (private spending, government investment, national defense) to cut resulted in large deficits, swollen incomes, and a rapidly rising money stock. This permitted the process of price-level inflation to inflict the cuts, but in a haphazard and inequitable fashion. Surrender to the demands of one group after another resulted in the support or increase of various prices, wages, and incomes. Direct controls were sometimes applied in a half-hearted fashion and were unable to cope with the strong inflationary pressures. Some key decisions were avoided or defaulted.

One of the consequences of government action, along with other factors, has been to build-in or reinforce an inflationary bias in the French economy. The large size of the budget nowadays, even when balanced, is an inflationary force. Also, the magnitude of the tax burden increases the difficulty of avoiding large deficits when sudden demands for new expenditures arise, as in a military crisis. The habit of settling income distribution according to the loudness of each group's complaint has also imparted an inflationary bias. Various groups soon sense this tendency and press their demands more vigorously, while the government becomes less and less capable of resisting. The broad sector of prices administered by private corporate bodies follows closely the rise in government-determined prices. Once a price or wage increase is granted, the government must see to it that the money supply necessary to support purchases at the higher price level is forthcoming, unless it is willing to risk unemployment.

2. *Control of Recession.* During the briefer periods of recession, government policies have worked for the most part in the right direction and have contributed to the recovery. This has been due in part to the built-in inflationary bias and to the impact of the worldwide economic prosperity. But the recessionary situations have involved fewer painful choices and open group conflicts, and this has made it easier to conceive and execute expansionary measures.

3. *Closing the Balance of Payments Gap.* While some of the direct controls adopted by the French government have helped towards closing the foreign exchange gap, the continued overvaluation of the franc has made it more difficult for France to balance its foreign accounts. The balance of payments gap has been appreciably narrowed over the postwar period, but this improvement has been due in considerable part to external factors. Viability remains a distant goal, since the present position is dependent on exceptional foreign earnings. There may now be a sort of built-in dollar gap bias, stemming from the inflationary bias of the internal economy and from the institutional and psychological barriers to devaluation.

C. EQUITY OF INCOME DISTRIBUTION

Many of the state's interventions have been aimed at changing the distribution of income in some direction or other on grounds of equity. Taxation and social security have been the principal means employed, but many other policies also have an income-redistribution effect.

Despite some drawbacks, taxation (that is, direct action on income and wealth) is probably the best way of redistributing income if that is what the society wishes to accomplish. But there is considerable doubt that the French tax system is sufficiently progressive for this purpose. As a result of fraud and legal exemptions in the calculation of income taxes and of the uncertain incidence of the excise taxes, it is not clear that the tax burden is borne most heavily by those with greatest ability to pay. There are also marked departures from the most generally accepted principle of equity, that equals should be treated equally.

Social transfers have reached the high proportion of 30 per cent of central government expenditures. The effect of the social security programs on the distribution of income has not been analyzed in detail here. For what it may be worth, the "expert" opinion is that the net effect has been a redistribution of income *within* the working class (from bachelors to parents, from the young to the aged) and not between labor and other groups (richer or poorer) in the population.

Other policies that indirectly affected equity were those that permitted or aggravated the postwar inflation. Sharp fluctuations in the price level (whether upwards or downwards) result in promiscuous, and therefore inequitable, impacts on the income position and relative well-being of different groups. In the case of the French inflations, it can be assumed that persons who happened to hold their assets in the form of money, bonds, or other fixed claims, or whose money income was "sticky," were expropriated. Those who owed money or owned real property probably benefited as a result of the drastic price rises.

Other policies also had important effects on the equity with which income is distributed. A multitude of benefits, advantages, or privileges of one sort or another to various groups in the population have been observed. Prices of goods or services provided by nationalized industries are lowered to sundry groups; subsidies are provided to various activities; tariffs are imposed; and various compensations, indemnities, equalization payments, bonuses, and rebates are provided. How far the process of compensation can go is indicated by the fact that fathers were granted a "compensatory indemnity" when the tax on wages and salaries was abolished in 1948, on the grounds that they received relatively less advantage from its abolition since they were largely exempted from it in the first place. The process through which these privileges tend to spread throughout the society is important to note. One group in the population receives a special advantage of some sort; other groups, which then regard themselves as "injured," attack these advantages. But, since "acquired rights" are considered sacred, and politically invulnerable, the government must resort to a compensatory advantage for the injured groups. Thus, tax rates are lowered as compensation to groups who claim that they have less opportunity for tax evasion, and the existence of these special rates encourages less favored groups openly to practice fraud.

A list of the beneficiaries of the paternalism of the state is almost endless. There is an apt French expression that "*chacun a son compte*" ("everyone has his deal"). Special advantages or privileges of some sort can be observed in the case of small farmers, young farmers, cooperative farmers, landless farmers, rural tenants, urban tenants, landlords, housing constructors, artisans, small businesses, veterans, wounded veterans, public employees and their families unto the second and third generation, pregnant women, wives who do not work, heads of large families, butchers, bakers, candlestick makers, home distillers, sugar beet growers, wine growers, wheat growers, infant industries, ancient industries, and so forth ad infinitum.

The subsidy effects of particular measures have not been traced in detail. Some direct benefits undeniably accrue to specific recipients. But the more widespread these measures become, the greater is the likelihood that the compensations and benefits given to different groups cancel each other out to some extent. And the system has become so involved and complex that no one knows, even very approximately, what the net effect of the state's actions on the distribution of income may be.

This uncertainty has sizable costs attached to it. Each group becomes embittered over what it believes to be the greater advantages afforded to others. As Aron has observed, the low income levels of many parts of the French population would be more tolerable were it not for the universal suspicion that the system as a whole is unjust.[2] This sense of injustice undoubtedly strengthens the positions, hostile to a republican regime, of extremists on the Left and Right. A high cost is also paid in terms of the inefficiency resulting from the multiple distortions of the cost-price mechanism. The mechanism for redistributing income, in which the state plays so large a part, becomes similar to the oft-cited situation where everyone is standing on tiptoes to watch a parade or football game: no one is better off (he can't see better than before); everyone is worse off (because of the discomfort of standing); but no one can get back down without suffering a further disadvantage.

D. ECONOMIC EFFICIENCY

While not an end in itself, efficiency in the use of existing resources helps to determine how much of certain ends or objectives can be accomplished. Some lip service is paid to economic efficiency in French government pronouncements, and, even when not explicitly emphasized, it is important for such objectives as higher living standards and stronger defenses. It is clear that relevant tests of economic efficiency have rarely played much of a role in policy formation. For instance, in operating the nationalized industries and in appraising their performance many dubious criteria unrelated to efficiency were applied (such as the investment trend, the production trend, the no-profit, no-loss criterion). There is consequently a presumption that a high degree of efficiency is unlikely to result.

1. Size and Technology. The forces that affect the efficiency of resource use by influencing the size or technological status of businesses and farms are much the same as those mentioned earlier in connection with growth. Some steps have been taken to promote larger or more modern business units and farming operations through investment loans, productivity assistance, and other measures. Increases in efficiency have undoubtedly resulted. But other measures have worked in the opposite direction; actions to protect small firms, small farms, and the artisan, and to provide shelter from the rigors of competition make possible the survival of units whose size and operating methods are inefficient. The extensive social security and subsidy programs may also dull incentives and hence competition among owners of productive resources. Because of the extent of these payments unrelated to productivity, and of the various shelters from competition, France is sometimes said to be an economy of rents rather than an economy of profits.[3]

2. The Market as an Allocator. On balance, the government's actions have served to sanction and sometimes stimulate the development of cartels and other forms of monopoly power. This is an important way in which the government has contributed to the malfunctioning of the market in its vital task of allocating resources efficiently among different uses. Furthermore, many interventions (whether or not they have merit on other grounds) work against an efficient resource allocation by distorting price relationships. All of a government's actions on prices need not be considered as distortions, for some may help prices to reflect "social" values and costs more accurately. There is little evidence, however, that the influences observed here operated systematically in this direction.

Distortions have been created through tax provisions, export subsidies, price-control regulations, and the below-cost pricing policies of the nationalized industries. The varying degrees of price support provided to different agricultural products have diverted resources into uses not justified on productivity grounds. Several interventions have contributed to an inflexibility of prices or price relationships; the protracted price freezes and the prescribing of minimum wages and of social security benefits are among the major examples. The inflexible costs and prices that result make for sluggish response to change, distorted price relationships, and a misuse of resources.

This type of intervention also tends to multiply. Thus rent control legislation, in effect without interruption for forty years, has helped to create a serious housing shortage by keeping rents at a level that has made it unprofitable to put resources into housing construction. This has obliged the government to stimulate housing construction through other cost and price distortions, such as interest rate subsidies and tax privileges, while the nationalized industries have had to devote a substantial proportion of their funds to workers' housing. The government has authorized some increases in the rent ceilings, but new rigidities have been introduced by linking these increases to the legal minimum wage. This minimum, which the government controls administratively, is in turn linked to other considerations (such as the size of family allowance payments under the social security program) and must be adjusted in the light of these considerations as well. As the housing shortage has persisted, a further cost-price distortion has developed from the imposition of a 1 per cent payroll tax, the proceeds of which must be devoted to housing construction. With under-the-table payments, "key" rents, black market leases, an entrenched layer of middlemen, and an endless round of legislation and litigation, the housing market has achieved such an awe-inspiring complexity that chaos would temporarily ensue if controls were to be removed tomorrow.

E. POLITICAL BEHAVIOR

The French government has not been given high marks for performance on any of the objectives considered so far. If it could be observed that state intervention in economic affairs had favorable effects on political behavior, then some of the shortcomings might weigh less heavily. But such evidence as has been gathered suggests that this is not the case. In fact the effects of economic interventions on political behavior seem more likely to have been unfavorable on the whole. Similar effects have been observed, and lamented, in the case of other countries, but most students of French politics believe that they are especially marked in France.

A particularly tough problem of "causality" arises in considering the implications of state intervention for political behavior. Were political instability, lack of civic responsibility, and the strength of pressure groups causes of intervention, or was the state's action itself conducive to instability of governments, disrespect for the laws, and uncompromising demands by various groups? No doubt the interaction among the people, the political system, and the state is highly complex. Yet there is perhaps a presumptive case that some of the observed attitudes and kinds of behavior have resulted from, or been influenced by, the action of the state.

One such case is that the extensive economic role of the state has contributed to the instability of individual ministries or governments. The increasing economic responsibilities assumed by the state mean that economic decisions that in the past were made by the market place have now entered the political arena. As the volume and importance of these decisions mount, a particularly strong and cohesive political system is required to support the added burden placed upon it. The French political system does not have these characteristics, and it can be inferred that the weight of economic responsibilities has contributed to the frequent breakdowns of the system. Some empirical corroboration can be found in the fact that disagreements on economic policies have frequently been the immediate cause of the downfall of governments. Some instances are: the overthrow of the Pinay government of 1952 on a problem of family allowances, of the Pleven government of 1952 on reform of the SNCF and the social security system, of the Bidault government of 1950 on the reclassification of civil servants, and of the Queuille government of 1949 on wage-price policies.[a] But the ultimate reasons for the downfall of governments are more complex, and the precise role occupied by economic decisions cannot be investigated here.

It is also possible that the privileges and inequities stemming from the government's actions have served to weaken the people's

[a] One observer has commented that "In one form or another the economic problem has been responsible for the fall of most post-war governments." (Philip Williams, *Politics in Post-war France* (London, 1955), p. 22.)

sense of civic responsibility. There is a danger that the unofficial motto of the Fourth Republic may become *"L'état, ce n'est pas moi."* As Premier Laniel observed, "We witness the paradox that everything is demanded of the state, while too many people seem to be striving to weaken its authority, to thwart its action."[4] In evidence of what is called *incivisme*, class after class has on some occasion challenged the authority of the state and refused to abide by its laws. Shopkeepers, organized by Poujade, not only refuse to pay their taxes but also threaten and obstruct tax officials. Farmers barricade the national highways, and winegrowers deliver ultimata to the government in insurrectionary language and threaten not to pay their social security contributions. The well organized butchers can publicly flout the government's regulations, while officials at all levels of government (nationalized industries, civil servants, local prefects) sometimes choose not to enforce the laws. Strikes of civil servants and employees of nationalized industries place the government (the largest employer in France) in the position of being a disputant rather than an arbitrator. These are more than just isolated episodes. They seem to fit into a pattern that has been described by Premier Reynaud as "every man for himself, and all against the state."[5]

The significance of this attitude is enhanced by the strength of organized pressure groups. The proper role of pressure groups in a democracy is exceedingly difficult to define. But in France everyone seems to be organized for all-out economic warfare—not only into the broad groups of labor, farmers, businessmen, and consumers, but also into more specific interests, such as alcohol producers, truckers, café owners, social security agencies, theatre operators, countless associations of taxpayers, the influential lobby of commission agents (*mandataires*) at Les Halles, and the "National Committee for the Defense of Labor-Intensive Industries." The government is constantly under pressure from many of these organized groups, in situations that sometimes evoke the symbols of military campaigns. Thus Premier Faure observed that France had become "a vast battlefield of conflicting claims," while Premier Pinay exclaimed, "I am besieged by the special interests."[6] In the face of organized groups pressing conflicting claims, the government at crucial times has seemed unable to arbitrate the conflict except by succumbing to each in turn. Some of the former heads of state would no doubt sympathize with the plaintive song of Ado Annie, of *Oklahoma!* fame: "I can't say no."

As this weakness before pressures has become apparent, the

authority of the state has been undermined. The government has been unable to enforce some of its laws. Or, in the face of resistance, it has sometimes been obliged to reverse itself and to assure "injured" parties that the laws would be interpreted "liberally" (i.e., disregarded). The executive may attempt more energetic action by special decree powers granted on occasion by Parliament, but the latter body is likely to vitiate the reform subsequently if important "acquired rights" are involved. In an address to the French people, President Coty observed that, "What we have most lacked in the past is not only stability but also and above all the authority of governments."[7] And his predecessor, Vincent Auriol, in his farewell address expressed the wish "that the men responsible for French policy have the strength to restore this authority [of the state] against the assaults of the great coalitions of interest groups and the feudalistic corporate entities."[8] These leaders were not advocating a more "authoritarian" form of government; they were concerned that, when a government is unable to enforce its laws, individual liberty may descend into anarchy or dictatorship.

BIBLIOGRAPHICAL NOTES

Chapter 1

1. Quoted in *Le Monde*, September 21, 1954, p. 3.
2. John Maynard Keynes, "The End of Laissez-Faire" written in 1926 and published in *Essays in Persuasion* (New York: Harcourt, Brace and Company, 1932), p. 313.
3. Frederick A. Hayek, *The Road to Serfdom* (Chicago: University of Chicago Press, 1944).
4. Barbara Wooton, *Freedom Under Planning* (Chapel Hill: University of North Carolina Press, 1945); Herman Finer, *Road to Reaction* (Boston: Little, Brown, and Company, 1946); John Jewkes, *Ordeal by Planning* (New York: Macmillan Company, 1948); John Maurice Clark, *Alternative to Serfdom* (New York: Alfred A. Knopf, 1948).
5. Quoted in *Le Monde*, April 28, 1955, p. 14.
6. Ministère des Finances, *Rapports sur les comptes provisoires de la nation des années 1951 et 1952 et sur le budget économique de l'année 1953* (Paris, 1953), p. 11. Hereafter referred to as the *Economic Report for 1951 and 1952.*

Chapter 2

1. United Nations, Economic Commission for Europe, *Economic Survey of Europe in 1954* (Geneva, 1955), p. 173.
2. J. H. Clapham, *The Economic Development of France and Germany, 1815-1914* (Cambridge, 1923) p. 232.
3. *Economic Survey of Europe*, pp. 174-175.
4. A. Viallate, *L'Activité économique en France de la fin du* XVIIIème *siècle à nos jours* (Paris, 1937), pp. 232-234, 246, 247.
5. Institut National de la Statistique et des Etudes Economiques (INSEE), *Annuaire statistique 1951* (Paris, 1952), p. 127.
6. *Economic Survey of Europe in 1954*, p. 177 and P. Delouvrier and R. Nathan, *Politique économique de la France* (Cours à l'Institut d'Etudes Politiques de l'Université de Paris, 1953-1954), Vol. I, p. 36.
7. Organization for European Economic Cooperation (OEEC), *Progress and Problems of the European Economy* (Paris, January 1954) p. 94.
8. Colin Clark, *The Conditions of Economic Progress* 2nd ed. (London: Macmillan and Co., Ltd., 1951) pp. 63, 80, and 101 offset.
9. *Progress and Problems of the European Economy*, p. 94.
10. Data from Ministères des Finances, du Budget, et des Affaires Economiques, *Inventaire de la situation financière* (Paris, 1951), pp. 119, 225; Maurice Lévy, *Histoire économique et sociale de la France depuis 1848*, Cours à l'Institut d'Etudes Politiques de l'Université de Paris 1951-1952, Vol. III, pp. 364-365; Delouvrier and Nathan, *op. cit.*, Vol. IV, pp. 122-128; and Delbert A. Snider, "French Monetary and Fiscal Policies Since the Liberation," *American Economic Review*, Vol. XXVIII, No. 3, June 1948, pp. 310-311.
11. INSEE, *Annuaire statistique* 1951, p. 128.
12. Ministère des Finances, *Economic Report for 1951 and 1952*, pp. 52-53.
13. Bernard Jarrier, "L'Etat investi par les intérêts," *l'Esprit*, June 1953, pp. 888-889.
14. *Inventaire de la situation financière*, p. 225.
15. Cf. the *Economic Report for 1951 and 1952*, p. 53.
16. Delouvrier and Nathan, *op. cit.*, Vol. V, pp. 5-7.
17. Cf. Edgar Beigel, "France Moves Toward National Planning," *Political Science Quarterly*, Vol. LXII, No. 3, September 1947, pp. 381-397; Louis-R. Franck, "Planisme français et démocratie," *Revue économique*, Vol. IV, No. 2, March 1953, pp. 194-219; and Delouvrier and Nathan, *op. cit.*, Vol. V, pp. 58-59.
18. Quoted in Beigel, *op. cit.*, p. 388.
19. Harold Lubell, *The French Investment Program, a Defense of the Monnet Plan*, (Multilithed, Paris, 1951), pp. 37-40.
20. Cf. Lubell, *op. cit.*, pp. 41-42.

21. *Ibid.*, p. 190; M. Lévy, *op. cit.*, p. 365; and Jacques Dumontier, *Budget économique et capital national* (Paris, 1951) pp. 70-73.
22. Commissariat Général du Plan, *Rapport général sur le premier plan de modernisation et d'équipement* (Paris, November 1946-January 1947) p. 24.
23. Economic Cooperation Administration, *European Recovery Program: France Country Study* (Washington, 1949) pp. 44-47.
24. J. O. Documents parlementaires—Assemblée Nationale, Deuxième Législature, 1954, Annexe No. 8555, *Projet de loi portant approbation du deuxième plan de modernisation et d'équipement*, p. 899.
25. *Ibid.*, p. 900.
26. Journal officiel, *Avis et rapports du Conseil Economique*, "Deuxième plan de modernisation et d'équipement," August 3, 1954, pp. 649-666 and Annexes.
27. *Ibid.*, pp. 651-652.
28. *Projet de loi portant approbation du deuxième plan*, p. 904.
29. Ministère des Finances, *Rapport sur les comptes de la nation* (Paris, 1955), Vol. I, p. 36, pp. 160-161 and 170-171.
30. OEEC, *Statistical Bulletins 1956*, No. 2 (April 1956) pp. 103 and 107.
31. OEEC, *Economic Conditions in France* (Paris, 1954) p. 12.
32. Data from *Rapport général sur le premier plan de modernisation*, p. 86; "Investissements pour l'exercice 1951," Journal officiel, *Avis et rapports du Conseil Economique*, January 27, 1951, pp. 9-10; and the annual reports of the Commission des Investissements.
33. Derived from data in the annual reports of the Commission des Investissements.
34. *Economic Survey of Europe in 1954*, p. 172.
35. OEEC, *Statistical Bulletins 1956*, No. 2 (April 1956), p. 45.

Chapter 3

1. Commissariat Général du Plan, *Perspectives des ressources et des besoins de l'économie française au cours du premier semestre et de l'année 1948, Rapport présenté au Gouvernement au nom de la Commission du Bilan National* (Paris, December 1947) *passim* and H. Lubell, *op. cit.*, pp. 72-76.
2. Val R. Lorwin, *The French Labor Movement* (Cambridge, Harvard University Press, 1954) p. 112.
3. Delouvrier and Nathan, *op. cit.*, Vol. V, pp. 32-35, 70.
4. Expression borrowed from Albert G. Hart, *Money, Debt, and Economic Activity* (New York, Prentice-Hall, 1948), p. 430.
5. Ministère des Finances, *Inventaire de la situation financière*, p. 130; Delouvrier and Nathan, *op. cit.*, Vol. V, pp. 71-74.
6. Louis-R. Franck, "Planisme français et démocratie," *Revue économique*, No. 2, March 1953, pp. 209-210.
7. *Inventaire de la situation financière*, pp. 129, 207.
8. Snider, *op. cit.*, pp. 318-320; *Inventaire de la situation financière*, p. 130.
9. Cf. Commissariat Général au Plan, *Rapport sur la réalisation du plan de modernisation et d'équipement de l'Union française* (Paris, 1953), pp. 87-88.
10. *Inventaire de la situation financière*, p. 257.
11. *Ibid.*, pp. 260-261.
12. Snider, *op. cit.*, p. 314.
13. *Inventaire de la situation financière*, pp. 478-482.
14. Ministère des Finances, *Statistiques et études financières*, No. 55, July 1953, p. 616.
15. Snider, *op. cit.*, pp. 313-317; Pierre Dieterlen and Charles Rist, *The Monetary Problem of France* (New York, King's Crown Press, 1948) pp. 16-18, 30-43; and Delouvrier and Nathan, *op. cit.*, pp. 10, 25-37, 100-105.
16. *Inventaire de la situation financière*, p. 532; *Statistiques et études financières*, No. 62, February 1954, pp. 140-142.
17. Cf. the first, second and third annual reports of the National Credit Council, sections on "La politique du crédit bancaire"; and P. C. Dupont, *Le Contrôle des banques et la direction du crédit en France* (Paris, 1952), pp. 298-315.
18. Cf. Dupont, *op. cit.*, pp. 309-315; "Credit Control in France," *The Economist* of November 15, 1952; and Pierre Dieterlen, *Quelques enseignements de l'évolution monétaire française de 1948 à 1952* (Paris, 1954).

19. Cf. Conseil National du Crédit, *Deuxième rapport annuel, 1947*, p. 52.

20. Cf. the article by Pierre Uri in *Réalités*, December 1950, and the discussion in Lubell, *op. cit.*, pp. 78-80.

21. Data from the second and third annual reports of the *Commission des Investissements* and from the monthly or bi-monthly economic surveys published by INSEE in *Etudes et conjoncture.*

22. Cf. Ruggles, "The French Investment Program and its Relation to Resource Allocation," *Modern France, Problems of the Third and Fourth Republics*, E. M. Earle, editor (Princeton University Press, 1951) pp. 375, 376 and 379.

23. For more details see the third and fourth reports of the National Credit Council, the *Economic Report for 1951 and 1952*, the third report of the Commission des Investissements, and *Etudes et conjoncture*, various issues for 1949 and 1950.

24. OEEC, *Europe—The Way Ahead* (Paris, December 1952), p. 256; *Inventaire de la situation financière*, pp. 135-136; and *Economic Report for 1951 and 1952*, p. 34.

25. Cf. *Economic Report for 1951 and 1952*, pp. 29-35.

26. Derived from Table 11.

27. *Statistiques et études financières*, No. 51, March 1953, p. 178.

28. Conseil National du Crédit, *Septième rapport annuel 1952*, p. 14.

29. Cf. the Annual Report for 1951, p. 41.

30. *Ibid.*, pp. 40-41.

31. Dieterlen, *op. cit.*, p. 167.

32. OEEC, *Progress and Problems of the European Economy* (Paris, January 1954) Table 7, p. 287.

33. Ministry of Labor data, cited in *Le Monde*, February 27, 1955, financial and economic supplement.

34. Data from *The Economic Report for 1954*, cited in *Le Monde*, August 9, 1955, p. 12; and *L'Economie*, August 25, 1955, p. 18.

35. Cf. the OEEC report referred to in *Le Monde*, December 14, 1954, p. 14.

36. OEEC, *Statistical Bulletins, 1955*, No. 3, May 1955, p. 8. See also the comments in OEEC, *Economic Conditions in France* (Paris, 1954), pp. 5-6.

Chapter 4

1. Estimates by Rist and Schwob, cited in INSEE, *Bulletin mensuel de statistique*, Supplement January-March 1953, pp. 61-62 and in Ministère des Finances, *Inventaire de la situation financière (1913-1946)* (Paris, 1946), p. 640.

2. Economic Cooperation Administration, *European Recovery Program, France Country Study*, pp. 25-27.

3. Prewar data from *Bulletin mensuel de statistique*, supplement January-March 1953, pp. 61-62.

4. *Inventaire de la situation financière, 1951*, p. 573.

5. Data from *Bulletin mensuel de statistique*, supplement January-March, 1953, pp. 76-77; and *Statistiques et études financières*, No. 68, August, 1954, p. 711.

6. J. Teissedre, "Evolution de la réglementation française du commerce extérieur (1945 à 1949)" *Droit social*, September-October, 1949, pp. 298-302.

7. *Inventaire de la situation financière, 1951*, pp. 574-585.

8. *Bulletin mensuel de statistique*, supplement January-March 1953, pp. 76-77.

9. United States Operations Mission to France, *France Data Book 1954*, Table J-1.

10. Delouvrier and Nathan, *op. cit.*, Vol. v, pp. 38-42.

11. *Ibid.*, pp. 94-96, 102-104.

12. OEEC, *Progress and Problems of the European Economy* pp. 78-79.

13. *Rapport général de la commission créée par arrêté du 6 janvier 1954 pour l'étude des disparités entre les prix français et étrangers* (the "Nathan Report") (Paris, 1954) p. 9.

14. *Etudes et conjoncture, économie française*, July-August, 1952, article on "Comparaison des prix français et étrangers," pp. 321-394.

15. Cf. the "*Nathan Report*," pp. 2, 7-11.

16. *Etudes et conjoncture, économie française*, July-August, 1952, article on "L'Evolution des termes de l'échange dans le commerce extérieur de la France," pp. 300-320.

17. The "*Nathan Report*," pp. 1-2.

18. La Documentation française, *Notes et études documentaires No. 1807*, "L'Evolution du commerce extérieur de la France metropolitaine de 1950 à 1953" (Paris, November, 1953), p. 36.

19. *Etudes et conjoncture*, July-August, 1952, p. 319.

20. Cf. the statement of Edgar Faure, then Finance Minister, quoted in the *New York Times*, January 11, 1955, p. 8 and the article on devaluation of the franc by Michel Drancourt in the issue of *Réalités* for March 1955.

21. This discussion is based primarily on Harry C. Eastman, "The Role of Speculation in France's Foreign-Exchange Crises," *Journal of Political Economy*, Vol. LXI, No. 3, June 1953, pp. 209-220.

22. *Ibid.*, pp. 210-213.

23. Information obtained from government sources.

24. Eastman, *op. cit.*, p. 81.

25. According to the *19th Annual Report* of the Bank for International Settlements (Basle, 1949), pp. 177-178.

26. *Progress and Problems of the European Economy*, p. 89.

27. *Notes et études documentaires No. 1807*, p. 13.

28. Cf. "La France et la politique de libération des échanges," article in *Statistiques et études financières*, No. 58, October, 1953, p. 903.

29. *From Recovery Towards Economic Strength, 6th Report of the* OEEC (Paris, March 1955) Vol. I, p. 133. William Diebold, Jr., *Trade and Payments in Western Europe* (New York, Harper & Bros., 1952), pp. 158-215.

30. See, for example, the French *Reply to the* GATT *questionnaire of January 8, 1953, on the discriminatory application of restrictions.*

31. See Diebold, *op. cit.*, pp. 167, 200-201 and *Le Monde*, April 10, 1954, p. 1.

32. *Agence économique et financière*, April 12, 1954, p. 4; April 20, 1954, p. 4.

33. The principal sources are the report of Maurice Byé, "L'Aide à l'exportation," *Avis et rapports du Conseil Economique, Journal officiel*, February 14, 1953, pp. 203-214; and J. Teissedre, *op. cit.*, *Droit social*, November, 1949, pp. 327-336.

34. In addition to the Byé report, see also: M. Barbier, "Les Remboursements des charges sociales et fiscales aux entreprises exportatrices," *Droit social*, March, 1954, pp. 171-173; and "Les Avantages fiscaux à l'exportation en France et à l'étranger," *Statistiques et études financières*, No. 60, December, 1953, pp. 1101-1118.

35. *Progress and Problems of the European Economy*, p. 90.

36. *Ibid.*, pp. 90-91; the Byé report, *op. cit.*; and *Le Monde*, July 19-20, 1953, p. 9 and September 15, 1953, p. 10.

37. Cf. *The 6th report of the* OEEC, Vol. II p. 50.

38. *Le Monde*, September 15, 1953, p. 10, and September 19, 1953, p. 10.

39. *Agence économique et financière*, December 18, 1954, p. 4.

Chapter 5

1. Cf. Louis Trotabas, *Précis de science et législation financières* (Paris, 1953), p. 5.

2. *Inventaire de la situation financière (1951)*, p. 18; and *Economic Report for 1951 and 1952*, pp. 132-133.

3. Derived from unpublished data prepared by the Foreign Operations Administration in Washington, D. C.

4. Cited in *Le Monde*, October 6, 1953, p. 4.

5. *Ibid.*

6. Quoted in the *Rapport de la Commission des Finances sur le projet de loi de finances pour l'exercice 1953* (No. 4794), Assemblée Nationale No. 4888, November 27, 1952, Vol. I, p. 74.

7. *Statistiques et études financières* No. 70, October 1954, p. 996.

8. *Bulletin mensuel de statistique*, Supplement April-June 1953, pp. 33-43.

9. *Le Monde*, January 17, 1954, financial and economic supplement.

10. Ministère du Budget, *Budget de la France en 1950* (Paris, 1950) pp. 9-10.

11. *Progress and Problems of the European Economy*, p. 99.

12. Ministère des Finances, Secrétariat d'Etat au Budget, *Le Budget de 1954* (Paris, 1954), pp. 52-53.

BIBLIOGRAPHICAL NOTES

Chapter 6

1. Material from: Julien Laferrière and Marcel Waline, *Traité élémentaire de science et de législation financières* (Paris, 1952), pp. 345-569; Henry Laufenburger, *Economie du système fiscal français national et local* (Paris, 1954), *passim* and *La Réforme fiscale de 1949* (Paris, 1949), pp. 1-48; and Louis Trotabas, *Précis de science et législation financières*, pp. 205-252. Among publications of the Ministry of Finance: *Code général des impôts; Inventaire de la situation financière, (1951)*, pp. 257-316; *Rapport général de la Commission de Réforme Fiscale* (Paris, 1952) (the "*Loriot Report*") *passim*; and *Statistiques et études financières, supplément finances comparées* Nos. 19-20 (1953), pp. 236-320.

2. Data for European countries from United Nations Economic Commission for Europe, *Economic Bulletin for Europe*, Third Quarter, 1950, Vol. 2, No. 3, p. 69; for the United States from U. S. Department of Commerce, *Statistical Abstract of the United States, 1953*, p. 391.

3. Unpublished data from the Ministry of Finance. The figures in the first column have been published in the *Rapport de la Commission des Finances de l'Assemblée Nationale sur le projet de loi (No. 6748) de finances pour l'exercice 1954 (No. 7270)* November 24, 1953, p. 158.

4. *The Loriot Report*, p. 148.

5. *Ibid.*, p. 146.

6. *Entreprise*, No. 22, February 15, 1954, p. 31.

7. The *Loriot Report*, p. 17.

8. *Economic Report for 1951 and 1952*, pp. 61-64. See also James L. Houghteling, "The Income Tax in France," *Public Policy*, Vol. v (Cambridge, Harvard University Press, 1954), pp. 334-338.

9. Cf. the articles on "incivisme" in *Esprit*, January, 1949.

10. Some useful references are: "Une 'Grande' réforme fiscale," *La Revue administrative*, May-June 1948, No. 3, pp. 23-29; "La Réforme fiscale," *Réalités*, No. 58, November 1950, pp. 57-58, 115-116; Georges Boissière, "De la fraude à l'incivisme fiscal," *Esprit*, January 1949, pp. 24-32; "Comment la fraude est installée dans le pays," *l'Express* No. 18, September 19, 1953, pp. 6-7; and the *Loriot Report*, pp. 17, 25-26.

11. Houghteling, *op. cit.*, pp. 337-338.

12. The *Loriot Report*, p. 53.

13. Carl S. Shoup, "Taxation in France," *National Tax Journal* Vol. VIII, No. 4, December 1955, p. 330.

14. Personal income from United States Operations Mission to France, *France Data Book 1954*, p. 5.

15. Cf. Maurice Lauré, *La Taxe sur la valeur ajoutée* (Paris, 1952), esp. pp. 44-52; Hubert Brochier, *Finances publiques et redistribution des revenus* (Paris, 1950) pp. 48-55, 60-63; Trotabas, *op. cit.*, pp. 183, 262-264; and the *Nathan Report*, pp. 16-18.

16. Cf. the comments in Commissariat Général au Plan, *Rapport général de la Commission du Financement du Deuxième Plan de Modernisation et d'Equipement* (Paris, November, 1953) pp. 23-24.

17. Cf. the report of the Committee on Productivity and the Tax System, reprinted in *Revue française de l'énergie* No. 37, December 1952, pp. 99-104.

18. In this sense, see Houghteling, *op. cit.*, p. 342.

19. Quotations, respectively, from P. Allix and F. Bloch-Lainé, *Finances publiques: les ressources publiques*, *Cours à l'Institut d'Etudes Politiques de l'Université de Paris* (Paris, 1953) p. 460; Louis Trotabas, *Les Finances publiques et les impôts de la France*, p. 136; and "La Réforme fiscale" article in *Réalités* No. 58, November, 1950, p. 57.

20. *Rapport fait au nom de la Commission des Finances sur le projet de loi de finances pour l'exercice 1953* (No. 4794), Assemblée Nationale No. 4888 Deuxième législature, 1952, Vol. I, p. 98. See also the criticism by Henri Ulver, then Secretary of State for the Budget, reported in *Agence économique et financière*, March 24, 1954, p. 4.

21. Quoted in *Le Monde*, March 4, 1955, p. 1.

22. Jacques Fauvet, in *Le Monde*, March 20-21, 1955, p. 1.

BIBLIOGRAPHICAL NOTES

Chapter 7

1. The estimate is cited by André Thiers in "Le Capitalisme d'état et la production industrielle," article in *Vingt ans de capitalisme d'état* (Paris, 1951), p. 110.

2. André Piettre, *Economie dirigée d'hier et d'aujourd'hui, du colbertisme à notre temps* (Paris, 1947), pp. 1-111; C. J. Gignoux, *L'Industrie française* (Paris, 1952), pp. 17-70; Bernard Chenot, *Organisation économique de l'état* (Paris, 1951), pp. 25-37, 46-49.

3. Marcel Ventenat, *L'Expérience des nationalisations* (Paris, 1947), pp. 66-67, 96-99; Henry Laufenburger, *L'Intervention de l'état en matière économique* (Paris, 1939), pp. 32-39.

4. Bernard Lavergne, *Le Problème des nationalisations* (Paris, 1946), pp. 46-51; and Ventenat, *op. cit.*, pp. 79-82.

5. René Gendarme, *L'Expérience française de la nationalisation industrielle* (Paris, 1950), Introduction; and Daniel Villey, "Les Etapes du capitalisme d'-état," article in *Vingt ans de capitalisme d'état*, pp. 22-25.

6. Jean Rivero, *Le Régime des nationalisations* (Paris, 1948), Nos. 20-25; Ventenat, *op. cit.*, pp. 82-96; Laufenburger, *op. cit.*, pp. 267-270.

7. Gendarme, *op. cit.*, p. 37.

8. Ventenat, *op. cit.*, p. 110.

9. Cf. the comments by David H. Pinkney, "The French Experiment in Nationalization, 1944-1950," article in *Modern France, Problems of the Third and Fourth Republics*: E. M. Earle, editor (Princeton, 1951), pp. 354-355.

10. Quoted by Louis-R. Franck in "Planisme français et démocratie," *Revue économique* No. 2, March, 1953, p. 208.

11. Cf. the preamble (*exposé des motifs*) of the Ordinance of January 16, 1945. See also Bernard Wilmet and Maurice Faber, "De la société anonyme à la Régie Nationale des Usines Renault," *Economie et humanisme*, No. 33, September-October, 1947, pp. 500-501.

12. According to the Minister of Finance, cited by Rivero, *op. cit.*, No. 66.

13. *Ibid.*, Nos. 67-70; and Ventenat, *op. cit.*, pp. 221-228.

14. *Inventaire de la situation financière (1913-1946)*, pp. 82-86; Gendarme, *op. cit.*, pp. 22-23; Bernard Chenot "Ambiguité de l'économie mixte," *Les Cahiers économiques*, August-September, 1953, pp. 4-7.

15. See two articles by Adolf Sturmthal: "The Structure of Nationalized Enterprises in France," *Political Science Quarterly*, Vol. LXVII, No. 3, September, 1952, and "Nationalization and Workers' Control in Britain and France," *Journal of Political Economy*, Vol. LXI, No. 1, February, 1953; also Gerard Lyon-Caen, "Les Nationalisations en Grande-Bretagne," *Droit social*, December, 1946, pp. 403-406.

16. For general references see: Pinkney, *op. cit.*, pp. 364-365; Sturmthal, "The Structure of Nationalized Enterprises in France," *op. cit.*, pp. 369-377; Ventenat, *op. cit.*, pp. 139-143, 173-179; and Gendarme, *op. cit.*, pp. 115-124.

17. Commission de Vérification des Comptes des Entreprises Publiques, *Troisième rapport d'ensemble, extrait du Journal officiel* October 3, 1952, pp. 41-42.

18. Etienne Audibert, quoted in *Le Monde*, February 18, 1948, p. 4.

Chapter 8

1. Material in this section from: Robert Fabre, "Les Houillères du Nord et du Pas-de-Calais," *Droit social*, April, 1945, pp. 138-153; "Structure et organisation des houillères du Nord et du Pas-de-Calais," *Droit social*, April, 1945, pp. 121-122; Bernard Chenot, "Premiers résultats de la nationalisation des mines," *Droit social*, July-August, 1949, pp. 242-246; Jean Personnaz, "La Nationalisation des houillères françaises," *Droit social*, March, 1947, pp. 81-83.

2. Data from Charbonnages de France, *Rapport de gestion exercice 1954* (Paris, 1955), p. 8.

3. Commissariat Général du Plan: *Premier rapport de la Commission de Modernisation des Houillères* (Paris, November 1946); *Rapport sur la réalisation du plan de modernisation et d'équipement de l'Union française, année 1952* (Paris, 1953), p. 101 and *Rapport annuel sur l'exécution du plan de modernisation et*

d'équipement de l'Union française, 1954 (Paris, 1955), p. 154. See also OEEC, *Coal and European Economic Expansion* (Paris, 1952) pp. 42-44.

4. United States Operations Mission to France, *France Data Book—1954*, Table H-3.

5. Data from the annual reports (*rapports de gestion*) of Charbonnages de France and the periodic reports of the Commission de Vérification des Comptes des Entreprises Publiques.

6. Data from the *rapports de gestion* of Charbonnages de France, except for 1945, which is given in Chenot, *Premiers résultats de la nationalisation des mines*, p. 244.

7. OEEC, *Coal Production and Supplies for Western Europe in 1952 and 1953* (Paris, January, 1953) Tables 7 and 8, pp. 30-31.

8. Electricité de France, *Rapport d'activité, comptes de gestion exercice 1954* (Paris, 1955), p. 18.

9. Data from the annual reports (*assemblée générale des actionnaires*) of the Société Nationale des Chemins de Fer Français.

10. Cf. *Le Monde*, January 8, 1955, p. 10.

11. Société Nationale des Chemins de Fer Français, *Assemblée générale des actionnaires*, 1954, p. 6.

12. Harold Lubell, *The French Investment Program: A Defense of the Monnet Plan*, Mutual Security Agency, Special Mission to France for Economic Cooperation (Paris, 1952), pp. 103-105; Commissariat Général du Plan, *General Report on the First Plan of Modernization and Equipment* (Paris, November, 1946, January, 1947), pp. 41-42; and *Premier rapport de la Commission de Modernisation des Houillères* (Paris, November, 1946), pp. 26-33.

13. Commissariat Général du Plan, *Premier rapport de la Commission de Modernisation de l'Electricité* (Paris, November, 1946), *passim*.

14. Calculated from data in Charbonnages de France, *rapports de gestion* for 1949, 1950, and 1951.

15. *Le Monde*, July 1, 1953, special supplement on *Electricité de France.*

16. Commissariat Général du Plan, *Etat des operations du plan de modernisation et d'équipement, projet de loi*, No. 4785, annexe No. III (Paris, 1952), pp. 37-41; *Economie et réalité mondiale*, No. 42, July, 1953, pp. 93-94.

17. "Perspectives d'avenir sur la production et le transport de l'énergie électrique en France," *Revue française de l'énergie*, No. 14, November, 1950, pp. 38-45. See also, in the same journal, Henri Varlet, "Le Plan Monnet et la production d'énergie électrique thermique," (No. 29, March, 1952, pp. 181-187); Pierre Massé, "L'Electricité devant un nouveau plan," (No. 30, April, 1952, pp. 214-225); Raymond Giguet, "Réalisations et perspectives de l'équipement électrique," (No. 32, June, 1952, pp. 282-292); Henri Varlet, "La Production de l'énergie électrique en France: répartition entre usines thermiques et hydrauliques," (No. 34, September, 1952, pp. 351-365); and R. Gaspard and Pierre Massé, "Le Choix des investissements énergetiques et la production d'électricité en France," (No. 35, October, 1952, pp. 5-14).

18. *Le Monde*, August 2, 1953, financial and economic supplement.

19. Cf. Lorwin, *The French Labor Movement*, p. 198.

20. Charbonnages de France, *Rapport de gestion 1954*, p. 64.

21. Commission de Vérification des Comptes des Entreprises Publiques, *Rapport d'ensemble*, *Journal officiel*, *Annexe administrative*, August 21, 1949, pp. 377-378; *Deuxième rapport d'ensemble*, *Journal officiel*, *Annexe administrative* January 26, 1951, p. 24; *Troisième rapport d'ensemble*, *Journal officiel*, *Annexe administrative*, October 3, 1952, pp. 7-8; Gendarme, *L'Expérience française de la nationalisation industrielle*, pp. 136-138; Ventenat, *L'Expérience des nationalisations*, pp. 176-177; Emmanuel Reboud, "Nationalisation de l'électricité et économie globale," *Economie et humanisme*, No. 81, September-October, 1953, pp. 58-69.

22. *Le Monde*, December 4, 1954, p. 14, November 6, 1953, p. 14; *Agence économique et financière*, December 14, 1953, p. 2; *L'Année ferroviaire 1953* (Paris, 1953), pp. 82-83.

23. Cf. Sturmthal, "Nationalization and Workers' Control in Britain and France," *passim*, and Lorwin, *The French Labor Movement*, pp. 198-199.

24. *Le Monde*, June 4, 1948, p. 4, June 10, 1948, p. 3, June 11, 1948, p. 4, June 13-14, 1948, p. 4; Jean Durand, "La Grève des mineurs," *Travaux de*

l'action populaire, No. 27, February, 1949, pp. 111-126; Charbonnages de France *Rapport de gestion, 1948*, (pp. 18-20).

25. Cf. *Le Monde*, August 7, 1953, p. 5, for the communiqué of the Cartel Force Ouvrière des Services Publics.

26. M. Levard, Secretary General of the *Confédération Française des Travailleurs Chrétiens*, quoted in *Le Monde*, August 11, 1953, p. 1.

27. Data from the annual reports of Charbonnages de France for 1949 and 1950.

28. M. Allais, *La Gestion des houillères nationalisées et la théorie économique* (Paris, undated), *passim.*

29. Gabriel Dessus, "Perspectives commerciales sur les fournitures d'énergie électrique à l'industrie," *Revue française de l'énergie*, No. 1, September, 1949, pp. 20-26; Robert Jouannet, "Les Tarifs de vente de l'énergie électrique en basse tension," *Revue française de l'énergie*, No. 3, November, 1949, pp. 85-92; Commission de Vérification, *Troisième rapport d'ensemble*, p. 8; Electricité de France, *Rapport de gestion des exercices 1946-1947, 1948, 1949* (Paris, 1950), pp. 27-28.

30. Cf. Roger Hutter, "La Théorie économique et la gestion commerciale des chemins de fer, le problème tarifaire," *Revue générale des chemins de fer*, July, 1950, pp. 318-332.

31. See the following issues of the *Revue générale des chemins de fer*: April, 1949, R. Hutter, "Les Tarifs de réglementation de la SNCF," pp. 155-168, and "A Propos des nouveaux tarifs marchandises en vigueur à la SNCF," p. 186; February, 1950, R. Hutter, "Qu'est-ce que le coût marginal?" pp. 53-63; May, 1951, G. Aubert, "La Tarification des marchandises de la SNCF," pp. 213-227; and March, 1953, M. Marcy, "L'Avenant du 10 juillet 1952 à la convention du 31 août 1937, dans le cadre des grands problèmes de gestion des chemins de fer," pp. 137-138.

32. R. Hutter, "La Théorie économique et la gestion commerciale des chemins de fer—la coordination des transports," *Revue générale des chemins de fer*, October, 1950, pp. 443-460; Pierre Uri, "La Querelle des nationalisations," *Les Temps modernes*, July, 1949, pp. 169-170; and M. Allais, "Le Problème de la coordination des transports et la théorie économique, *Revue d'économie politique*, Vol. LVIII, 1948, pp. 212-271. See also *Le Monde* October 1, 1954, p. 16; November 7-8, 1954, p. 7; and November 14, 1954, financial and economic supplement.

33. Cf. the annual report of Electricité de France for 1954, p. 25.

34. Cf. the annual reports of the SNCF for 1951 (p. 9) and 1954 (p. 33), *Revue générale des chemins de fer*, May 1953, p. 296; and *Economic Report for 1951 and 1952*, p. 48.

35. M. Allais, "Le Problème de la coordination des transports," pp. 249-252. See also Pierre Uri, "La Querelle des nationalisations," p. 170.

36. *Le Monde*, November 7-8, 1954, p. 7; January 6, 1955, p. 10; May 2, 1955, financial and economic supplement.

37. Commission de Vérification, *Deuxième rapport d'ensemble*, p. 20.

38. Data from the annual reports of Electricité de France.

39. Data from the annual reports of the Société Nationale des Chemins de Fer Français.

40. *Journal Officiel, débats parlementaires, 1952*, No. 79, Assemblée Nationale, October 25, 1952, pp. 4425-4426, statement of the Minister of Public Works, Transportation, and Tourism.

41. Data from Commission de Vérification, *Rapport d'ensemble*, p. 382; *Deuxième rapport d'ensemble*, p. 38; *Troisième rapport d'ensemble*, pp. 30-31; and from Régie Nationale des Usines Renault, *Rapport annuel de gestion*, fiscal year 1952, pp. 41-47, fiscal year 1953, pp. 49-53.

Chapter 9

1. Data from the Stanford Research Institute, reprinted in the *Bulletin du Conseil National du Patronat Français*, March 20, 1954, pp. 21-23. See also La Documentation française, *Notes et études documentaires* No. 1296, March 15, 1950, "Recueil de documents sur la productivité," pp. 7, 15.

2. *Economic Report for 1951 and 1952*, p. 65. See also *Merchants of France*, a pamphlet published by France Actuelle, October 1953, pp. 5-7.

3. *The Nathan Report*, p. 29.

4. *Economic Report for 1951 and 1952*, p. 67. See also *Merchants of France*, pp. 7-8.
5. *The Economist*, March 26, 1955, p. 1069.
6. Cf. David S. Landes, "French Business and the Businessman: A Social and Cultural Analysis," *Modern France, Problems of the Third and Fourth Republics*, p. 335.
7. The *Economic Report for 1951 and 1952*, p. 66.
8. *Ibid.*
9. Gabriel Chevry, "La Structure industrielle et commerciale de la France," Journal de la Société de Statistique de Paris, January-March 1952, p. 28.
10. "Effectifs des salariés du commerce en 1950," *Bulletin du Conseil National du Patronat Français*, June 20, 1953, pp. 27-30.
11. See *Bulletin mensuel de statistique*: supplement October-December, 1952, pp. 46-62; supplement October-December, 1953, pp. 40-59.
12. *Le Monde*, January 30, 1954, p. 14 and March 21, 1954, financial and economic supplements; and U. S. Department of Commerce, *Statistical Abstract of the United States, 1953*, p. 785.
13. Pierre Maillet "Les Disparités de consommation d'énergie en France et dans quelques pays étrangers," *Revue française de l'énergie* No. 51, March, 1954, p. 215.
14. *Notes et études documentaires*, No. 1296, p. 8; *Le Monde*, January 30, 1954, p. 14. See also the individual reports of the various committees which formed part of the initial studies of the Commissariat Général du Plan.
15. Quoted in *Agence économique et financière*, December 3, 1953, p. 4.
16. La Documentation française, *Notes et études documentaires* No. 1736, "Ententes et monopoles dans le monde: France" (Paris, May 5, 1953), pp. 87-88; and J. Mérigot, "Le décret du 30 juin 1952 portant aménagement du régime fiscal des sociétés et des valeurs mobilières," *Revue de science et de législation financière*, January-March, 1953, pp. 132-145.
17. Cf. Conseil Economique, "Etude sur le rôle économique du crédit, sa situation actuelle, et les réformes que celle-ci appelle," *Journal officiel, Avis et rapports du Conseil Economique*, May 29, 1953, pp. 363-377.
18. Data from *Rapport sur la réalisation du plan de modernisation et d'équipement* (Paris, 1953) and from the annual reports of the Commission des Investissements.
19. Comité National de la Productivité, *Actions et problèmes de productivité* (Paris, 1954) Part I; and *France actuelle*, Vol. II, No. 37, October 5, 1953.
20. *Le Monde*, March 12, 1954, p. 16; and *Bulletin du Conseil National du Patronat Français*, June 5, 1953, pp. 26-29.
21. Preamble to the *projet de loi No. 9034 (rectifié) autorisant le Gouvernement à mettre en oeuvre un programme d'équilibre financier, d'expansion économique et de progrès social.* See also *Le Monde*, December 8, 1954, p. 14; *L'Economie*, December 10, 1954, pp. 6-7; and *Bulletin du Conseil National du Patronat Français*, March, 1955, pp. 31-34.
22. *Le Monde*, August 4, 1954, p. 12, October 27, 1954, p. 12.
23. *Le Monde*, September 26, 1954, financial and economic supplement, December 16, 1954, p. 14, March 3, 1955, p. 14. See also the French chapter of the Economic Commission for Europe's *Economic Survey of Europe in 1954* (e.g., pp. 178-187).
24. Robert Buron, "La Sclérose des structures économiques de la France," *Les Cahiers économiques*, April, 1954, pp. 3-4. See also the comments by Alfred Sauvy in *Droit social*, January, 1953, p. 16; *Le Monde*, December 29, 1953, p. 10, and December 30, 1953, p. 4; and *Agence économique et financière*, February 22, 1954, p. 3.
25. *Le Monde*, July 14, 1953, p. 14; *Agence économique et financière*, October 21, 1953, p. 2.
26. *Le Monde*, February 25, 1954, p. 10.
27. Cf. the discussion in Louis-R. Franck, "Planisme français et démocratie," pp. 210-211, 217-218.
28. Commission des Finances de l'Assemblée Nationale: *Rapport No. 9506 sur le projet de loi relatif aux comptes spéciaux du Trésor pour l'année 1950* (1950 Session) pp. 8-10 and 197-198; *Rapport No. 4888 sur le projet de loi de finances pour l'exercice 1953 (4794)* (1952 Session) pp. 132-133.

Chapter 10

1. Cf. *Economic Report for 1951 and 1952*, pp. 57-58.
2. *Rapport sur la réalisation du plan de modernisation et d'équipement, année 1952* (Paris, 1953), Introduction.
3. *Economic Report for 1951 and 1952*, p. 55.
4. Conseil Economique, "L'Aide à l'exportation," *Journal officiel, Avis et rapports du Conseil Economique*, February 14, 1953, p. 204.
5. *Journal officiel, Lois et décrets*, January 4-5, 1954, pp. 145-150.
6. *Statistiques et études financières* No. 14, February, 1950, pp. 83-94; *Inventaire de la situation financière (1951)*, pp. 309-316; *Inventaire de la situation financière (1913-1946)*, pp. 444-459; Assemblée Nationale, Rapport de la Commission des Finances sur le projet de loi relatif aux comptes spéciaux du trésor pour l'année 1950, No. 9506, 1950 session, *passim* and *Rapport de la Commission des Finances sur le projet de loi des finances pour l'exercice 1953 No. 4888*, 1952 session, Vol. I, pp. 126-131; and Paul Nollet, "La Parafiscalité," *Droit social*, February, 1953, pp. 65-73.
7. *Le Monde*, February 12, 1954, p. 10; *Agence économique et financière*, November 4, 1953, pp. 2, 4 and February 11, 1954, p. 4.
8. See, for example, Conseil Economique, "Contrôle des ententes professionnelles," *Etudes et travaux No. 13*, Paris, 1950.
9. Pierre Bauchet, "La Structure d'une branche d'industrie française: l'automobile," *Economie appliquée* April-September, 1952, pp. 359-399.
10. "Contrôle des ententes professionnelles," pp. 38-39.
11. Ibid., pp. 36-43; Herbert Multzer, "Les Ententes dans l'industrie pétrolière," *Nouvelle revue de l'économie contemporaine*, August-September, 1950, pp. 17-18; Bertrand de Jouvenel, "Les Ententes sur le marché mondial du pétrole," *Revue française de l'énergie*, No. 35, October, 1952, pp. 22-25; and Giles Pasqualaggi, "Les Ententes en France," *Revue économique*, January, 1952, pp. 63-82.
12. Quoted in Jean Mazard, "Prix imposés et prix d'entente," *Droit social*, March, 1953, p. 133.
13. Landes, "French Business and the Businessman: A Social and Cultural Analysis," p. 334. See also the *Bulletin du Conseil National du Patronat Français*, April 15, 1952, pp. 1-8 (supplement).
14. Landes, *op. cit.*, p. 348.
15. "L'Economie française aux rayons X," article in *Réalités*, November, 1953, p. 46.
16. *Progress and Problems of the European Economy*, p. 95.
17. La Documentation Française, *Notes et études documentaires No. 1736*, "Ententes et monopoles dans le monde, France" (Paris, 1953), pp. 40-42. See also J. Tchernoff, *Ententes économiques et financières* (Paris, 1953) *passim*.
18. Mazard, *op. cit.* pp. 129-133; *Notes et études documentaires No. 1736*, pp. 85-87, and *No. 1737* (Vol. II), pp. 118-128.
19. *Le Monde*, August 20, 1953, p. 10.
20. M. Gros, quoted in "Contrôle des ententes professionelles," p. 38.
21. Report of the Finance Committee of the National Assembly, quoted in *Agence économique et financière*, November 26, 1953, p. 3.
22. William Diebold, Jr., *Trade and Payments in Western Europe* (New York, Harper & Bros., 1952), pp. 141-143, 354-376. See also several reports by the Conseil Economique (*Avis et rapports* dated January 27, 1949, May 26, 1949, March 24, 1950, May 11, 1950, and November 22, 1950).
23. Henry W. Ehrmann, "The French Trade Associations and the Ratification of the Schuman Plan," *World Politics*, Vol. VI No. 4, July, 1954, pp. 453-481.
24. Cf. Pierre Ricard, first Vice President of the *Chambre Syndicale de la Sidérurgie Française* quoted in the *Bulletin du Conseil National du Patronat Français*, January 5, 1953, pp. 15-19; the report of the Senatorial committee on the Coal and Steel Community cited in *Le Monde*, July 1, 1953, p. 5; and *Le Monde*, May 20, 1954, p. 14.
25. See, for example, the articles by Henri Maurice in *Le Monde* (January 14, 15, 16 and 17-18, 1954), the reply of the High Authority (*Le Monde*, February 9, 1954), and the article by Raymond Aron (*Le Figaro*, January 28, 1954, p. 9).
26. *Le Monde*, March 25, 1954, p. 5.

27. Cour des Comptes, *Rapport au Président de la Republique années 1948-1949, Journal officiel, Annexe administrative*, June 30, 1950, p. 271.

28. Chenot, *Organisation économique de l'état*, pp. 186-191; and L. Gingembre, "Le Syndicalisme patronal et l'administration," *La Revue administrative*, November-December, 1949, pp. 589-593.

29. *Le Monde*, October 2, 1953, p. 14; *Agence économique et financière*, December 2, 1953, p. 4 and February 11, 1954, p. 4; *L'Economie* No. 443, May 6, 1954, p. 17.

30. *Droit social*, July-August, 1952, p. 452. See also *Notes et études documentaires No. 1736*, p. 85.

31. *Le Monde*, September 5, 1953, p. 1, September 6-7, 1953, p. 1, and *Paris-Match* No. 233, September 5-12, 1953, p. 13.

32. *Agence économique et financière*, March 5, 1954, p. 4; *Le Monde*, May 8, 1954, p. 14.

33. "Contrôle des ententes professionnelles," pp. 33-35. See also *Agence économique et financière*, March 31, 1954, p. 3.

34. "Contrôle des ententes professionnelles," pp. 35-36 and Pierre Fromont, "Le Capitalisme d'état et la production agricole," article in *Vingt ans de capitalisme d'état* (Paris, 1951) pp. 123-125.

35. *Le Monde*, December 23, 1954, p. 16.

36. Delouvrier and Nathan, *Politique économique de la France*, Vol. III, p. 21. See also Diebold, *op. cit.*, pp. 222-223.

37. Diebold, *op. cit.*, p. 223.

38. The *Nathan Report*, pp. 3-4.

39. *Economic Report for 1951 and 1952*, p. 56.

40. See two reports by the Conseil Economique on the allocation of import licenses (*Journal officiel, Avis et rapports du Conseil Economique*, March 11, 1949, pp. 62-71 and February 14, 1953, pp. 195-201). See also Buron, "La Sclérose des structures économiques de la France," p. 3.

41. Lorwin, *The French Labor Movement*, Chapters IV and V.

42. See the three articles by Paul Durand in *Droit social*, issues of March, April, and May, 1950.

43. A. Philbert, "Le Problème de l'échelle mobile des salaires," *Droit social*, November, 1952, pp. 592-599.

44. Cf. Lorwin, *op. cit.*, pp. 221-223.

45. *Agence économique et financière*, February 13, 1954, p. 4.

46. Cf. the comments of Minister of Labor Bacon, *Le Monde*, May 21 1953, p. 6.

47. Quoted in Lorwin, *op. cit.*, p. 190. See also pp. 134-135.

48. Val R. Lorwin, "French Trade Unions Since Liberation, 1944-1951," *Industrial and Labor Relations Review*, Vol. 5, No. 4, July, 1952, p. 536.

49. *Statistiques et études financières* No. 25, January, 1951, pp. 5-21 and No. 27, March, 1951, pp. 266-285.

50. The *Nathan Report*, p. 33.

51. INSEE data, reprinted in *Le Monde*, July 28, 1954, p. 10.

52. *Bulletin mensuel de statistique*, supplement April-June, 1953, p. 53.

53. Cf. Paul Durand, *La Politique contemporaine de sécurité sociale* (Paris, 1953), pp. 163-165, 287-291, and 613-618 and "Les Equivoques de la redistribution du revenu par la sécurité sociale," *Droit social*, May, 1953, pp. 292-298; Alfred Sauvy, "La Situation économique," *Droit social*, January, 1954, pp. 21-24; the *Nathan Report*, p. 33; and *Etudes et conjoncture* August, 1954, pp. 754-759 and January-February, 1955, pp. 40-42.

54. Louis-R. Franck, *op. cit.*, p. 206.

55. A. Croizat, quoted in *L'Economie*, July 2, 1953, p. 9. See also "L'Expérience des comités d'entreprise, bilan d'une enquête," *Droit social*, January, 1952, pp. 14-33, February, 1952, pp. 92-104, and March, 1952, pp. 163-179; and Lorwin, *The French Labor Movement*, pp. 262-276.

56. *Le Monde*, December 4, 1953, p. 14.

57. *Troisième rapport de la Commission des Investissements* (Paris, 1950), pp. 48-49.

58. "La Réglementation actuelle des prix," *Statistiques et études financières* No. 74, February, 1955, pp. 113-122.

59. Cf. Louis-R. Franck, *op. cit.*, pp. 210-211.
60. Conseil Economique, "Etude générale sur le problème du logement" *Journal officiel, Avis et rapports du Conseil Economique*, August 21, 1953, *passim.*
61. Jean Benard, "La Répartition des dépenses de la population française en fonction de ses besoins," Institut National d'Etudes Démographiques, *Population 1953*, p. 233.

Chapter 11

1. M. Nove-Josserand, of the Fédération Nationale des Syndicats des Exploitants Agricoles, quoted in *Le Monde*, February 16, 1955, p. 10.
2. *Le Monde*, August 11, 1954, p. 2.
3. United Nations Food and Agriculture Organization, *Yearbook of Food and Agricultural Statistics 1953*, Vol. VII, Part I, Tables 1 and 3, pp. 3-4 and 13.
4. *Rapport sur la réalisation du plan de modernisation et d'équipement de l'Union française, année 1952*, pp. 30-31.
5. *Recensement général de la population effectué le 10 mars 1946*, Vol. VII, "Exploitations agricoles" (Paris, 1950), pp. XLV ff.
6. J. Klatzmann, "La Place de l'agriculture dans le revenu national français—dangers et incertitudes de son évaluation," *Etudes et conjoncture*, March-April, 1953, pp. 180-192.
7. UN/FAO, *1953 Statistics Yearbook*, Vol. VII, Part I, Table 5A, pp. 18-19.
8. Cf. the data in UN/ECE and FAO, Joint Secretariat, *Output and Expenses of Agriculture in Some European Countries* (Geneva, 1953), Table 8, p. 21.
9. UN/ECE and FAO, Joint Secretariat, *European Agriculture, A Statement of Problems* (Geneva, 1954), Chart 3, p. 16.
10. *Recensement général de la population*, pp. XXII ff.
11. Cited in *Le Monde*, December 9, 1954, p. 14.
12. Commissariat Général au Plan, *Rapport de la Commission de l'Equipement Rural* (Paris, 1953), p. 37.
13. La Documentation Française, *Situation et perspectives de l'agriculture française* (Paris, undated), p. 10, and Jean Fauchon, *Economie de l'agriculture française* (Paris, 1954), p. 122.
14. La Documentation Française, *Notes et études documentaires No. 1545* "Quelques aspects de l'équipement agricole en France" (Paris, 1951), p. 11.
15. *Rapport de la Commission de l'Equipement Rural*, pp. 169-170.
16. Estimate of the *Comité National de l'Habitat Rural*, cited in Fauchon, *op. cit.*, p. 122.
17. *Rapport de la Commission de l'Equipement Rural*, pp. 17-18, and *Coopération Agricole* February-March, 1955, p. 35.
18. *L'Economie* No. 484, March 17, 1955, p. 15.
19. *Economic Survey of Europe in 1954*, Table 86, p. 184.
20. Ministère de l'Agriculture, *Bulletin d'information* No. 30, 1955, pp. C-C3.
21. *Economic Survey of Europe in 1954*, Table 86, p. 184.
22. *Ibid.*
23. See H. Richard, *Physionomie de la fertilisation en France* (Paris, 1951) *passim* and "Quelques aspects du problème des engrais," *Etudes et conjoncture* August, 1953, pp. 871-885.
24. Jacques Lépicard, quoted in *Le Monde*, March 7-8, 1954, p. 10.
25. *Economic Survey of Europe in 1954*, Table 86, p. 184.
26. Colin Clark, *The Relation Between the Pace of Technical Change in Farming and the Level of Agricultural Prosperity*, paper presented at the International Conference of Agricultural Economists, Helsinki, August, 1955, p. 6.
27. *Rapport sur la réalisation du plan de modernisation et d'équipement de l'Union française, année 1952*, p. 80.
28. Commissariat Général au Plan, *Deuxième plan de modernisation et d'équipement—rapport général des Commissions de la Production Agricole et de l'Equipement Rural* (October, 1953) pp. 134-138.
29. *Rapport général des Commissions de la Production Agricole et de l'Equipement Rural*, p. 97.
30. *Ibid.*, p. 98; *Rapport sur la réalisation du plan de modernisation et d'équipement de l'Union française, année 1952*, p. 206.

31. *Rapport général des Commissions de la Production Agricole et de l'Equipement Rural*, p. 137 and *Rapport annuel sur l'exécution du plan de modernisation et d'équipement de l'Union française, 1954*, p. 135.

32. *Rapport sur la réalisation du plan de modernisation et d'équipement de l'Union française, année 1952*, p. 199; and *L'Economie*, March 17, 1955, p. 15.

33. *L'Economie*, March 11, 1954, p. 7.

34. Commissariat Général au Plan, *Document de synthèse et de coordination des travaux de la Commission de l'Equipement Rural* (Paris, 1953) pp. 20-21.

35. See D. R. Bergmann, *Cooperative Use of Machinery on French Farms*, OEEC AG/PP (49) 15, September 29, 1949.

36. See "Quelques aspects du problème des engrais," *Etudes et conjoncture*, August 1953, pp. 871-890.

37. *Rapport sur le réalisation du plan de modernisation et d'équipement de l'Union française, année 1952*, pp. 203-218.

38. OEEC data cited in "Les Problèmes actuels de l'agriculture européenne," La Documentation Française, *Notes et études documentaires No. 1826*, January 22, 1954, p. 13.

39. *Rapport sur la réalisation du plan de modernisation et d'équipement de l'Union française, année 1952*, p. 202; and *Bulletin hebdomadaire du Cabinet du Ministre de l'Agriculture* No. 26, 1954, pp. B2-B3.

40. Fauchon, *op. cit.*, p. 130.

41. "Le Revenu de l'agriculture en France, en 1952-1953," *Etudes et conjoncture*, December, 1953, p. 1265.

42. *Rapport de la Commission de l'Equipement Rural*, p. 21.

43. *Rapport sur la réalisation du plan de modernisation et d'équipement de l'Union française, année 1952*, p. 205.

44. "Plan d'Investissement Agricole 1948/1952" in *Revue du Ministère de l'Agriculture*, July, 1952, p. 390.

45. F. O. Sargent, "Fragmentation of French Land: Its Nature, Extent and Causes" in Land Economics, August, 1952, pp. 221-229 and D. R. Bergmann, "Regrouping of Farm Holdings in France," in *International Journal of Agrarian Affairs*, May 1952, pp. 24-32.

46. Fauchon, *op. cit.*, p. 142; *Le Monde*, August 24, 1954, p. 10.

47. *Rapport sur la réalisation du plan de modernisation et d'équipement de l'Union française, année 1952*, p. 204.

48. Denis R. Bergmann, "Les Obstacles matériels et psychologiques à l'accroissement de la productivité agricole," *Cahiers des ingénieurs agronomes*, No. 2, 1954, p. 19. Figure for the United States from T. W. Schultz, *Economic Organization of Agriculture* (New York, 1953) p. 115.

49. Cited by J.-F. Gravier, "La Clé du problème agricole: enseignement et vulgarisation" in *Droit social*, November, 1950, special issue on *Les Aspects économiques, techniques et sociaux de l'expansion agricole*, pp. 19-23. See also "L'Enseignement agricole," *Terres de France*, special issue No. x, 1954.

50. M. Chatelain, *L'Agriculture française et la formation professionnelle* (Paris, 1953), p. 218.

51. "Economie et sociologie rurale de la Bretagne," *Etudes d'économie rurale*, September, 1953, p. 27.

52. *Le Monde*, November 5, 1954, p. 6.

53. *Le Monde*, October 24, 1954, financial and economic supplement.

54. Data on France from the budgets of the Ministry of Agriculture, on the Netherlands from J.-F. Gravier, *op. cit.*, p. 21.

55. OEEC, *Agricultural Advisory Services in European Countries* (Paris, 1950) *passim*.

56. Cf. "Fecondité urbaine et rurale mesurée par les naissances ramenées au domicile," *Revue du Ministère de l'Agriculture*, Supplement to No. 61-62, August-September 1951, p. 203.

57. *Recensement général de la population effectué le 10 mars 1946*, Vol. VII, pp. LVIII-LIX.

58. "La Population: producteurs et consommateurs," *Etudes et conjoncture*, January-February, 1955, p. 19.

59. M. de Juglart, *Droit rural*, Vol. 1, "L'Exploitation rurale" (Paris, 1949) p. 198; and R. Montagne, "La Notion de l'exploitation agricole et son évolution," *Bulletin de la Société Française d'Economie Rurale*, December, 1950, p. 67.

60. Caisse Nationale de Crédit Agricole, *Rapport sur la situation du crédit agricole mutuel au 31 décembre 1954*, p. 38.
61. "Plans d'Investissements agricoles," *Revue du Ministère de l'Agriculture*, July, 1953, p. 390.
62. F. Robin, "L'Evolution des marchés de la terre en France depuis la libération," *Economie rurale*, January, 1955, p. 46.
63. Cf. the two reports of the Conseil Economique, "La Réforme du statut du fermage et du métayage," *Etudes et travaux No.* 2, 1949, and "Les Diverses formes du métayage," *Etudes et travaux No. 23* (2 Vols.) 1953
64. Cf. "La Réforme du statut du fermage et du métayage," p. 23.

Chapter 12

1. Cf. *Le Monde*, August 6, 1955, p. 1.
2. Journal officiel, *Avis et rapports du Conseil Economique*, "Problème de la viande," December 11, 1948, p. 264.
3. *L'Economie*, December 17, 1954, p. 11.
4. Data from *L'Economie*, October 21, 1954, pp. 7-8.
5. Georges Bréart, *Le Fleuve blanc* (Paris, 1954), p. 165.
6. Ruth Cohen, "Contrôle des prix agricoles dans certains pays d'Europe occidentale," UNFAO, *Etudes sur les politiques en matière de produits* No. 2, Rome, September, 1953, p. 66. See also F. Clerc, "La Commercialisation des laits de collecte dans la région toulousaine," *Economie rurale*, April, 1954, p. 17.
7. Fauchon, *op. cit.*, pp. 51-54.
8. Material from the *Recueil méthodique des dispositions législatives en vigueur en matière de céréales*, published by the Office National Interprofessionnel des Céréales (ONIC) in 1952.
9. Fauchon, *op. cit.*, p. 52 and *Le Monde*, September 14, 1954, p. 10.
10. Data from *L'Economie*, February 18, 1954, p. 26.
11. *Le Monde*, June 19, 1955, financial and economic supplement.
12. Alfred Sauvy, in *Droit social*, December, 1952, p. 669.
13. Conseil Economique, *Etudes et travaux No. 15* "Le Statut de l'alcool" (Paris, 1950), p. 92.
14. *Agence économique et financière*, September 24, 1954, p. 2; "Le Statut de l'alcool," p. 134.
15. *Agence économique et financière*, September 30, 1954, p. 4.
16. *Le Monde*, July 19, 1955, p. 10 and November 9, 1955, p. 10.
17. See "Le Problème de l'alcool," *Etudes et conjoncture*, September, 1953, p. 1003, and "Les Problèmes posés par les excédents d'alcool," Conseil Economique, *Etudes et travaux No. 29* (Paris, 1953), p. 56.
18. "Le Problème de l'alcool," pp. 993-994.
19. Cf. the data presented in *Le Monde*, December 17, 1954, p. 7 and October 22, 1955, p. 14.
20. *Le Monde*, November 29, 1955, p. 10.
21. Cf. "Le Problème de l'alcool," p. 998 and the Ministry of Finance study cited in *Le Monde*, November 9, 1955, p. 10.
22. *Le Monde*, September 12, 1954, financial and economic supplement; *Agence économique et financière*, September 24, 1954, p. 2.
23. Cf. "Le Problème de l'alcool," pp. 1013-1016.
24. "Les Problèmes posés par les excédents d'alcool," p. 58.
25. *Agence économique et financière*, September 30, 1954, p. 4.
26. Statement of the Fédération des Associations Viticoles, *Le Monde*, August 10, 1955, p. 10.
27. Material from R. Badouin, "Analyse économique et détermination du prix du vin," *Bulletin du Centre Régional des Etudes Economiques de Montpellier*, 3rd quarter 1953, pp. 115-158; and J. Milhau, "L'Avenir de la viticulture française," *Revue économique*, September, 1953, pp. 700-738.
28. "Le Problème de l'alcool," p. 985.
29. *Ibid.*
30. *Ibid.* and *Rapport sur la réalisation du plan de modernisation et d'équipement de l'Union française, année 1952*, p. 29.
31. *Le Monde*, October 9, 1955, financial and economic supplement and August 11, 1955, p. 1.

32. "Le Problème de l'alcool," p. 984.
33. *Le Monde*, October 7, 1955, p. 10.
34. Cf. *Time Magazine*, August 22, 1955, p. 28.
35. *Le Monde*, August 11, 1955, p. 1 and August 18, 1955, p. 10.
36. La Documentation Française, *Situations et perspectives de l'agriculture française* (Paris, undated), p. 13.
37. *Rapport général des Commissions de la Production Agricole et de l'Equipement Rural*, pp. 43-47.
38. Based on unpublished studies of the Ministry of Agriculture.
39. Mendès-France, quoted in *Le Monde*, November 10, 1954, p. 14.
40. Cf. *Ibid.*, *Le Monde*, March 23, 1955, p. 10, and April 9, 1955, financial and economic supplement.

Chapter 13

1. "France's Economic Ills," *The Economist*, August 22, 1953, p. 517.
2. *Le Figaro*, October 16, 1953, p. 13.
3. Cf. the *Economic Report for 1951 and 1952*, p. 57.
4. Quoted in *Le Monde*, November 10, 1953, p. 6.
5. *Le Monde*, March 30, 1955, p. 5.
6. *Le Monde*, March 20-21, 1955, p. 5 and *Paris-Match*, June 6-13, 1953, p. 9.
7. *L'Express*, October 23, 1954, p. 5.
8. *Le Monde*, January 1, 1954, p. 5.

BIBLIOGRAPHY

GOVERNMENT PUBLICATIONS

Assemblée Nationale, "Projet de loi portant approbation du deuxième plan de modernisation et d'équipement," *Journal officiel, Documents parlementaires*, Deuxième Législature 1954, Annexe No. 8555.

———, *Rapport No. 4888 de la Commission des Finances sur le projet de loi de finances pour l'exercice 1953 (No. 4794)*, 3 vols. Paris, November 27, 1952.

———, *Rapport No. 7270 de la Commission des Finances sur le projet de loi de finances pour l'exercice 1954 (No. 6748)*, Paris, November 24, 1953.

———, *Rapport No. 9506 de la Commission des Finances sur le projet de loi relatif aux comptes spéciaux du Trésor pour l'année 1950*, Paris, 1950.

Bank for International Settlements, *19th Annual Report*, Basle, 1949.

Caisse Nationale de Crédit Agricole, *Rapport sur la situation du crédit agricole mutuel au 31 décembre 1954*, Paris, 1955.

Charbonnages de France, *Rapports de gestion*, Paris, 1947-1954.

Comité National de la Productivité, *Actions et problèmes de productivité*, Part I, Paris, 1954.

Commissariat Général au Plan, *Deuxième plan de modernisation et d'équipement - rapport général des Commissions de la Production Agricole et de l'Equipement Rural*, Paris, October, 1953.

———, *Document de synthèse et de coordination des travaux de la Commission de l'Equipement Rural*, Paris, 1953.

———, *Etat des opérations du plan de modernisation et d'équipement, projet de loi No. 4785, annexe No.* III, Paris, 1952.

———, *Perspectives des ressources et des besoins de l'économie française au cours du premier semestre et de l'année 1948: Rapport présenté au Gouvernement au nom de la Commission du Bilan National*, Paris, December, 1947.

———, *Premier rapport de la Commission de Modernisation de l'Electricité*, Paris, November, 1946.

———, *Premier rapport de la Commission de Modernisation des Houillères*, Paris, November, 1946.

———, *Quartre ans d'exécution du plan de modernisation et d'équipement de l'Union française*, Paris, 1954.

———, *Rapport annuel sur l'exécution du plan de modernisation et d'équipement de l'Union française, 1954*, Paris, 1955.

———, *Rapport de la Commission de l'Equipement Rural*, Paris, 1953.

———, *Rapport général de la Commission du Financement du Deuxième Plan de Modernisation et d'Equipement*, Paris, November, 1953.

———, *Rapport général sur le premier plan de modernisation et d'équipement*, Paris, November 1946-January 1947.

———, *Rapport sur la réalisation du plan de modernisation et d'équipement de l'Union française, année 1952*, Paris, 1953.

Commission de Vérification des Comptes des Entreprises Publiques, *Rapports d'ensemble, Journal officiel, Annexe administrative*, Paris, 1949, 1951, 1952.

Conseil Economique, "L'Aide à l'exportation," *Avis et rapports du Conseil Economique, Journal officiel*, February 4, 1953.

———, "L'Attribution des licenses d'importation," *Avis et rapports du Conseil Economique, Journal officiel*, March 11, 1949 and February 14, 1953.

———, "Contrôle des ententes professionnelles," *Etudes et travaux, No. 13*, Paris, 1950.
———, "Deuxième plan de modernisation et d'équipement," *Avis et rapports, Journal officiel*, August 3, 1954.
———, "Les Diverses formes du métayage," *Etudes et travaux, No. 23*, 2 vols., Paris, 1953.
———, "Etude générale sur le problème du logement," *Avis et rapports, Journal officiel*, August 21, 1953.
———, "Etude sur le rôle économique du crédit, sa situation actuelle, et les réformes que celle-ci appelle," *Avis et rapports, Journal officiel*, May 29, 1953.
———, "Investissements pour l'exercice 1951," *Avis et rapports, Journal officiel*, January 27, 1951.
———, "Problème de la viande," *Avis et rapports, Journal officiel*, December 11, 1948.
———, "Les Problèmes posés par les excédents d'alcool," *Etudes et travaux No. 29*, Paris,· 1953.
———, "La Réforme du statut du fermage et du métayage," *Etudes et travaux, No. 2*, Paris, 1949.
———, "Le Statut de l'alcool," *Etudes et travaux, No. 15*, Paris, 1950.
———, L'Union douanière Franco-Italienne," *Avis et rapports, Journal officiel*, January 27, 1949, May 26, 1949, March 23-24, 1950, May 11, 1950 and November 22, 1950.
Conseil National du Crédit, *Rapports annuels*, Paris, 1947-1955.
Cour des Comptes, *Rapport au Président de la Republique pour les années 1948-1949, Journal officiel, Annexe administrative*, Paris, June 30, 1950.
La Documentation Française, "Ententes et monopoles dans le monde: France," *Notes et études documentaires, Nos. 1736, 1737*, Paris, May 5, 1953.
———, "L'Evolution du commerce extérieur de la France métropolitaine de 1950 à 1953," *Notes et études documentaires, No. 1807*, Paris, November 25, 1953.
———, "Les Problèmes actuels de l'agriculture européenne," *Notes et études documentaires No. 1826*, Paris, January 22, 1954.
———, *Problèmes économiques*, Paris, February 24, 1953.
———, "Quelques aspects de l'équipement agricole en France," *Notes et études documentaires, No. 1545*, Paris, 1951.
———, "Recueil de documents sur la productivité," *Notes et études documentaires, No. 1296*, Paris, March 15, 1950.
———, *Situation et perspectives de l'agriculture française*, Paris, (n.d.).
Electricité de France, *Comptes de gestion et rapport d'activité* for 1950-1954, Paris, 1951-1955.
———, *Rapport de gestion des exercices 1946-1947, 1948, 1949*, Paris, 1950.
Institut National de la Statistique et des Etudes Economiques (INSEE), *Annuaire statistique 1951*, Paris, 1952.
———, "La Balance des payements de la zone Franc, de 1945 à 1951," *Bulletin mensuel de statistiques*, Supplement, January-March, 1953, pp. 42-80.
———, "Comparaison des prix français et étrangers," *Etudes et conjoncture*, July-August, 1952, pp. 321-394.
———, "Les Etablissements industriels et commerciaux du secteur privé en France en 1950," *Bulletin mensuel de statistiques*, Supplement, April-June, 1952, pp. 40-58.

———, "L'Evolution des termes de l'échange dans le commerce extérieur de la France," *Etudes et conjoncture*, July-August, 1952, pp. 300-320.

———, "L'Evolution récente des revenus salariaux modestes en France," *Etudes et conjoncture*, August, 1954, pp. 754-779.

———, "La Place de l'agriculture dans le revenu national français—dangers et incertitudes de son évaluation," *Etudes et conjoncture*, March-April, 1953, pp. 180-192.

———, "La Population: Producteurs et consommateurs," *Etudes et conjoncture*, January-February, 1955, pp. 12-21.

———, "Le Problème de l'alcool," *Etudes et conjoncture*, September, 1953, pp. 980-1016.

———, "Quelques aspects du problème des engrais," *Etudes et conjoncture*, August, 1953, pp. 871-890.

———, "Résultats du recensement des fonctionnaires de l'Etat effectué en 1952," *Bulletin mensuel de statistiques*, Supplement, April-June, 1953, pp. 33-43.

———, "Le Revenu de l'agriculture en France en 1952-1953," *Etudes et conjoncture*, December, 1953, pp. 1253-1274.

———, "Le Revenu de l'agriculture en France en 1953-1954," *Etudes et conjoncture*, December, 1954, pp. 1059-1087.

———, "Les Salaires dans l'industrie et le commerce en 1951," *Bulletin mensuel de statistiques*, Supplement, October-December, 1953, pp. 40-59.

———, "Les Salaires en France en 1952," *Bulletin mensuel de statistiques*, Supplement, April-June, 1953, pp. 50-63.

———, "Statistiques des chiffres d'affaires fiscaux," *Bulletin mensuel de statistiques*, Supplement, October-December, 1952, pp. 46-62.

Ministère de l'Agriculture, "Fecondité urbaine et rural mesurée par les naissances ramenées au domicile," *Revue du Ministère de l'Agriculture*, Supplement to Nos. 61-62, August-September, 1956.

———, "Plans d'investissements agricoles," *Revue*, July, 1953.

———, "Plans d'investissements agricoles 1948-1952," *Revue*, July, 1952.

Ministère des Finances, "Analyse des résultats de l'emprunt 3.50% 1952," *Statistiques et études financières*, No. 51, March, 1953, pp. 177-198.

———, "Les Avantages fiscaux à l'exportation en France et à l'étranger," *Statistiques et études*, No. 60, December, 1953, pp. 1101-1118.

———, "La Balance des payements en 1953," *Statistiques et études financières*, No. 68, August, 1954, pp. 709-728.

———, "Le Budget de 1953," *Statistiques et études financières*, No. 52, April, 1953, pp. 269-295.

———, *Le Budget de 1954*, Paris, 1954.

———, *Code général des impôts*, Paris, November 5, 1956.

———, "L'Evolution de la Trésorerie au cours de l'année 1953," *Statistiques et études*, No. 66, June, 1954, pp. 535-547.

———, "L'Evolution de la Trésorerie en 1952, *Statistiques et études financières*, No. 55, July, 1953, pp. 611-625.

———, "Exploitations agricoles," *Recensement général de la population effectué le 10 mars 1946*, Vol. VII, Paris, 1950.

———, "Exposé général des motifs du projet de loi de finances pour 1955," *Statistiques et études financières*, No. 73, January, 1955, pp. 5-21.

———, "La Fiscalité française," *Statistiques et études financières, supplément finances comparées*, Nos. 19-20, 1953, pp. 236-320.

———, "La France et la politique de libération des échanges," *Statistiques et études financières*, No. 58, October, 1953, pp. 873-903.

———, "L'Impôt sur le revenu des personnes physiques en 1952," *Statistiques et études financières*, No. 57, September, 1953, pp. 807-815.

———, *Inventaire de la situation financière*, Paris, 1951.
———, *Inventaire de la situation financière (1913-1946)*, Paris, 1946.
———, "La Parafiscalité," *Statistiques et études financières*, No. 14, February, 1950.
———, "Premier rapport de la Commission 'Productivité et Fiscalité,'" *Statistiques et études financières*, No. 42, June 1, 1952, pp. 516-544.
———, *Rapports annuels de la Commission des Investissements*, 1948-1954.
———, "Les Rapports entre le Trésor et l'institut d'émission en France," *Statistiques et études financières, supplément finances comparées*, No. 10, 1951, pp. 385-409.
———, *Rapport général de la commission créée par arrêté du 6 Janvier 1954 pour l'étude des disparités entre les prix français et étrangers*, Paris, 1954.
———, *Rapport général de la Commission de Réforme Fiscale*, Paris, 1952.
———, *Rapports sur les comptes provisoires de la nation des années 1951 et 1952 et sur le budget économique de l'année 1953*, Paris, 1953.
———, "La Réglementation actuelle des prix," *Statistiques et études financières*, No. 74, February, 1955, pp. 113-122.
———, "La Situation financière de la Société Nationale des Chemins de Fer Français," *Statistiques et études financières*, No. 76, April, 1955, pp. 341-353.
———, "Les Variations du taux d'escompte de la Banque de France," *Statistiques et études financières*, No. 62, February, 1954, pp. 140-142.
———, *Statistiques mensuelles du commerce extérieur de la France, Année 1954*, No. 12, December, 1954.
Ministère du Budget, *Budget de la France en 1950*, Paris, 1950.
Office National Interprofessionnel des Céréales, *Recueil méthodique des dispositions législatives en vigueur en matière de céréales*, Paris, 1952.
Organization for European Economic Cooperation (OEEC), *Agriculture Advisory Services in European Countries*, Paris, 1950.
———, *Coal and European Economic Expansion*, Paris, 1952.
———, *Coal Production and Supplies for Western Europe in 1952 and 1953*, Paris, January, 1953.
———, *Economic Conditions in France*, Paris, 1954.
———, *Europe: The Way Ahead*, Paris, December, 1952.
———, *From Recovery Towards Economic Strength, 6th Report of the* OEEC, Paris, March, 1955.
———, *Progress and Problems of the European Economy*, Paris, January, 1954.
———, *Statistical Bulletins 1955*, No. 3, Paris, May, 1955.
Régie Nationale des Usines Renault, *Rapports annuels de gestion*, for 1949-1954, Paris, 1950-1955.
Société Nationale des Chemins de Fer Français, *Assemblée générale des actionnaires*, 1948-1954, Paris, 1948-1954.
United Nations, Economic Commission for Europe (UN/ECE), *Economic Survey of Europe in 1954*, Geneva, 1955.
———, "Modifications in the Tax Structure in Europe," *Economic Bulletin for Europe*, Vol. 2, No. 3, 1950, pp. 66-90.
UN/ECE and Food and Agriculture Organization, Joint Secretariat, *European Agriculture: A Statement of Problems*, Geneva, 1954.
———, *Output and Expenses of Agriculture in Some European Countries*, Geneva, 1953.
United Nations Food and Agriculture Organization, *Yearbook of Food and Agricultural Statistics 1953*, Vol. VII, Geneva, 1954.

United Nations Statistical Office, *Statistical Yearbook 1948*, Lake Success, New York, 1949.

U. S. Bureau of the Census, *Statistical Abstract of the United States: 1953*, Seventy-fourth edition, Washington, 1953.

United States Economic Cooperation Administration, *European Recovery Program: France Country Study*, Washington, 1949.

United States Operations Mission to France, *France Data Book, 1954*, Paris, 1954.

OTHER PUBLICATIONS

Books and Pamphlets

Allais, Maurice, *La Gestion des houillères nationalisées et la théorie économique*, Paris (n.d.).

Allix, Pierre and Bloch-Lainé, François, *Finances publiques: Les Ressources publiques*, Cours à l'Institut d'Etudes politiques de l'Université de Paris, Paris, 1953.

Bergmann, D. R., *Cooperative Use of Machinery on French Farms*, Paris, 1949.

Bloch-Lainé, François, *Le Trésor public et la politique financière*, Cours à l'Institut d'Etudes Politiques de l'Université de Paris, Paris, 1953.

Bréart, Georges, *Le Fleuve blanc*, Paris, 1954.

Brochier, Hubert, *Finances publiques et redistribution des revenus*, Paris, 1950.

Chatelain, M., *L'Agriculture française et la formation professionnelle*, Paris, 1953.

Chenot, Bernard, *Organisation économique de l'état*, Paris, 1951.

Clapham, J. H., *The Economic Development of France and Germany*, 1815-1914, Cambridge, 1923.

Clark, Colin, *The Conditions of Economic Progress*, 2nd edition, London, 1951.

Cohen, Ruth, "Contrôle des prix agricoles dans certains pays d'Europe occidentale," UN/FAO, *Etudes sur les politiques en matière de produits*, No. 2, Rome, September 1953.

Delouvrier, Paul and Nathan, Roger, *Politique économique de la France*, Cours à l'Institut d'Etudes Politiques de l'Université de Paris, Paris, 1953.

Diebold, William Jr., *Trade and Payments in Western Europe*, New York, 1952.

Dieterlen, Pierre and Rist, Charles, *The Monetary Problem of France*, New York, 1948.

Dieterlen, Pierre, *Quelques enseignements de l'évolution monétaire française de 1948 à 1952*, Paris, 1954.

Dumontier, Jacques, *Budget économique et capital national*, Paris, 1951.

Dupont, P. C., *Le Contrôle des banques et la direction du crédit en France*, Paris, 1952.

Durand, Paul, *La Politique contemporaine de sécurité sociale*, Paris, 1953.

Fauchon, Jean, *Economie de l'agriculture française*, Paris, 1954.

Fromont, Pierre, "Le Capitalisme d'état et la production agricole," *Vingt ans de capitalisme d'état*, Paris, 1951.

Gendarme, René, *L'Expérience française de la nationalisation industrielle*, Paris, 1950.

Gignoux, C.-J., *L'Industrie française*, Paris, 1952.

Houghteling, James L., "The Income Tax in France," *Public Policy*, Vol. v, Harvard University Press, 1954.

Juglart, M. de, *Droit rural*, Vol. 1, Paris, 1949.

Laferrière, Julien and Waline, Marcel, *Traité élémentaire de science et de législation financières*, Paris, 1952.
Landes, David S., "French Business and the Businessman: A Social and Cultural Analysis," *Modern France, Problems of the Third and Fourth Republics*, E. M. Earle, ed., Princeton University Press, 1951.
Laufenburger, Henry, *Economie du système fiscal français national et local*, Paris, 1954.
———, *L'Intervention de l'état en matière économique*, Paris, 1939.
———, *La Réforme fiscale de 1949*, Paris, 1949.
Lauré, Maurice, *Impôts et productivité*, Paris, 1953.
———, *La Taxe sur la valeur ajoutée*, Paris, 1952.
Lavergne, Bernard, *Le Problème des nationalisations*, Paris, 1946.
Lévy, Maurice, *Histoire économique et sociale de la France depuis 1848*, Cours à L'Institut d'Etudes Politiques de l'Université de Paris, Paris, 1951.
Lorwin, Val R., *The French Labor Movement*, Harvard University Press, 1954.
Lubell, Harold, *The French Investment Program, a Defense of the Monnet Plan*, Multilithed, Paris, 1951.
Piettre, André, *Economie dirigée d'hier et d'aujourd'hui, du colbertisme à notre temps*, Paris, 1947.
Pinkney, David H., "The French Experiment in Nationalization, 1944-1950," *Modern France, Problems of the Third and Fourth Republics*, E. M. Earle, ed. Princeton University Press, 1951.
Richard, H., *Physionomie de la fertilisation en France*, Paris, 1951.
Rivero, Jean, *Le Régime des nationalisations*, Paris, 1948.
Ruggles, Richard, "The French Investment Program and its Relation to Resource Allocation," *Modern France, Problems of the Third and Fourth Republics*, E. M. Earle, ed., Princeton University Press, 1951.
Tchernoff, J., *Ententes économiques et financières*, Paris, 1933.
Thiers, André, "Le Capitalisme d'état et la production industrielle," *Vingt ans de capitalisme d'état*, Paris, 1951.
Trotabas, Louis, *Les Finances publiques et les impôts de la France*, Paris, 1953.
———, *Précis de science et législation financières*, Paris, 1953.
Veisseyre, R., *Contribution à l'étude de la consommation du lait et des products laitiers en France*, Conseil Supérieur de l'Agriculture, Paris, 1954.
Ventenat, Marcel, *L'Expérience des nationalisations*, Paris, 1947.
Viallate, A., *L'Activité économique en France de la fin du* XVIIIème *siècle à nos jours*, Paris, 1937.
Villey, Daniel, "Les Etapes du capitalisme d'état," *Vingt ans de capitalisme d'état*, Paris, 1951.
Williams, Philip, *Politics in Postwar France*, London, 1955.

Journals and Newspapers

Allais, M., "Le Problème de la coordination des transports et la théorie économique," *Revue d'économie politique*, Vol. LVIII, 1948, pp. 212-271.
Aubert, G., "La Tarification des marchandises de la SNCF," *Revue générale des chemins de fer*, May, 1951, pp. 213-227.
Badouin, R., "Analyse économique et détermination du prix du vin," *Bulletin du Centre Régional des Etudes Economiques de Montpellier*, 3rd quarter, 1953, pp. 115-158.
Barbier, M., "Les Remboursements des charges sociales et fiscales aux entreprises exportatrices," *Droit social*, March, 1954, pp. 171-173.

Bauchet, Pierre, "La Structure d'une branche d'industrie française: l'automobile," *Economie appliquée*, April-September, 1952, pp. 359-400.

Beigel, Edgar, "France Moves Toward National Planning," *Political Science Quarterly*, Vol. LXII, No. 3, September, 1947, pp. 381-397.

Benard, Jean, "La Répartition des dépenses de la population française en fonction de ses besoins," Institut National d'Etudes Démographiques, *Population 1953*, Paris, 1953.

Bergmann, Denis R., "Les Obstacles matériels et psychologiques à l'accroissement de la productivité agricole," *Cahiers des ingénieurs agronomes*, No. 2, 1954, pp. 18-22.

———, "Regrouping of Farm Holdings in France," *International Journal of Agrarian Affairs*, May, 1952, pp. 24-32.

Buron, Robert, "La Sclérose des structures économiques de la France, *Les Cahiers économiques*, April, 1954, pp. 1-10.

Chenot, Bernard, "Ambiguité de l'économie mixte," *Les Cahiers économiques*, August-September, 1953, pp. 4-7.

———, "Premiers résultats de la nationalisation des mines," *Droit social*, July-August, 1949, pp. 242-246.

Chevry, Gabriel, "La Structure industrielle et commerciale de la France," *Journal de la Société de Statistique de Paris*, January-March, 1952, pp. 17-40.

Clark, Colin, *The Relation Between the Pace of Technical Change in Farming and the Level of Agricultural Prosperity*, paper presented at the International Conference of Agricultural Economists, Helsinki, August, 1955.

Clerc, F., "La Commercialisation des laits de collecte dans la région toulousaine," *Economie rurale*, April, 1954, pp. 17-23.

"Credit Control in France," *The Economist*, November 15, 1952, pp. 506, 509-510.

Dessus, Gabriel, "Perspectives commerciales sur les fournitures d'énergie électrique à l'industrie," *Revue française de l'énergie*, No. 1, September, 1949, pp. 20-26.

Dijon, H., "Alcool, ou lait et viande?" *Economie et réalités mondiales*, August 3, 1954, pp. 66-69.

Durand, Jean, "La Grève des mineurs," *Travaux de l'action populaire*, No. 27, February, 1949, pp. 111-126.

Durand, Paul, "Les Equivoques de la redistribution du revenu par la sécurité sociale," *Droit social*, May, 1953, pp. 292-298.

Eastman, Harry C., "The Role of Speculation in France's Foreign-Exchange Crises," *Journal of Political Economy*, Vol. LXI, No. 3, June, 1953, pp. 209-220.

"Economie et sociologie rurale de la Bretagne," *Etudes d'économie rurale*, September, 1953, pp. 1-35.

"L'Economie française aux rayons X," *Réalités*, November, 1953, pp. 46-48.

Ehrmann, Henry W., "The French Trade Associations and the Ratification of the Schuman Plan," *World Politics*, Vol. VI, No. 4, July, 1954, pp. 453-481.

"L'Enseignement agricole," *Terres de France*, special issue No. x, 1954.

"L'Expérience des comités d'entreprise, bilan d'une enquête," *Droit social*, January, 1952, pp. 14-33, February, 1952, pp. 92-104, March 1952, pp. 163-179.

Fabre, Robert, "Les Houillères du Nord et du Pas-de-Calais," *Droit social*, April, 1945, pp. 138-153.

"France's Economic Ills," *The Economist*, August 22, 1953, pp. 516-517.

Franck, Louis-R., "Planisme français et démocratie," *Revue économique*, Vol. IV, No. 2, March, 1953, pp. 195-219.

Gaspard, R., and Massé, Pierre, "Le Choix des investissements énergetiques et la production d'électricité en France," *Revue française de l'énergie*, No. 35, October, 1952, pp. 5-14.

Giguet, Raymond, "Réalisations et perspectives de l'équipement électrique," *Revue française de l'énergie*, No. 32, June, 1952, pp. 282-292.

Gingembre, L., "Le Syndicalisme patronal et l'administration," *La Revue administrative*, November-December, 1949, pp. 589-593.

"Une 'Grande' réforme fiscale," *La Revue administrative*, No. 3, May-June, 1948, pp. 23-29.

Gravier, J.-F., "La Clé du problème agricole: Enseignement et vulgarisation," *Droit social*, November, 1950, a special issue on *Les Aspects économiques, techniques et sociaux de l'expansion agricole*, pp. 19-23.

Hoüel, Pierre, "Comment fonctionne en France le secteur nationalisé?" *La Tribune des peuples*, No. 4, September-October, 1953, pp. 82-99.

Hutter, R., "Qu'est-ce que le coût marginal?" *Revue générale des chemins de fer*, February, 1950, pp. 53-63.

———, "Les Tarifs de réglementation de la SNCF," *Revue générale des chemins de fer*, April, 1949, pp. 155-168.

———, "La Théorie économique et la gestion commerciale des chemins de fer: la Coordination des transports," *Revue générale des chemins de fer*, October, 1950, pp. 443-460.

———, "La Théorie économique et la gestion commerciale des chemins de fer: le Problème tarifaire," *Revue générale des chemins de fer*, July, 1950, pp. 318-332.

"L'Incivisme," *Esprit*, January, 1949, pp. 1-86.

"Industry Pushes Productivity Drive," *France actuelle*, Vol. II, No. 37, October 5, 1953.

"Informations économiques mondiales," *Economie et réalités mondiales*, No. 42, July, 1953, pp. 83-98.

Jarrier, Bernard, "L'Etat investi par les intérêts," *l'Esprit*, June, 1953, pp. 878-903.

Jouannet, Robert, "Les Tarifs de vente de l'énergie électrique en basse tension," *Revue française de l'énergie*, No. 3, November, 1949, pp. 85-92.

Jouvenel, Bertrand de, "Les Ententes sur le marché mondial du pétrole," *Revue française de l'énergie*, No. 35, October, 1952, pp. 15-25.

Lorwin, Val R., "French Trade Unions Since Liberation, 1944-1951," *Industrial and Labor Relations Review*, Vol. 5, No. 4, July, 1952, pp. 524-539.

Lyon-Caen, Gérard, "Les Nationalisations en Grande-Bretagne," *Droit social*, December, 1946, pp. 403-407.

Maillet, Pierre, "Les Disparités de consommation d'énergie en France et dans quelques pays étrangers," *Revue française de l'énergie*, No. 51, March, 1954, pp. 212-224.

———, "Politique de l'énergie et expansion économique," *Les Cahiers économiques*, May, 1954, pp. 5-16.

Marcy, M., "L'Avenant du 10 juillet 1952 à la convention du 31 août 1937, dans le cadre des grands problèmes de gestion des chemins de fer," *Revue générale des chemins de fer*, March, 1953, pp. 123-162.

Massé, Pierre, "L'Electricité devant un nouveau plan," *Revue française de l'énergie*, No. 30, April, 1952, pp. 214-225.

Mazard, Jean, "Prix imposés et prix d'entente," *Droit social*, March, 1953, pp. 129-134.

Merchants of France, France Actuelle, Washington, 1953.

Mérigot, Jean, "Le décret du 30 juin 1952 portant aménagement du régime fiscal des sociétés et des valeurs mobilières," *Revue de science et de législation financières*, January-March, 1953, pp. 132-146.

Milhau, J., "L'Avenir de la viticulture française," *Revue économique*, September, 1953, pp. 700-738.

Montagne, R., "La Notion d'exploitation agricole et son évolution," *Bulletin de la Société Française d'Economie Rurale*, December, 1950, pp. 66-70.

Multzer, Herbert, "Les Ententes dans l'industrie pétrolière," *Nouvelle revue de l'économie contemporaine*, August-September, 1950, pp. 17-18.

Nollet, Paul, "La Parafiscalité," *Droit social*, February, 1953, pp. 65-74.

Pasqualaggi, Giles, "Les Ententes en France," *Revue économique*, January, 1952, pp. 63-82.

"Paye-t-on en France plus d'impôts qu'à l'étranger?" *Entreprise*, No. 22, February 15, 1954, pp. 31-34.

Personnaz, Jean, "La Nationalisation des houillères françaises," *Droit social*, March, 1947, pp. 81-88, April, 1947, pp. 121-126.

"Le Personnel et l'activité financière de la SNCF," *L'Année ferroviaire 1953*, Paris, 1953, pp. 81-90.

"Perspectives d'avenir sur la production et le transport de l'énergie électrique en France," *Revue française de l'énergie*, No. 14, November, 1950, pp. 38-45.

Philbert, A., "Le Problème de l'échelle mobile des salaires," *Droit social*, November, 1952, pp. 592-599.

"Les Principaux fonds économiques de caractère général," *Bulletin du Conseil National du Patronat Français*, March, 1955, pp. 31-34.

"La Productivité industrielle par tête en France et à l'étranger," *Bulletin du Conseil National du Patronat Français*, March 20, 1954, pp. 21-23.

"Le Programme français d'accroissement de la productivité et l'amendement Blair-Moody," *Bulletin du Conseil National du Patronat Français*, June 5, 1953, pp. 26-29.

"Rapport de la délégation française sur les causes de la haute productivité américaine," *Bulletin du Conseil National du Patronat Français*, April 15, 1952, Supplement, pp. 1-8.

Reboud, Emmanuel, "Nationalisation de l'électricité et économie globale," *Economie et humanisme*, No. 81, September-October, 1953, pp. 58-69.

"La Réforme fiscale," *Réalités*, No. 58, November, 1950, pp. 57-58, 115-116.

"Le Régime fiscal des carburants" (Rapport de la Commission Fiscalité et Productivité), *Revue française de l'énergie*, No. 37, December, 1952, pp. 99-104.

Rist, C., and Pirou, G., "De la France d'avant guerre à la France d'aujourd'hui, vingt-cinq ans d'évolution de l'économie française," special issue of the *Revue d'économie politique*, Paris, 1939.

Robin, F., "L'Evolution du marché de la terre en France depuis la libération," *Economie rurale*, January, 1955, pp. 43-47.

Sargent, F. O., "Fragmentation of French Land: Its Nature, Extent and Causes," *Land Economics*, August, 1952, pp. 218-229.

Sauvy, Alfred, "La Situation économique," *Droit social*, January, 1953, pp. 14-17, December, 1953, pp. 591-594.

Shoup, Carl S., "Taxation in France," *National Tax Journal*, Vol. VIII, No. 4, December, 1955.

Snider, Delbert A., "French Monetary and Fiscal Policies Since the Liberation," *American Economic Review*, Vol. XXXVIII, No. 3, June, 1948, pp. 309-327.

"Structure et organisation des 'Houillères nationales du Nord et du Pas-de-Calais,' " *Droit social*, April, 1945, pp. 121-131.

Sturmthal, Adolf, "Nationalization and Workers' Control in Britain and France," *Journal of Political Economy*, Vol. LXI, No. 1, February, 1953, pp. 43-79.

———, "The Structure of Nationalized Enterprises in France," *Political Science Quarterly*, Vol. LXVII, No. 3, September, 1952, pp. 357-377.

Teissedre, J., "Evolution de la réglementation française du commerce extérieur (1945 à 1949)," *Droit social*, September-October, 1949, pp. 297-305.

Uri, Pierre, "La Querelle des nationalisations," *Les Temps modernes*, July, 1949, pp. 165-170.

Varlet, Henri, "Le Plan Monnet et la production d'énergie électrique thermique," *Revue française de l'énergie*, No. 29, March, 1952, pp. 181-187.

———, "La Production de l'énergie électrique en France: répartition entre usines thermiques et hydrauliques," *Revue française de l'énergie*, No. 34, September, 1952, pp. 351-365.

Wilmet, Bernard, and Faber, Maurice, "De la société anonyme à la Régie Nationale des Usines Renault," *Economie et humanisme*, No. 33, September-October, 1947, pp. 494-522.

INDEX

GPSR Authorized Representative: Easy Access System Europe - Mustamäe tee 50, 10621 Tallinn, Estonia, gpsr.requests@easproject.com

www.ingramcontent.com/pod-product-compliance
Ingram Content Group UK Ltd.
Pitfield, Milton Keynes, MK11 3LW, UK
UKHW020909230826
474546UK00008B/27

9780691626468